BC

Transitions in Mental Retardation

Volume 3,

The Community Imperative Revisited

Transitions in
Mental Retardation

An Official Series of Northeast Region X of the
American Association on Mental Deficiency

Series Editor

James A. Mulick
Ohio State University

Associate Series Editor

Richard F. Antonak
University of New Hampshire

TRANSITIONS IN MENTAL RETARDATION
Volume 3

The Community Imperative Revisited

Edited by
Richard F. Antonak
University of New Hampshire

and

James A. Mulick
Ohio State University

Ablex Publishing Corporation
Norwood, New Jersey 07648

Printed in the United States of America.

ISBN: 0-89391-408-8
ISSN: 0749-3924

Ablex Publishing Corporation
355 Chestnut Street
Norwood, New Jersey 07648

Contents

CONTENTS

This volume is dedicated to Burton Blatt who taught us that:

All people are equally valuable and deserve to be part of a normal world; that the world isn't now, but *can* be, hospitable and normal; so we must try to change the world, else we contribute to its evil.

In and Out of Mental Retardation: Essays on Educability, Disability, and Human Policy

Preface to the Series

James A. Mulick

Richard F. Antonak

Adaptation to change is a hallmark of development of the individual; it is the key to prospering in a complex and evolving environment. The dynamic interplay of biological, experiential, and environmental variables is well known to those of us concerned with disorders of human development. Similarly, the strategies we select for our therapeutic interventions are the adaptive products of events and forces both within our field (e.g., research) and external to our field (e.g., technology). The field and the strategies available to us are constantly changing—are constantly in transition.

To meet the challenges of transition, we need: (a) a mandate for innovation, (b) adequate human and material resources, (c) knowledge of previous relevant experience, and (d) an analytic strategy to evaluate this experience. The first condition is not typically within the scope of a professional association. Rather, a mandate for change is derived from the values held generally by the larger society and reflected in the policies of its institutions. However, the values held by society can be influenced by the presentation of information and the demonstration of new practices by professionals.

The well known sequence of research, demonstration, and dissemination in our field has been fostered in part by resources allocated by the federal government. Today, these resources are being diverted away from education and human services to other applications and in the service of other interests. While federal support may someday return to the level enjoyed in past decades, we cannot stop and wait for it to return. Rather, we must develop and apply alternate sources of support for the initiation of research and development projects, and we must seek alternate means for the dissemination of the results of these studies. Presentations at professional meetings and the publication of archival collections of papers based on those presentations is a sound alternative to the traditional grant-supported publication and dissemination of results.

The last two conditions required to meet the challenges of transition are addressed by the purposes of the American Association on Mental Deficiency (AAMD). As a professional organization devoted to the dissemination of knowledge in the field of mental retardation, the AAMD preserves past experiences in the proceedings of its meetings and its publications. While there are other methods to evaluate experience, such as cost-benefit analysis or historical comparisons, the scientific method has been the favored analytic strategy by most of the biological, behavioral, and social disciplines represented within AAMD.

The series *Transitions in Mental Retardation* was created in 1983 by the leadership of AAMD Northeast Region X to assist professionals who serve people who are mentally retarded to adapt to the changes in our field. This series will present papers selected for their scholarly merit and scientific rigor, papers presenting advances in the field of mental retardation and developmental disabilities which are relevant to the scholar, practitioner, and policy maker. Moreover, this series will highlight successful demonstrations of innovative practices in order to stimulate the adoption of these practices. Priority for the inclusion of works in the volumes of the series will be given to those papers based on presentations at the annual conferences of AAMD Northeast Region X.

Contributions will be considered which are derived from basic as well as applied research programs, descriptions of program evaluation technology, theoretical analyses of the literature in a particular area, and papers describing methodological innovations. Special emphasis will be placed on interdisciplinary research and progress reports of programmatic research. Recognition of emerging professional and research talent will be afforded whenever possible. Contributions will be solicited from members of all professions involved in this multidisciplinary field, with preference given to those who are members of AAMD.

We invite readers to participate in the transitions in mental retardation which this series will attempt to document. We invite authors to contribute to this series in order to ease these transitions and promote improvements in services to people with mental retardation and other developmental disabilities.

Preface to Volume 3
The Community Imperative Revisited

Richard F. Antonak

James A. Mulick

This volume presents 13 chapters, each concerned with some aspect of the development, implementation, or evaluation of community-based services for people who are mentally retarded. These processes, which collectively we will refer to as communization, can be traced to the pioneering work of Charles Bernstein, the superintendent of Rome (NY) State School at the turn of this century (Antonak, 1984). Although there was never a time when the majority of people with mental retardation lived in institutions, the watershed year for communitization is considered to be 1967. In that year, the population of American public residential facilities for the mentally retarded totaled 194,650 (Lakin, Krantz, Bruininks, Clumpner, & Hill, 1982). This marks the first year since 1848, when the first institution for the mentally retarded was opened in the United States, in which the average daily population showed a decline. Since 1967, there has accumulated a rich and controversial aggregate of research and conceptual literature on communitization and the associated topics of normalization and deinstitutionalization. Only recently, however, have there appeared edited texts which provide overviews and ctitical evaluations of this literature (e.g., Bruininks & Lakin, 1985; Bruininks, Meyers, Sigford, & Lakin, 1981; Lakin & Bruininks, 1985). To this small set of books we add the present volume of *Transitions in Mental Retardation*.

The 13 chapters of this volume are roughly divisible into four sections. The first section, comprising the first chapter alone, provides the title for the volume and a framework for the reader to consider the issues raised in the subsequent chapters. The next section includes Chapters 2 and 3, complimentary discussions of the problems involved in conducting communitization research. The third and largest section comprises the next eight chapters. The order which we selected to present the chapters in this section will be explained shortly. The final section includes two chapters illustrating the range of views on the future role of institutions.

The chapters in this volume are intended to be representative rather than exhaustive of the issues of communitization. Each is remarkable for the potential to challenge our beliefs, to prick our professional conscience, and to provoke our contemplation of topics we may prefer to avoid. We are convinced that the work reported on will enhance future conceptualization and stimulate well-designed research in this complex social policy domain.

In the opening chapter, Biklen and Knoll begin by reiterating *The community imperative: A refutation of all arguments in support of institutionalizing anybody because of mental retardation* (Center on Human Policy, 1979). This position is presented in the conclusion of the syllogism; that is, "All people, regardless of the severity of their disabilities, are entitled to community living." The authors sketch the history of the declaration, and present a review of its philosophical basis. The literature opposing communitization since the publication of the declaration is organized by the authors into eight categories—fallacies, in the authors' view. In the middle section of the chapter, these eight fallacies are presented and systematically refuted with cogent analyses of logic, summaries of empirical studies, and appeals to rational beliefs and values. Various points of these arguments are highlighted by quotes from interviews with a number of disabled people. The last section of the chapter presents a summary of the communitization controversy, and identifies the barriers which are delaying the continuation of the movement. In their view, the principal barrier is our lack of moral conviction to the community imperative.

At this point, many readers will be asking themselves "Where is the proof of these assertions?" Typically, we turn to the research literature to provide the proof. But before we do that, some forewords about communitization research are in order. The next two chapters provide these forewords.

In Chapter 2, Deborah Allen makes explicit what she refers to as "The Identity Crisis in Community Research." She argues that, without a coherent definition of applied research on the community placement of people who are mentally retarded, the demand for naturalistic investigations (Brooks & Baumeister, 1977) can only exacerbate this crisis. Allen highlights the forces and events which demand more and better communitization research, and proceeds to consider four questions whose answers should provide the necessary definition. The reader who is confused by the presumed dichotomy of quantitative and qualitative research paradigms (or "world views," as Allen calls them) will be particularly pleased with this section of the chapter. The author concludes that community researchers have erroneously tried to adhere to laboratory standards and values when the real world demands otherwise. She urges community researchers to stop apologizing for the weakness of their studies, because what may be a weakness from the perspective of the laboratory may in fact be a strength from the perspective of the community.

The third chapter of this volume illustrates and elaborates one of Allen's crisis-defining questions. In their chapter, "Investigating the Impact of Communitization: Issues in Research Methodology," Mallory and Herrick take up the question of how can we design a study of the impact of the policy of communitization. They begin by addressing the first of the eight communitization fallacies presented in the first chapter of the volume; namely, that there is a lack of empirical data to support deinstitutionalization. Research on the impact of community placement of people who are mentally retarded has been a major concern of researchers for more than 20 years. In their view, the data are available. What is lacking, however, is the leadership necessary to forge an interaction of research data and social policy. That is, the research enterprise and the policy-making enterprise are proceeding on parallel tracks but, at least for the moment, in the same direction. This chapter proceeds with the exploration of two complimentary themes. The first theme is the problem of designing and conducting research in natural environments. The second theme is the author's view that communitization research cannot escape being an advocacy ideology.

Mallory and Herrick (1985) designed and conducted a comprehensive study of the 180 mentally retarded children who lived at the Laconia (NH) State School between 1970 and 1985, of which 70 left as children. In preparation for this study, they reviewed the empirical literature from 1980 to 1985 on the impact of community placement of previously institutionalized people with mental retardation. The studies in this review are presented in a taxonomy comprising six classes, defined by the variables which constitute the focus of the study. This matrix alone will delight researchers, and should be of considerable value to students and administrators who are making an initial assault on the literature on community adjustment. The middle section of the chapter discusses barriers to communitization research—loss of subjects, obtaining subjects' consent, inadequacy of records, transportation, and many others. This leads the authors to propose a theoretical model which is a unique blend of the characteristics of both the quantitative and qualitative world views. In the closing section of the chapter, we are returned to the concern for the social validity of communitization research.

In a conclusion which many classical researchers will find unsettling, Mallory and Herrick suggest that researchers should not pretend to have no biases. Rather, they should explicate their biases in advance to allow the research consumer to reach sound judgments about the meaning of the results. Joining the ranks of other researcher-advocates, the authors assert that the question of whether communitization works is irrelevant. Rather, the questions are: How can we make it work? How can we identify the barriers? How can we overcome these barriers? How can we change society?

The third section of this volume includes eight chapters. Using the structure of the eight fallacies provided by Bicklen and Knoll in Chapter 1, these chapters are arranged sequentially based upon which of the fallacies is the primary concern of the chapter. While some of the chapters deal with more than one of the eight fallacies, it is our view that each chapter has one fallacy as its primary focus. An alternative organization is suggested by the sixfold taxonomy of communitization research variables of Chapter 3. For the chapters which concern communitization research, we will present our taxonomic classification in the brief introductions which follow.

In Chapter 4, the first chapter in this third section, Kaminer and Jedrysek take up the theme of the first of the communitization fallacies; that is, that normalization implies normal (equal) treatment for people who are mentally retarded. The manifestation of this argument that these authors investigate is that of risk. Is it rational to adopt the "dignity of risk" philosophy as a social policy? They begin by reviewing the literature on risk of injury to normal and mentally retarded children and adolescents. In general, it appears to the authors that considering level of adaptive behavior, the person who is mentally retarded is at greater risk for injury than is the non-retarded person in similar environments. The difficulty of defining risk, of measuring risk, and of removing the influences of confounding variables from a study of the occurrence of injury (such as intelligence, experience, and environmental control) leads the authors to caution against overinterpretation of their conclusion. The authors then present a compelling argument in support of autonomy as the concept which links risk with dignity. We must assist people who are mentally retarded to assess the risks and benefits associated with choices of behavior in the community environment, skills which may be impossible to teach and to learn in an artificial environment. And we must be aware of, and resolve, conflicts which we create when we establish policies, which parents and guardians must carry out, based on philosophies which they cannot understand or accept.

In Chapter 5, Haney and Heal deal with both the second and the third of the eight fallacies. Their comprehensive review of studies published between 1970 and 1984, concerned with the impact of residential environments on the adaptive behavior of people who are mentally retarded (Mallory and Herrick define this as Class 1 in their taxonomy), demonstrated that communitization has an empirical base, and that the data favor community environments. The 20 studies they selected to review are organized by the factors studied and are critiqued, in turn, with reference to design, instrumentation, and control of extraneous variables. Haney and Heal conclude that, in general, community placement of mentally retarded people who previously lived in institutions leads to an increase in adaptive behavior. Within the community, small group homes seem to be preferable. The research concerning changes in maladaptive behavior following placement is equivocal in their view. The reader will discover in the final part of this chapter a critique of the application of quantitative methodology to communitization research with recommendations, similar to those of Chapter 3, for future research in this area.

The fourth of the eight fallacies presented in Chapter 1 is that there are some people who are so severely handicapped that the community cannot hope to meet their needs. For example, a specialized residential institution, it is argued, is necessary for medically fragile people who have intense needs. The chapter by

Silverman and his colleagues confronts this argument. (The studies bearing on this communitization question are referred to as Class 3 in the taxonomy of Chapter 3). These researchers investigated whether community-based programs can provide the health services needed by people who are profoundly mentally retarded and multiply handicapped. They reasoned that if the needs of those living in the community are the same as the needs of those living in the institution, then it could be shown that the medical fragility argument is groundless. Using the comprehensive databae available for New York Stae's mentally retarded citizens, and a specially designed instrument that others will undoubtedly find useful, the researchers analyzed data comparing a group of profoundly mentally retarded people living in a specialized institution with a similar group of people living in small community facilities in New York City. The results of these comparisons showed that the community residents' needs for medical services did not differ significantly from the needs of the institutional residents, and that all of the needed services were available in the community. The authors correctly caution that the setting in which the study took place is unique.

Parnel Wickham-Searl tackles, in Chapter 7, what is perhaps the most confusing and perplexing set of human service policies of the federal government, those concerning Intermediate Care Facilities for the Mentally Retarded (ICFs/MR). In so doing, she illustrates for us the sixth of the communitization fallacies, as well as the dilemma of policy and practice proceeding on parallel tracks. In this carefully researched chapter, Wickham-Searl details the legislative and social history of the federal government's involvement in mental retardation services through the Medicaid program, from the extension of Medicaid to cover mentally retarded people in ICFs/MR in 1971, to the Home and Community-Based Care Waiver Authority in 1981. The intent of Senator Chaffee's (R-RI) proposed Community and Family Living Ammendments (CFLA) of 1983, and their 1985 revisions—to remove the incentive for states to invest resources in large facilities rather than smaller community-based facilities—are outlined in terms of the political and economic environment of the 1980s. The author contends that institutional forms of services are not more efficient and are certainly not less expensive than comparable community-based services. The chapter will assist readers to understand the reasons for Senator Chaffee's CFLA legislation through a balanced presentation of the issues as seen by both proponents and opponents at the time of the 1986 legislative debate on the proposals.

The seventh fallacy of communitization is that by grouping people with similar needs in congregate care facilities we can provide unique services which are not available in the community. To understand this fallacy, we need to know what services are needed (the data of Chapter 6 are relevent here), whether the needed services are available in the community, and whether we can make them available through the use of existing or enhanced generic services (e.g., hospitals, schools, YMCAs, etc.). In her chapter, "The Availability of Community Resources to Group Homes in New York City," Gothelf provides not only the necessary data but also a methodology for others to use in their communities. Analyses of data obtained from residence administrators lead the author to conclude that, in general, those resources and services needed by people who are developmentally disabled are available in community neighborhoods. Most of the obstacles to service use and satisfaction identified in her survey—petty crime, lack of recreational facilities nearby, traffic congestion, and few job opportunities—are the same obstacles faced by all people who live in the community.

Some readers may point to Gothelf's data on the gaps in services and resources as justification for the perpetuation of isolated speciality institutions. The research advocacy model of Chapters 2 and 3, however, is evident in Gothelf's conclusion: "If there are unsatisfactory neighborhoods, they present a problem for everyone who lives there." We must take the steps necessary "to add or modify the services" needed to achieve community integration of all people, including people who are mentally retarded.

One of the services which must be added is respite services for people who are developmentally disabled and for their families. This is the conclusion of the authors in Chapter 9, based on data from their interviews of 39 families using respite services in central New York State. The questions asked by Schultz and her colleagues concerned why families needed respite, the type of respite preferred, the benefits they and their handicapped family member obtained, and what they see as needed enhancements of this service. This presentation of a timely topic will be particularly useful to planners of family support systems, offering specific recommendations for both the establishment and evaluation of respite programs.

If generic community services, such as those discussed in the two preceeding chapters, are or can be made available, can we assume that they will be used by people who are mentally retarded? As Kaminer and Jedrysek point out in Chapter 4, the skills necessary to display such autonomous behavior cannot be taken for granted with previously institutionalized people or with those who have a history of overprotection at home. The conservative approach of some professionals would lead to the establishment of mechanisms in the community to bring the necessary services to the person (the phenomenon of the dentist who makes house calls). The communitization advocacy approach would lead to programs which prepare people who need services to locate and use existing services.

In the tenth chapter, Keul, Spooner, Grossi, and Heller describe just such a program developed at the University of North Carolina at Charlotte. The authors describe the philosophy, setting, and goals of the Community Resources Training Program, and present analyses of data which support its efficacy. These data are obtained from their unique Assessment of Independent Living Skills instrument which others should find useful. Variables which the authors considered to be important in influencing the success of the project are discussed—in particular, the participation of parents and family members in the training. The chapter concludes with a set of recommendations for replication of the project and for field-based evaluation of similar empowerment projects. This chapter illustrates the kind of communitization research called for in Chapter 2, and is a demonstration of the research ideology of barrier identification and elimination called for in Chapter 3.

The preceeding chapters show us that communitization is a twofold process. On the one hand, we must return people who are institutionalized to the freedom of the neighborhood. Eight of preceeding chapters have provided us with rationales and means for this component. The other component of the communitization process is to prevent people from leaving and losing the freedom of our neighborhoods. Chapters 4 and 7 help us to appreciate our responsibilities in this regard. The next chapter extends our appreciation by examining a complex and controversial issue raised by the community imperative.

Basic rights of people who are mentally retarded to live, learn, and work in integrated communities have been asserted and are being secured through concerted advocacy efforts (Sailor & Guess, 1983). This advocacy has generally failed, however, to reach into intimate areas of human rights, including the rights to sexual expression, to marry, and to parenthood. Parenting by people who are mentally retarded has been an unsettling topic throughout history. The major arguments and solutions are evident in the most recent eugenic period in Western society, from 1880 to 1945. During this period, the philosophy of Social Darwinism and the gross misunderstanding of genetic transmission of human characteristics (Gould, 1981) lead to cries for institutionalization, segregation, and nontherapeutic sterilization of mentally retarded and other devalued people. In the words of Charles Sherman Little (*Sixth Biennial Report, 1912*), society must be protected from those who, ''endowed with abnormal desires which are allied with defective judgment and will-power, spread abroad in the community the most loathsome and infectious of diseases, and beget children, often times illegitimate, who are defective and who eventually become public charges, whether in the county farms, insane hospitals, jails, or prisons. . . . If provision is not made for them very soon by the State, these children will grow into manhood and womanhood ignorant and untrained, their vicious tendencies unrestrained'' (pp. 8–9). Although they are couched in less vehement words, similar arguments are still proposed. In 1980s parlance, the supporting arguments focus on issues of parental adequacy and the quality of life for the offspring of parents who are labelled mentally retarded.

Sirota and Hoffman present in Chapter 11 a brief review of the history of the legislation permitting or compelling the practice of sterilization of people who are mentally retarded in North America, and discuss the contemporary rationales for this procedure. Their review of a sample of empirical investigations in the past 40 years on the parental adequacy of people who are mentally retarded leads them to conclude that it is prejudice and not evidence which supports denial of parenthood. The studies reviewed lack control of confounding variables (such as poverty and lack of parenting education in special education programs), fail to adequately define and measure parental adequacy, and use obviously biased sampling procedures. In their view, the lack of community social support systems, not the lack of intelligence, accounts for the reported incidence of parental inadequacy among people who are mentally retarded (as well as those who are poor, uneducated, and otherwise devalued). Rather than deny the right to parenthood to people who are mentally retarded while we wait for the community to modify their prejudicial attitudes, the authors call for the establishment of the necessary parent education and social support systems.

The last section of this volume presents two chapters with contrasting views on the future of institutions for people who are mentally retarded. Walsh and McCallion are administrators at one of the oldest mental retardation institutions in the United States, founded at Vineland, New Jersey, in 1888 by S. Olin Garrison. In Chapter 12, they present a defense of the congregate facility as one endpoint of the continuum of residential alternatives for people who are mentally retarded. These authors begin their chapter with an interesting historical perspective on the evolution of institutional models: from the tutorial programs established for one or two students in the home of a philanthropic physician (for example, Hervey Wilbur's "institution" at Barre, Massachusetts, established in his home in 1848 to serve the feeble-minded son of a prominent lawyer), to schools for the feeble-minded operated at state expense (for example, the New York State Asylum at Syracuse, established by Hervey Wilbur in 1851, originally at Albany; or the program for mentally retarded children established by Samuel Gridley Howe within the larger program for the blind which he directed at Perkins Institute in Boston, in 1848; or by James B. Richards' school at Elwyn, in 1852; or Henry Martyn Knight's school at Lakeville, now Mansfield, Connecticut, in 1858), to custodial institutions (for example, the transition of Elwyn under the direction of Isaac N. Kerlin in 1887, or the transition of the Massachusetts School for the Feeble-Minded at Waltham by Walter E. Fernald in 1891), to the institutional warehouses (such as the facilities at Letchworth Village or Sonoma or Beatrice or Faribault or Pennhurst, which housed 3,000, or 4,000, or even 5,000 inmates as recently as 1965).

Litigation of the '70s, changing social forces and philosophies, and improving technology are leading, in the authors' view, to reductions in size and improvement of services in public residential facilities. The current trend is to make institutions more homelike, to prevent them from becoming the dumping grounds they once were. Walsh and McCallion argue (as Fernald and Bernstein and Humphreys did 40 years ago, or as Miller and Warren and Thorne did 15 years ago, or as Melton and MacNamara and Zitnay did 5 years ago) that institutions must be transformed into regional resource centers and transitional facilities which provide short-term intensive treatment and crisis intervention. In addition, the new institution should be a catalyst for the development of community programs by providing the experts and equipment necessary to help communities develop human services for people who are mentally retarded. To illustrate their arguments, the authors describe a model for the small (300-bed) facility, such as the one they administer at Vineland.

The evidence cited to defend the position of the authors of Chapter 12 is derived in part from the analysis of data on the relationship of program size to the quality of care for the residents. The studies Walsh and McCallion suggest support larger institutional facilities (Class 6 studies in the taxonomy of Chapter 3) are some of the same ones cited by Biklen and Knoll in Chapter 1 in reaching their conclusion in support of smaller community facilities (Communitization Myth #5). Another expression of this paradox concerns the set of studies on the relationship of environmental setting to the behavior of residents. Again, the conclusion derived in Chapter 12 from an analysis of the evidence of these studies is diametrically opposite to the conclusion reached by Haney and Heal in Chapter 5 from their analysis of essentially the same studies. How can these apparent contradictions be accounted for?

Burton Blatt, in the concluding chapter of this volume, provides an answer. The reason that two researchers (or educators or administrators or policy makers) can look at the same evidence and derive opposite conclusions is that the question which led to the evidence is fatally flawed! As we have come to expect of Professor Blatt (we know of few others in our profession more deserving of the title Professor), this chapter challenges our beliefs and our behavior toward people we label mentally retarded.

Similar to Chapter 1, Professor Blatt begins Chapter 13 with an explication of six arguments against the deinstitutionalization of people who are mentally retarded, exploding each in turn. This is followed by a review of the definition of normalization and a brief history of the concept. The communitization paradox is taken on next. If institutions clearly are no good for the people who live there (Blatt, 1981), why hasn't communitization research shown that communities are better places to live? Why is there no conclusive proof of the superiority of community living to institutional living? The reason, Blatt tells us, is that "it is simply not a fair question." Normal environments are good by definition, and what is normal does not need to be justified by research, only observed.

In the next section of this provocative chapter, Professor Blatt appears to attack science by challenging the utility of research for studying the communitization paradox. Yet Professor Blatt was both a preeminent scientist and a preeminent humanitarian. The two are not contradictory. His view is that the application of science to the question of communitization is misguided, it misses the point. The issue is not one of science but rather one of values. The issue is freedom, and our failure to let people who are mentally retarded be free. "People are entitled to live free in a natural setting, irrespective of what particular environment most enhances their reading capability or vocational aptitude." For Professor Blatt, the question which we all must confront before we can profess our position on communitization is "What are your values?" The answer to that question will reveal the "real problem embedded in this controversy," and the answer to the paradox.

This book is the third in an annual peer-reviewed series. Beginning with Volume 3, an open submission policy was implemented in which chapters need not be based on presentations made at the annual conference of AAMD Northeast Region X. However, the theme for the volume will be related to the theme of the associated conference. Manuscripts for Volume 4, subtitled "Implications and Applications of Technology," are currently being reviewed. The tentative subtitle for Volume 5 is "Life Cycles" and is intended to present reviews of the research and theoretical literature at each stage of human development: prenatal, infancy, early childhood, childhood, adolescence, young adulthood, adulthood, and senesence. Potential authors are directed to the "Instructions for Authors," which appears at the end of this volume, for more information.

We encourage readers and contributors to join us in meeting the challenge of changing conditions in the field of mental retardation and developmental disabilities through careful study, research, and quality program development. Let's begin by revisiting the community imperative.

REFERENCES

Antonak, R.F. (1984). First among equals. In J.A. Mulick & B.L. Mallory (Eds.), *Transitions in mental retardation: Volume 1. Advocacy, Technology, and Science* (pp. 275–287). Norwood, NJ: Ablex.

Blatt, B. (1981). *In and out of mental retardation: Essays on educability, disability, and human policy.* Baltimore, MD: University Park Press.

Brooks, P.H., & Baumeister, A.A. (1977). A plea for the consideration of ecological validity in the experimental psychology of mental retardation: A guest editorial. *American Journal of Mental Deficiency, 81,* 407–416.

Bruininks, R.H., & Lakin, K.C. (1985). (Eds.). *Living and learning in the least restrictive environment.* Baltimore, MD: P.H. Brookes.

Bruininks, R.H., Meyers, C.E., Sigford, B.B., & Lakin, K.C. (1981). (Eds.). *Deinstitutionalization and community adjustment of mentally retarded people.* Washington, DC: AAMD.

Center on Human Policy (1979). *The community imperative: A refutation of all arguments in support of institutionalizing anybody because of mental retardation.* Syracuse, NY: Author.

Gould, S.J. (1981). *The mismeasure of man.* New York: W.W. Norton.

Lakin, K.C., & Bruininks, R.H. (1985). (Eds.). *Strategies for achieving community integration of developmentally disabled citizens.* Baltimore, MD: P.H. Brookes.

Lakin, K.C., Krantz, G.C., Bruininks, R.H., Clumpner, J.L., & Hill, B.C. (1982). One hundred years of data on public residential facilities for mentally retarded people. *American Journal of Mental Deficiency, 87,* 1–8.

Mallory, B.L., & Herrick, S.C. (1985, May). *The impact of deinstitutionalization on children and their families: Research findings and policy implications.* Paper presented at the meeting of the American Association on Mental Deficiency, Philadelphia.

Sailor, H. & Guess, D. (1983). *Severely handicapped students.* Boston, MA: Houghton-Mifflin.

Sixth Biennial Report of the Trustees of the New Hampshire School for Feeble-Minded at Laconia. (1912, October 31). Manchester, NH: John B. Clarke.

About the Editors and Contributors

Richard F. Antonak received the BA degree in mathematics from Rutgers College, and the M.Ed. and Ed.D. degrees in special education from Temple University, specializing in mental retardation research and teacher training. His early professional experiences with people with mental retardation were as a teacher of adolescents at the Woods Schools in Langhorne, Pennsylvania, and as a work-study coordinator at Penncrest High School in Media, Pennsylvania. While completing his doctorate, he supervised teachers of exceptional children and taught courses in special education for the Pennsylvania State University. He joined the faculty of the education department at the University of New Hampshire in 1975 where he designed and established the university's first special education teacher training courses and the Master's degree program in developmental disabilities. He is currently an Associate Professor of Education and Coordinator of Special Education Programs at UNH.

Dr. Antonak's research specialities are in attitude measurement, psychometrics, multivariate statistics, and the history of mental retardation. He has published research instruments and statistical analysis programs, as well as articles, monographs, and book chapters on topics in developmental disabilities. He has appeared as an expert witness on behalf of people with mental retardation and their advocates in 18 court cases, including *Garrity v. Gallen* concerning Laconia (NH) State School, and *CARC v. Thorne* concerning Mansfield (CT) State School. Dr. Antonak was elected to Phi Beta Kappa and Pi Mu Epsilon (the National Honorary Mathematics Society) while at Rutgers, and was advanced to Fellow of the American Association on Mental Deficiency in 1983. He was also elected a member of the American Academy on Mental Retardation and the American Statistical Association. An incorporator of AAMD Northeast Region X, he served as president in 1980 and is presently completing a second 3-year term as secretary-treasurer. He is also a co-founder and incorporator of the New Hampshire State Chapter of AAMD which he serves as secretary-treasurer.

James A. Mulick received his A.B. degree in psychology from Rutgers College, and then completed graduate studies at the University of Vermont, where he received his M.A. and Ph.D. degrees in psychology, specializing in learning and behavioral development. He completed a postdoctoral fellowship in clinical child psychology at the Child Development Institute, Division for Disorders of Development and Learning at the University of North Carolina, Chapel Hill. He has held clinical positions at Murdoch Center in Butner, North Carolina, the Eunice

Kennedy Shriver Center in Waltham, Massachusetts, the Child Development Center of Rhode Island Hospital in Providence, and Columbus Children's Hospital in Ohio. Dr. Mulick has held faculty appointments at Northeastern University, the University of Rhode Island, and the Brown University Program in Medicine, and presently holds a joint appointment as Associate Professor of Pediatrics and Psychology at The Ohio State University in Columbus.

Dr. Mulick has published widely in the areas of learning, developmental psychobiology, and mental retardation. He is co-editor of *The handbook of mental retardation, Parent-professional partnership in developmental services,* and *Prevention of developmental disabilities: Strategies for the 80's.* In addition to serving as series editor for *Transitions in Mental Retardation,* he is a member of the editorial boards of *Applied Research in Mental Retardation, Analysis and Intervention in Developmental Disabilities,* and *Computers in Human Behavior.* He has been chairperson of the psychology division and president of AAMD Northeast Region X, and the psychology division chairperson of the Ohio State Chapter of AAMD. He is a Fellow of the American Psychological Association and a Clinical Fellow of the Behavior Therapy and Research Society. His current research interests include experimental and applied behavior analysis, instructional technology and computer applications, parent training, severe childhood psychopathology, and public policy analysis relating to children and the handicapped.

THE CONTRIBUTORS

Deborah A. Allen completed her Ph.D. degree in experimental psychology at the State University of New York at Albany. She is currently an Assistant Professor at the University of Connecticut School of Medicine and Director of Research at the Research and Training Center for Pediatric Rehabilitation. Her current research interests include early intervention for infants who have been in neonatal intensive care, and community services for minority groups with handicapped infants. She is also active in program evaluation and research consultation in behavioral pediatrics.

Douglas Biklen received the B.A. degree in history from Bowdoin College, and the master's degree in regional planning and the Ph.D. degree in social science from Syracuse University. Formerly the Director of the Center on Human Policy at Syracuse, Dr. Biklen is currently Professor and director of Syracuse's Division of Special Education and Rehabilitation. He has published widely on the topics of community integration, legal policy, attitudes, and ethics, and is perhaps best known for his work on handicapism and advocacy. He served on the AAMD task forces which wrote the monographs concerning consent and least restrictive environments, and presently serves on the legislative and social issues committee of AAMD Northeast Region X. In addition to his position on the faculty at

Syracuse, Dr. Biklen is a senior investigator for the federally funded Research and Training Center on Community Integration.

Burton Blatt (1927–1985) was awarded the B.S. degree in education from New York University, the M.A. degree in counseling from Teachers College Columbia University, and the Ed.D. degree in special education from the Pennsylvania State University. Dr. Blatt was a teacher of English and of mentally retarded children in the city of New York, the Coordinator of Special Education Programs at Southern Connecticut State College, Chairman of Special Education at Boston University, and Centennial Professor and Dean of the School of Education at Syracuse University. For 1 year (1968), Dr. Blatt served as the first nonmedical director of the Division of Mental Retardation of the Massachusetts Department of Mental Health, an experience he shared with us in his book *Exodus from Pandemonium*. With Seymour Sarason of Yale University, Dr. Blatt created the psycho-educational clinic at SCSC, a model he would re-create at Boston University and Syracuse for the training of special education teachers. In 1971, he founded the Center on Human Policy at Syracuse "for the study and promotion of open settings." Dr. Blatt's publication list included over 300 entries; perhaps the most widely known of these is *Christmas in purgatory,* a photographic essay on institutionalization he published with Fred Kaplan in 1965. Throughout his life, he served people with mental retardation: by writing and speaking, by teaching, by testifying, by training teachers, and by leading professional societies. He received many awards and honors, including an Honorary Doctorate of Humane Letters from Ithaca College in 1974, a citation from the President's Committee on Mental Retardation, and the AAMD's Humanitarian Award. Dr. Blatt was president of AAMD in 1976–1977. He served Northeast Region X as chairperson of the education division and national councilor, and was the recipient of the region's Education award in 1973. It is to the continuation of the work of Burton Blatt that we dedicate this volume of *Transitions in Mental Retardation*.

Betsy Edinger holds a B.A. degree in art from the State University of New York at Oswego. She is currently a Program Specialist with Transitional Living Services, Inc. of Onondaga County, New York, responsible for developing respite services for families with relatives with a developmental disability.

Carole R. Gothelf earned the Ed.D. degree from Teachers College, Columbia University, and is currently affiliated with Hunter College of the City University of New York, coordinating a federal grant project to develop a training curriculum for administrators of community residences. Her major area of research interest is service delivery in community-based residential alternatives for people with mental retardation and other developmental disabilities.

Theresa A. Grossi received her B.A. degree from Marshall University and is currently completing her M.Ed. degree in administration at the University of North Carolina at Charlotte. She is employed as a supported work coordinator for a transition from school to work project of UNCC and the Charlotte-Mecklenburg schools.

Janell I. Haney received her M.A. degree from the University of Pittsburg and is currently working on her Ph.D. degree in special education at the University of Illinois. She has been a consultant to parent groups and teachers of mentally retarded children, and has published on topics related to adaptive skill training. Her research interests include the acquisition and generalization of adaptive behavior by people who are mentally retarded, particularly those living in community residential settings.

Laird W. Heal was awarded the Ph.D. degree in psychology from the University of Wisconsin, and then joined the faculty at George Peabody College in Nashville, Tennessee. Dr. Heal was the Director of Research for the National Association for Retarded Citizens from 1972 to 1974, where he developed an interest in deinstitutionalization, especially strategies for assessing the cost-effectiveness of residential alternatives. For the past 10 years, he has been on the faculty of the special education department at the University of Illinois at Urbana-Champaign. The focus of his current research and scholarly work is communitization ideology.

Harold W. Heller received his B.S. degree from Southern Illinois University, his M.A. degree from Northern Illinois University, and his Ed.D. degree from the University of Northern Colorado. He is currently Dean of the College of Education and Allied Professions and Professor of Special Education at the University of North Carolina at Charlotte. His previous experiences include faculty and administrative positions at the University of Alabama and at Indiana State University, director of the Division of Personnel Preparation of the U.S. Office of Education's Bureau of Education for the Handicapped, and superintendent of Bryce Hospital in Tuscaloosa, Alabama. Dr. Heller served as Vice Chairperson of the 1977 White House Conference on Handicapped Individuals and chaired the Professional Standards Committee of the Council for Exceptional Children. His research interests are in the areas of teacher training, career education for the handicapped, and ethical practices of special education practitioners.

Susan C. Herrick earned her M.A. degree in psychology at Hunter College of the City University of New York, and is currently a doctoral student in sociology at the University of New Hampshire. She has served as a recreation therapist in psychiatric facilities in New York City, and has participated in research studies of family problem solving and the impact of work on family life.

John W. Jacobson received the B.S. degree from Union College in Schenectady, New York, and the M.S. degree in psychology from the University of Bridgeport. He is currently pursuing doctoral studies at the University of Vermont. His clinical involvement in the field includes positions as director of admissions for an independent living center, a consultant on organizational management in community settings, and a staff psychologist. Mr. Jacobson is currently a planner and research analyst for the New York State Office of Mental Retardation and Developmental Disabilities where he is engaged in research on topics involving group homes, foster placements, and aging.

Matthew P. Janicki was awarded the B.A. degree in psychology from American International College in Springfield, Massachusetts, the M.A. degree from the State University of New York at Albany, and the Ph.D. degree from the State University of New York at Buffalo. He is currently the director of planning for the New York State Office of Mental Retardation and Developmental Disabilities. Previous positions included staff psychologist in a community mental health program, director of hostels for a private agency, probation officer, and staff psychologist for a community mental retardation program. He is the author of research publications in the areas of community living and population demographics, and is currently pursuing projects on aging and program management of community residences. Dr. Janicki is the chairperson of the administration division of AAMD Northeast Region X.

Eleonora Jedrysek was awarded a degree from the University M. Curie, Sklodowska, Poland, and is a diplomate of the Institut de psychologie of the Sorbonne. She has had more than 30 years of experience in a variety of roles working with children with developmental disabilities, and has taught at the university level. She is currently the Senior Psychologist of the Infant and Preschool Unit of the Children's Evaluation and Rehabilitation Center in Bronx, New York. She has published widely on topics relating to counselling parents of handicapped children and social class influences on intellectual development.

Ruth Kahan Kaminer was awarded her M.D. degree from New York University School of Medicine, and is board certified in pediatrics with fellowship training in developmental disabilities. She is currently the director of the Infant and Preschool Unit of the Children's Evaluation and Rehabilitation Center in Bronx, New York, and Associate Professor of pediatrics at Albert Einstein College of Medicine. Dr. Kaminer has been active in training pediatricians and other developmental disabilities professionals in the management of handicapped children. She has published in the medical and mental retardation literature on topics relating to early identification, behavioral interventions, and parent training.

Patricia K. Keul earned her B.S. degree from Appalachian State University and her M.S. degree from Winthrop College, both in special education. She is currently a doctoral candidate at the University of North Carolina at Greensboro, and serves as the Parent–Community Coordinator for a transition from school to work program of UNC Charlotte and the Charlotte-Mecklenburg schools.

James Knoll is a doctoral candidate in special education at Syracuse University and the coordinator of information for the Community Integration Project of the Center on Human Policy. In this role, he assists in the development of community-based programs for individuals with severe disabilities. Mr. Knoll worked for 12 years in a variety of direct service positions which included managing a community residence and teaching adolescents. He is currently involved with research on the influence of media on attitudes toward people with disabilities and the development of training materials for residential providers.

Robert A. Lubin holds the B.A. degree in psychology from Rutgers College, the Master's degree in public health from Columbia University, and the Ph.D. degree in psychology from the University of Vermont. He is currently a Research Scientist and the Head of the Department of Epidemiology and Community Health at the New York State Institute for Basic Research in Developmental Disabilities. He has held faculty positions at Columbia's School of Public Health, and at the New School for Social Research in New York City. Dr. Lubin has served as a consultant in program planning and evaluation in educational, governmental, and industrial settings, and has published research on a variety of topics in developmental disabilities, including epidemiology, prevention, communitization, and aging.

Bruce L. Mallory received his Ph.D. degree from George Peabody College, and is currently an Associate Professor of Education at the University of New Hampshire where he coordinates the Master's degree program in early childhood special needs. Previous positions include service as a VISTA volunteer, Head Start director, and legislative researcher. His research and teaching interests include support for families with handicapped children, analysis of policies affecting handicapped children and their families, and the preparation of professionals to work with young children with developmental disabilities. He has served as publications committee chairperson of AAMD Northeast Region X, and as chairperson of the legislative and social issues committee of the New Hampshire State Chapter of AAMD. He is currently the chairperson of the AAMD research advisory committee.

Philip McCallion was born in Belfast, Northern Ireland, and completed his training in sociology at Queen's University in Belfast. In Ireland, he was involved with the provision of day activity, respite, and vacation programs for disabled people. In the United States, Mr. McCallion was awarded the MSW degree from the State University of New York at Albany. He is currently the Assistant Executive Director for Programmatic Operations at American Institute—The Training School at Vineland, New Jersey. Mr. McCallion's research interests focus on the operation of complex human service organizations.

Meg Morse holds a B.A. degree in English from Michigan State University. She is currently a respite provider with Transitional Living Services, Inc. of Onondaga County, New York.

Bernice Schultz received her B.A. from Syracuse University, and is working toward her Master's degree at the New School for Social Research. Associated with Syracuse's Center on Human Policy since 1977, she is presently involved with the development of community-based residential and support services for people with developmental disabilities. She was the recipient of the Onondaga County Mental Health Department's Community Services Board Award for outstanding service on behalf of people with mental retardation.

Ellen Johnson Silver received her M.S. degree in educational psychology and statistics from the State University of New York at Albany, and is currently a statistical analyst for the Preventative Intervention Research Center for Child Health at the Albert Einstein College of Medicine and Montefiore Medical Center. In this role, she serves as a consultant on computer applications and research design for projects focusing on the prevention of mental health problems in chronically ill children. Previously, Ms. Silver served as a research scientist with the New York State Institute for Basic Research in Developmental Disabilities.

Wayne P. Silverman received his Ph.D. degree in cognitive psychology from the State University of New York at Buffalo. He is currently the head of the cognitive psychology research program at the New York State Institute for Basic Research in Developmental Disabilities. Dr. Silverman has conducted and published research on topics related to perceptual learning and information processing, epidemiology, and community services for people with profound and multiple handicaps.

Perry Sirota and *Diane Hoffman* are doctoral candidates in the department of psychology at Queen's University, Kingston, Ontario, Canada.

Fred Spooner received his B.S. and M.S. degrees from Butler University, and the Ph.D. degree from the University of Florida. Currently, he is Visiting Assistant Professor at the University of North Carolina at Charlotte, and Senior Research Associate with the Human Development Research and Training Institute at Western Carolina Center, Morganton, North Carolina. His previous experiences included positions as a researcher or administrator in programs in

Washington, Illinois, and North Carolina. A member of the editorial boards of several publications in mental retardation, including Education and Training of the Mentally Retarded, Dr. Spooner's research interests center on comparisons of training procedures for people with severe handicaps, the role of peer review in the protection of client's rights, and criminal offenders with mental retardation.

Kevin K. Walsh received his master's and doctoral degrees in life-span developmental psychology from the University of Akron, Ohio. He has held a variety of position in treatment settings for people with mental retardation, including staff psychologist at the Broome Developmental Center in New York, and Director of Residential Services at the Training School at Vineland, New Jersey, where he is currently the Director of Psychology and Habilitation. His research interests are in the areas of programming for skill development and reduction of maladaptive behavior, and management practices of residential facilities. Dr. Walsh is currently the chairperson of the psychology division of AAMD Region IX.

Parnel Wickham-Searl earned her Master's degree in public administration and the Ph.D. degree in special education administration from Syracuse University. The parent of a child with developmental disabilities, she founded the Center for Handicapped Children, a family-oriented program in Buffalo, New York, and currently serves as coordinator of the Eastern Suffolk Center for Developmental Disabilities, a program she founded in Cutchogue, New York. Dr. Wickham-Searl conducts research on federal policy for individuals with developmental disabilities, with particular interest in the transition of people from institutions to communities.

Warren B. Zigman was awarded the B.A. degree from New York University, and the M.A. and Ph.D. degrees from Columbia University. He is currently a research scientist in the Department of Epidemiology and Community Health at the New York State Institute for Basic Research in Developmental Disabilities. His research interests are in the area of premature aging in people with Down's syndrome.

Acknowledgements

This volume is an official publication of Northeast Region X of the American Association on Mental Deficiency. The theme was selected by the program committee of the association's 47th Annual Conference, held at Kiamesha Lake, New York, in October, 1984. We are grateful to Michael R. Dillon, 1984 program committee chairperson, and to the members and officers of the Association for continued support of this series.

The following individuals served as guest reviewers for Volume 3 to resolve conflicting reviews received from members of the editorial board, or to provide expertise in particular areas: Richard Ashbrook, Stephen N. Calculator, Craig R. Fiedler, Bruce L. Mallory, Lori Jeanne Peloquin, and L. Kaye Rasnake.

The series editor was supported during preparation of this volume in part by U.S. Department of Health and Human Services MCH Special Project MCJ-009053-01-0. The series associate editor was supported in part by U.S. Department of Education Personnel Preparation Grant G008535064. Editorial work was facilitated by the use of Valdocs supplied through the generosity of Rising Star Industries of Torrance, California.

The Community Imperative Revisited

Douglas Biklen and James Knoll
Division of Special Education and Rehabilitation
Syracuse University

This chapter reviews the philosophical, legal, and empirical underpinnings of the Community Imperative Declaration (Center on Human Policy, 1979), which asserts that, "All people, regardless of the severity of their disabilities, are entitled to community living." A systematic refutation of eight major arguments which oppose this position provides the framework for this review. In addition, the experiences of a number of disabled people, who have formerly resided in mental retardation institutions, are cited as a further affirmation of the imperative. In the process of this review, a number of obstacles which continue to hinder complete realization of the community imperative's goal are highlighted.

In November of 1983, in hearings before the New York State Commissioner for Mental Retardation and Developmental Disabilities, a young man named Michael Kennedy testified:

> Well, I hear you talking about making institutions smaller. I want to make sure that you know that smaller isn't acceptable. You have to close them down completely. There are still people in there and they need good care. Instead of just taking a few people out, you've got to get everybody out.[1]

What distinguished Mr. Kennedy from most of the other people gathered to testify in the ballroom of the Sheraton Hotel that day was the fact that he knew first hand the meaning of institutional life and of deinstitutionalization. He had spent 16 of his 23 years living in three different institutions administered by the commissioner's department. But, since August of 1982, an apartment has been

---

[1] This and all subsequent unattributed quotes and descriptions are from an observational study of life in a community residence. With the exception of Mr. Kennedy, whose statements are a matter of public record, the names of all participants in this study have been changed to protect their privacy.

his home. He shares it with three other men. On the commissioner's books, Mr. Kennedy's home is listed as a community residence administered by a local voluntary agency.

The presence at such hearings of people whom the bureaucracy calls clients is a recent phenomena. In fact, when Mr. Kennedy signed up to testify and described himself as a "consumer advocate," he had to explain the term and convince a seemingly disbelieving aide to the commissioner that he had a right to speak. The tacit assumption has been, and largely continues to be, that people with mental retardation and other developmental disabilities are merely the passive recipients of services.

Michael Kennedy's words and those of other consumer activists are uncompromising in their advocacy for the right of all people, no matter how severely disabled, to live in the community. Their challenge bears striking resemblance to a syllogism composed by a group of faculty and students the Center on Human Policy at Syracuse University in 1979. The Syracuse statement read as follows:

The Community Imperative:
A Refutation of All Arguments
in Support of
Institutionalizing Anybody
Because of Mental Retardation.

In the domain of human rights:
All people have fundamental moral and constitutional rights.
These rights must not be abrogated merely because a person has a mental or
    physical disability.
Among these fundamental rights is the right to community living.

In the domain of educational programming and human service:
All people, as human beings, are inherently valuable.
All people can grow and develop.
All people are entitled to conditions which foster their development.
Such conditions are optimally provided in community settings.

Therefore:
In fulfillment of fundamental rights and
In securing optimum developmental opportunities,
All people, regardless of the severity of their disabilities, are entitled to
    community living.

The community imperative statement was signed by more than 100 scholars, consumers, and other leaders in the field of mental retardation during the ensuing months. It was adopted by the President's Committee on Mental Retardation, the National Association for Retarded Citizens, and the community residential interest group of the American Association on Mental Deficiency. The Association for Persons with Severe Handicaps passed its own version of the imperative, and went a step further, calling for a cessation of institutional construction. But, despite a broad base of professional support for the community imperative, the policy of deinstitutionalization has continued to evoke enormous professional and political controversy nationally.

In the years since the community imperative was first published, it has become increasingly apparent that the affirmation that all people have a right to live in typical neighborhoods is only part of what is implied by the term "community." The community imperative, deinstitutionalization, and the least restrictive alternative speak to a deeper vision, the right to be treated as equal with others. That is why the perspective and experiences of individuals who are directly affected by the policy of deinstitutionalization merits consideration on a par with that afforded to the opinions of politicians, administrators, professionals, and researchers, since the questions really are: "Where should this person live?" and "How should this person live?"

Most of the recent criticisms (e.g., Barbakow, 1982; Clifford, 1984; Issues of Concern, 1984; Kupfer, 1982) of the imperative are relatively subtle and often presented as being in full agreement with the basic ideals of deinstitutionalization. In reviewing the critiques of the community imperative, we found that one of eight major arguments is generally invoked to prove it is an unrealistic and even uncaring attempt to impose an abstract social agenda on the daily lives of people who are mentally retarded within the nation's neighborhoods. We also found that the very barriers which hamper efforts to implement the imperative are cited, in these arguments, as part of the rationale for negating it. These eight arguments provide us the framework for refuting them.

1. Normalization promotes a fallacy. It is true that, through the systematic use of behavioral technology, you can change people's behavior, but even this cannot make them normal. So just moving everyone into middle class housing certainly is not going to bring about this metamorphosis.

No one who understands the principle of normalization has ever proposed that its aim is to make people "normal" or to force everyone into conformity with some inflexible model of a socially acceptable lifestyle. This interpretation views normalization from the perspective of the individual pathology model, which defines the root of all problems within the person, and finds that the only answer to a problem is to change the person. In fact, normalization is grounded in a more ecological framework which sees problems as multifaceted and evolving from the interaction of the person with the environment. From this ecological perspective, intervention must be global and systemic—not merely individualistic.

In 1959, Bank Mikkelson, then head of mental retardation services for Denmark, articulated the principle of normalization or, in simple terms, the permitting of retarded people to live in as normal a fashion as possible. A decade later, another Scandinavian, Bengt Nirje, executive director of the Swedish Association for Retarded Children, explained the concept to an American audience in the President's Committee on Mental Retardation publication entitled *Changing pat-*

terns in residential care of the mentally retarded. Nirje's article described normalization as "making available to the mentally retarded patterns and conditions of everyday life which are as close as possible to the norms and patterns of the mainstream of society" (Kugel & Wolfensberger, 1969, p. 181).

Perhaps one of the clearest visions of normalization was provided more than a decade ago, when a group of retarded people themselves articulated a vision of what they wanted their lives to look like. Nirje reports on a statement of "beliefs, questions, and demands" which was drafted by retarded adults at a conference sponsored by the Swedish Association for Retarded Children. These comments suggest some of the specific implications of normalization. Among the demands made at the national conference in Malmo, Sweden, were the following:

Leisure Time Activities

Under no circumstances do we want to walk in large groups in town. There should be more possibilities for sports and exercises. We think, further, that the financial situation of the handicapped today is such that he cannot afford the leisure-time activities or organizations he wants to take part in. We have all agreed that we want more power of participation in decision making, especially in planning and implementation of leisure-time activities.

Vacation

We all think one should decide oneself what to do during vacations. We think travel abroad is good, but one should travel with other non-retarded young adults of the same age. We have all agreed that summer camps for adults should be banished (this refers to segregated camps for both retarded adults and children).

Living Conditions

We wish to have an apartment of our own and not be coddled by personnel; therefore, we want courses in cooking, budgeting, etc. We want to have a right to our own apartment but without priority in the waiting list (in Sweden, one may have to sign up for an apartment well in advance.) We want the right to move together with the other sex when we feel ready for it, and we also want the right to marry when we ourselves find the time is right. We want to have more personal freedom, and not as it is now in certain institutions and boarding homes where you have to ask permission to shop for fruit, newspapers, tobacco, etc. When we are living in institutions, we want social training to be able to move out into society and manage on our own. We who live at home have found that: it is largely good, but one ought to move out when the time is right to a sheltered apartment or hostel; one cannot for his whole life be dependent on his parents. We want, however, to have our own key when we live at home.

Vocational Schools

We demand more training in a wider range of vocational fields so that we can have larger freedom of choice in determining our vocations. We want to choose our vocations ourselves and have influence over our education.

Questions Concerning Work

We demand more interesting jobs. We do not want to be used on our jobs by doing the worst and the most boring tasks we do at present. We demand that our capacity for work should not be underestimated. We think that we should be present when our situation is discussed by doctors, teachers, welfare workers, floor men, etc. Now it feels as if they talk behind our backs. (Cited in Wolfensberger, 1972, pp. 190–193)

The message from Malmo was clear. People wanted support to achieve independence, dignity, and personal fulfillment.

In the U.S., normalization has often meant the chance for people with retardation to live more independently. For example, for many years Morey Post lived in a New York State institution where he had his meals served to him and his laundry done for him. Now he lives in an apartment. And he makes choices about *how he wants to live.* He is not particularly enchanted with the idea of doing the his own laundry. But he delights in demonstrating how, after it has reached the point of no return, he is able to manage an over-loaded basket on his wheel chair and make his way down in the elevator to the laundry room. But meals are another matter. Its very important to Morey that he has free access to the kitchen. You see, Morey is a bit of an insomniac; every morning, he is awake by 4:30 or 5:00. For the first time in his 34 years he can get up—he does not need permission. He boosts himself into his wheelchair and wheels himself into the kitchen. He no longer has to wait for someone to bring him what's on the menu for everyone's breakfast that day. He makes a pot of coffee, rummages up some breakfast, then sits back and listens to the radio while the rest of the people in his house get up and get ready for work.

More recently, Wolfensberger has argued that the term "normalization" no longer serves the field adequately. First, people frequently misunderstand or misinterpret it. Second, people often trivialize normalization, not recognizing its conceptual roots and operational utility. And third, the term normalization may not communicate well enough the kind of societal changes needed to enhance the lives of people with disabilities. Hence, Wolfensberger recommends a term that more narrowly describes the principal goal of normalization, to fashion, support, and defend "valued social roles for people who are at risk of social devaluation" (Wolfensberger, 1983, p. 234). He would have us call this "social role valorization." His point, obviously, is that the power of stigma leveled against people with disabilities demands an affirmative, even activist response, something more than an accommodation or what might be implied by the phrase "making normal."

2. Normalization, deinstitutionalization, mainstreaming, and the least restrictive alternative are nice concepts for consciousness-raising but really they are little more than slogans without any empirical base.

This argument embodies a pair of related fallacies which are refuted by the historical evolution of these concepts.

The first fallacy is to deny the empirical basis of these interrelated concepts. In fact, their empirical roots are twofold: (a) the history and experience of the human species testifies to the fact that the best environment for human growth is provided by participation in the life of a person's natural community; and (b) the experience of the absolute bankruptcy of the institutional model of service for people with mental retardation. While such data do not conform to the canons for statistical significance it is pre-eminently empirical in the fullest sense of the word. As we shall see the data have been substantial enough to meet the criteria for legal evidence.

The essential problems of institutional life were embedded in the very idea of institutions for retarded people. As Wolfensberger (1975) points out, in an historical analysis of how mental retardation institutions emerged on the American scene, the abusive quality of institutional life could easily have been predicted when institutions were first developed. Their physical designs foreshadowed custodial, dehumanizing treatment. Wolfensberger likened their growth and permanence to the story of the mythical Greek figure, Procrustes, who would lengthen or shorten his guests to fit the bed that he had prepared for them:

> It did not matter who or what the resident was, whether young or old, whether borderline or profoundly retarded; whether physically handicapped or physically sound; whether deaf or blind; whether rural or urban; whether from the local town or from 500 miles away; whether well-behaved or ill-behaved. We took them all, by the thousands, 5,000 and 6,000 in some institutions. We had all the answers in one place, using the same facilities, the same personnel, the same attitudes, and largely the same treatment. And if our guest did not fit, we made him fit! What we need to do is to take an entirely fresh look at the needs of the retarded, and increase the goodness of fit between their needs and our programs. And we must face the possibility that we may need a new bed. (Wolfensberger, 1975, p. 69)

Michael Kennedy remembers the one-size-fits-all approach of the institution where he spent 8 years of his life. He was on a ward with 52 other young men. They all stayed in bed all day, every day, because no one thought it was important to get them up. But Michael was lucky. He was the one person on that ward who was able to sit up. So he was moved to another ward that had a little more activity. This meant that, instead of lying in bed all day, he got to sit around in the day room and watch television. It did not matter that these were the years of his life which most people spend in elementary school, since there was no educational program available for him. In recounting his life in this institution, Michael makes a special point of telling about the identification which each resident carried with him. Since the ward was very crowded, the staff found it hard to remember who was who; in order to overcome this difficulty, they painted each person's name on his back.

The normalization principle as the model for a "new bed" spread quickly through the ranks of mental retardation professionals and parent organizations in America. Not surprisingly, its chief proponents were people who had first hand knowledge of life in the nation's mental retardation institutions, and had managed to keep their eyes open to the truth of what they saw. One of the principal advocates was Dr. Burton Blatt, author of the major institutional expose, *Christmas in Purgatory* (Blatt & Kaplan, 1966), which started the critique of institutions as we know it today. Dr. Blatt, who, with photographer Fred Kaplan, visited a number of institutions and published accounts of them both in *Christmas in Purgatory* and in *Look* magazine, knew the horrors of institutional life. During his observational visits, he had seen people tied to benches and chairs, locked in barren isolation rooms, left to languish in boring, sparse "dayrooms." He had seen people washed down with hoses like so many cattle in a slaughter house. He had seen people bound up in straight jackets. Blatt's accounts of institutional life portrayed the inhuman conditions imposed upon institutionalized retarded personnel. He observed and recounted the many bathrooms with toilets that had no toilet seats, stall walls, or toilet paper, the broken plumbing and decaying ceilings. His writing revealed meals in which residents were given only ground-up food. He showed how trays of tranquilizing drugs and hours of boredom characterized institution life. He describes seeing children locked in so-called "therapeutic" cages, and rooms for sleeping where people were so crowded that it was necessary to literally walk across the tops of beds to get from one side of the room to another.

The scenes described by Blatt were not unlike those documented by other scholars, journalists, and film makers. Erving Goffman prepared what is still the most detailed account of institutional life in his scholarly, sociological treatise entitled *Asylums* (1961). Kenneth Wooden brought the litany of institutional abuse to Congress and to the American public through his book *Weeping in the Playtime of Others* (1974). Edwin Newman narrated the now classic NBC News documentary "This Child is Rated X" (Carr & Newman, 1971) describing again the horrors of institutional life. And Frederic Wiseman, a one-time law professor turned film producer, shocked the nation with his first documentary, "Titticut Follies" (1969), which sketched a stunning and disturbing portrait of dehumanization in a mental hospital for the criminally insane.

Not surprisingly, as the exposés proliferated, parents and advocates who had long suffered in the silent knowledge of these American Dachaus realized that to need help did not mean you had to accept second class citizenship. They went to court. One of the most famous confrontations between lawyers and state mental retardation officials occurred in Alabama, where, on April 13, 1972, U.S. District Court Judge Frank Johnson ordered state officials to implement stringent standards for the care of mentally retarded residents at the Partlow State School. Among the standards were requirements that residents be served in community based, noninstitutional settings as much as possible. That decision (*Wyatt v. Stickney*, 1972), known within the field of mental retardation as the "Wyatt

case," adopted the notion that people with retardation should be served in the
least restrictive (i.e., most free) environment possible.

As litigation mushroomed throughout the country, the litany of institutional
abuse was sung, over and over again. Plaintiffs' briefs at Willowbrook explained
that 100% of all residents in the institutions contracted hepatitis within 6 months
of entering the facility. Scabies, pneumonia, and roaches were present at
Willowbrook in epidemic proportions. The Willowbrook briefs read like the
worst from Blatt's *Christmas in Purgatory*. It was alleged that 80% of the
school-aged youngsters at the Willowbrook State School received no educational
programming. Plaintiffs charged that experimental research programs, including
those which utilized noxious stimuli, were being carried out at Willowbrook,
with inadequate and unethical provisions for obtaining consent from clients or
their families. Plaintiffs claimed that 96% of the facility's adults received no
educational or habilitative programming. The Willowbrook suit was filed in
March of 1972. Three years later, when a consent decree (*New York State
Association for Retarded Children et al. v. Carey et al.*, 1975) was finally
signed, a newspaper account of conditions at Willowbrook showed nearly no
improvement:

> Willowbrook is atrocious—an exercise in surrealism that seems to have sprung full
> blown from one of the inner circles of Dante's Inferno. To label Willowbrook "a
> developmental center" is to mutilate the phrase beyond recognition . . . there were
> children laying on floors . . . abandoned in shower stalls . . . sitting in pools of
> urine . . . beds were crowded head to head, side to side in some wqrds, only inches
> separating them . . . there were broken windows . . . the overall pattern from floor
> to floor, building to building, was one of repetition . . . no supervision, no struc-
> tured activities . . . the only forms of "recreation" a television set . . . or a
> blaring phonograph. (Action not words, 1975).

During the ensuing decade, New York State had difficulty meeting the spirit
of the Willowbrook consent decree, which called for deinstitutionalization of the
facility for all but 250 of the most severely disabled residents. Many residents
were "repatriated" (a term that the state mental retardation bureaucracy used to
describe a policy of moving people back to the institutions that were identified as
serving the counties from which the residents originally were placed) to other
state institutions. Finally, in 1984, New York State announced plans to close
Willowbrook altogether.

From the sound of life at Willowbrook, one might think it an extremely bad
institution. However, accounts of abuse surfaced at Beatrice State Hospital in
Nebraska, Sandhaven in North Dakota, Pennhurst in Pennsylvania, Solomon
State Hospital in Maryland, Cloverbottem in Tennessee, and Belchertown in
Massachusetts. The conditions of institutional life across America were shock-
ingly similar one to the other.

The second fallacy in this argument is the claim that the principles we are
considering are mere slogans with no substantive content. While tracing the

history of normalization and the course of anti-institutional litigation should have largely laid this to rest, one thing remains to be said. To equate normalization, deinstitutionalization, mainstreaming, and the least restrictive alternative with mere slogans is to trivialize some of the basic moral and legal underpinnings of our society. These principles remind our culture that the statement that all people "are created equal" does not come with any qualifiers.

Normalization meant opportunities for people with retardation to achieve greater independence and self-determination and to escape the stigma of being seen as incompetent. Initially, at least, it appeared that the concept of normalization as a moral and programmatic position within the field of mental retardation would be further enhanced by legal developments in the delivery of human services, particularly residential services. The legal concept "least restrictive alternative" provided what seemed an authoritative base for normalization. The concept first arose in constitutional law through a corporate lawsuit (*Dean Milk v. Madison, WI,* 1951). Then, in 1960 (*Shelton v. Tucker*), the Supreme Court examined and made a determination on the state's right to abridge personal, constitutionally protected freedoms:

> Even though the governmental purpose be legitimate and substantial, the purpose cannot be pursued by means that broadly stifle fundamental personal liberties when the end can be more narrowly achieved. The breadth of legislative abridgment must be viewed in the light of less drastic means for achieving the same basic purpose. (*Shelton v. Tucker,* 1960)

After the Wyatt case, this principle came to mean that, if the state needed to provide protective or habilitative care, it must do it in a manner which least intrudes upon the liberty interests of individuals with mental retardation. If the provision of day services in a community based setting could achieve the needs of the individual, then the state would not be constitutionally justified to incarcerate the person for 24 hours a day.

The concept of least restrictive alternative became frequently cited in state and federal legislation affecting a broad range of human service areas, including education, rehabilitation, medical care (i.e., sterilization), and residential programming. Public Law 94-142, the Education for All Handicapped Children Act, incorporated the concept. Similarly, Section 504, the nondiscrimination part of the 1973 Rehabilitation Act, required that organizations which receive federal funds adhere to the principle and practice of providing services to the disabled in a non-discriminatory (i.e., nonsegregated, least restrictive) fashion.

3. Sure the institutions of the past were awful, but we can develop high quality institutions. After all, there really is no data that people develop more in noninstitutional settings than in institutional ones.

Apart from the exposés and courtroom accounts of institutional abuse, researchers have provided extensive data on the stultifying effects of life in institutions. As we reported in 1979, we know that interaction between people who have been institutionalized with each other or with staff drops precipitously (Goffman, 1961; Provence & Lipton, 1962). Because of high employee turnover and institutional staffing patterns residents are likely to be cared for by hundreds of different staff over a several year time period, rather than by a few "primary" care givers (Hobbs, 1975). Holland (1971) found that within the first 24 hours of placement in an institutional setting, residents are transformed, both in appearance and in interaction with others, confirming Blatt's (1970) and Goffman's descriptions of the process by which people being inducted into the institutional setting are stripped of their individuality and dignity.

Further, we know that institutionalized children frequently become either apathetic and isolated or overly anxious to gain recognition and attention (Yarrow, 1962). Desire for attention obviously reflects the neglect of being routinized and alienated (Goffman, 1961). Simply put, institutions do not on the whole provide a stimulating environment in which children can develop (Flint, 1966). The atmosphere of institutions is generally bleak and unstimulating.

The evidence marshalled in the extensive literature review of Dr. Zigler's Yale group over a 20 year period (Zigler & Balla, 1977) proves damning to the institutional setting. Earlier, in 1963, Zigler had concluded: "It seemed that the effects of institutionalization depended on the pre-institutional history of the individual, with such institutionalization being more socially depriving for individuals from relatively good homes than for individuals from extremely deprived backgrounds." (Zigler & Balla, 1977, p. 3) Zigler and Williams (1963) had found that the only ones of their subjects in institutions whose IQs rose were from the "high deprived group". In short, the institution improved the test scores of those who came from the worst circumstances. But when Zigler, Balla, and Butterfield (1968) began another longitudinal study, this time in "what was considered to be one of the finest public institutions" (Zigler & Balla, 1977, p. 4) in the country, they found that the subjects did show increases in IQs over time. This finding contradicted the 1963 report. Their conclusion was that the effects of institutionalization were influenced not only by the person's pre-institutional experiences but by the particular institution in question.

The studies went on. In 1977, Zigler and Balla reported that the retarded individuals who maintained contact with their parents or parent-surrogates were more likely to display autonomous behavior characteristic of non-retarded children. It might well be argued from this finding, that retarded people can benefit from more personal contact than is available in the institution.

Next, Butterfield and Zigler (1965) compared one institution that made efforts to create homelike living arrangements within its cottage system and another that seemed to take no measures to simulate a homelike environment. They found, as they expected, that the latter institution was more socially depriving than the former. It caused readers of the study, ourselves included, to wonder. Would not a real home be even better still?

The data are in and with a few exceptions, are unequivocal. On the whole the institutions have fostered institution-like treatment, and among other things, greater dependency among residents. While it is true that one can find some isolated examples of humane "good" institutions and inhumane "bad" community residential facilities, the data consistently point to the community and to smaller programs for quality, resident-oriented programming.

Pamela Jenkins, is a 33-year-old woman who is blind and confined to a wheelchair because of cerebral palsy. After having lived for 18 years in two state institutions, she now shares an apartment with Morey Post and two other people who are disabled. Pamela admits that the last institution that she lived in is probably what most people would call a "good" institution. It was clean, the administration was sensitive to the need for people to be treated as individuals, abuse was not an accepted fact of life, and the staff was reasonably nice. Nevertheless, she feels no one should have to live in an institution. By their very nature, institutions "keep people held back against their will." When she was asked to describe the difference between "good" institutions and community life, Ms. Jenkins outlined four main points:

> For me I guess the main thing is meeting other people, a lot of different people. It's just that I find that interaction with people is better when you are living in the community. People are more likely to see you as you, not just as part of a bunch of wheelchairs. . . . Living in the community also means that you can make choices. It's not easy to have to make choices, but it's important to feel you decide your own future. You can always learn from that. In the institution you are laid back and kept back from having a say in what you want. . . . Another big difference is the way the staff treat you. In the institution they always tell you what to do; they don't ask you. In the apartment the staff ask if you want assistance or I can ask them for help. Also they are there for you, they can sit down and talk with you as a friend. . . . I can see myself change. I can say to myself "well today wasn't perfect" and then go on the next day and make it better. I can now feel as if I am productive. In the institution I didn't ever feel productive.

The principal change since the publication of the community imperative is that the evidence of the positive effects of living in noninstitutional settings has multiplied dramatically (e.g., Conroy, Efthimiou, & Lemanowicz, 1982; Eyman, Demaine, & Lei, 1979; Hull & Thompson, 1981; Keith & Ferdinand, 1984; Kleinberg & Galligan, 1983; Thompson & Carey, 1980; Willer & Intagliata, 1981). In addition, some of the findings hint at the radical difference between life in institutional and community settings. For example, Pratt, Luszcz, and Brown (1980) point out that, when they attempted to use an instrument constructed to observe behavior within an institution in a community site, the findings were confounded. Quite simply, the residents were found to be doing things which were beyond the instrument, because these things (e.g., extensive conversations between residents) *never* occurred within the institution.

There is also increasing evidence of the ability of community settings to handle a whole constellation of problems which at one time were used to justify the need for some individuals to remain in more restrictive settings. The primary factor influencing "success" seems to be the careful matching of the person to an environment or a service provider that is attuned to the needs of the individual (Willer & Intagliata, 1982). We know, for example, that, when retarded people have advocacy and support services, they tend to achieve success in community residential placements; this is often true even when the residents exhibit "maladaptive" behavior (Schalock, Harper, & Genung, 1981). Of course, when support and programming are unavailable in the community, residents of group homes are more likely to be institutionalized or reinstitutionalized (Polivka, Marvin, Brown, & Polivka, 1979). The complement of this is also true. That is, "when residential environments [community residences] are more normalized, along the lines of increased training opportunity, increased opportunity to assume responsibility for in-house tasks, more autonomy, clearer expectations on the part of staff members, and increased access to resources, residents are more likely to perform mastered skills and be satisfied with the residential setting" (Seltzer, 1981, p. 629).

Another look at some earlier studies of community life is instructive, since it reminds us that none of the more recent findings should come as a surprise. Two such studies (Edgerton, 1967; Fernald, 1919) on desinstitutionalization suggested that retarded people tended to succeed in community living arrangements when they enjoyed the assistance of benefactors or what we might today call "support networks." Without such support, retarded people were assumed incapable of achieving, or not competent enough to achieve, independence. This early finding would seem to support the importance of citizen advocacy and other support programs.

On the other hand, more recent research suggests the difficulty of predicting precisely those factors which influence success in community living. When Edgerton and Bercovici (1976) did a follow-up study 12 to 14 years after Edgerton's original *Cloak of Competence* (1967) study, many of those deinstitutionalized retarded persons who had been expected to "succeed" in adjustment, in a conventional sense (jobs, friends, family ties, increased steady income, etc.), had not. Yet they lived in and seemed to prefer the community to the institution. Others, who had been predicted as headed for disaster, fooled the researchers. They succeeded. In other words, Edgerton and Bercovici found that it was difficult, if not impossible, to tell who would successfully adapt to community life. In a second, albeit less extensive follow-up study—it is becoming increasingly difficult to locate the original research subjects—Edgerton and his colleagues (Edgerton, Bollinger, & Herr, 1984) find that the researchers' notions of success, as they themselves readily admit, were often inconsistent with the perspectives of retarded people themselves. Invariably, despite terribly difficult conditions and seemingly quite limited life opportunities, the deinstitutionalized people regarded their own adjustment to community living positively, and had a remarkably optimistic outlook. We might conclude, then, that, in regard to adjustment to community living, whatever measures are used, whether the client's own perspectives on happiness or satisfaction, or externally devised measures, the consistent pattern is one of moderate, though unpredictable, success.

> 4. Some people have such profound retardation that they cannot benefit from educational programming, and certainly not from community placement. Rather, this group—this "hopeless" remnant—needs enriched care in an institutional setting.

This argument has become the rallying cry for most opponents of deinstitutionalization. It is used to prove that there will always be a need for institutions, since, they contend, it would be cruel to subject the most severely handicapped individuals to the complexity of a life in the community. Indeed, it is this very argument as it was presented in the Wyatt case, by a group of consultants known collectively as the Partlow Committee (Ellis, Balla, Estes, Hollis, Isaacson, Orlando, Palk, Warren, & Siegel, 1978), which was part of the impetus behind the original publication of the community imperative. The committee said that the standards of care which the court had elaborated in its 1972 decision, particularly the mandates for community living and a specific amount of programming within the institution, were unrealistic, inflexible, and precluded informed professional judgments, and should therefore be set aside and replaced with "enriched" institutional life for those who could not learn.

The available research evidence provides the basis for asserting that small community based settings are the most enriched environment for facilitating people's growth and providing for their comfort. There is *absolutely no evidence* to support the contention that any institution has ever provided any kind of environment that we would judge to be enriched. Certainly, it makes absolutely no sense to subject people who apparently have a very difficult time processing their perceptions, and are among the least efficient learners, to environments which involve a very large number of people and are many times more complex than a family home. However, the position presented by proponents of this argument, under the mantle of a true empiricism, is not data-based.

Essentially, this hopeless-remnant argument is the most recent incarnation of a myth which has formed an integral part of the individual pathology model from its inception. Operating under this myth, professional clinicians, on the basis of an a priori theoretical construct such as the shape of the skull, the nation of origin, or the normal curve, define some individuals as being so different that their own good and the good of society demands that they be excluded from the community. These individuals are excommunicated. It is true that, with the passage of time, the size of the remnant has shrunk considerably and the methods of exclusion have become somewhat more benign. Nevertheless, this does not change the nefarious nature of the hopeless remnant myth, because it establishes a test for humanness. It says, "If you pass on the scale of adaptive behavior, or

IQ, or daily living activities then you can earn the privilege of community living.'' It errs on the side of exclusion.

The essential position in the community imperative is that history has shown it is better to err on the side of inclusion. Hence, there can be no test. By birth, we are all members of the same community. Privilege is not at issue. Even if someone cannot learn anything which *we* judge to be of value, that does not alter their right to the richest possible life in the community.

Despite the weakness of its logic and data base, the Partlow Committee's resurrection of the myth of the hopeless remnant has stimulated an ongoing debate over the educability of severely handicapped persons. The debate continues to be played out on the pages of professional publications (e.g., Lehr & Brown, 1984; Noonan, Brown, Mulligan, & Rettig, 1982). It is ironic that these shock waves, set off by an argument in the Wyatt case, would later be used by a conservative Supreme Court in another case to support its dismantling of the right to treatment in the least restrictive environment as it was originally outlined in the Wyatt decision.

On June 12, 1974, a severely retarded man by the name of Nicholas Romeo was admitted to the Pennhurst State School. His father had died recently. In the absence of sufficient community support services, his mother found it difficult to tend to his needs, and so institutionalized him. The facility served 2,000 other residents at the time. During the next 9 years that led to the Supreme Court's consideration of his case, Nicholas Romeo was injured (bruised, cut, scarred) 200 times. The questions that Nicholas Romeo's attorneys put before the Supreme Court were numerous, but central among them were:

1. When a state institutionalizes a retarded person, is that person entitled to a treatment program (i.e., something more than custodial care)?
2. Is an institutionalized resident entitled to safe living conditions?
3. Is a retarded person who needs protective and habilitative care entitled to receive such services in the least restrictive setting possible?

The negative side of Nicholas' story lies in how the Supreme Court decided his case. Just at the time when the concept of least restrictive alternative had gained acceptance in professional circles (e.g., planning, education, psychology), a conservative Supreme Court all but abandoned it as a principle that could help institutionalized retarded people. The Court's interpretation of the concept deserves careful attention, for it will surely influence public policy and, particularly, state deinstitutionalization practices. While the Supreme Court agreed with Nicholas Romeo's attorneys that he must be guaranteed bodily safety, it implied that he need not be served in the least restrictive setting. In skirting the broad issue of whether an institutionalized resident enjoys the right to treatment, the Court specifically cited the professional argument over the educability of severely retarded persons as one reason for its defining the issue in the narrowest possible terms (cf. *Youngberg v. Romeo,* 1982, p. 4683). The Court declared that habilitation or treatment need only be provided where its availability will preclude the necessity of "unreasonable restraints" (e.g., straight jacket, isolation cell).

Numerous legal policy analysts (e.g., Ellis, 1982; Menolascino, McGee, & Casey, 1982; Turnbull, 1982) tried to interpret the Romeo decision positively, but lower courts and state level officials were quick to see in Romeo a significant retreat from an imperative for the least restrictive alternative (see, for example, *Society for Goodwill to Retarded Children, Inc. v. Cuomo,* 1984). The principle of normalization makes the presumption that everyone can benefit by living in normal community settings. Or at least the presumption is made until proven false. Yet, as the courts have now interpreted the concept of "least restrictive environment or alternative" as applied to treatment models for retarded persons, we can no longer assume that this presumption enjoys high court backing.

There is a positive side to the story which stands in sharp contrast to the myth of the hopeless remnant. On April 5, 1983, Nicholas Romeo, who "is profoundly retarded . . . has the mental capacity of an eighteen month old child . . . cannot talk and lacks the most basic self-care skills," and whose counsel conceded "no amount of training will make possible his release" (*Youngberg v. Romeo,* 1982, pp. 4681, 4683), left the institution for a group home in a typical Philadelphia neighborhood. His living conditions changed dramatically as a result. Once again he could enjoy homelike surroundings. Slowly, Nicholas' behavior began to change as well. A news reporter described the changes this way:

> Nick's good behavior has been reinforced with snacks, praise, or pats on the hand, or back for every 15 seconds he goes without hurting himself or others. His "aggressions" . . . hitting himself or others . . . have dropped from 80 an hour to 12 an hour, and to even fewer than that. And a new Nick has begun to emerge, the affectionate, happy one Paula [his mother] remembers from a decade ago. Every weekday morning, his lunch bag in hand, Nick goes to the workshop where he receives physical therapy and vocational training. At 3 p.m., staff members of the group home pick him up. Sometimes, if he has had a toileting accident at the workshop, he returns carrying a large hefty bag containing his soiled clothes but those accidents too have decreased. And he recently completed his first production work at the workshop (putting an auto part in a box) and was paid for the job. (Woestendiek, 1984).

Interestingly, the high court rebuff of the least restrictive alternative as a guiding principle comes at a time when researchers are finding more and more evidence to support the positive side of Nicholas Romeo's story. As we mentioned above, it is clear that all people seem to benefit from small homelike placements, but the benefits are greatest for those with more severe disabilities (Conroy, Efthimou, & Lemanowicz, 1982; Hemming, Lavender, & Pill, 1981; Keith & Ferninand, 1984; Raynes, 1980). This finding stands in sharp contradiction to the claim that we need institutions to serve individuals with the most severe disabilities.

George Blake shares Ms. Jenkins's and Mr. Post's apartment with them. Before he moved into this apartment, Mr. Blake, although he was only 20 years old, lived in a nursing home because of the extensive amount of "care" he needs. Mr. Blake is unable to speak and communicates with facial expressions and one or two gestures. His use of muscles is so limited that he is unable to eat without assistance. His food must be ground up for him, since he cannot chew properly. If he falls over while sitting, someone must help him back to an upright position—he is unable to do that for himself. Although he is able to walk short distances with support, his problems with balance necessitate that, most of the time, he be pushed around in a wheelchair. When we asked Ms. Jenkins how Mr. Blake's life was different now that he was living in the community, she said:

> Sure he can't talk, but look at him in the apartment; he's happy all the time. When he was up at the nursing home, he spent most of his time crying. Once you get to know him, he's a real nice person and you can begin to understand him and what he wants and needs. Besides, he goes out in the community all the time and gets to experience stores, movies, and all kinds of things he couldn't before.

5. The matter of the size of living arrangement is not a factor that explains quality of experience for residents.

This argument is contradicted by a systematic examination of the relevant research. For example, in 1980, Baroff examined the eight major studies, available at that time, which related size to behavior and found; "Seven of them show some advantage to the smaller settings and one shows no difference. None show any advantage to the larger one" (p. 116). But, since size challenges the potential survival of larger settings (e.g., institutions and large "community" residences), it continues to re-surface in the research literature as a key variable.

Recently, the press to create small community-based programs has afforded researchers a unique opportunity to thoroughly study, on a wide scale, how size of residential facilities influences the life experiences of retarded persons. One set of systematic studies has been carried out by Conroy and a research group at Temple University (Sokol-Kessler, Conroy, Feinstein, Lemanowicz, & McGurrin, 1983). They have compared developmental and behavioral progress of people who are retarded in a large institutional facility with those in small group homes (two to six residents each). They gathered data on 713 residents of the institution and 174 residents in community living arrangements (CLAs) or group homes. The researchers matched clients in initial adaptive, and maladaptive behavior scores, gender, and age. They then re-examined these behaviors 2 years later. In adaptive behavior, the two groups did not differ. But in the area of maladaptive behavior, residents in the small community based facilities showed greater developmental progress. A second research group, this one in Minnesota, found similar benefits in small community based programs. Smaller programs were found to be more homelike than larger, institutional settings. Of the smaller programs, namely those ranging in size from one to eight residents, the Minnesota research team "found resident activity and autonomy to be higher (although not significantly so) in facilities with five to eight residents than in those with one to four residents" (Rotegard, Hill, & Bruininks, 1983, p. 55).

The experience of sitting at the dinner table with Pamela, Morey, George, their other housemate, and a couple of staff people offers some of the best evidence that supported residential settings should be as small as possible. Morey and a staff person had together made dinner for everyone—six regulars and one guest, not the 15 people we observed in a larger "small" community residence. Everyone, including George, was part of the conversation, which took place in a nice, pleasant tone of voice. There was no need to speak up to be heard over the din of clashing dishes. Nor was there the deadly silence of a rushed meal where the only aim is to empty the serving dishes as quickly as possible. The staff made a conscious, but natural, effort to insure this was a relaxed social occasion. They were able to do this at the same time they were attending to special needs or problems, such as Morey having difficulty pouring. The staff had to assist only four people, not ten.

It was striking that, throughout this mealtime, one staff person was able to devote most of his efforts to assisting George eat. This is a long process, which continued for well over an hour. George was able to pace his own meal. The staff person did not rush him. The three other residents were able to see to their own needs. In other words, apart from the small size of this residential group, the heterogeneous nature of the people living here means that the special needs of the more severely handicapped person can be seen to in an individualized manner. This differs markedly from situations where the numerous demands of a homogeneous grouping of severely disabled people tend to create, or are associated with, an environment and care that is "characteristically unstimulating, undifferentiated [not individualized], depersonalized, and rigid" (Raynes, 1980, p. 220).

Perhaps the most frequently cited research on size is the work of Landesman-Dwyer and her colleagues (Landesman-Dwyer, Sackett, & Kleinman, 1980). This work is distinctive because it is the only research to date that purports to find clear benefits for residents in larger community settings. Needless to say, this has led to it becoming a favorite citation of those who are looking for support for their attempts to build large "institutional" community residences (e.g., *New York State Association for Retarded Children et al. v. Carey et al.*, 1982, p. 41). These researchers found that "residents in larger group home [18–20 persons] interacted with more peers, were more likely to have a 'best friend,' [i.e., a peer with whom a person was observed more frequently than with any other person] and spent more time with their best friend than did residents in smaller group homes. . . . Clearly, the smallest facilities did not foster better interpersonal relationships than did the larger facilities" (Landesman-Dwyer et al., 1980, p. 14).

A moment's reflection makes it clear that Landesman-Dwyer's findings are not the unqualified endorsement of larger settings which they are presented to be.

As with all research, any generalization of the findings is constrained by the limitation inherent in the method. In this case, the focus is on providing a quantifiable picture of life *within the walls* of 20 community residences. The fact that the essence of community living involves integration into the larger community outside the walls of a person's abode is ignored. Indeed, these findings on relationships are consistent with other research (Willer & Intagliata, 1983) which found that residents of larger homes tended to have more of their social needs met within the place of residence, while individuals who lived in smaller settings had a broader network of relationships and social activities in the community. From this perspective, the most that can be said about Landesman-Dwyer's research is that it provides us with a great deal of information about how people occupy themselves within their place of residence, but it really does not address the qualitative differences among the social relationships of individuals living in settings of various sizes.

What needs to concern researchers is the degree to which true social integration into the community is taking place, and how that can be facilitated. Service providers need to know more about how the severely disabled residents of even the smallest settings develop relationships outside of these settings. Then they can begin to act on this knowledge so that residents are not left to be dependent solely on relationships with their housemates or with paid staff members. When the active development of extramural relationships begins to happen, community residences become more than just residences in typical neighborhoods; they become gateways into the larger community. This expectation seems to be justified in light of findings such as those of Hull and Thompson (1980) that residences in more populated areas, and ones which promote "socially integrated vocational, educational, recreational, and social activities" (p. 260), tend to promote more culturally normative appearance and behavior (including social interaction) than those that are more isolated or less promoting of social integration.

6. Larger settings may be a more efficient and less expensive ways to provide services, particularly to people with severe and profound retardation.

Obviously, many factors play a part in the troubles which beset deinstitutionalization. But one of the most important of these, the economics of institutions and the question of who pays the cost of deinstitutionalization, has only recently been recognized for its enormous influence. For the average citizen this cost question becomes a shell game—now you see the money, now you don't. Is it state money? Is it federal money? Is it Social Security? All the same, it is still tax money. As we shall see, the only place that this process makes any sense at all is in the state budget office. But, for the mentally retarded people who are affected by this juggling, funding formulas are often the unseen determinant of where and how they live.

In 1963, the federal government formally adopted deinstitutionalization as a major new thrust. The purpose of this policy was to improve the care and treatment of people classified as mentally retarded. The federal plan was to reduce admissions to institutions (prevent them if possible), find and create alternative programs in local communities, and improve conditions in existing institutional facilities (Comptroller General, 1977). Over more than a 20-year period, 135 federal agencies, located diversely in eleven major executive departments and agencies, became involved in affecting the lives of mentally disabled people. According to the Comptroller General's report to Congress on the effectiveness of deinstitutionalization, it is nothing less than a national problem; some might call it a national failure. As the subtitle of the Comptroller General's report indicates, "government needs to do more."

But perhaps doing more of the same is not the answer. Mentioned in the Comptroller's report is the fact that the federal government has, through grants and loans, facilitated the construction and refurbishing of institutions. As a result of previous federal and state commitments, the states are left with a difficult financial problem that, whatever our rhetoric about deinstitutionalization and the least restrictive environment, will be hard to solve. Federal Medicaid funding (Title XIX) of Intermediate Care Facilities for Mentally Retarded persons (ICFs/MR) has proven popular in state mental retardation agencies because it reimburses states anywhere from 50%–78% of residential services cost (Taylor, McCord, & Searl, 1981). So, through the availability of Medicaid money, the states which have bonded or mortgaged these facilities, have a ready flow of federal funds into their general state institutional budgets, as long as the institutions remain filled with residents eligible for Medicaid. Moreover, this program underwrites the cost of totally new facilities and new construction at existing institutions in order to assist the states in meeting the standards for ICF certification. In the period 1977–80, $821,456,000 in Medicaid funds went to support institutional construction (Taylor, Brown, McCord, Giambetti, Searl, Mlinarick, Atkinson, & Lichter, 1981). This situation speaks for itself. The existence of the Medicaid program provides an incentive for states to continue supporting the institutions, even at the expense of developing community based programs. [Ed. note. Refer to Chapter 9 by Wickham-Searl for a detailed exposition of this observation.]

While there are provision in the ICF/MR regulations for so-called community ICFs, there are no incentives to keep these facilities small. A 1979 report revealed that, of 524 ICFs in 23 states, 224 served 16 or more people (Human Services Associates, 1979). The same report showed California with 28 privately operated ICFs/MR, with an average of 96 residents each. And, by 1978, Minnesota had used Medicaid funds to pay for 25 facilities housing 16–50 persons each, and for three facilities housing over 100 persons each.

But the fiscal advantage to states maintaining existing institutions or building new smaller institutions is not the end of this economic "Catch 22" of deinstitutionalization. For a time, it appeared that community-based services would be far more cost effective than the large congregate institutions. Yet, while some experts have claimed that deinstitutionalization saved public funds (e.g., Templeman, Gage, & Fredericks, 1982), that claim is fast losing its credibility as the cost of community programming escalates. There are literally no incentives to keep overall program costs down or to keep down the cost of Medicaid-funded ICFs. It makes no difference if a facility is a traditional institution or one of the new smaller community-based ICFs; the regulations call for high levels of professional (i.e., expensive) staffing. In the years 1978 to 1984, New York State community ICFs/MR increased in annual per resident cost from $45,069 to $52,475, and per resident institutional ICF/MR cost for 1984–85 was anticipated at $68,866 (Pezzolla, 1984). Non-Medicaid-funded residences (group homes) in New York State in 1981–82 cost $23,530 and, in 1984–85, cost $27,384, just slightly more than half of the ICF/MR cost. It was within this context that New York State officials spoke of the need for a "critical mass" (*NYSARC v. Carey,* 1982, p. 43) of at least 50 beds if they were going to obtain federal funds to underwrite the movement of some of the most severely handicapped individuals out of Willowbrook.

The apartment where Pam, Morey, and George live is certified as an ICF/MR. Medicaid was the only funding vehicle the state would make available to the sponsoring agency in its attempt to provide service to severely or multiply handicapped people. Karen Campbell, the coordinator of the agency's residential services, explained some of the difficulties involved in trying to balance a firm commitment to normalization with the federal regulations:

> Yes, we really try to create a homelike environment and at the same time remain in compliance with the state's regulations. They constantly are trying to get us to run an institution-like environment. But, we think we do a pretty good job of trying to keep an atmosphere that is pretty close to what someone's home should be like. . . . As it is they have all these silly rules about keeping things—so called dangerous substances, like dish soap—under lock and key. So we defeat that regulation by giving all the residents their own keys to everything in the apartment. After all, it's their home! They can't have part of their own home inaccessible to them.

Perhaps the distinction between the perspectives of a person who is committed to community integration and those who are solely responsible for regulatory compliance were most clearly drawn when we observed the State review team audit Morey, Pamela, and George's home. During a break in the audit, Karen Campbell and the head of the review team had a conversation about the agency's desire to open a couple of new homes. Karen pointed out the difficulty she was having in finding good locations that would take a minimal amount of renovation in order to provide small homes or apartments for 3 or 4 people. The auditor responded, "Well, you should get in touch with the central office. They have some great plans for some totally accessible, built-from-the-ground facilities for 12 people which are extremely cost-effective." It did not occur to him that he was talking about something that entirely contradicted Karen's goal of small, normalized setting.

The obvious effect of Medicaid funding has been as follows:

1. To shift the cost of funding for residential services from the states to the federal government.
2. To inflate the cost of community based residences by nearly 100% over the cost of non-ICF-funded programs.
3. To expand the numbers of large institution-like facilities in the community.

The long term effect of ICF/MR funding will likely be to create a public backlash against institutional and noninstitutional residences alike, on the grounds that they are cost inefficient. Such a backlash would place greater stress on families with retarded family members.

7. The human service professions are notorious for being susceptible to fads. Isn't deinstitutionalization just another fad that's become entrenched in public policy and will be repudiated by the next generation?

All that we have presented thus far should adequately prove that deinstitutionalization is not a piece of intellectual fluff, but a well-reasoned, empirically sound position. What is clear is that the mode of delivery for residential services is changing. And, while it may appear to those caught in the middle (parents) that human services is a sea of ever-shifting sand, history shows that, once a particular system of services is in place, it might as well be etched in granite (Rothman, 1979). It will endure for generations. Our concern is to create a new community-based service system which can provide a good foundation for future generations.

The difficulties of converting from an institutional model to a small, community-based one are numerous. It has been difficult to get those who are ideologically trained to work in and for an institutional setting to adopt and truly integrate an ideology of normalization and its policies and practices in communities. In addition, failure to develop an orderly transition from institution to community reflects the intransigence of many state bureaucracies which have been accustomed to thinking of mental retardation services as synonymous with institutional care. In fact, some critics contend that, with the incentive of Medicaid reimbursement and the tendency of many states to turn to private-for-profit service providers, what we are really seeing is a trans-institutionalization (Scull, 1981; Warren, 1981). If this is true, our new system of service will involve smaller settings and will no doubt make some people rich, but it will not integrate mentally retarded people into the community. It will be a tragic perversion of the community imperative.

The data show that, while the number of retarded people institutionalized in mental retardation facilities has declined, the numbers of retarded people in nursing homes has increased by an equal amount (Conroy, 1977). In 1970–71, nearly 190,000 mentally retarded people lived in public residential facilities. That number dropped dramatically during the ensuing decade, to a figure of 125,799 in 1980–81 (Scheerenberger, 1982). The average size of public residential facilities in 1982 was 478, one third what the average size was in the mid-1960s (Rotegard, Bruininks, & Krantz, 1984). Those remaining in institutions tend to be "the most seriously impaired mentally retarded persons" (Eyman & Borthwick, 1980, p. 65), this despite the fact that the most disabled people derive the greatest benefit from deinstitutionalization. In recent years, the rate of decline in institutional populations has been slightly greater than 3% per year (Rotegard et al., 1984). Thus, the trend in residential services seems to be in the direction of somewhat fewer and smaller institutions, more "institutional" group homes, and a propensity to congregate more severely disabled people in institutions. This was confirmed in the figures from the most recent survey (mid-1982) of all public and private residential facilities (Hauber, Bruininks, Hill, Lakin, Scheerenberger, & White, 1984), which reported that, of the 243,669 mentally retarded people living in some type of supported residential setting, 58% lived in settings serving 64 or more people and 72% were in settings for 16 or more. Of the total, nearly half (115,032) live in privately operated facilities, and 46.4% of these people live in settings for more than 16 people. Although the smallest settings (1–5 persons) are increasing at the highest rate, they still serve only 10.5% of the people in residential settings.

8. The community is not prepared to accept profoundly and severely retarded people, and may never be willing to accept such people.

It is true that professionals and bureaucrats are not the only ones to balk at across-the-board efforts at deinstitutionalization. In neighborhoods throughout America, we see similar, if somewhat differently articulated, concern over the national policy of deinstitutionalization. If we ask, for example, "Do you think retarded people should be allowed to live in group homes or other independent living programs in the community," most people will say yes (Kastner, Reppucci, & Pezzoli, 1979; also see Gallup Organization, 1976). But face these same respondents with the possibility that the group home is actually moving into their neighborhoods, and most of them lose their enthusiasm for retarded people living in the community (Kastner et al., 1979). Group home opponents cite such concerns as potential harm to property values in the neighborhood, fear that retarded adults might harm area children, concern that retarded people might get hurt by traffic, and concern that residence staff will disrupt the tranquility (particularly in suburban areas) of the neighborhood by coming and going in their cars at all hours of the day and night (for a discussion of community opposition, see the account by Rothman and Rothman, 1984). One theory about how best to achieve community acceptance for residents suggests the value of public education campaigns prior to establishing a group home. But research has shown that prior public education campaigns do not improve the likelihood that neighbors will accept a community residence. In fact, such efforts tend to consolidate and intensify neighborhood opposition (Seltzer, 1984).

Some of the fears are totally unfounded, others the result of handicapist prejudice which is reinforced by continued institutional segregation, while still others are an expression of the person-in-the-street's common sense version of normalization. After all, it is one thing to open a house which a couple of people share and where they are provided with some assistance to help them deal with their limitations. It is something else altogether when an agency opens a "facility" serving 10 or 12 or 15 or more people with all the necessary staff and accoutrements—anyone can see that's not a home, it's an institution. Who wants to live next to an institution? But one thing is clear, there is a way to gain community acceptance—move in a small group, and live there. Amazingly, when that happens, the "retarded people" soon become just other neighbors who are some people's friends, whom some people avoid, but who most often are the recipients of the benign neglect with which most Americans treat their neighbors (Perske & Perske, 1980; Rothman & Rothman, 1984).

CONCLUSION

What future lies ahead for the community imperative? The past has seen a rather remarkable concurrence of moral conviction in support of deinstitutionalization, with nearly 20 years of empirical research on institutional and community living. There is no question that a different system of residential services for people with mental retardation is here to stay. Whether this new system will be a vehicle for social integration or a renovated asylum has, now, largely been left in the hands of the professionals in the field.

The courts have failed to support, particularly in the most recent decisions, the notion that retarded people must have the right to live in typical American communities. Faced with an opportunity to either defend the rights of retarded people, or accept the judgment and discretionary power of state mental retardation officials, the Supreme Court chose the latter. In effect, the court has declared that, in cases involving people with the most severe disabilities, they look to professionals to determine what is helpful and what is harmful or debilitating. While the courts' deference to professional judgment is understandable within the context of the majority's political philosophy, the position of many professionals and state agencies on the right of all people with disabilities to live in the community is less comprehensible. Why are they so confused about the benefits of living in small community settings, when the evidence is so clear? Why do they continue to support and develop new institutions and institution-like (i.e., large) community-based facilities?

Our own view is that the principal barriers to deinstitutionalization are not technical ones. Federal program incentives such as the Medicaid law can be redirected. Conversion plans to find alternative uses for institutions can be fashioned. Community opposition can be overcome. Exclusionary zoning laws can be and are being reshaped in courts and legislatures. And community support services can put an end to the practice of "dumping." But no amount of tinkering with technical planning matters alone can bring about community integration. The real issue concerns how people view other people and, more specifically, how people classified as retarded are perceived. Policies of forceably segregating groups of labeled people, whether for protection, punishment, or treatment, reflects their marginal, devalued status. In our culture, and in many others, institutions have provided the mechanism for large scale devaluation of certain labeled groups, including people with mental retardation. As long as retarded people are socially, economically, and politically rejected, the institution will seem acceptable.

By definition, institutions deny people community living experiences and limit the opportunities of non-disabled people to interact with their disabled peers. To allow for continued segregation of retarded people into institutions and other forms of residential ghettoes can only lend credence to the many fears, myths, and prejudices against people with disabilities. Segregation benefits no one. We find no reasons, either based in data or moral belief, to support the practice of isolating or segregating retarded people from the mainstream of communities. If people need services, let them receive them in typical communities. Rational scientific inquiry and moral convictions can support no other conclusion. Indeed, we ask, when is it time to express one's moral beliefs? When is it time to declare and enforce constitutional rights? And when is there enough data to support a fundamental social change? At what point must we cease to ask "Does it work?" and instead ask "How can we help make it work?"

REFERENCES

Action not words needed at Willowbrook. (1975, May 5). *Times Union.*

Barbakow, D. (1982). Partlow and the Wyatt case: A personal experience. *Mental Retardation, 20,* 141–144.

Baroff, G. (1980). On size and the quality of residential care: A second look. *Mental Retardation, 18,* 113–117.

Biklen, D. (1979). The case for deinstitutionalization. *Social Policy,* May/June, 48–54.

Blatt, B. (1970). *Exodus from pandemonium: Human abuse and the reformation of public policy.* Boston: Allyn & Bacon.

Blatt, B., & Kaplan, F. (1966). *Christmas in purgatory.* Boston: Allyn & Bacon.

Butterfield, E.C., & Zigler, E. (1965). The influence of differing institutional social climates on the effectiveness of social reinforcement in the mentally retarded. *American Journal of Mental Deficiency, 70,* 48–56.

Carr, M. (Director-writer), & Newman, E. (correspondent). (1971, May 2). *This child is rated X* [Television program]. New York: N.B.C. News.

Center on Human Policy, (1979). *The community imperative: A refutation of all arguments in support of institutionalizing anybody because of mental retardation.* Syracuse,NY: Author.

Clifford, L.X. (1984). A reaction to "social role valorization." *Mental Retardation, 22,* 147.

Comptroller General (1977). *Report to Congress: Returning the mentally disabled to the community—government needs to do more.* Washington: General Accounting Office.

Conroy, J.W. (1977). Trends in deinstitutionalization of the mentally retarded. *Mental Retardation, 15*(4), 44–46.

Conroy, J., Efthimiou, J., & Lemanowicz, J. (1982). A matched comparison of the developmental growth of institutionalized and deinstitutionalized mentally retarded clients. *American Journal of Mental Deficiency, 86,* 581–587.

Dean Milk Co. v. Madison, WI., 340 U.S. 349 (1951).

Edgerton, R.B. (1967). *The cloak of competence.* Berkeley, CA: University of California Press.

Edgerton, R.B., & Bercovici, S.M. (1976). The cloak of competence: Years later. *American Journal of Mental Deficiency, 80,* 485–497.

Edgerton, R.B., Bollinger, M., & Herr, B. (1984). The cloak of competence: After two decades. *American Journal of Mental Deficiency, 88,* 345–351.

Ellis, J.W. (1982). The Supreme Court and institutions: A comment on Youngberg v. Romeo. *Mental Retardation, 20,* 197–200.

Ellis, N.R., Balla, D., Estes, O., Hollis, J., Isaacson, R., Orlando, R., Palk, B.E., Warren, S.A., & Siegel, P.S. (1978). Memorandum. Wyatt v. Hardin, C.A. 3195-N (Mid. D. Ala.).

Eyman, R.K., & Borthwick, S.A. (1980). Patterns of care for mentally retarded persons. *Mental Retardation, 18,* 63–66.

Eyman, R.K., Demaine, G.C., & Lei, T. (1979). Relationship between community environments and resident changes in adaptive behavior: A path model. *American Journal of Mental Deficiency, 83,* 330–338.

Fernald, W. (1919). After-care study of the patients discharged from Waverly for a period of 25 years. *Ungraded, 5,* 25–31.

Flint, B. (1966). *The child and the institution.* Toronto, Canada: University of Toronto Press.

Gallup Organization. (1976). Report for the President's Committee on Mental Retardation: Public attitudes regarding mental retardation. In R. Nathan (Ed.) *Mental retardation: A century of decision* (No. 040-000-00343-6). Washington, DC: U.S. Government Printing Office.

Goffman, E. (1961). *Asylums.* Garden City, NY: Anchor.

Hauber, F.A., Bruininks, R.H., Hill, B.K., Lakin, C., Scheerenberger, R., & White, C.C. (1984). National census of residential facilities: A 1982 profile of facilities and residents. *American Journal of Mental Deficiency, 89,* 236–245.

Hemming, H., Lavender, T., & Pill, R. (1981). Quality of life of mentally retarded adults transferred from large institutions to small units. *American Journal of Mental Deficiency, 86,* 157–169.

Hobbs, N. (1975). *Issues in the classification of children.* San Francisco, CA: Jossey-Bass.

Holland, H. (1971). The social experiences of newly committed retarded children. In B. Blatt & F. Garfunkel (Eds.), *Massachusetts study of educational opportunities for handicapped and disadvantaged children* (pp. 101–149). Boston, MA: Commonwealth of Massachusetts.

Hull, J.T., & Thompson, J.C. (1980). Predicting adaptive functioning of mentally retarded persons in community settings. *American Journal of Mental Deficiency, 85,* 253–261.

Hull, J.T., & Thompson, J.C. (1981). Factors contributing to normalization in residential facilities for mentally retarded persons. *Mental Retardation, 19,* 69–73.

Human Service Associates. (1979). *Personalized living: Homes for Californians with special developmental needs.* Santa Rosa, CA: Author.

Issues of concern regarding senate bill 2053. (1984). Baton Rouge, LA: Louisiana Association for Retarded Citizen.

Kastner, L.S., Reppucci, N.D., & Pezzoli, J.J. (1979). Assessing community attitudes toward mentally retarded persons. *American Journal of Mental Deficiency, 84,* 137–144.

Keith, K.D., & Ferdinand, L.R. (1984). Changes in levels of mental retardation: A comparison of institutional and community populations. *Journal of the Association for Persons with Severe Handicaps, 9*(1), 26–30.

Kleinberg, J., & Galligan, B. (1983). Effects of deinstitutionalization on adaptive behavior of mentally retarded adults. *American Journal of Mental Deficiency, 88*, 21–27.

Kugel, R.B., & Wolfensberger, W. (1969). *Changing patterns in residential services for the mentally retarded.* Washington, DC: President's Committee on Mental Retardation.

Kupfer, F. (1982, December 13). Institution is not a dirty word. *Newsweek*, p. 170.

Landesman-Dwyer, S., Sackett, G.P., & Kleinman, J.S. (1980). Relationship of size to resident and staff behavior in small community residences. *American Journal of Mental Deficiency, 85*, 6–17.

Lehr, D.H., & Brown, F. (1984). Perspectives on severely multiply handicapped. In E.L. Meyen (Ed.), *Mental retardation: Topics of today—issues of tomorrow.* (CEC—Mental Retardation Monograph No. 1, pp. 41–65). Reston, VA: Division on Mental Retardation, Council for Exceptional Children.

Menolascino, F.J., McGee, J.J., & Casey, K. (1982). Affirmation of the rights of institutionalized retarded citizens (Implications of *Youngberg v. Romeo*). *Journal of the Association for Persons with Severe Handicaps, 7*(3), 63–72.

New York State Association for Retarded Children et al. v. Carey et al., 393 F. Supp. 715 (E. D. NY 1975).

New York State Association for Retarded Children et al. v. Carey et al., 72-C-356/357 (E.D. NY 1982).

Noonan, M.J., Brown, F., Mulligan, M., & Rettig, M.A. (1982). Educability of severely handicapped persons: Both sides of the issue. *Journal of the Association for Persons with Severe Handicaps, 7*(1), 13–19.

Perske, R., & Perske, M. (1980). *New life in the neighborhood.* Nashville, TN: Abingdon.

Pezzolla, P. (1984). *OMRDD Developmental Centers and Community residential program cost and population trends* (Internal Memoes). Albany, NY: Office of Mental Retardation and Developmental Disabilities.

Polivka, C.H., Marvin, W.E.C., Brown, J.L., & Polivka, L.J. (1979). Selected characteristics, services and movement of group home residents. *Mental Retardation, 17*, 227–230.

Pratt, M.W., Luszcz, M.A., & Brown, M.E. (1980). Measuring dimensions of the quality of care in small community residences. *American Journal of Mental Deficiency, 85*, 188–194.

Provence, S., & Lipton, R. (1962). *Infants in institutions.* New York: International Universities Press.

Raynes, N.V. (1980). The less you've got the less you get: Functional grouping, a cause for concern. *Mental Retardation, 18*, 217–220.

Rotegard, L.L., Bruininks, R.H., & Krantz, G.C. (1984). State operated residential facilities for people with mental retardation July 1, 1978–June 30, 1982. *Mental Retardation, 22*, 69–74.

Rotegard, L.L., Hill, B.K., & Bruininks, R.H. (1983). Environmental characteristics of residential facilities for mentally retarded persons in the United States. *American Journal of Mental Deficiency, 88*, 49–56.

Rothman, D.J. (1979). Can deinstitutionalization succeed? *New York University Education Quarterly*, Fall, 16–22.

Rothman, D.J., & Rothman, S.M. (1984). *The Willowbrook wars.* New York: Harper & Row.

Schalock, R.L., Harper, R.S., & Genung, T. (1981). Community integration of mentally retarded adults: Community placement and program success. *American Journal of Mental Deficiency, 85*, 478–488.

Scheerenberger, R.C. (1982). Public residential services, 1981: Status and trends. *Mental Retardation, 20*, 210–215.

Scull, A. (1981). A new trade in lunacy: The recommodification of the mental patient. *American Behavioral Scientist, 24*, 741–754.

Seltzer, G.B. (1981). Community residential adjustment: The relationship among environment, performance, and satisfaction. *American Journal of Mental Deficiency, 85*, 624–630.

Seltzer, M.M. (1984). Correlates of community opposition to community residences for mentally retarded persons, *American Journal of Mental Deficiency, 89*, 1–8.

Shelton v. Tucker, 364 U.S. 349 (1960).

Society for Good Will to Retarded Children v. Cuomo, 83-7621, 83-7663 (2nd Cir. 1984).

Sokol-Kessler, L.E., Conroy, J., Feinstein, C.S., Lemanowicz, J.A., & McGurrin, M. (1983). Developmental progress in institutional and community settings. *Journal of the Association for Persons with Severe Handicaps, 8*(3), 43–48.

Taylor, S.J., Brown, K., McCord, W., Giambetti, A., Searl, S., Mlinarcik, S., Atkinson, T., & Lichter, S. (1981). *Title XIX and deinstitutionalization: The issue for the 80's.* Syracuse, NY: Center on Human Policy.

Taylor, S.J., McCord, W., & Searl, S.J. (1981). Medicaid dollars and community homes: The community ICF/MR controversy. *Journal of the Association for Persons with Severe Handicaps, 6*(3), 59–64.

Templeman, D., Gage, M.A., & Fredericks, H.D. (1982). Cost effectiveness of the group home. *Journal of the Association for Persons with Severe Handicaps, 6*(4), 11–16.

Thompson, T., & Carey, A. (1981). Structured normalization: Intellectual and adaptive behavior changes in a residential setting. *Mental Retardation, 18*, 193–197.

Turnbull, H.R. (1982). *Youngberg v. Romeo:* An essay. *Journal of the Association for Persons with Severe Handicaps, 7*(3), 3–6.

Warren, C.A.B. (1981). New forms of social control: The myth of deinstitutionalization. *American Behavioral Scientist, 24*, 724–740.

Willer, B., & Intagliata, J. (1981). Social-environmental factors as predictors of adjustment of deinstitutionalized mentally retarded adults. *American Journal of Mental Deficiency, 86*, 252–259.

Willer, B., & Intagliata, J. (1982). Comparison of family-care and group homes as alternative to institutions. *American Journal of Mental Deficiency, 86*, 588–595.

Willer, B., & Intagliata, J. (1983). *Promises and realities for mentally retarded citizens.* Austin, TX: Pro-Ed.

Wiseman, F. (Director). (1969). *Titticut Follies* [Film]. New York: Grove Press.

Woestendiek, J. (1984, May 27). The unwitting revolutionary of Pennhurst. *Philadelphia Inquirer Magazine,* pp. 18–24, 30.

Wolfensberger, W. (1972). *The principle of normalization in human services.* Toronto, Canada: National Institute on Mental Retardation.

Wolfensberger, W. (1975). *The nature and origin of our institutional models.* Syracuse, NY: Human Policy Press.

Wolfensberger, W. (1983). Social role valorization: A proposed new term for the principle of normalization. *Mental Retardation, 21*, 234–239.

Wooden, K. (1974). *Weeping in the playtime of others.* New York: McGraw Hill.

Wyatt v. Stickney, 344 F. Supp. 387 (M. D. Ala. 1972).

Yarrow, M. (1962). *Maternal deprivation.* New York: Child Welfare League of America.

Youngberg v. Romeo, 50 U.S. Law Week 4681 (1982).

Zigler, E., & Balla, D.A. (1972). Developmental course of responsiveness to social reinforcement in normal children and institutionalized retarded children. *Developmental Psychology, 6*, 66–73.

Zigler, E., & Balla, D.A. (1977). Impact of institutional experience on the behavior and development of retarded persons. *American Journal of Mental Deficiency, 82*, 1–11.

Zigler, E., Balla, D.A., & Butterfield, E.C. (1968). A longitudinal investigation of the relationship between pre-institutional social deprivation and social motivation in institutionalized retardates. *Journal of Personality and Social Psychology, 10*, 437–445.

Zigler, E., & Williams, J. (1963). Institutionalization and the effectiveness of social reinforcement: A three year follow-up study. *Journal of Abnormal and Social Psychology, 66*, 197–205.

2

The Identity Crisis in Community Research*

Deborah A. Allen
American University in Cairo
Cairo, Egypt

Community research is currently experiencing an identity crisis. The field is plagued by criticisms and self-doubts in spite of an increasing need and growing demand for studies of people who are mentally retarded who live in the community environment. The definition of the subject matter of community research, the rigor of its methodology, and the nature of its relationships with the service system and with the political process are all being questioned. These uncertainties are rooted in a laboratory science tradition which produces defensiveness rather than conviction among community researchers. Some of the debates hinge on nonissues in which the unique contributions of community research are obscured. This chapter attempts to place these debates into perspective, and calls for interdisciplinary collaboration as a way to realize the promise of community research.

Community research lacks a coherent identity. It is true that most of us can cite examples of community studies, and would maintain that we can recognize community research when we see it. Still, beyond the unhelpful tautology that community research has to do with the community, any defining characteristics of the field are elusive. This state of affairs is revealed in the typically unorthodox career paths of most professionals who call themselves community researchers, and of the larger number who think they may fall into this category but are not really sure. With the exception of some anthropologists and sociologists, many of these people have had experiences similar to my own, which I will use to set the theme of this chapter.

Like most young researchers, I was delivered to the professional world from

* I owe a great debt to Maria McQueeney who taught me the benefits of interdisciplinary collaboration. Suzanne Hudd assisted with technical aspects of this chapter. Karen Majeski and Sandra Anderson provided administrative and secretarial support.

the protective sac of the laboratory indoctrinated with a code of honor regarding experimental control, a pristine moral sense of "clean" data, and an aesthetic worship of elegant research design. This was all well and good until one day I found myself journeying across our state (mercifully a small one) to interview parents of developmentally disabled children in their homes. To my dismay, the integrity of my experimental control was repeatedly insulted by gossipy neighbors, ringing telephones, and household emergencies. The virtue of my "clean" data endured countless violations from the pernicious tendency of subjects to relocate, children's uncanny ability to develop disorders which were not a part of my coding scheme, and the alarming disarray of medical records. And if this were not enough to bear, even the simple beauty of my no-treatment control group was besmirched by the stubborn persistence of control group subjects to require and receive treatment.

Fortunately, several years of making a fool of myself rehabilitated me to the point where I acquired the following skills which are critical to the success of a community researcher: (a) the ability to locate an address when the only direction provided by the parent is "near a fire hydrant in Mudtown"; (b) the ability to perform heroic feats to remove sources of experimental contamination, e.g., dislodging a pigeon that gets stuck in the family's chimney during an interview; and (c) proficiency in the judicious use of dog biscuits to make one's way past three Doberman pinschers.

After a time, I began to keep what my graduate advisers would have considered unsavory company. I could be found lurking about anthropology conventions and hobnobbing with community nurses. Alarmed by my debaucherous decline, my academic friends hauled me off to such purification rites as the university colloquium and the psychometricians' workshop—all to no avail. I am now a fallen woman, and would like to make a case for a more painless way to be corrupted.

Most discussions of community research are as dry and sterile as the usual treatises on laboratory methods. They also have a distinctly apologetic tone, instructing in how to compensate for some methodological deficiency or at least how to muddle through with a minimum of scientific embarrassment. What is vital and vibrant about research in the community rarely comes through in print. It is no wonder that community investigation is often shunned as the black sheep of the research family. Goldenberg's (1971) statement about action research makes the point:

> Given the frame of reference of its critics, one would be hard pressed to try to justify the existence of action research on the basis of the criteria (i.e., objectivity, control and replication) usually associated with the process of scientific inquiry . . . All too often, those involved in the area of action research have been placed in the position of first apologizing for and then defending what has come to be labeled parochially as an "inferior" (rather than a "different") approach to the problems of assessing highly volatile and complex settings. (p. 334)

Despite this attitude, research in mental retardation is becoming more applied and community-oriented. When Detterman (1983) compared reports published in the *American Journal of Mental Deficiency* for the years 1976 and 1980, he found a marked decline in the proportion of basic research relative to applied research. For 25 randomly selected studies each year, the decrease in basic research was from 79% to 67%. This result was obtained using rigid criteria for applied research which required evidence of immediate application. When the same studies were reclassified using more lenient criteria for applied research which included suggested as well as immediate applications, the decrease in basic research was even more dramatic—from 68% to 40%.

Most people have been aware of a trend toward more applied research and have heard the chorus of recent pleas for naturalistic investigation. Brooks and Baumeister (1977), for example, urged researchers to "leave the security of their laboratories, tolerate greater ambiguity, and go where people actually live in order to analyze adaptive behavior" (p. 415). The trend has been initiated and hastened by a host of converging social, legislative, economic, and scientific factors which have pushed the focus from specialized settings into the community.

I shall summarize the events impelling greater community research, and then discuss each of several problems that contribute to the identity crisis in this field.

THE MOVEMENT INTO THE COMMUNITY

Beginning with the report of the President's Panel on Mental Retardation in 1962, the concept of "the continuum of care" was described in a way that clearly implied community-level organization:

> Thus, "care" is used in its broadest sense and the word "continuum" underscores the many transitions and liaisons, within and among various services and professions by which *the community* [italics added] attempts to secure for the retarded the kind and variety of help and accomodation he requires. (U.S. Department of Health, Education and Welfare, 1976, p. 2)

By the mid 1970s, terms like "mainstreaming," "normalization," and "least restrictive alternative" became popular, signaling a movement toward integration of handicapped and retarded individuals into more generic and less specialized activities. A greater diversity of service alternatives became available, including various types of decentralized residential services and vocational and recreational programs. It was recognized that the health care needs of disabled young children had to be considered in the context of the child's total service needs with the involvement of the family in nonhospital, community settings (Healy, 1983). Interagency collaborative relationships were undertaken in response to the Rand Corporation's findings of fragmentation and poor coordination in programs for handicapped children (Brewer & Kakalik, 1979), and strong arguments were made for working out these relationships at the local community level (Elder & Magrab, 1980).

It became apparent that the new community programs for people who are handicapped and mentally retarded were proliferating largely on faith, without a sound database to inform their development, and without adequate evidence of program effectiveness. For that matter, we still do not have very much basis for predicting which mentally retarded individuals will do well in normalized environments, nor do we know much about the coping of mentally retarded people once they are placed in the community (Edgerton, 1977). The evaluation crunch was heralded by the recent federal policy of fiscal retrenchment following years of expansion of federally sponsored social programs during the 1960s. This meant that programs could no longer count on automatic increases or renewals in their funding. They needed to be justified in terms of effectiveness and efficiency.

Not only did the programs need to be evaluated, but they also needed to be examined on new dimensions. Implicit in the movement toward more normalized service settings was an emphasis on the quality of life of mentally retarded and handicapped individuals (Vitello, 1984), creating a demand for the measurement of daily living variables which had heretofore received scant attention. Moreover, greater knowledge of people's lives, attitudes and concerns was needed to bring about cooperation toward service goals. Basic research, after all, can go only so far in reducing the incidence of mental retardation and improving the functioning of retarded people without a concentrated effort to ensure implementation of innovations. For instance, the discovery of amniocentesis is limited in its impact by the knowledge, willingness, and ability of high-risk women to seek the service. Thus, applied research was increasingly called upon to examine factors in service consumption. This function allied it more closely with primary rather than with secondary and tertiary prevention.

Opportunities for basic researchers to abandon their ivory towers were accompanied by good theoretical reasons for doing so. Psychology, a discipline with a laboratory science tradition, awakened to the fact that a thorough understanding of environmental influences on behavior depends upon an understanding of the environment (Lehmann, 1975). Bronfenbrenner (1979) argued for studying the ecology of human development, and set off a new generation of studies designed to determine optimal environmental conditions to foster the psychological growth of the child. In this spirit, Masterpasqua (1981) recommended a cross-fertilization between an ecology of human development and community psychology. Techniques for measuring the home environment (Caldwell & Bradley, 1979) and family systems theories (Olson & McCubbin, 1983) were developed, and they influenced researchers in the field of mental retardation (e.g., Crnic, Friedrich, & Greenberg, 1983; Nihira, Meyers, & Mink, 1983). The role of social support networks in coping with a range of life crises (Gottlieb, 1983) was extended to the community adaptation of mentally retarded persons (Edgerton, 1984).

The imperative for community research is real and growing. Since few fields except anthropology and sociology offer professional training in community research, a legion of converts from other disciplines is filling the gap. As a group, they tend to lack a professional identity and, because of lingering values from laboratory doctrine, feel vaguely defensive about their new roles. Their uncertainties are reflected in several identity crises in the field, issues and non-issues central to the very essence of what community research is about.

COMMUNITY RESEARCH IDENTITY CRISES

Identity Problem Number One: What Is "the Community"?

Ideally, the community should be defined in functional terms (Lehmann, 1975). It is an interdependent system in which the individual's behavior is shaped, needs are satisfied, and major functions of life are carried out. More often than not, however, geographic or political boundaries are followed. A study's "catchment area" may refer to any of these units or to none of them. It may simply be an arbitrarily circumscribed area whose limits are suggested by convenience, as, for example, the area within a specified radius of the research base. Frequently, it makes sense to adopt the boundaries of a particular service region or to insure that a range of service areas have been sampled.

In the past, "community" referred to little more than what could be glimpsed from the window of the university. It is likely that a preponderance of studies were conducted in university towns. Certainly, there was an overemphasis on urban settings. Very recently, concern about services for handicapped individuals living in rural areas has begun to right the balance. All communities are different, and high expectations for generalizability may be unrealistic. A substantial amount of variance can usually be attributed to site-specific effects, but it would be impractical if not impossible to catalog the effects of all possible combinations of site-specific variables. The wisest course may be to acknowledge local individuality, while at the same time investigating and describing processes whereby local conditions exert an influence.

The greatest challenge in delineating a community is that it encompasses far more than a physical setting. Instead, it is a set of interlocking physical, social, political, economic, cultural, and interpersonal systems. Further, as Seltzer (1983) pointed out, the environment is not the same for all persons who experience it. Environmental features take on different meanings for different people. A related problem is that of the level of complexity of analysis needed to describe the community. On the one extreme, a narrow focus on a few isolated variables misses so much that it may be irrelevant. The other extreme is to study an exceedingly large number of presumably relevant variables and rely on statistics to sort out the mess. That strategy has, unfortunately, been oversold.

The multiplicity of systems and perspectives involved makes the definition and description of a community a formidable task. Even so, the need to persist is underscored by Moos's (1973) observation that "no matter how much information about the individual one adds to the predictive equation, one cannot bring the correlation coefficient between individual characteristics and prediction criteria much above .40" (p. 653). Several instruments to measure the environment have now been developed. The largest number appear to have been designed in connection with the evaluation of community residences, perhaps because here the central questions have been directed at the setting per se (see Jacobson & Schwartz, 1983, for a review). By and large, however, environmental measurement is still in its infancy.

It is understandable if community research seems a bit confused and unsure of itself given the difficulties in defining its very subject. This will continue to be so if community research holds itself accountable to the same standards of "environmental" description employed in the laboratory, where it is easy to provide the dimensions of the testing room and the model types of the apparatus. More suitable field models must be developed.

Identity Problem Number Two: Can There Be Legitimate Methodologies?

Community research is most often criticized for inadequate experimental control and for lack of objectivity. These are two separate issues.

Control.   Control has several different meanings, all of which involve ruling out threats to valid inference. Control may mean the ability to (a) exclude interference from extraneous factors, (b) determine which experimental units receive treatment at a particular time, or (c) eliminate identified threats to valid inference statistically or procedurally (Cook & Campbell, 1979). In field settings, the first form of control (over the environment) is generally not possible, so the researcher must rely on the latter two forms of control alone. This makes causal inference more difficult.

The ability to determine the delivery and timing of experimental treatment (control over the independent variable) is optimized through randomization. Yet, there are major obstacles to conducting randomized experiments in field settings. Cook and Campbell (1979) identified the following problematic situations: (a) withholding the treatment from no-treatment control groups, (b) faulty randomization procedures, (c) sampling variability and choice of the units for randomization, (d) treatment-related refusals to participate in the planned experiment, (e) treatment related attrition from the experiment, (f) heterogeneity in extent of treatment implementation, (g) treatment in the no-treatment control group, and (h) unobtrusive treatment implementation.

The list seems imposing enough to send all but the most courageous re-searcher scurrying back to the security of the laboratory. Although control is more elusive in field settings, the situation is not completely hopeless. Cook and Campbell (1979) discuss each of the problems, and propose ways to resolve or reduce them in the conduct of quasi-experimental designs. Quasi-experimental designs are those in which randomized procedures are not employed. The ap-plication of three kinds of quasi-experimental designs (nonrandomized control group design, interrupted time series design, and statistical control design) to mental retardation field research has been described by Seltzer (1983).

The third form of control, statistical control, involves the attempt to remove extraneous influences through covariate methods, a technique which can do only so much, or the attempt to make statistically based inferences about cause from passive observations. On the latter topic, Cook and Campbell (1979) outline several approaches to the statistical analysis of concomitancies in time series, such as path analysis, cross-lagged panel correlations, and the like. They point out that each method has its shortcomings, which boil down to the inability to entirely rule out third-variable causation.

A special problem of control has to do with the fact that communities are hardly static. Changes continually occur in the environment, in demographics, and in the political and social climate. It is important to monitor and attempt to gauge the effects of major environmental fluctuations that occur during the course of the study. While this is troublesome, shifting conditions also afford unique research opportunities. A "treatment" which naturally evolves in the community may not be the same as one which has been imposed. Further, it is sometimes possible to anticipate natural changes and adopt an active rather than a passive research stance. For example, Cook and Campbell (1979) suggest that social scientists and government administrators collaborate in making policy changes, so that causal assertions buttressing these changes can be cross-validated.

Objectivity. The debate about objectivity often centers on the merits of quan-titative versus qualitative research. This is misguided, since there is no reason why both types of research cannot be equally objective or, for that matter, equally subjective. Nonetheless, community research has generally been per-ceived as more subjective than laboratory research since it has relied more heavily on qualitative methods. (Indeed, it may be true that community research has been more subjective, but this is not a necessary consequence of qualitative techniques.) The issues and nonissues need to be clarified.

Cook and Reichardt's (1979) volume offers a range of viewpoints on the debate. By and large, quantitative methods have come to mean randomized experiments and sometimes quasi-experiments, using "objective" tests, sur-veys, or ratings which yield numerical data, typically on a limited number of variables and relatively large samples. Qualitative methods have come to imply ethnographies, case studies, in-depth interviews, and participant observations, using "subjective" methods of data collection such as diaries, life histories, or recorded impressions which yield detailed descriptive material, typically on small samples. As these popular definitions suggest, the trend has been to view quantitative and qualitative methods as diametrically opposed to each other. The result is that researchers "take sides" and argue the superiority of one method or the other. Those who favor quantitative methods see them as the only way to obtain valid, reliable information and to make causal inferences (Riecken et al., 1974; Rossi & Wright, 1977). Supporters of qualitative methods criticize quantitative research as artificial, restricted in scope, and inadequate for elucidating complex problems (Guba, 1978; Parlett & Hamilton, 1976; Weiss & Rein, 1972).

Reichardt and Cook (1979) observed that the controversy goes beyond a disagreement about methodology. Rather, it is a fundamental clash between paradigms, between quantitative and qualitative world views. For instance, Rubinstein (1984) states:

My thesis is that the anthropological understanding of the nature of the scientific study of human behavior is inconsistent with many non-anthropological views, and that the latter have so thoroughly influenced discussions of the nature, causes, and distributions of mental disorders that a clash between the policy recommendations made by anthropologists and by others working in research on mental disorders is inevitable. (p. 164)

The quantitative paradigm is said to be positivistic, hypothetical-deductive, particularistic, objective, outcome-oriented, and grounded in natural science. In contrast, the qualitative paradigm is described as phenomenological, inductive, holistic, subjective, process-oriented, and based in social anthropology.

Reichardt and Cook (1979) believe the dichotomy stems from two fallacious assumptions. The first is that the choice of method type is irrevocably linked to the researcher's paradigm. The second is that the only choice is between quantitative and qualitative paradigms, and that each is unmodifiable. The paradigm need not dictate the choice of research method, since quantitative procedures have been used to answer qualitative questions and vice versa. For example, quantitative procedures have been used to investigate topics associated with a phenomenological perspective. There have been qualitative outcome measures and quantitative process measures as well. It is also possible to adopt elements of each paradigm, depending on the situation and research problem.

Use of *both* methods may be even better, if one can overcome the barriers of cost, time, and professional intransigence about "competing" paradigmatic perspectives. Use of both methods is more likely to satisfy the demands of multi-purpose research. In addition, each method offers insights which the other can build upon, and employing both methods affords triangulation, or converging operations, in which each method serves as a check on the other. This was why

Seltzer (1983) advocated use of several methods of data collection in mental retardation research, since the validity of data can be more confidently established when two or more methods of measuring the same dimension are in agreement (Campbell & Fiske, 1959).

Use of both quantitative and qualitative methods in this fashion in community research is rare. At present, consumers of the research literature may broaden their understanding by considering ethnographic findings along with the more numerous results of surveys, ratings, and behavioral tests. Ethnography, which endeavors to learn about the community "from the inside out," is exemplified by the work of Edgerton and his colleagues (Edgerton, 1967, 1984; Edgerton & Bercovici, 1976). They have used long-term ethnographic methods based on participant observation to intensively study the social adaptation of mildly retarded people living in the community. Edgerton's research program was designed to produce a continuous record of community adaptation with data from several sources. The methods include direct observation as well as life history interviewing on a subsample. In addition, each subject keeps a record of daily activities.

This approach is unusual. Other than brief case histories, most of the few detailed accounts of the lives of retarded people have been autobiographies or have been done by popular writers or journalists, not researchers. However, Edgerton (1977) believes that people who are mentally retarded are both willing and able to provide detailed, meaningful recollections of their lives, which can provide a rich supplement to other sources of data.

Another debate in community research has been unnecessarily linked to the question of objectivity. It concerns the relative roles of program evaluation versus research aimed at other, usually theoretically derived, questions. The primary objectives of the two areas of inquiry differ, program development and evaluation versus production of scientific knowledge, and they usually depend upon different funding sources. It is probably fair to say that more community researchers are engaged in program evaluation than in other research activities. Their more "academically-inclined" colleagues have often berated the scientific value of program evaluation, despite increasingly sophisticated evaluation methodologies (Struening & Guttentag, 1975). Once again, a dichotomy has been established which need not exist. Gray and Wandersman (1980) recognized this when they suggested that the evaluation of home-based early interventions be designed as longitudinal developmental research. A model for the analysis of data from this sort of model was suggested by Dunst (1984). It considers treatment as but one of a number of variables in a multiple regression equation.

Concerns about control and objectivity in community research, though often justified, do not necessarily doom the field to a non-science as some misleading dichotomies imply. Not only do methods exist to remedy or alleviate many of the research problems, but these very problems in community research have a positive side. They exist because of characteristics of field settings which can, as new methodologies emerge, contribute a unique and much needed perspective.

Identity Problem Number Three: What is the Relationship with Service Providers?

Researchers and practitioners have traditionally followed nonintersecting career pathways (Begab, 1977). The resulting communication gap between the discoverers and potential users of new knowledge has serious consequences. Many service programs have been implemented on a massive scale without an adequate scientific base, many irrelevant research findings have been produce, and much potentially useful knowledge has not found its way into the hands of those who could benefit from it. Rational program development is predicated on research that is closely linked with service and administration. Yet most community services do not perceive research as a means of meeting their needs, nor do they offer what most scientists would consider a favorable climate for research.

Part of the difficulty lies in ideological differences between service providers and researchers (Twain, 1975). Service providers are likely to have implicit faith in the value of what they are doing. Their "hands-on" sense of clients' problems may make research data seem narrow and superfluous. The researcher, on the other hand, has an obligation to challenge existing values and develop new approaches, which can have profound and threatening implications for the service system. Consider, for example, the potential impact of results such as those reported by Durlak (1979). He analyzed 42 studies comparing the effectiveness of professional and paraprofessional helpers and found that paraprofessionals achieved clinical outcomes equal to or significantly better than those obtained by professionals. It is, therefore, not surprising that professionals should feel threatened. Levy (1984) described the evaluation of a self-help group whose members, when asked about their program's dropouts and apparent failures, replied that those individuals simply were not ready for what the group had to offer. Shown negative results of the evaluation, they questioned the outcome measures and concluded that their judgment was better than the research.

Misunderstandings between practitioners and researchers often arise around program evaluation. One reason is because most community programs are saddled with bloated expectations. Overly optimistic goals may have been stated to secure funding, or as a naive reflection of an ideal situation. The programs are therefore destined to fall short in any evaluation against such goals. In addition, practitioners' expectations for what individual research programs can accomplish may be too high. In order to "sell" a research project, the project may be presented in such simplistic and glowing terms that service providers count on a panacea. Practitioners fail to recognize, and researchers fail to admit, that most knowledge is gained by slow, sometimes faltering, steps rather than in startling breakthroughs. Another source of conflict pertains to differences in priorities placed on the smooth delivery of service versus the flawless conduct of research, goals which can sometimes be at odds. What the service provider sees as a bothersome intrusion the researcher may perceive as a prerequisite to valid experimentation.

Lavoie (1984) discussed problems in doing research with self-help groups, and offered two approaches to formulating a study which can also be profitably applied to interactions with service providers. The first is to carry out research to solve problems identified by the providers themselves. The second is to formulate research which develops explanatory models, such as a model of the causes and evolution of problems, drawing from the providers' clinical experiences. These steps give service providers an investment in the research and should increase the likelihood of their support and cooperation. They also lead to more meaningful research.

Even community researchers who are not engaged in program evaluation will probably sooner or later have to work out arrangements with service providers. Services are a part of the community and are an integral aspect of the lives of individuals who are handicapped and mentally retarded. Relationships with service providers should be approached not as an inevitable source of frustration which compromises professional identity, but rather as a resource which can broaden the scope and depth of one's research.

Identity Problem Number Four: Does Community Research Sell Its Soul to Politics?

Community research is a community enterprise and, as such, is inextricably bound to political influences. As Gurel (1975) pointed out, "information and knowledge are not neutral quantities once they enter the public domain. Knowledge is power. Depending on whether the information is withheld, and if disseminated, how and where it is disseminated, information can be made to serve political ends" (p. 15). It can even be argued that there is a political statement inherent in the fact that some variables are selected for study, while others go unexamined. Thus, community research is likely to have political implications, whether the researcher wants it to or not. It affects social policy, and it affects fiscal decision making.

Of the various community research functions, program evaluation is the most clearly associated with a political context. The common resistance of community groups to evaluation, combined with a mandate for evaluation from their funding agencies, creates an atmosphere of political fractionation and distrust. In these situations, it is better to be politically informed than to close one's eyes and hope the politics will go away. One must take care to be responsive to the needs of the groups studied and to clarify what they will get out of the research. It is probable that they will get more out of the research if the criteria for evaluation are consistent with the values and assumptions of the decision makers. Otherwise, the findings will not be heeded. More generally, community research would do well to study variables that are meaningful to the community if it expects community members to care about the results. Another factor that influences how results will be received is the extent to which specific reforms have been advocated as though they were certain to be successful. This practice traps the administrator in the event of an unfavorable evaluation. Campbell (1975) recommends that the administrator be advised to acknowledge the seriousness of the issue rather than advocate a specific reform. In this way, a reform can be proposed as one of several alternatives which require testing.

The community researcher may be involved in politics at several levels. On one level, the researcher can gain awareness of the political forces helping or hindering a project, capitalizing on the former and performing rear guard actions against the latter. At a greater level of involvement, the researcher may attempt to influence policy. And, finally, it is possible for policy itself to be the object of research, as in legislative analysis.

Since the findings of community research are likely to effect policy regardless of what the researcher does, active attention to the manner in which results are received by policy makers and the public may be appropriate. Researchers have traditionally been uncomfortable with public relations activities, but it behooves them to become more astute in this area. Publicity is generally unmerited until a project has reached its goals. Moreover, premature publicity for longitudinal research may constitute a "treatment" in and of itself, altering subjects' attitudes toward participation (Jordan, 1984). This risk must be balanced with the natural desire of the sponsoring agencies to receive recognition and their need to justify continuing support for long-term projects. Community endorsement and cooperation may be greater for well publicized projects as well. Research is most likely to be favorably received by policy makers if it is readable, suggests specific actions that can be taken, and arrives before a decision is to be made. This requires keeping up with the political scene, an activity which many researchers regard with disdain because of mistaken assumptions about inevitable corruption of the scientific enterprise.

In short, community research cannot escape its political and social implications and it is better to be aware of them. This does not mean a "sellout." On the contrary, it can mean a broader picture of the community if the research takes account of political and social factors. On this score, social science has yet to offer much in the way of methodologies. Sjoberg (1975) indicts social science for its failure to incorporate the ideological orientation of the researcher and the political constraints imposed upon the research. And further, "after examining the activities of social researchers, I am forced to conclude that most treatises on research methods propound ideal norms which often have no, and at best only a vague, relationship to what occurs in practice" (p. 31). Sjoberg (1975) suggests a new evaluation methodology which would incorporate ethical and political issues. In this scheme, social criticism becomes an essential ingredient and, beyond criticism, a major thurst is constructive analysis. A "countersystem analysis'' is proposed which puts forward a utopian model embodying the dialectical alternative to the existing system against which future programs can be evaluated.

CONCLUSION

An evaluation of the identity crisis in community research suggests that researchers may be overly sensitive to shortcomings in the field, while failing to promote its strengths. This is no doubt a product of having been nurtured in laboratory traditions. The key to resolving the identity conflict is, I believe, to be found in fostering cooperative relationships across two dimensions. The first, which I will call the vertical dimension, is a relationship between service, research, and training. This should be a circular relationship in which service suggests research problems, whose solution informs professional training, which in turn improves service. The second dimension, the horizontal dimension, involves interdisciplinary relationships at all levels of the vertical dimension. It would formalize and legitimize the cooperative roles of educational, medical, social service, and other disciplines in service, research, and training.

My thesis is that community research should not be defined by its perceived liabilities (difficulties in determining its subject matter, methodological problems, service constraints, and political indebtedness). Rather, it should be defined by its potential for unique and valuable contributions which may be best realized through interdisciplinary, service–research–training links. Perhaps then, community researchers will venture to rendezvous with social workers and nurses in broad daylight, will be decorated for heroism in data collection, and will be confident of the identity of their field.

REFERENCES

Begab, M.J. (1977). Barriers to the application of knowledge. In P. Mittler (Ed.), *Research to practice in mental retardation. Vol. 1—Care and intervention.* (pp. A1–A5). Baltimore, MD: University Park Press.

Brewer, G.D., & Kakalik, J.S. (1979). *Handicapped children: Strategies for improving services.* New York: McGraw-Hill.

Bronfenbrenner, U. (1979). *The ecology of human development.* Cambridge, MA: Harvard University Press.

Brooks, P.H., & Baumeister, A.A. (1977). A plea for consideration of ecological validity in the experimental psychology of mental retardation. *American Journal of Mental Deficiency, 81,* 407–416.

Caldwell, B., & Bradley, R. (1979). *Home observation for measurement of the environment.* Manual. Little Rock, AK: University of Arkansas, The Center for Child Development and Education.

Campbell, D.T. (1975). Reforms as experiments. In E.L. Struening & M. Guttentag (Eds.), *Handbook of evaluation research* (Vol. 2, pp. 71–100). Beverly Hills, CA: Sage.

Campbell, D., & Fiske, E. (1959). Convergent and discriminant validation by the multitrait-multimethod matrix. *Psychological Bulletin, 56,* 81–105.

Cook, T.D., & Campbell, D.T. (1979). *Quasi-experimentation: Design and analysis issues for field settings.* Chicago, IL: Rand McNally.

Cook, T.D., & Reichardt, C.S. (Eds.). (1979). *Qualitative and quantitative methods in evaluation research.* Beverly Hills, CA: Sage.

Crnic, K., Friedrich, W., & Greenberg, M. (1983). Adaptation of families with mentally retarded children: A model of stress, coping, and family ecology. *American Journal of Mental Deficiency, 88,* 125–138.

Detterman, D.K. (1983). Some trends in research design. In J.L. Matson & J.A. Mulik (Eds.), *Handbook of mental retardation* (pp. 527–539). New York: Pergamon.

Dunst, C. (1984, December). *Issues in experimental design.* Paper presented at the conference Comprehensive Approaches to Disabled and At-Risk Infants, Toddlers and Their Families, sponsored by the Division of Maternal and Child Health (U.S. HHS), the Office of Special Education and Rehabilitative Services (U.S. DOE), and the National Center for Clinical Infant Programs, Washington, D.C.

Durlak, J.A. (1979). Comparative effectiveness of paraprofessional and professional helpers. *Psychological Bulletin, 86,* 80–92.

Edgerton, R.B. (1967). *The cloak of competence: Stigma in the lives of the mentally retarded.* Berkeley, CA: University of California Press.

Edgerton, R.B. (1977). The study of community adaptation: Toward an understanding of lives in process. In P. Mittler (Ed.), *Research to practice in mental retardation, Vol. 1—Care and intervention* (pp. 371–376). Baltimore, MD: University Park Press.

Edgerton, R.B. (Ed.). (1984). *Lives in process: Mildly retarded adults in a large city* (Monograph No. 6). Washington, DC: American Association on Mental Deficiency.

Edgerton, R.B., & Bercovici, S.M. (1976). The cloak of competence: Years later. *American Journal of Mental Deficiency, 80,* 485–497.

Elder, J.O., & Magrab, P.R. (1980). *Coordinating services to handicapped children: A handbook for interagency collaboration.* Baltimore, MD: Paul H. Brookes.

Goldenberg, I. (1971). *Build me a mountain: Youth, poverty and the creation of new settings.* Cambridge, MA: MIT Press.

Gottlieb, B.H. (1983). *Social support strategies: Guidelines for mental health practice.* Beverly Hills, CA: Sage.

Gray, S.W., & Wandersman, L.P. (1980). The methodology of home-based intervention studies: Problems and promising strategies. *Child Development, 51,* 993–1009.

Guba, E.G. (1978). *Toward a methodology of naturalistic inquiry in educational evaluation.* Los Angeles, CA: University of California, Los Angeles, Center for the Study of Evaluation.

Gurel, L. (1975). The human side of evaluating human services programs: Problems and prospects. In M. Guttentag & E.L. Struening (Eds.), *Handbook of evaluation research* (Vol. 2, pp. 11–28). Beverly Hills, CA: Sage.

Healy, A. (1983). *The needs of children with disabilities: A comprehensive view.* Monograph. Division of Developmental Disabilities, University of Iowa.

Jacobson, J.W., & Schwartz, A.A. (1983). The evaluation of community living alternatives for developmentally disabled persons. In J.F. Matson & J.A. Mulik (Eds.), *Handbook of mental retardation* (pp. 39–66). New York: Pergamon.

Jordan, T.E. (1984). Prospective longitudinal study of retarded children. In J.M. Berg (Ed.), *Perspectives and progress in mental retardation. Vol. 1—Social, psychological, and educational aspects* (pp. 143–153). Baltimore, MD: University Park Press.

Lavoie, F. (1984). Action research: A new model of interaction between the professional and self-help groups. In A. Gartner & F. Riessman (Eds.), *The self-help revolution* (pp. 173–182). New York: Human Sciences Press.

Lehmann, S. (1975). Psychology, ecology and community: A setting for evaluation research. In M. Guttentag & E.L. Struening (Eds.), *Handbook of evaluation research* (Vol. 2, pp. 485–496). Beverly Hills, CA: Sage.

Levy, L.H. (1984). Issues in research and evaluation. In A. Gartner & F. Riessman (Eds.), *The self-help revolution* (pp. 155–172). New York: Human Sciences Press.

Masterpasqua, F. (1981). Toward a synergism of developmental and community psychology. *American Psychologist 36,* 782–786.

Moos, R.H. (1973). Conceptualization of human environments. *American Psychologist, 28,* 652–655.

Nihira, K., Meyers, C.E., & Mink, I.T. (1983). Reciprocal relationship between home environment and development of TMR adolescents. *American Journal of Mental Deficiency, 88,* 139–149.

Olson, D.H., & McCubbin, H.I. (1983). *Families: What makes them work.* Beverly Hills, CA: Sage Publications.

Parlett, M., & Hamilton, D. (1976). Evaluation as illumination: A new approach to the study of innovatory programs. In G.V. Glass (Ed.), *Evaluation studies: Review Annual* (Vol. 1, pp. 140–157). Beverly Hills, CA: Sage.

Reichardt, C.S., & Cook, T.D. (1979). Beyond qualitative versus quantitative methods. In T.D. Cook & C.S. Reichardt (Eds.), *Qualitative and quantitative methods in evaluation research* (pp. 7–32). Beverly Hills, CA: Sage.

Riecken, W.R., Boruch, R.F., Campbell, D.T., Caplan, N., Glenan, T.K., Jr., Pratt, J.W., Rees, A., & Williams, W. (1974). *Social experimentation: A method for planning and evaluating social intervention.* New York: Academic.

Rossi, P.H., & Wright, S.R. (1977). Evaluation research: An assessment of theory, practice, and politics. *Evaluation Quarterly, 1,* 5–52.

Rubinstein, R.A. (1984). Epidemiology and anthropology: Notes on science and scientism. *Communication and Cognition, 17,* 163–185.

Seltzer, M.M. (1983). Nonexperimental field research methods. In J.L. Matson & J.A. Mulick (Eds.), *Handbook of mental retardation* (pp. 557–570). New York: Pergamon Press.

Sjoberg, G. (1975). Politics, ethics and evaluation research. In M. Guttentag & E.L. Struening (Eds.), *Handbook of evaluation research* (Vol. 2, pp. 29–51). Beverly Hills, CA: Sage.

Struening, E.L., & Guttentag, M. (Eds.). (1975). *Handbook of evaluation research.* Beverly Hills, CA: Sage.

Twain, D. (1975). Developing and implementing a research strategy. In E.L. Struening & M. Guttentag (Eds.), *Handbook of evaluation research* (Vol. 2, pp. 27–52). Beverly Hills, CA: Sage.

U.S. Department of Health, Education, and Welfare. (1976). *The role of higher education in mental retardation and other developmental disabilities.* Washington, DC: Author. (ERIC Document Reproduction Service No. ED 148 078)

Vitello, S.J. (1984). Deinstitutionalization of mentally retarded persons in the United States: Status and trends. In J.M. Berg (Ed.), *Perspectives and progress in mental retardation. Vol. 1— Social, psychological, and educational aspects* (pp. 345–349). Baltimore, MD: University Park Press.

Weiss, R.S., & Rein, M. (1972). The evaluation of broad-aim programs; Difficulties in experimental design and an alternative. In C.H. Weiss (Ed.), *Evaluating action programs: Readings in social action and education.* Boston: Allyn and Bacon.

3

Investigating the Impact of Communitization: Issues in Research Methodology*

Bruce L. Mallory and Susan C. Herrick
University of New Hampshire

A review of the purposes and characteristics of 30 recent empirical investigations of the impact of deinstitutionalization is discussed. A six-category taxonomy of such studies is suggested, common characteristics and research gaps are presented, and barriers to research on the effect of community placements are discussed. An investigation of the educational and residential consequences of community placement for institutionalized children is described, with emphasis on methodological and field work techniques leading to valid conclusions. The role of values in communitization research is emphasized throughout the chapter. Suggestions are offered for the use of multiple perspectives and techniques in conducting socially valid, policy-relevant investigations.

The dramatic and consistent shift in public policy resulting in the deinstitutionalization and community integration of people with developmental disabilities is now entering its third decade. If we view the passage of P.L. 88-164, the Community Mental Health and Mental Retardation Facilities Construction Act of 1963, as the watershed in federal policy, and Hobbs' (1964) recognition of the "third revolution in mental health" as the watershed in theoretical and programmatic models, we can assert that one of the most sweeping and significant social experiments in United States history is now over 20 years old. Although there are signs that the momentum of the communitization movement is slowing, and the dangers of public backlash are ever present, it appears that the principles of normalization and the commitment to community-based services as close to home as possible are here to stay. The field of developmental disabilities has emerged from the half-century era in which there was a "loss of rationales"

* Partial support for this chapter was provided by The Spencer Foundation through a research grant to the University of New Hampshire. Additional support was provided by the Research Office and Central University Research Fund at UNH.

(Wolfensberger, 1969), and embarked on a persistent and apparently successful effort to severely curtail the use of residential institutions.

As is usually the case, changes in social policy have created new directions and paradigms in social science. Research activities have, in turn, supported the refinement and evolution of social policy. Thus, it is possible to detect significant new research developments as the policy of communitization becomes established. Between 1920 and 1970, investigation of community placement outcomes proceeded at a constant, albeit low, rate. Gibson and Fields (1983) have identified 44 community placement follow-up studies beginning in 1920, and found an average of 8.8 studies in each decade through the 1960s. By the 1970s, communitization was in full swing, and the number of studies increased exponentially. We have not calculated the number of community placement studies for the decade of 1970–79, but we are confident that the number exceeds the previous averages. In reviewing studies reported in major professional journals and book chapters from 1980 to early 1985, we discovered 30 empirical investigations of the impact of community placement on previously institutionalized people with developmental disabilities. This number is not meant to represent *all* studies in that time period, but it is an indication of the continuing and expanding interest in determining the outcomes of social policies enacted in the 1960s and 1970s.

After reviewing some of the recent investigations of the impact of communitization, this chapter will describe some barriers to current research, discuss design and methodological issues, describe the authors' present study of the impact of communitization on school-age children, and consider some issues in the analysis and reporting of findings.

RECENT RESEARCH ON COMMUNITIZATION

The overriding purpose of communitization studies has been policy evaluation. That is, these studies are asking, either directly or indirectly, how have the policies of institutional reduction and community care worked? Are people with developmental disabilities ''better off'' as a result of these policies? What factors have hindered successful community placement, and what factors enhance the likelihood of successful integration? How many people return to institutions after a period of community living? Do community-based services meet various criteria for normalized and least restrictive environments? How do communitization policies affect family and community groups? What are the costs and benefits of these policies?

Most empirical studies answer one or more of these questions in some fashion. However, it should be noted that some writers have argued that policy evaluation is not enough. For example, one group of scholars has declared that research to determine whether community-based care is better than institutional care is irrelevant and outdated (Bogdan, Biklen, Blatt, & Taylor, 1981). Rather, the barriers to normalization and least restrictive services should be the primary targets of research. They further contend that "the transformation of a society rather than the deinstitutionalization of individuals" should be the focus of research in this area (p. 237). Kiernan (1981) is also skeptical of the policy evaluation orientation. He suggests that the policy evaluation paradigm has led to a "horse race" mentality in which the expectation is created that one best system will be validated as the most effective and efficient approach to care. Both Kiernan (1981) and Bogdan et al. (1981) call for investigation into broader socio-political and "professionalism" factors that interfere with community integration. In sum, these writers argue that the question is not "Does it work?" but "How can the ideologies of normalization, conversion, and social role valorization be advanced?" We will return to these questions later in the chapter.

Taxonomy of Empirical Studies

Under the broad rubric of policy evaluation, it is possible to identify specific categories of research activities. After reviewing 30 studies that have been published since 1980, we generated six categories. These include: (a) studies which analyze the impact of community placement on the behaviors or skills of previously institutionalized people, (b) studies which measure attitude change in family or community members as a result of community integration, (c) studies which measure physical and psychological stress (e.g., transition shock) associated with community placement, (d) studies which track recidivism rates after community placement, (e) studies which assess community and environmental factors that may affect placement, and (f) studies which illustrate release patterns and subsequent community placements for large numbers of people across numerous sites. As is the case with any taxonomy, some studies may fall into more than one category, and the decision to place a study in any particular category is open to debate. It is also clear that some studies (such as Conroy's major investigation of the depopulation of Pennhurst) generate multiple findings which cut across several categories.

The criteria for including these particular studies were that: (a) the study was published in a professional journal or book chapter between 1980 and early 1985; (b) the study compared the institutional and community experiences of the same mentally retarded subjects, or of matched subjects, some of whom remained at the institution and some of whom left; and (c) the study followed subjects who left large, public residential facilities to live in a community-based alternative such as a group home, family home, or an independent living situation. In cases where family or community attitudes were assessed (category b), we chose studies that either measured attitudes in families directly affected by the community placement of a family member or measured the attitudes of community members toward the practice of communitization in general.

Table 1 indicates several clear trends in recent communitization studies. First, the studies reported include sample sizes sufficient to draw generalizable conclu-

Table 1
Taxonomy of Empirical Communitization Studies

Type of Study and Names of Investigators	Year of Publication	N	Age of Subjects	Level of Retardation	Length of Community Placement	State
A. *Impact on Behaviors or Skills*						
1. Reduction in maladaptive behaviors and/or increase in adaptive behaviors						
Conroy, et al.	1982	140[a]	36	IQX̄ = 28	2 years	PA
Kleinberg & Galligan	1983	20	46.3	IQX̄ = 23.8 range 10–51	up to 1 year	NY
Schalock, et al.[a]	1981	166	34[b]	IQX̄ = 48	1–9 years	NE
Schalock, et al.[b]	1981	69	31[b]	IQX̄ = 66	5 years	NE
Seltzer, et al.	1982	153	64 & 33[c]	IQX̄ = 49 & 54[c]	n.s.	MA
Sutter, et al.	1980	77	over 18	all levels	1–3 years	HI
Thiel	1981	49	31[b]	IQX̄ = 44	less than 1 year	NE
Walsh & Walsh	1982	40	26.42	n.s.	X̄ = 40.85 weeks	MT
2. Employment-related factors						
Seltzer, M.M.	1981	153	38.4	all levels	X̄ = 4.3 years	MA
B. *Attitude Change*						
1. Family						
Conroy	1985	321	n.s.[d]	n.s.	n.s.	PA
Frohboese & Sales	1980	58	n.s.	n.s.	n.s.	NE
Meyer	1980	273	29.3	all levels	n.a.[e]	PA
Rudie & Riedl	1984	74	29	n.s.	1–5 years	MN
2. Community						
Roth & Smith	1983	600	n.a.	n.a.	n.a.	AR
C. *Transition Shock*						
Heller	1982	50	0–17	severe and profound	n.a.[f]	IL

	Year	N	Age	Level	Follow-up	Location
D. Recidivism						
Intagliata & Willer	1982	301	45.1	all levels	2 years	NY
Lakin, et al.	1983	244	0–63+	all levels	n.s.	multiple states
E. Community and Environmental Factors						
Edgerton, et al.	1984	15	56	$IQ\bar{X} = 61.7$	over 20 years	CA
Kielhofner	1981	43	adults	mild to severe	1–3 years	CA
Reagan, et al.	1980	186	$\bar{X} = 15$ range 5–23	$IQ\bar{X} = 70$	up to 18 months	MN
Seltzer, G.B.	1981	153	38.4	all levels	4 years	MA
Sutter	1980	167	30–37	n.s.	n.s.	HI
Turnbull, et al.	1985	12 families	n.s.	n.s.	n.s.	KS
Willer & Intagliata	1981	338	13 @ placement 46 @ follow-up	all levels	2–4 years	NY
Willer & Intagliata	1982	338	46	all levels	over 2 years	NY
Willer, et al.	1981	43 families	24.5	all levels	2 years	NY
F. Release Patterns						
Best-Sigford, et al.	1982	474	31.6[b]	all levels	less than 1 year	multiple states
Bruininks, et al.	1982	4,999 foster homes	0–63+	all levels	n.s.	multiple states
Ellis, et al.	1981	100	9.4[b]	$IQ\bar{X} = 17.6$	over 5 years	LA
Seltzer & Kraus	1984	761	19.5	all levels	4–8 years	MA

Notations
[a] 70 movers and 70 stayers
[b] Ages given are at placement rather than at time of follow-up
[c] Older and younger groups compared
[d] 291 parents of adults, 30 parents of children
[e] Prospective survey
[f] Ss moved from CLF into large institution
n.s. = not specified
n.a. = not applicable

sions. Largest sample sizes come from those projects operating in multiple states (e.g., the work of Bruininks and his colleagues—Bruininks, Hill, & Thorsheim, 1982) and in states with large population bases (Willer & Intagliata in New York—1981, 1982; Willer, Intagliata, & Atkinson, 1981; Seltzer, 1981, and her colleagues, Seltzer & Krauss, 1984; Seltzer, Seltzer, & Sherwood, 1982, in Massachusetts). Not surprisingly, qualitative studies such as those by Edgerton, Bollinger, and Herr (1984), Kielhofner (1981), and Turnbull, Brotherson, and Summers (1985) contain smaller samples. Second, all studies reviewed except four focused primarily on adults. There seems to be a dearth of information on the community placement and integration of children. Third, the studies include subjects from all ranges of retardation. Fourth, the length of time the subjects have lived outside of an institution at the time of follow-up ranges from less than 1 year to 20 years, with a typical length of 2–3 years. This would seem to provide the opportunity to make valid statements about the short-term and long-term consequences of communitization. Finally, we were somewhat surprised at the small number (one) of community attitude studies. This may reflect either less concern in recent years with community opposition to people who have been released from institutions, or the influence of court decisions and state policies that have tended to override local resistance to community programs.

Common Methods and Variables

The studies reviewed relied on quantitative methods of structured assessment, record review, structured interview protocols, and statistical analyses of personal and sociological data. The few qualitative studies were based on participant observation, open interviews, and analysis of unsolicited documents. The most common assessment and observation instruments were the Adaptive Behavior Scale (Nihira, Foster, Shellhaas, & Leland, 1974) and the Behavior Development Survey (cf. Conroy, Efthimiou, & Lemanowicz, 1982). Almost all the studies gathered data on subjects at a single point rather than longitudinally (Reagan, Murphy, Hill, & Thomas, 1980, and Edgerton et al., 1984, are exceptions). Many studies used cross-sectional samples to approximate longitudinal analysis. Outcome or dependent variables concentrated on behavior change or the environmental characteristics of post-release placements, with a particular emphasis on the degree of independent functioning and adaptive behavior as a consequence of the type and quality of community residence.

Many investigators, particularly those conducting studies in categories a and e in Table 1, have examined "quality of life" variables. However, there is no uniform definition of such outcome variables, and the measures and criteria used in this area vary widely. This is due in part to the varying definitions of community placement success found in the literature. Shadish, Thomas, and Bootzin (1982) present a useful analysis of this problem. They argue that the definition of placement success varies with the interest group doing the defining. Their model of interest group discrepancies is based on nursing home care, but it is readily acceptable to community living facilities for people with developmental disabilities.

Shadish et al.'s (1982) analysis found that federal bureaucrats, academics, and state legislators tend to value treatment-oriented variables for the measurement of successful placement. These variables include the availability of active treatment and habilitative programs, the use of current and appropriate individual service plans, elimination of aggressive or maladaptive behaviors, active efforts to move clients into less restrictive settings, stable and well-trained staff, and active community integration programs. Relatives of residents and direct care staff, on the other hand, value creature comforts such as privacy, facility cleanliness, client cleanliness, adequate nutrition, isolation from psychiatrically involved clients, and sufficient care to prevent reinstitutionalization. This model illustrates the persistent gap in perceptions and values between policy-makers and practitioners or consumers. The implication here is that studies of the quality of life of deinstitutionalized people should assess multiple variables related both to mandated treatment efforts and individual client well-being. Such an orientation is more useful than relying on standardized, quantifiable measures of quality of life. Ultimately, such a single measure would lack social validity and generalizability.

Barriers to Communitization Research

Aside from basic problems such as obtaining adequate funding to carry out large scale studies, the central problem in communitization research is that of locating subjects and obtaining their informed consent to participate. Retrieval rates, or the percentage of deinstitutionalized people found from the total possible research population, have declined markedly since the early studies of the 1920s. Through the 1950s, most studies reported locating 80% to 98% of the possible sample. In the 1960s, retrieval rates plunged to around 55%, due largely to the emergence of human subject protections and a highly diversified, decentralized community service system (Gibson & Fields, 1983). Although most recent studies do not report their retrieval rates, it is safe to assume the trend is continuing in light of further concern with the privacy of disabled people and the absence of centralized service and tracking systems for people who are deinstitutionalized.

Siegel and Ellis (1985) summarize the major barriers to research as follows:

1. Delays and unnecessary work related to obtaining parental or guardian consent for nonintrusive research, resulting in weakening of sample quality.
2. Apprehension on the part of administrators, teachers, and community staff who are sensitive to the potential for litigation, resulting in a general suspicion of outsiders (especially researchers).
3. Anti-intellectual attitudes concerning the value of research and the related unrealistic desire for immediate benefits from research studies. These factors contribute to both initial difficulties in recruiting subjects and in subsequent problems during data collection.

An additional barrier is incomplete and inaccurate clinical records, making pre- and post-placement comparisons quite difficult. Changing or inaccurate use of terms creates problems with detecting developmental change over time. Changes in diagnostic codes, such as occurred in the 1983 revision of the AAMD classification manual (Grossman, 1983), also lead to problems in interpreting longitudinal records. Community service records often undergo frequent changes in format due to the rapid implementation of new programs.

A negative consequence of public funding may be that relatives of subjects and community service providers resent the use of public funds for research. Skeptical relatives and staff members who wanted to know who was paying for our research were receptive to our questions when they learned that no public dollars were involved. Parents did not perceive our activities as competing for scarce dollars with the direct services their relatives needed. Staff were no longer concerned that our work was really a covert evaluation of their effectiveness.

DESIGN CONSIDERATIONS

The Ideology of the Researcher

The design of a specific investigation, including the formulation of empirical questions, the methods used to answer those questions, and the analysis of the answers, is determined to a large degree by the ideological perspective of the researcher. Even those who claim to do "value-free" research operate within the context of prevailing social values and scientific paradigms. Certainly the field of communitization research reflects these realities.

Although researchers rarely and unfortunately do not make their ideological biases explicit in their reports, commonly accepted assumptions seem to be that: (a) large residential institutions are not conducive to human development, (b) the most effective treatment occurs as close to home as possible, and (c) disabled people have inalienable rights to progressive, effective treatment and to an independent, self-determined lifestyle. There is ample empirical evidence found in the professional literature, as well as in court testimony, to support the first two assumptions. Beyond that, there is an extensive body of literature arguing that community living is philosophically and normatively the better system. Economic rationales are also invoked, although the empirical support is not as well established. Courts and legislatures have fostered the "inalienable rights" rationale, occasionally independent of significant amounts of empirical data. Researchers are not immune to the attitudes and beliefs these forces create. The result is value-laden research and analysis.

Recalling Bogdan et al.'s (1981) call for the study of the transformation of society, it may be argued that many researchers are engaged in advocacy on behalf of disabled people. For this group, the primary research question is not so much, "Are they better off as a result of community placement?"; rather, it is

"How can community services be improved to create better lives for previously institutionalized people?" The a priori assumption is that institutions are inherently restrictive and capable of only custodial care. Thus, the term "deinstitutionalization" is replaced with the notion of "communitization" in this chapter and elsewhere. The use of the term "community integration" advances the belief that the current trend is part of a larger civil and human rights movement, not simply an empirical experiment.

Additional evidence of an advocacy ideology is found in recent interest in treating people with mental retardation as legitimate and valid sources of data. Efforts to have people who have moved from institutions into local communities speak on their own behalf are increasing. Major activity in this area has been undertaken by Sigelman and her colleagues at Texas Tech University (e.g., Sigelman et al., 1983). Given that community-based services are mandated in court orders and state legislation, there need to be opportunities for the beneficiaries to voice their assessment of the impact and success of these policies. Perhaps this recognition of the legitimacy of the disabled person's voice is a result of the policy itself. That is, people who are relegated to institutional care are inherently voiceless and incompetent. People who live and work among us, who prepare our food, build our computers, or work in our factories are perceived as competent and valued. We have an obligation to hear their side of things, even if that takes extra effort on our part.

Identification of Research Variables

Table 2 presents a model of the critical variables in communitization research on school-age children. This model is the basis for the data collection and analysis we are presently conducting. The model is specific to the experiences of school-age children; thus, factors such as adult employment, marital status, and economic independence are not included. The model attempts to take into account individual characteristics and their interaction with ecological conditions (family, community, and the policy context). The essential research question posed in this model is, "What are the consequences of community placement of previously institutionalized school-age children?" Secondary questions include: What effect have the implementation of court orders and legislative policies had on the process of communitization? How do family and community characteristics interact with the individual child's characteristics and needs to influence the consequences of community placement?

The answers to these questions can lead to improvement of programs and policies which affect severely handicapped children and their families. Given the value stance described earlier, the analysis and recommendations which result from our work are intended to improve the transition of children from public residential facilities into the community service system. Negative outcomes of community placement (e.g., recidivism, developmental regression, increased

Table 2
Theoretical Model of Communitization Variables Affecting Children

Individual Characteristics	Family Characteristics	Community Characteristics	Mandates and Policies
• Age at admission • Level of retardation • Medical condition • Behavioral charcteristics • Community of origin • Age at community placement • Length of institutional residence • Institutional experiences	• SES • Attitudes toward institutional and community care • Age of parents • Size and structure • Availability and utilization of support networks (extended family, neighbors, church, etc.) • Degree of contact with disabled child during institutional residence (visits, vacations, staff conferences)	• Type and size of community (rural, suburban, urban/traditional, progressive) • Availability of services • Accessibility of services • Opportunities for social integration • Attitudes toward institutional and community care • Attitudes and norms relative to acceptable appearance and behavior • Historical experiences with disabled people • Size of community tax base and utilization of state and federal dollars • Economic conditions (competition for employment, philanthropic resources)	• Court orders • Federal and state policies • Zoning ordinances • Degree of enforcement

Placement Outcomes

- Quantity of educational services
- Quality of educational services
- Type of residential arrangement
- Degree of restrictiveness of educational and residential services
- Stability of educational and residential services
- Individual's developmental status
- Individual's satisfaction with community living
- Changes in family and community attitudes
- Family adjustment to community placement

family stress) are viewed as resolvable problems associated with the evolution of communitization, not as evidence that communitization itself is unworkable.

However, there are two critical factors that temper the influence of this advocacy ideology. First, the assessment of "restrictiveness" and "quality" in judging placement outcomes must occur with the individual child in mind. The match between the child's abilities and disabilities and the nature of the learning and living environments is what determines quality and degree of restrictiveness. Here it is not possible to refer to some universal standard applicable to all cases. Beyond the injunctions that children be free from harm and that they be given equal (but not optimal) educational opportunities, the notions of "appropriateness" and "normalizing" require an analysis of the individual child–environment match. (It should be noted that we do not support the position that some children are incapable of benefitting from community services, and should remain in the protective custody of institutions. We have the technological and financial capacity to serve *all* children in or near their homes.)

The second reservation about the advocacy ideology in research is that family members are critically affected by communitization. Problems that occur in the service system may be remediable through staff training, additional resources, or enforcement of regulations. These steps are not so easily applied to families. Although training family members and providing support services are desirable steps, families are vulnerable to pathologies and dissolution in ways that formal service systems are not. Families have individual histories related to early stresses of the child's birth and infancy, decisions to institutionalize the child, attempts to maintain contact and attachment during institutional placement, and uncertainties about the child's return to the community. Researchers and service providers have not experienced these traumas. In fact, we are often the source of them (Mallory, 1986). Thus, recommendations based on analysis of research must take into account the degree to which family stress is exacerbated or reduced, even if such reduction of family stress may be in conflict with ideologically based communitization goals. This implies an obligation to consider multiple perspectives (philosophical, normative, familial, and individual) when making sense out of research data and developing recommendations for future practice.

AN EXAMPLE OF COMMUNITIZATION RESEARCH

The Population

With the preceding discussion of the purposes, theories, and value bases for communitization research in mind, we will describe the study with which we are currently engaged. The study is examining the experiences of 180 individuals who resided in a public residential institution between 1970 and 1985. All of the subjects were born after January 1, 1949, so they were under 21 years old at some point in the 15-year period being reviewed. The year 1970 was chosen as the beginning point because that is the year in which the population of the institution reached its peak (1150). The resident population has declined steadily since then, to an early 1985 level of 250. Our primary interest is in the group of people ($n = 70$) who left the institution prior to reaching adulthood, during a period of rapid and sweeping change in the educational service system for handicapped children. Although state-level special education mandates were in place beginning in the late 1960s, implementation of community-based services and enforcement of statutory regulations was not fully underway until 1978, when P.L. 94-142 went into effect and when state laws were amended to conform more closely with federal requirements.

We examined the effects of the implementation of state and federal policies by reviewing the community experiences of children who left the institution prior to 1978 and after 1978. The institution, like so many others, was the subject of litigation in the late 1970s. The resulting court order, issued in late 1981, also acts as a benchmark for the evolution of community services. Again, the experiences of children placed in the community before and after the court order are of major concern. Of the 70 children who left between 1970 and 1985, there are three subgroups that can reveal something about the impact of laws and court orders on the communitization of children—those who left between 1970 and 1978, those who left between 1978 and the end of 1981, and those who left after 1981.

The Methodology

"Triangulation" in research requires the use of two or more methods to measure the same trait, for the purpose of insuring reliable and valid observation and definition of that trait (Campbell & Fiske, 1959; Denzin, 1970). The term triangulation refers not only to the distinctly different methods that are used, but also includes different sources of data to measure the same trait. That is, multiple tools of measurement are applied to multiple populations.

Recall that the guiding question in the present study is, "What are the consequences of community placement of previously institutionalized school-age children?" To answer this question, we must know what factors determine the distribution of community-based services to the research population. Therefore, we considered medical and behavioral descriptions of each child, their diagnosed levels of retardation, pre-institutional experiences in the community service system, family social and economic background, and parent attitudes toward institutional and community care. Table 3 summarizes the key traits of interest in the study and the data sources used to examine each of these traits.

The interviews were of the schedule standardized type (Denzin, 1970). However, interviewers were allowed some leeway in the order in which they asked the questions and in the phrasing of questions, so that the interviewee understood exactly what he or she was being asked. Face-to-face interviews were chosen

Table 3
Data Sources and Types

Type of Data / Source of Data	Family Background	Reasons for Admission	Medical and Behavioral Characteristics	Community Services		Attitudes Toward Deinstitutionalization
				Residential	Educational	
Institutional Records	x	x	x	1	1	
Parent/Relative/Guardian	x	x	x	x	x	x
Case Manager or Service Provider	x		x^2	x	x	
Ex-Resident		x		x	x	x

Notes: [1]Community services data only available during trial placements prior to final discharge
[2]Only for post-institutional period

55

over mailed questionnaires because the interviewer can answer questions, reducing ambiguity and incorrect responses.

The drawbacks of the interview are that (a) they are measures taken at one point in time, (b) information is subject to the exigencies of the memory of the respondent, and (c) there is usually no information about the period of time prior to the point in time being covered by the interview. In order to compensate for these shortcomings, institutional records were examined to provide an historical context to the data. In this way, archival analysis provided the pre-test information.

In order to better understand the process of communitization, cases were chosen from among those children still residing at the institution, but who were scheduled to leave the institution within the time period of the study. By this method, the process of communitization may be observed as it occurs. Thoughts and feelings of the observed and the observer are also considered valuable data contributing to the understanding of what transpires in this process.

Because of memory bias and decay, parents were asked only to answer whether their child received educational services before and after going to the institution. Though we asked for the length of time the child went to school, these data are less reliable. However, in some cases, parents were able to document this information from their own collection of medical and social histories on their children. In other cases, service providers would substantiate the information. The field researchers were instructed to encourage the parent or service provider to consult his or her records whenever possible.

Another aspect of triangulation is the use of multiple theoretical and value perspectives in designing the research and in the analysis of the resulting data. In the analysis stages, data will be examined in terms of the pros and cons of placing a child in community settings. Some policymakers (and parents) would have the institution stay just as it is, and prefer keeping children in the institution, regarding it as the least restrictive environment. If it appears that many people do not get needed services in the community and some people return to the institution, do we conclude, then, that the community is not the proper place for this group? Not necessarily. Further analysis is based on such questions as, Who are the people who do not get services in the community? Are they the most severely handicapped? Are they people who lack strong advocates? Do they come from regions which do not have their service delivery system in as advanced a working order as other regions? Is there a correlation between communitization and family attitudes?

To summarize, the methodology used in the current study incorporates multiple measures of communitization outcomes. We are tracing the sequence of residences and educational services obtained before and after a child's residency at the institution. The pre-institutional data are obtained from parents and therefore are subject to the frailties of human memory. Nevertheless, it will be possible to say whether a child received *any* pre-institutional education. Post-institutional data come from parents, service providers, community records, and, to some extent, from institutional records (with regard to institutional experiences and trial community placements). Thus, it is possible to discuss, not only the length of stay in the community, but also the stability of placement (i.e., the length of time spent at any one residence or any one educational program).

Subject Recruitment

Locating those subjects who met our population criteria presented a classic "Catch-22" situation. In order to know who would be included in the study (and therefore from whom we needed to obtain consent), we had to determine which past and current residents of the institution met our specific age and residency criteria. This determination required access to clinical records at the institution. But in order to have such access, we needed prior consent from all those individuals whose records we would examine. The institution had no way of knowing which residents met our criteria, requiring that someone review *all* client records, including those stored in the state archives. The problem was partially solved by hiring one of the investigator's graduate students as a staff member of the institution. This person then had access to the records, because she was now a legitimate member of the institutional staff. After 2 months reviewing the records, she was able to develop a list of those people whom we needed to locate. However, she technically could not share those names with the University research team.

The next step, then, was to have her give the list of potential subjects to institutional staff in the community integration department. They agreed to mail letters, including consent forms and an explanation of the study, to all those on the list. Not surprisingly, many of the addresses available from the institutional records were outdated. Of 181 letters mailed to potential members of Population One (those who had left prior to their 21st birthdays), 63 (34.8%) were returned by the post office as undeliverable.

Of those that were returned, 10 denied consent. The most common reasons for denying consent included current family stress that precluded participation in interviews, fear of intrusive questions, and a misconception that participation in the study would lead either to reinstitutionalization in the case of community residents, or to deinstitutionalization in the case of institutional residents. This last misconception occurred partly because the cover letter sent to the parents or guardians was on institutional letterhead, although the consent documents were on University stationery. Thus, for those parents or guardians who feared that the study meant their child might be recommitted, the letterhead only served to reinforce this notion. We emphasized the independent nature of the study, but parents or guardians were often unable to make the subtle distinction between the state university (acing as an independent agency) and the state institution.

Community Networks.   Given the problems encountered in soliciting consent through the mails, our next step was to develop community networks of people and organizations that could assist us in locating subjects, including community agency staff and parent organizations such as the Association for Retarded Citizens (ARC). In order to obtain the support and cooperation of these groups, we went through a four-stage process of: (a) telephoning and meeting leaders of the various community groups, (b) arranging time on the group's meeting agenda to describe the study and solicit support, (c) distributing "contact packets" to the group members, and (d) maintaining contact with the group to assure that they followed through on the agreed-upon procedures. The "contact packets" included a one-page description of the study, a list of the personnel involved, an informed consent document, and a self-addressed stamped postcard that parents or guardians could return directly to us to indicate that they would like more information before giving their consent.

This approach was well received by ARC groups. Parents were able to see the potential benefits of the study, although some had inappropriate expectations that participation would lead to better services for their individual children. In general, ARCs were enthusaistic about the project and devoted time and energy to mailing the contact packets to members and publicizing the study in their newsletters. A secondary benefit of this process was that many more people became aware of the study in its early stages. The initial meetings with these groups also led to discussions about parents' perceptions and evaluation of communitization in its present state. This knowledge has been useful in guiding us to more meaningful interview questions, and in analyzing the data to generate policy recommendations.

Service Providers as Informants.   Developing rapport with case managers and other service providers was a somewhat different experience. The case management and community services system in New Hampshire was in development when the study began. Because many of the staff in these agencies were new to their positions, and because many had no previous experience with research projects, they resisted participating because of a concern that our study would reflect on their ability to perform their jobs. Case managers, who rightfully saw themselves as overworked, expressed concern about our demands on their time. Some questioned the value of research, arguing that our questions were either too general to be of help to them, or that our presence would create problems in their relations with their clients. Many times, case managers and others wanted us to add specific questions that would respond to their immediate concerns. After repeated meetings with groups and individuals to clarify the goals and limits of the study, most of this resistance and fear dissipated.

Similar reactions were encountered with institutional staff and public guardians. At the institution, in the early stages of record review and interviews, staff assumed that the study was directly related to recent litigation involving the institution. Some staff thought that our workers were attorneys, and many perceived our role as primarily evaluative. After the first month, when we paid a great deal of attention to protocol at the institution, staff relaxed and opened up to us, accepting our presence as routine.

Public guardians, who had legal responsibility for many of our potential subjects, were also skeptical in the early stages. Their concerns focused on informed consent and the intrusiveness of our procedures. As guardians of our subjects, they closely scrutinized our consent documents, requested meetings with us, and questioned our purposes and procedures. They clearly had a protective stance relative to their wards, expressing fear that family members could interfere with their role as guardians. There was a belief that the parent interviews could result in some parents wanting to re-establish contact with their children, which could lead to tension between the legal guardian and the subject's parents. It was agreed that parents who had not had contact with their children since they left the institution would not be interviewed. For our purposes, they would not be valid sources of data anyway. In the end, the public guardians provided consent and were fully cooperative as the study progressed.

Meetings were held with parents of children still residing at the institution, and state-level administrators. While it was frustrating to repeat the same information and encounter the same questions and concerns on many occasions, the lesson was clear. Research is often perceived as of little immediate value, threatening to those whose jobs are affected, and having some ulterior motive. These reactions must be addressed before subject recruitment, consent, and data gathering can proceed.

Informed Consent. As potential subjects were identified, the next step was to obtain their informed consent to participate in the study. Because people with mental retardation are less likely to be capable of providing truly informed and voluntary consent, due to both their intellectual limitations and to their dependence on bureaucratic systems for their survival, they are viewed as a special class for whom consent is a particularly crucial matter. (See Turnbull, 1977, for a more complete discussion.)

Research which focuses primarily on children with mental retardation presents some unique considerations in the area of informed consent. On the one hand, people under 18 years old are minors and legally incapable of giving their own consent, whether or not they are also mentally retarded. This group presented no real problems in obtaining consent. All of our subjects who were still below 18 had parents or guardians who were accessible to us. On the other hand, many of our subjects were no longer minors. Some were still below 21, and therefore viewed as children for the purposes of the study (that is, they were still eligible for educational services under P.L. 94-142). Most of the remaining group were in their early to mid-20s. Some of these young adults had been assigned public guardians, and obtaining consent was a straightforward process.

But the remaining group had not been adjudicated as incompetent, and therefore they were legally their own guardians. Yet they still lived at home. In fact, almost all of the parents contacted believed that they still had legal authority over their adult children. Even when subjects were no longer living at home, parents viewed themselves as having the right to make decisions for their children.

This situation presented us with an interesting dilemma. Should we take a strictly legal approach and obtain consent solely from the adult retarded person, bypassing the parent, or should we view the retarded person as de facto incompetent and seek substitute consent from a person who had some social and personal responsibility for the individual (in this case, his or her parent or nearest relative)? We chose the latter alternative. We believed that to bypass the role and concern of the parent would unnecessarily introduce confusion and stress. For us to introduce the notion that the parents no longer had any legal relationship to their child, and that we could enter into their lives without the parents' permission, was seen as intrusive. We were also concerned that we establish positive relationships with parents, so they would participate as respondents to our interviews. Because the service providers also seemed to be acting as though the parents were still guardians, we wanted to act in a consistent fashion. Interestingly, none of the state agencies, community staff, or institutional staff raised this issue as a concern. It was one that we identified and resolved internally.

Interviews of Community Residents

Because people with mental retardation may be valid sources of data, we asked those people who left the institution to live in the community to participate in brief face-to-face interviews. The community residents were approached as consumers in the service delivery system. We wanted to know what *they* wanted and believed. Where do they want to live? Do they want to go to school? How do they compare life at the institution with life in the community?

The sample of respondents was chosen from a pool of those people who were classified at the institution as mildly or moderately retarded and who did not have a psychiatric diagnosis. Only those individuals who could communicate and understand language were included in this part of the study. Sigelman et al. (1983) have suggested that verbal interviewing is generally most successful with persons who are moderately and mildly retarded, noting that, beginning in the severe range of retardation, verbal interviewing techniques yield unreliable and invalid responses.

In addition to these criteria, screening questions were used, the answer to which could be corroborated by other sources (e.g., parents, case managers). The respondents were asked to tell the interviewer their names, birthdays, gender, hometown, and whether they had ever resided at the institution. The responses were coded as either correct, incorrect, no response, or inappropriate response. If the respondent answered three or more questions correctly, he or she was included in the study. However, whether or not a person answered to criterion, we continued with the interview to explore the reliability of the screening procedure.

Interviews were conducted at the community residences of the subjects, at times that were most convenient for them. In most instances, parents were present during the interview. The parents were a hindrance when they prompted their children to make socially acceptable responses. However, their presence served to orient their child to the situation and to help him or her to stay on task. Parents also helped by their ability to translate our questions into forms more comprehensible to their children, and to assist us in understanding their children's responses.

The guiding question of the interview was, What are the residential, educational, and vocational preferences of people who have left the institution? In order to insure the reliability and validity of our information, questions were asked using multiple formats.

To demonstrate the utility and importance of multiple formats, we can examine the central question of the interview, concerning the respondents' residential preferences. In order to get at this, seven questions were posed with and without the aid of photographs: Would you rather live here or at the institution? Why would you rather live at [previous response]? After naming the array of pictures, we asked: Which picture looks like where you live? Which picture looks like the place where you would most like to live, if you could live anywhere you wanted? With new pictures, we asked: Which picture [happy and sad circle faces] shows how you usually feel? Which shows how you usually felt at the institution? Thirteen questions (about 10 minutes) later, we asked again: Would you rather live at the institution or here? (We referred to the institution by its name in these questions.)

A final, open-ended question asked was: If you could have anything you wanted (in the whole world), what would it be? The purpose of this question was to understand the scope of possibilities envisioned by the respondents, and get some sense of their unfulfilled aspirations and desires. It was also a pleasant way to conclude the interview.

Taping all the interviews seemed the most expedient means to obtain verbatim all that was said, and to record the process of each interview. Since many parents also participated, it was difficult for the field researchers to write all the dialogue. They did, however, write the ex-residents' verbatim responses to the questions of the interview schedule. Interestingly, in many instances, the tape recorder was a means of engaging respondents, for they enjoyed holding the microphone and operating the machine.

Issues in Data Collection

After subjects have been located and consent obtained, the next step required gathering data from the various sources described previously. The critical, and potentially problematic, sources are archival records, parents, and the ex-residents themselves. Each of these sources will be briefly discussed with respect to their inherent threats to reliability, and suggestions will be offered for increasing their usefulness and accuracy.

Review of Clinical Records.   Analysis of clinical records describing the past experiences of institutionalized people is a process that by its nature is retrospective. Therefore, the two most common problems encountered here are the threats to internal validity related to history and measurement (Campbell & Stanley, 1966; Heal & Fujiura, 1984). At a "clerical" level, the reliability of the records is affected by the care, accuracy, and completeness with which information was recorded. When very little information is entered for a particular time period, it is not possible to know whether that is because nothing of significance occurred, or staff neglected to make any entries, or significant events occurred that were consciously not recorded (e.g., a resident injury or a questionable behavior modification procedure). This means that the level of analysis must be superficial. Rich details of a resident's history, details which would have a bearing on later community placement, remain unknown to the investigator.

At a more substantive design level, history affects the collection and analysis of data, because the period of most rapid communitization occurred when changes in federal and state policies created the need to compare the experiences of those who left in the earlier era (pre-1978) with those who have left more recently. The social and historical context of these two groups was quite different when they left the institution. In addition, those who left in the earlier period were less severely impaired, increasing the likelihood that they could successfully "pass" in normal society without formal assistance. This is a form of attrition that frustrates the researcher, but may be a sign of positive outcome for the ex-resident. Although the stories of these successful individuals is an important part of the total picture of the communitization process, it is a part that is largely impossible to explicate. Likewise, case management and client tracking systems have only been developed in New Hampshire since the late 1970s. The accuracy and detail of records is thus quite different for those who entered community programs in recent years.

These historical threats to validity may also be seen in a positive light. That is, history is also an independent variable. If we can develop samples large enough to represent those who left before and after policy enactment and the issuance of court orders, then we can begin to answer the critical question, "Have communitization policies and programs improved the lives of people with mental retardation?" By relying on time series designs or quasi-experimental designs, such as the use of pretest and posttest procedures on intact groups or prematched control groups (assuming that the enactment of policies can be viewed as an "intervention"), the effect of historical factors can be assessed. Large sample sizes are necessary in order to control for subject characteristics, and a broad time frame is necessarv due to the lag time that occurs between the initial enactment of a policy and the ability to detect its impact at the community level.

Closely related to the threat created by history are the issues of changing measurement procedures, changing definitions, and reliance on reported rather than observed data (Campbell & Stanley, 1966, refer to these as threats of instrumentation). Until the late 1970s, systematic observation of behavior was not common practice in the particular institution we have been studying. The first attempt at complete documentation of all residents' behaviors took place in 1979. Subsequent assessments have been based on the ABS or other scales, with no known correlation to the scales used in 1979. Comparable measures of resident progress are therefore not available. This major problem of instrumentation makes a definitive conclusion about the developmental outcomes of communitization virtually impossible.

We have been plagued by the changes in diagnostic labels and codes caused by revisions in the AAMD diagnostic manuals. It is difficult to track precisely the progress of individual residents and ex-residents during the 1970–84 time period because of these changes. We have had to limit the diagnostic descriptors to the general terms mild, moderate, severe, or profound. In addition, it seems that the level of disability assigned to a particular individual is occasionally independent of IQ score. That is, different clinicians may refer to a person as moderately or severely retarded at different points in time even though there has been no new assessment of intellectual functioning to verify those judgments. This forces us to rely solely on IQ level and code retardation level according to AAMD standards. The possibility for detecting developmental change is, therefore, limited. The problem is exacerbated by infrequent re-assessment during the period of institutionalization, particularly in the earlier part of the 1970s.

A final measurement problem was revealed when we compared written data contained in the clinical records with the oral reports of direct care staff. In the process of looking closely at a group of profoundly and multiply disabled children still living at the institution, it became clear that the written behavioral descriptions were deficit oriented. This is due in part to the floor effect inherent in the instruments (and, to some degree, inherent in the attitudes of clinical staff who believed that a profoundly disabled child simply was not capable of manifesting much behavior). When direct care staff were asked to describe the abilities and limitations of the residents, they made an effort to focus on positive attributes and emerging, albeit subtle, skills. And several staff emphasized to us their concern that the clinicians who conducted formal assessments were not familiar with the residents and the progress they were making.

These threats to validity related to history and measurement require the use of multiple sources of data for each subject. If institutional records, direct care staff, family members, and community-based case managers are each used as data sources for a particular person, then a more complete and reliable picture may be obtained. When conflicting data emerge, it would seem necessary to follow three basic rules. First, rely on written records rather than oral recall. This approach is not trouble-free, but it does lead to greater consistency when looking at large amounts of data for large numbers of people. Second, rely on those people who are closest to the individual subject and who have known him or her over the longest period of time. Sometimes these people are family members, sometimes case managers, and sometimes direct service providers (teachers, therapists, group home counselors). Finally, use multiple data sources to corroborate each other. Because each data source has its own inherent weaknesses (memory bias, incomplete records, professional bias, etc.), none is a complete source by itself. In the end, the research inevitably makes judgments about who or what to believe. The more one attempts to corroborate through multiple sources, the more confident one can be that those judgments are correct.

Interviewing Parents.   Parents of children who have been institutionalized are important sources of information. Although their information may be distorted by time, emotion, or periods of reduced contact with their children, they still must be recognized as legitimate sources of specific types of data. They knew the child best prior to institutional placement. They often maintain intense interest and some degree of contact with their child during the period of placement, and they often assume some level of involvement when the child returns to his or her community. The parents' attitudes, resources, and skills thus are important in understanding the communitization process.

Parent interviews can be intrusive and painful occasions. Because of the retrospective nature of the interview questions (e.g., Why did your child go to live in the institution? Who recommended the placement? How often did you visit your child? What are your attitudes toward deinstitutionalization?), painful memories are recalled. Earlier feelings of guilt, anger, or confusion related to placing their child out of the home may come back to the surface, perhaps for the first time in a decade or more. This possibility requires well-trained interviewers who can balance the need to be good listeners with the need to solicit specific personal information. We have used interviewers with backgrounds and skills that enabled parents to open up with minimum embarrassment or pain. One interviewer was the mother of a severely, multiply handicapped 21-year-old son. Another was a woman with extensive experience as a nurse and psychologist in residential institutions and as a community advocate for disabled adults. Another had experience as a teacher at the institution involved in the study; he had known many of the children when they first lived there. To an unexpected degree, parents readily opened up. Although the experience was obviously a painful one (many cried and openly expressed their pain and anger during the interviews), it also seemed beneficial. Many of the parents said that no one had ever asked them these questions, particularly in a neutral context. Because the interviewers did not represent the service system, their questions provided the opportunity for parents to give information and express deeply-held beliefs without fear of judgment or loss of services for their children. Parents frequently said they were glad that someone cared enough to listen to their stories.

For some parents, the pain experienced over the years of caring for their handicapped child precluded their participation in our study. Of the 10 parents who denied consent for their son or daughter to be included, half said it was due to the fear that to do so would create even greater stress for themselves or their children. In some cases, husbands expressed concern for the emotional state of their wives ("She has been through enough. I don't want anything else to upset her.") Some parents were concerned that the study would add stress to their children's lives ("She's doing very well now, and I don't want anybody to bother her." "He's lived in a gold-fish bowl long enough. We just want to let things rest at this point.")

Another clue to the stress of parent interviews came from a father who had initially given consent on behalf of his son, and subsequently gave us permission to interview him and his wife. When the interview began, the father became very upset at the personal nature of the questions. ("It's none of your damn business! What does this [a question about his occupation] have to do with my son's treatment, anyway? Everybody from the secretary up will know my business. That's not confidential. Confidential is when I tell you something and you don't tell anyone else.") This man's severely disabled son still lived at the institution, and he greatly feared that his son was soon going to be placed in the community. His anxiety led to an unsuccessful interview, and revealed emotions felt to a lesser degree by many of the parents we interviewed.

Parent interviews have the potential for creating feelings of anxiety, pain, anger, and relief. Interviewers must be prepared to encounter this range of emotions, and act as empathetic listeners during the course of the interview. Because the information and perceptions held by parents are critical, the interviews are an important part of the data collection process. In general, parents readily shared difficult experiences and memories with us. But the potential for harm exists. Great sensitivity and respect are required throughout this delicate encounter, and interviewers must be prepared to listen, console, and not push any further than can be justified in the cause of social science.

ANALYSIS CONSIDERATONS

There are at least two major considerations affecting the analysis phase of communitization research. First, as with any social science, the research must report on the reliability and validity of the data collected. Heal and Fujiura (1984) covered the territory thoroughly (see also Heal, 1985, for additional discussion of methodological issues). They place communitization research within the design and analysis framework developed by Campbell and Stanley (1966), and conclude that such work rarely meets those rigorous standards. Given the present state of consent requirements, confidentiality, and decentralized services, communitization research will very rarely meet those standards. The best we can do is describe our data sources and data collection procedures as clearly as possible, and be careful that our analysis does not lead to unsupportable claims. As studies are conducted with narrow population groups, limited residential alternatives, in geographically small areas, a cumulative knowledge base is beginning to emerge. In light of the increased frequency of communitization studies described at the beginning of this chapter, the possibility of meta-analysis (Glass, McGaw, & Smith, 1981) seems not so remote. After 50 years of research into the effects of early intervention for young handicapped children, meta-analysis of outcome studies is now occurring at the Early Childhood Research Institute at Utah State University (Casto, White, & Taylor, 1983). Similar work should be attempted on the large body of community integration studies, in order to identify under what circumstances, with what populations, and at what cost communitization can succeed.

The second issue of analysis to be raised here is that of social validity (Heal & Fujiura, 1984). It would seem that communitization research is inherently socially valid. The central research questions of most studies in some way evaluate the effects of social policies that affect large numbers of disabled people, their families, and the community of practitioners and policy-makers. Yet much of the existing research focuses exclusively on people who have moved from institutional into community settings. The impact of community placement on family members, neighborhoods, school systems, health care systems, social welfare agencies, and taxpayers has not been investigated. The work of Turnbull et al. (1985) and Conroy (1985) are important beginnings in examining family consequences, but the impact on bureaucratic organizations, community groups, and other components of the larger social context also requires attention.

In keeping with the value framework described earlier, the purpose of this new area of work should not be, "Should communitization proceed?" but rather, "How can community systems and formal organizations enhance the process so that disabled people continue to move toward full independence, and the goals of normalization and social role valorization can be achieved?" If organizations and individuals resist the realization of the Community Imperative (see Biklen & Knoll, Chapter 1 in this volume), research must discover the causes of that resistance and some strategies for reducing it. In this way, the social validity of communitization research may be increased. It is important to note that researchers who adopt this position must adhere to rigorous methodological principles, and be cautious not to propose spurious interpretations that are not supported by their findings. To the extent that research reports include both a description of the investigator's inherent biases and the details of his or her data collection and analysis procedures, consumers of that information will be better equipped to reach sound judgements about the implications of the findings.

There are probably several avenues to this kind of research. The multiple interests framework suggested by Shadish et al. (1982), described earlier, is one approach. Another could be the use of Family Impact Analysis (Hubbell, 1981). This approach, developed as part of a national family policy that was debated in the late 1970s, has several basic tenets. First, the local implementation of federal and state policies must be examined relative to their impact on families. Just as environmental impact analysis seeks to predict the consequences of government action on the physical environment, family impact analysis proposes to predict how families as holistic entities would be affected by certain policies.

Essentially, the question asked is, How will a given policy (e.g., community-based care for people who are mentally retarded or disturbed) affect the ability of families to perform their basic domestic, economic, and social functions? Second, family impact analysis examines the values which underlie a particular policy. For example, value analysis questions relevant to the present topic would be: Do the interests of individual disabled people and their constitutional rights to freedom and treatment override the interests of family systems which might be harmed by the reintegration of their disabled members? If such harm is a likelihood, what obligation does government have to assist families and minimize the disruption and costs of community-based care? Third, this approach suggests certain criteria to be considered before policy is enacted. These involve the qualities of staff, administrative auspices, convenience for families, sensitivity to family needs, and the degree to which policies treat families as independent, proactive systems. Fourth, family impact analysis focuses on the ways in which policies affect families with varying socioeconomic, structural, and life cycle characteristics. The pluralistic aspects of policies are thus measured. Finally, an ecological perspective is emphasized in order to understand the broader historical and social context in which a policy is implemented.

The Institute for Educational Leadership at George Washington University has applied these principles to policies related to foster care, employee flexitime, and teenage pregnancy, and the state of Minnesota has incorporated Family Impact Analysis into many areas of social policy planning. What is needed is an expansion of this approach to include extrafamilial systems affected by social policies such as the community integration of disabled children and adults. For example, local school districts are directly affected by the communitization of children. As children return to their home communities, increased burdens on budgets, classroom space, teachers' workloads, transportation systems, administrative time, and so on are likely to occur. To the extent that communitization is a planful process subsidized with state and federal dollars, and supported by technical assistance to teachers and administrators, it may enjoy greater chances of success and community acceptance. If, on the other hand, the process is arbitrary, unanticipated, and unsupported by additional resources, it will, of course, be resisted and even sabotaged. Similarly, if health care providers such as hospitals, community clinics, and mental health centers feel they have been given a new and unanticipated responsibility with little prior notice and preparation, they too will be less likely to cooperate.

Research that examines the sociological effects of communitization (as opposed to the more narrow personological focus of most studies), is an important next step. One example of such work is the Kirschner Associates' study (1970) of the impact of Project Head Start on health care and social service agencies in the communities in which centers were established. What is needed, then, is something that might be called Community Impact Analysis. If the multiple perspectives and voices of those affected by communitization are to be heard and respected, it would seem necessary for researchers concerned with social validity to move into this promising, albeit complex, arena.

SUMMARY AND CONCLUSIONS

This chapter has been concerned with the recent history of research investigations on the community placement of people with mental retardation. Most of the recent and current work has focused on behavioral and developmental changes in those individuals who have left public residential facilities and moved into smaller public and private community living facilities. Less attention has been paid to family and community attitudes, the characteristics of varying social contexts, and the costs (financial and psychosocial) of communitization. Because of the major barriers to valid research caused by subject recruitment, confidentiality requirements, the use of multiple and unreliable measurement tools, and a general suspicion of the value of social science, our efforts have not had immediate effects on policy and program reform. Policy-making and the generation of new knowledge have more often been parallel than complementary activities.

The purpose of communitization research is essentially to evaluate the outcomes of social policy. Whether we examine the effects on disabled people, their families, or communities, the core question is not simply, Is it a good idea? The values and political ideologies of the last 30 years provide an answer to that question. The critical questions in this light are, How can the process achieve the social and political goals articulated by legislatures, judges, and consumer advocacy groups? Under what circumstances does the process succeed, and when does it not? What additional resources are needed to make it succeed? What, in fact, is success? How will we know when our goals have been achieved? What do we do if they are?

Suggestions for methodological strategies have been offered. These include the triangulation of data sources, face-to-face interviews with ex-residents of institutions and their parents or guardians, and consideration of unsolicited comments and other qualitative data. Obstacles to truly valid research are enormous, although important models such as Conroy and Bradley's (1985) are emerging. In the long run, cumulative knowledge from myriad sources may lead to meta-analysis that can guide subsequent research and policy development. In addition, broader conceptions of research which take into account family and community impact are beginning to be considered. If we can say with confidence that disabled people who are living, learning, and working in their own communities are better off, then the next set of questions will focus on how community organizations and agencies can benefit from the integration of such people.

REFERENCES

Best-Sigford, B., Bruininks, R.H., Lakin, C.K., Hill, B.K., & Heal, L.W. (1982). Resident release patterns in a national sample of public residential facilities. *American Journal of Mental Deficiency, 87,* 130–140.

Bogdan, R., Biklen, D., Blatt, B., & Taylor, S.J. (1981). Handicap, prejudice, and social science research. In H.C. Haywood & J.R. Newbrough (Eds.), *Living environments for developmentally retarded persons* (pp. 235–247). Baltimore, MD: University Park Press.

Bruininks, R.H., Hill, B.K., & Thorsheim, M.J. (1982). Deinstitutionalization and foster care for mentally retarded people. *Health and Social Work, 7,* 198–205.

Campbell, D.T., & Fiske, D.W. (1959). Convergent and discriminant validation by the multitrait-multimethod matrix. *Psychological Bulletin, 56,* 81–105.

Campbell, D.T., & Stanley, J.C. (1966). *Experimental and quasi-experimental designs for research.* Chicago, IL: Rand McNally.

Casto, G., White, K., & Taylor, C. (1983). An early intervention research institute: Studies of the eficacy and cost effectiveness of early intervention at Utah State. *Journal for the Division of Early Childhood, 7,* 5–17.

Conroy, J.W. (1985). Reactions to desinstitutionalization among parents of mentally retarded persons. In R.H. Bruininks & K.C. Lakin (Eds.), *Living and learning in the least restrictive environment* (pp. 141–152). Baltimore, MD: Paul H. Brookes.

Conroy, J.W., & Bradley, V.J. (1985). *The Pennhurst longitudinal study: A report of five years of research and analysis.* Philadelphia, PA: Temple University Developmental Disabilities Center.

Conroy, J., Efthimiou, J., & Lemanowicz, J. (1982). A matched comparison of the developmental growth of institutionalized and deinstitutionalized mentally retarded clients. *American Journal of Mental Deficiency, 86,* 581–587.

Denzin, N.K. (1970). *The research act: A theoretical introduction to sociological methods.* Chicago, IL: Aldine.

Edgerton, R.B., Bollinger, M., & Herr, B. (1984). The cloak of competence: After two decades. *American Journal of Mental Deficiency, 88,* 345–351.

Ellis, N.R., Bostick, G.E., Moore, S.A., & Taylor, J.J. (1981). A follow-up study of severely and profoundly mentally retarded children after short-term institutionalization. *Mental Retardation, 19,* 31–35.

Frohboese, R., & Sales, B.D. (1980). Parental opposition to deinstitutionalization: A challenge in need of attention and resolution. *Law and Human Behavior, 4,* (1–2), 1–87.

Gibson, D., & Fields, D.L. (1983). Fifty years of institutional habilitation outcomes: Inventory and implications. *Education and Training of the Mentally Retarded, 18,* 82–89.

Glass, G.V., McGaw, B., & Smith, M.L. (1981). *Integrating research studies: Meta-analysis of social research.* Beverly Hills, CA: Sage Publishers.

Grossman, H.J. (Ed.). (1983). *Classification in mental retardation.* Washington, DC: American Association on Mental Deficiency.

Heal, L.W. (1985). Methodology for community integration research. In R.H. Bruininks & K.C. Lakin (Eds.), *Living and learning in the least restrictive environment* (pp. 199–224). Baltimore, MD: Paul H. Brookes.

Heal, L.W., & Fujiura, G.T. (1984). Methodological considerations in research on residential alternatives for developmentally disabled persons. In N.R. Ellis & N.W. Bray (Eds.), *Inter-*

national review of research in mental retardation, Vol. 12 (pp. 205–244). New York: Academic Press.

Heller, T. (1982). Social disruption and residential relocation of mentally retarded children. *American Journal of Mental Deficiency, 87,* 48–55.

Hobbs, N. (1964). Mental health's third revolution. *American Journal of Orthopsychiatry, 34,* 822–833.

Hubbell, R. (1981). *Foster care and families: Conflicting values and policies.* Philadelphia, PA: Temple University Press.

Intagliata, J., & Willer, B. (1982). Reinstitutionalization of mentally retarded persons successfully placed into family-care and group homes. *American Journal of Mental Deficiency, 87,* 34–39.

Kielhofner, G. (1981). An ethnographic study of deinstitutionalized adults: Their community settings and daily life experiences. *The Occupational Therapy Journal of Research, 1,* 125–142.

Kiernan, C. (1981). Residential provision for the mentally handicapped. In H.C. Haywood & J.R. Newbrough (Eds.), *Living environment for developmentally retarded persons* (pp. 209–234). Baltimore, MD: University Park Press.

Kirschner Associates, Inc. (1970). *A national survey of the impacts of Head Start centers on community institutions.* Washington, DC: Office of Child Development, Department of Health, Education, and Welfare.

Kleinberg, J., & Galligan, B. (1983). Effects of deinstitutionalization on adaptive behavior of mentally retarded adults. *American Journal of Mental Deficiency, 88,* 21–27.

Lakin, K.C., Hill, B.K., Hauber, F.A., Bruininks, R.H., & Heal, L.W. (1983). New admissions and readmissions to a national sample of public residential facilities. *American Journal of Mental Deficiency, 88,* 13–20.

Mallory, B.L. (1986). Interactions between community agencies and families over the life cycle. In R.R. Fewell & P.F. Vadasy (Eds.), *Families of handicapped children: Needs and supports across the life span.* Austin, TX: Pro-Ed.

Meyer, R.J. (1980). Attitudes of parents of institutionalized mentally retarded individuals toward deinstitutionalization. *American Journal of Mental Deficiency, 85,* 184–187.

Nihira, K., Foster, R., Shellhaas, M., & Leland, H. (1974). *AAMD Adaptive Behavior Scale.* Washington, DC: American Association on Mental Deficiency.

Reagan, M.W., Murphy, R.J., Hill, Y.F., & Thomas, D.R. (1980). Community placement stability of behavior problem educable mentally retarded students. *Mental Retardation, 18,* 139–142.

Roth, R., & Smith, T.E.C. (1983). A statewide assessment of attitudes toward the handicapped and community living programs. *Education and Training of the Mentally Retarded, 18,* 164–168.

Rudie, F., & Riedl, G. (1984). Attitudes of parents/guardians of mentally retarded former state hospital residents toward current community placement. *American Journal of Mental Deficiency, 89,* 295–297.

Schalock, R.L., Harper, R.S., & Carver, G. (1981). Independent living placement: Five years later. *American Journal of Mental Deficiency, 86,* 170–177.

Schalock, R.L., Harper, R.S., & Genung, T. (1981). Community integration of mentally retarded adults: Community placement and program success. *American Journal of Mental Deficiency, 85,* 478–488.

Seltzer, G.B. (1981). Community residential adjustment: The relationship among environment, performance, and satisfaction. *American Journal of Mental Deficiency, 85,* 624–630.

Seltzer, M.M. (1981). Deinstitutionalization and vocational adjustment. In P. Mittler (Ed.), *Frontiers of knowledge in mental retardation, Vol. 1, Social, educational, and behavioral aspects* (pp. 347–355). Baltimore: University Park Press.

Seltzer, M.M., & Krauss, M.W. (1984). Family, community residence, and institutional placements of a sample of mentally retarded children. *American Journal of Mental Deficiency, 89,* 257–266.

Seltzer, M.M., Seltzer, G.B., & Sherwood, C.C. (1982). Comparison of community adjustment of older vs. younger mentally retarded adults. *American Journal of Mental Deficiency, 87,* 9–13.

Shadish, W.R., Thomas, S., & Bootzin, R.R. (1982). Criteria for success in deinstitutionalization: Perceptions of nursing homes by different interest groups. *American Journal of Community Psychology, 10,* 553–566.

Siegel, P.S., & Ellis, N.R. (1985). Note on the recruitment of subjects for mental retardation research. *American Journal of Mental Deficiency, 89,* 431–433.

Sigelman, C.K., Scheonrock, E.C., Budd, J.L., Winer, C.L., Spanhel, P.W., Martin, S.H., & Bensberg, G.J. (1983). *Communicating with mentally retarded persons: Asking questions and getting answers.* Lubbock, TX: Texas Tech University, Research and Training Center in Mental Retardation.

Sutter, P. (1980). Environmental variables related to community placement failure in mentally retarded adults. *Mental Retardation, 18,* 189–191.

Sutter, P., Tadashi, M., Call, T., Yanagi, G., & Yee, S. (1980). Comparison of successful and unsuccessful community-placed mentally retarded persons. *American Journal of Mental Deficiency, 85,* 262–267.

Thiel, G.W. (1981). Relationship of IQ, adaptive behavior, age, and environmental demand to community-placement success of mentally retarded adults. *American Journal of Mental Deficiency, 86,* 208–211.

Turnbull, H.R. (1977). *Consent handbook.* Washington, DC: American Association on Mental Deficiency.

Turnbull, A.P., Brotherson, M.J., & Summers, J.A. (1985). The impact of deinstitutionalization on families: A family systems approach. In R.H. Bruininks & K.C. Lakin (Eds.), *Living and learning in the least restrictive environment* (pp. 115–140). Baltimore, MD: Paul H. Brookes.

Walsh, J.A., & Walsh, R.A. (1982). Behavioral evaluation of a state program of deinstitutionalization of the developmentally disabled. *Evaluation and Program Planning, 5,*(1), 59–67.

Willer, B., & Intagliata, J. (1981). Social-environmental factors as predictors of adjustment of deinstitutionalized mentally retarded adults. *American Journal of Mental Deficiency, 86,* 252–259.

Willer, B., & Intagliata, J. (1982). Comparison of family-care and group homes as alternatives to institutions. *American Journal of Mental Deficiency, 86,* 588–595.

Willer, B.S., Intagliata, J.C., & Atkinson, A.C. (1981). Deinstitutionalization as a crisis event for families of mentally retarded persons. *Mental Retardation, 19,* 28–29.

Wolfensberger, W. (1969). The origin and nature of our institutional models. In R.B. Kugel & W. Wolfensberger (Eds.), *Changing patterns in residential services for the mentally retarded* (pp. 35–82). Washington, DC: U.S. Government Printing Office.

4

Risk in the Lives of Children and Adolescents who are Mentally Retarded: Implications for Families and Professionals

Ruth Kahan Kaminer and Eleonora Jedrysek
Rose F. Kennedy Center, Albert Einstein College of Medicine

Independent functioning is a goal of intervention with individuals who are mentally retarded. However, independent functioning carries with it the risk of physical harm, and this risk may be greater than average for individuals with limited competence. This paper reviews the literature on risk of physical injury during the childhoods of individuals who are mentally retarded. Only a few reports were found on risk assessment, which is measurable. On the other hand, recent literature urges greater risk acceptance, which is a policy decision. The implications of this policy for the autonomy of individuals who are mentally retarded and their parents are discussed.

Interventions by members of the helping professions are based on assumptions about desirable levels of function and the quality of life of the individuals being helped. Independence and self-determination are generally agreed upon goals, However, independent function carries with it the risk of a harmful outcome. This paper will review the literature on risk of injury or harm to children and adolescents in the general population, and to individuals who are mentally retarded. We will evaluate the risk assessment information available to professionals who serve individuals who are mentally retarded, and their families. The implication of this information for the relationships between parents, children, and professionals in making choices that involve risk of harm will be discussed.

Risk is defined as the measure of the association between exposure to a particular factor and the likelihood of a certain undesirable outcome (Rapoport, 1979). In this context, we are referring to the risk of physical injury or bodily harm, not psychological trauma. In a strict sense, risk describes a relationship between the event or characteristic being studied and its result, each of which must be stated. However, the word is often used more loosely as a synonym for danger and harm, or for unpredictability and adventure.

The "dignity of risk," a concept that has been popularized by Perske (1972), applies this thinking to the lives of individuals who are mentally retarded. Perske states that "many who work with the handicapped, impaired, disadvantaged and aged tend to be overzealous in their attempts to 'protect' . . ." (p. 195). "We now need to ensure this dimension of human dignity for the handicapped and prepare them for facing real but prudent risk in a real world" (p. 200). The principle of prudent risk is not problematic, but its implementation raises two important questions: What information is needed to assess prudent risk in a given situation for a particular person? Who should decide how much risk is prudent? Perske urges a greater degree of risk acceptance by professionals on behalf of individuals who are mentally retarded, without offering data on risk assessment for this population.

At the same time those experts speaking for the normalization movement recommend greater freedom from protection and encourage more risk taking for handicapped individuals of all ages, those experts writing in the pediatric and public health literature emphasize the high morbidity and mortality caused by unintended injuries in the general population of children and youth. The risk of harm to children and adolescents who are mentally retarded must be viewed against a background of injury risk for an unselected population of similar age.

INJURIES IN CHILDHOOD AND ADOLESCENCE

The General Population

Injury is the leading cause of death and disability in childhood and early adult life (Committee, 1983). Approximately 22,000 injury deaths occur yearly in the 0–19 year old population in the United States, for a crude death rate of 30.3/100,000 (Guyer & Gallagher, 1985). The 1980–81 Statewide Childhood Injury Prevention Program (SCIPP) established a surveillance system to collect data on injury related deaths, hospitalizations, and emergency room visits for children and adolescents from a defined geographic area of Massachusetts over a 1-year period. They found that 20% of the 87,000 children living in the area required an emergency room visit or hospitalization for an injury each year (Gallagher, Finison, Guyer, & Good-enough, 1984). Increasing awareness of the extent of the need for injury prevention has led to careful analysis of what constitutes accidents.

The concept of "accident" as an unavoidable occurrence which cannot be controlled has been replaced by a more scientific view of injury epidemiology. This view utilizes the same agent–host–environment model used in describing the epidemiology of communicable disease. This concept assumes that the injury occurs when the agent, host, and environment come together in a critical manner. The agent is the form of energy causing the damage, the host or injured individual can be described by age, sex, and developmental level, and the environment includes both physical and psychosocial elements. Study of these three factors permits the identification of populations and of circumstances at high risk for specific types of injuries. Such identification is the first step in planning strategies for injury prevention (Guyer & Gallagher, 1985).

The Mentally Retarded Population

Several types of injury are specifically associated with individuals who are mentally retarded. Well-described categories include pica and self-injurious behavior. There is also a category of injuries each of which is characteristically associated with a particular cause of mental retardation.

Pica is defined in two different ways, either as the ingestion of nonfood items (nonfood pica), or as deviant eating behaviors (food pica) (Danford & Huber, 1982). The latter type of pica includes eating food from the garbage or floor, and constant compulsive eating of certain foods. The tasting or mouthing of objects is common in unselected infants and toddlers, but "pica after the second year of life is a symptom needing investigation" (Forman, Hetznecker, & Dunn 1983, p. 73).

In a review of 991 institutionalized children and adults with mental retardation, pica by either definition was noted in 25.8%. Among those aged 11–20 years, the youngest individuals in the study, nonfood pica was present in 20.2% and food pica in 3.9%. The incidence of nonfood pica decreased with age and was related to a lower level of functioning. Food pica was not related to the level of retardation, but rather to behavioral problems. Some medical complications, such as intestinal obstruction and foreign body ingestion, occurred only in individuals with pica (Albin, 1977; Danford & Huber, 1982). Food pica is also a characteristic behavior of children with the Prader-Willi Syndrome, in which constant craving for food leads to harmful obesity (Stephenson, 1980).

Self injurious behavior (SIB) is defined as "a self-inflicted repetitive action that leads to lacerations, bruising or abrasions of the client's body" (Singh & Millichamp, 1985, p. 257). This behavior is more frequently observed in individuals who are severely and profoundly retarded, is seen mostly in institutionalized populations, and constitutes a significant danger to the involved person (Bates & Wehman, 1977). In reviewing 56 studies of maladaptive behaviors, including self injury, Bates and Wehman found SIB described only for institutionalized individuals and not reported in schools, homes, or vocational programs. The average prevalence of SIB in the institutionalized populations reviewed was 16% for all ages. With the exception of very few mildly and moderately retarded children, individuals manifesting SIB were severely and profoundly retarded. However, Tavormina, Henggeler, and Gayton (1976) reported SIB in children living with their own families. They conducted interviews concerning their children's behavior with 52 mothers of children aged 2 to 17 years, and reported self-injurious behavior in 17% of the children.

In a study using a questionnaire to obtain information from 75 institutions for the mentally retarded, Lakin, Hill, Hauber, Bruininks, and Heal (1983) found that 22% of 430 randomly selected first admissions and readmissions manifested self-injurious behavior. Of those successfully discharged from the institution to a community setting, only 11% manifested SIB. Approximately half of the individuals studied were 5–21 years old, and three fourths of the population were of a moderate to profound level of mental retardation.

Certain forms of injury may be specifically associated with the medical condition causing the child's mental retardation. In Lesch-Nyhan disease, self-mutilation, most often biting the fingers or lips, is a characteristic behavior. In a report on 19 individuals with this diagnosis, self-injurious behavior was present in each one (Christie, Bay, Kaufman, Bakay, & Nyhann, 1982).

Individuals with Down's syndrome are susceptible to joint dislocations, even under conditions of normal activity. In a study of 161 individuals with Down's syndrome admitted to three acute care centers, partial and complete dislocations of knees, hips, and the atlanto-axial joint of the neck were commonly observed (Diamond, Lynn, & Sigman, 1981). Atlanto-axial dislocation in the neck is particularly dangerous, since it can cause injury to the spinal cord. In a prospective study by Pueschel et al. (1984) of 236 individuals with Down's syndrome, 40 were found to have atlanto-axial instability, and 7 of them displayed neurological symptoms. Awareness of this susceptibility has led to the authors' recommendation that children with Down's syndrome be carefully evaluated for this condition prior to participating in sports involving forceful movements of the neck.

Aside from the specific injuries which are seen primarily among individuals with mental retardation of organic etiology or a well-defined clinical syndrome, individuals who are mentally retarded are subject to the same dangers as the rest of the population. It must be noted, however, that studies of accidents among children with mental retardation are typically based on institutionalized samples. For example, Berggreen (1972) studied casualties and surgical emergencies reported over a 3-year period in an institution for mentally retarded children in Denmark. The population of 300 children, with an average age of 9.5 years, was studied retrospectively by means of records of injuries requiring treatment at the institution and discharge summaries from acute care hospitals. Medical emergencies, such as poison ingestions, and emergencies requiring dental, eye, or ear, nose, and throat consultations, were excluded. The total number of injuries in the 3-year period was 408, and would have been almost double if dental injuries were included. This figure is about three times the figure reported among normal Danish children living in the community. Almost half of the injuries were to the head and face, and the peak age for these injuries was 9 to 11 years, whereas the peak for such injuries among nonretarded children is at a much younger age. The accidents noted in this study were thought to correspond, by and large, to accidents occurring in the home. Furthermore, they took place in spite of sheltered conditions with a maximum of supervision. It is worthy of note that most children who suffered head injuries had an additional handicap besides mental retardation. Epilepsy and cerebral palsy, singly or combined, were present in about three fourths of the children who sustained head injuries.

In a similar study, Williams (1973) reported on a review of all casualty forms completed during a 6-month period at an institution for children with mental retardation in Great Britain. Twenty-three injuries were reported for the 109 children aged 16 years and under, but only 10 of the injuries required treatment in the casualty department. Of interest is the fact that the most frequent cause of injury was aggression by other patients.

A report by Nihira and Nihira (1975) is of particular relevance to the question of injury risk in a community setting. The adaptive behavior of 424 community placed individuals who are mentally retarded was studied by means of tape recorded interviews of their caretakers. All the subjects were living in family care homes and nursing homes, in suburban and semi-urban neighborhoods in California. The tapes were evaluated to analyze incidents of problem behavior. Seventy-seven percent of the 1,252 incidents noted involved jeopardy to health or safety, and in four fifths of the hazardous incidents the client had jeopardized his or her own self. Incidents primarily involving health were found in the area of eating habits, physical violence against one's self, and peculiar habits. Safety was jeopardized by wandering away, poor sense of direction, noncompliance with rules, eccentric and immature behavior, temper tantrums, and problems in heterosexual adjustment. The population consisted of individuals from 1 to 90 years of age, with 76% being 13 to 49 years old, and 78% mildly to moderately retarded. Of the 145 youngsters aged 3–18 years, 64% were cited in incidents of problem behavior, while only 27% of the 279 adults were thus cited. The authors concluded that there was greater health risk to individuals who were below adolescent age.

RISK IN RETARDED AND NONRETARDED POPULATIONS

Early Childhood Risk

The SCIPP Surveillance System (Gallagher et al., 1984) confirmed previous observations that injury rates varied by age and sex, with injury rates higher for males at all ages except among infants and 2-year-olds. The rate of injuries was highest for adolescents and lowest for the 0- to 5-year-old group. However, there was a peak in the rate of emergency room visits for both girls and boys between 1 and 3 years of age, which was exceeded only by that of male adolescents. The types of injuries most characteristic of the preschool age are non-sport-related falls, poisonings, and burn injuries, most of which occur in the kitchen. Foreign body injuries and choking are not frequent, but are seen almost exclusively at this age and usually as a result of mouthing small objects or inserting them in the nose or ear.

Both age and developmental level are characteristics of the child found to be relevant in assessing the magnitude of the risk of injury and the kind of injury likely to occur (Guyer & Gallagher, 1985). The developmental level of children who are mentally retarded is below that expected for their chronologic age. As a result, some circumstances are hazardous to them on the basis of their developmental level at an age when they cease to be a serious concern in an unselected population. One example described previously is the eating of nonfood items past toddler age. Another illustration is the high prevalence of head and face injuries, many of them lacerations from falls, reported by Berggreen (1972) to occur in a group of institutionalized children. In this population, they occurred most often at 9 to 11 years, while similar injuries are reported at a much younger age in the general population.

A recent study of the adaptive functioning of children with mental retardation aged 3 to 5 years 11 months was based on interviews with the parent or caretaker, using the Behaviour Screening Questionnaire (BSQ—Richman, Stevenson, & Graham, 1975) and the Vineland Social Maturity Scale (Doll, 1965). The population consisted of 100 children living in the community who were seen consecutively by the psychologist as part of their developmental evaluation at a university-based evaluation center in the Bronx, New York (Jedrysek, 1985). The level of intelligence of the children was borderline for 46, 26 were mildly, 15 moderately, 10 severely or profoundly mentally retarded, and 3 were not testable. The mothers who were interviewed stressed the need for constant supervision of the children, since 28% of the youngsters did not discriminate edible substances (Vineland item 30) and 43% failed to avoid simple hazards (Vineland item 41). Specific problem behaviors mentioned by the parents included leaning out of the window, jumping from high places, breaking property, or running away in public places. On the BSQ, 47% of the children were reported to be difficult to manage, 53% overactive, and 39% had severe temper tantrums. In comparison, the prevalence of these behaviors as reported by their parents for normal 3-year-olds in the London area was 5.5% difficult to manage, 23.5% overactive, and 5.5% prone to severe temper tantrums (Richman et al., 1975).

Children who are hyperactive or difficult to manage are reported in the literature to be prone to accidents. This information comes both from retrospective studies of the behavioral styles of children hospitalized for injuries or ingestions, as well as from prospective studies of the children's temperament. For example, a group of 113 preschool children from the Boston area admitted to the hospital with accidental injury during a 12-month period was studied by a multidisciplinary team to elucidate factors associated with injuries (Meyer, Roelofs, Bluestone & Redmond, 1963). They were compared to a group of preschool children who had never been hospitalized for this cause. Aside from significant family and other environmental factors, several child factors distinguished the accident group from the contrast group. The study children were described by their parents as overactive, as having behavior problems, and as manifesting pica significantly more often than the contrast children.

In a British study of similar design, Sibert and Newcombe (1977) studied 105 children under 5 years of age admitted to the hospital for ingestion of poisons. The parents of these patients were asked to give information on their children's behavior. Compared to the matched controls, the study children were harder (not defined), more anxious, and more active. They were also more likely to put other than food substances in their mouths.

Carey (1972) studied the temperament of 200 infants in his private practice by means of a questionnaire he developed. The mother fills out the questionnaire during a visit when the infant is between 4 and 8 months old. Fourteen percent of the 200 babies fell into the ''difficult'' category, meaning they were irregular in eating and sleeping, low in adaptability, intense, responded to new situations by initial withdrawal, and had a predominantly negative mood. These difficult babies had a significantly higher incidence of lacerations requiring sutures in the first 2 years compared to the rest of the infants studied. In another prospective study, a longitudinal follow-up of twins in Kentucky was used to identify the behavioral antecedents of accidental injury (Matheny, Brown, & Wilson, 1971). The interview data from the 1-year visit for 49 pairs of same sex twins were used to provide within-pair behavioral comparisons on frequency of temper tantrums, attention span during play, and amount of spontaneous activity. The twins with more accidents were found to be more active, temperamental, and less attentive than their co-twin.

School Age Risk

The new challenges for children during school age years consist of increased interaction with peers and with the larger community. In the general population, the changing nature of the hazards is reflected in a different pattern of injuries in this group than was seen in preschool age group. Elementary school children have the lowest rate of burns and poisoning, but the highest risk of injury as pedestrians, twice that of preschool children. In the SCIPP survey, more than one of every 80 school-age children required hospital treatment for a bicycle accident not involving a motor vehicle during a 1-year period (Gallagher et al., 1984).

Comparable data for school age children who are mentally retarded are not available. As noted previously, institutionalized children of school age were noted to have the types of accidents characteristic of preschool children in the general population (Berggreen, 1972). However, unlike nonretarded preschool aged children, school aged children with mental retardation are expected to regularly function in a school setting which may be less sheltered than the home environment.

Since it is usual for children with retardation of a moderate or greater degree to be in special class placement and receive transportation, their interaction with the general community is limited during school hours. Such a setting minimizes risk from the outside environment, but may expose the child to the specific dangers of this environment. For example, parents report hyperactive-aggressive behaviors among youngsters with mental retardation, with a tendency to fight, to have severe tantrums, and to be difficult to control (Tavormina et al., 1976). We did not find any reports in the literature on the risk of physical harm from classmates in special classes. However, in an institutionalized group of children, the most common cause of injuries was aggression by peers (Williams, 1973).

Overall behavior disturbance and behavior classified as emotional disturbance, hyperactive behavior, aggressive conduct disorder, and antisocial behavior were all more frequent and more severe among mentally retarded males and females in childhood, according to a follow-up study in a British city (Koller, Richardson, Katz, & McLaren, 1982). The population studied consisted of 221 subjects, and included all the children born in that city from 1951 to 1955 who were placed in a special school, training center, or hospital for retarded children before age 16, as well as some severely retarded children not receiving any services. Their IQ scores were obtained when they were 7 to 10 years old, and records kept by home health visitors, schools, residential institutions, and social workers were available. The cohort was compared to matched controls. Though information on injuries and accidents is not given, the hyperactive behavior seen more frequently in this group may place them at risk for a higher rate of injuries, while the antisocial and aggressive behaviors may contribute to injuries in peers.

Mildly retarded children of school age may be mainstreamed, and, even when they are in special classes, they are more likely to be permitted to play unsupervised in the neighborhood. It is, therefore, of interest to know whether they are more or less likely than nonretarded children to take risks in similar situations. To test the hypothesis that children who are retarded would take fewer risks due to a presumed low expectancy of success, Hayes (1973) used an experimental situation consisting of a game of chance. The responses of 30 boys and 30 girls with mildly retarded intelligence in special education classes were compared to those of an equal number of nonretarded youngsters of comparable mental ages in grades 3 and 5. They were shown a game consisting of 10 switches, nine of which would release a penny, while the tenth one sounded a buzzer and all the pennies won so far would be lost. The children with mental retardation took as many or more risks as the controls.

Adolescent Risk

Achieving independent adult functioning is the major task of adolescence, and thus issues of risk are central for all adolescents. The areas in which the risk may be evident are work, independent travel (including the possibility of getting a driver's license), sexual activity, and the capacity to give consent.

The most common type of injury in the 13- to 19-year-old population surveyed in the SCIPP (Gallagher et al., 1984) study was sports injury. Teenagers had a rate of motor vehicle occupant injuries six times that of younger children; in one year's time, one out of every 50 teenagers was injured as a motor vehicle occupant. Burns and poison ingestions were not very common; the former were usually work-related, and the latter often involved alcohol and drug abuse.

Studies of work training of individuals with retardation indicate that their lack of awareness of safety rules may interfere with their ability to keep a job (Rusch, 1979). The ability to travel independently in a city is often a prerequisite for obtaining a job, and thus presents a challenge for mildly and moderately retarded adolescents and young adults. The risk of being lost is real and, as described by Birenbaum and Seiffer (1976), may be regarded with enthusiasm as an adventure. Where public transportation is not readily available, a driver's license may be necessary to enable an individual to obtain work or live independently. Mental retardation is not considered to be a reason for withholding a driver's license, and there is available assistance for functionally illiterate drivers (Chinn, Drew, & Logan, 1979).

Parents express great concern about adolescent sexual activity. They fear that increasing independence will lead to greater opportunities for heterosexual contacts, with the resulting risk of sexual exploitation or pregnancy. These views are reflected in the responses given by a group of parents of retarded young people to a questionnaire on the subject of sterilization. Wolf and Zarfas (1982) mailed questionnaires to 300 Canadian parents of individuals with mental retardation who were under 40 years old, and obtained a 55% response rate. The parents were a random sample obtained from lists of residents of institutions, members of parent organizations, and students in schools for retarded people. The parents' estimate of their offspring's functional level was reported as educable in 23% of cases, trainable in 48%, and severely impaired in 17%; 52% of the group were males and 28% were below 15 years old. Sixty-seven percent of the parents favored voluntary, and 71% favored involuntary, sterilization of their offspring, though only 7% were actually sterilized.

A study of sexual knowledge and attitudes of adolescents with mental retardation by Hall, Morris, and Barker (1973) revealed that noninstitutionalized adolescents with mild and moderate retardation had more liberal attitudes toward sex than anticipated by their parents. Knowledge about sex was somewhat more extensive among those individuals classified as educable than among those considered trainable, but both groups lacked important information in such crucial areas as conception, contraception, and venereal diseases.

Since drug and alcohol abuse are identified hazards during adolescence for an unselected population, information on the scope of the problem among individuals with retardation is of importance. Krishef and Di Nitto (1981) used a double survey approach to study the extent of alcohol abuse among persons with mental retardation. One questionnaire was sent to 100 Associations for Retarded Citizens (ARC) and another to 100 Alcohol Treatment Centers (ATC) in American cities of a population of more than 100,000. The return rate was 52%, and the ARCs identified 115 male and 24 female mentally retarded alcohol abusers, while the ATCs reported 224 males and 51 females of this description. An intriguing finding which can not be interpreted on the basis of information available in this study was the fact that mentally retarded persons lving alone were much more likely to be identified as alcohol abusers than those living in group care facilities. This study revealed that alcoholism is found in the mentally retarded population, but it was not designed to assess how the prevalence of this problem compares to that of the general population.

In the previously mentioned longitudinal British study of children with mental retardation (Koller et al., 1982), follow-up was obtained when the young people were 22 years old by separate interviews with them and with their parents. The study reported a lower prevalence of alcoholism and drug-related problems among the retarded young men than in the matched contrast group, while there were no differences in the two groups of young women.

In the general population of adolescents, burns are not especially common, their rate being higher than in school age but lower than among preschoolers. However, the fire safety requirements of residences for individuals who are mentally retarded is an important issue in their ability to live in the community. Current concepts in building design of community group homes are given as an example of a shift from overprotection to normal risk. MacEachron and Janicki (1983) examined the fire safety of the 46,000 developmentally disabled individuals within the New York's Disability Information System in February 1982. They used the available records to assess the subjects' self-preservation abilities, and they evaluated the extent of fire protection embedded in the building design. The group consisted of 56% males, and 32% of the subjects were below 21 years of age. Eighty-six percent were mentally retarded, more than half of them severely or profoundly, and 47% had a physical impairment. Self-preservation was defined as the ability to respond quickly, appropriately, and independently to fire emergencies, and was assessed by using an Evacuation Assistance Score developed by the Center for Fire Research. Sixty-one percent of the disabled individuals had scores indicating they would require no evacuation assistance. The two risk factors most difficult to pass were ability to respond to instructions and adequate independent mobility. It still remains to be proven that the Evacuation Assistance Score predicts actual self-preservation behavior in fire emergencies.

RISK, AUTONOMY, AND HUMAN RIGHTS

Review of the literature on risk of harm in the lives of individuals with mental retardation reveals that there are few studies on this topic. There is a large body of literature on injuries in the general child population, and injuries are known to be the leading cause of death and disability in childhood and early adult life. Temperamental and behavioral characteristics which correlate with higher rates of injuries have been described. Some of these characteristics, such as high level of activity, and being difficult to manage, are reported to be more common in children who are mentally retarded. Most of the reviewed studies of individuals with mental retardation were reports of adaptive functioning, which include maladaptive behaviors. In the studies of institutionalized children, physical handicaps, seizures, and aggression from peers have been identified as relevant factors in injuries. Some forms of injury, such as pica and self-injury, are seen predominantly among individuals with mental retardation. Certain other injuries are characteristically associated with particular causes of mental retardation—for example, self-injury among individuals with Lesch-Nyhan syndrome.

The available information suggests that, for a given level of independent function, an individual who is mentally retarded runs a greater risk of harm than the average person. A handicapped individual who masters a task in spite of the handicap performs the task with a greater degree of effort and concentration and without the flexibility other people have. He or she is closer to the limits of his or her capacity, and lacks the reserve which may be needed in an emergency. If an individual who is mentally retarded was taught a particular strategy for coping with a hazardous situation, and circumstances change unexpectedly, generating an alternate strategy may present a problem. Since one definition of intelligence is the ability to solve problems one has not encountered before, an individual with mental retardation may be at a disadvantage in a new and hazardous situation. Reserve capacity is crucial for situations which provide more exploration but also more danger.

Personal Autonomy and Risk

Nevertheless, professionals are being urged to recognize the ''dignity of risk'' and to press for greater risk taking by individuals who are mentally retarded in pursuit of independence. We question the assumption that there is inherent dignity *in* risk, either for handicapped individuals or for others, though we agree that there is a relationship between risk and dignity. The concept that ties the two together is autonomy, that is, making one's own choices. ''The most general idea of personal autonomy is still that of self-governance: being one's own person'' (Beauchamp & Childress, 1983, p. 59). Beauchamp and Childress (1983) state that ''diverse figures in philosophy, ranging from Kant, Mill, Nietzche, and Sartre to Robert Paul Wolff, have held that morality requires autonomous persons'' (p. 59). Therefore, the dignity resides in having autonomy, and the exercise of autonomy demands taking risks. The exercise of autonomy involves constant risk–benefit assessments and subsequent decisions on a course of action. Risk is only dignified if it is chosen by an autonomous individual, not if it is imposed by another person. Imposing more risk on someone else is as paternalistic as imposing less risk, since it is a constraint on someone else's action. Since decisions about risk are central to the exercise of autonomy, examining the former concept leads to an exploration of the latter.

Individual autonomy is a central value in our society, but one which raises dilemmas when applied to individuals whose competence is limited. Though the moral principle of preserving autonomy applies to individuals throughout their lifespan, the same is not true of the competence to make decisions. The task of rearing children is based on guiding them from a state of total dependency to one of a comfortable level of independence. This process requires a constant assessment of the degree of risk involved in engaging in any activity versus the benefit accruing from it. It also involves teaching the child to make these risk–benefit assessments and eventually turning this task over to the child, that is, guiding him or her to assume autonomy. Thus, each individual spends at least part of life being entitled to autonomy in theory, but unable to exercise it in practice. On a pragmatic level, decision making is a shared process more often than the principle of autonomy implies.

Susceptibility to suggestion by individuals with retardation is an issue in their decision making and even in eliciting factual information from them. The techniques used in interviewing them can alter the responses obtained from such individuals (Sigelman, Budd, Winer, Schoenrock, & Martin, 1982). Three groups were interviewed concerning their daily activities, using several different techniques of eliciting information. The samples consisted of 52 institutionalized children aged 11 to 17 years with a mean IQ of 42, 42 adults in the same institution with a mean IQ of 40, and 57 children aged 11 to 17 years with a mean IQ of 48 who lived in the community and received special educational services. Information obtained was compared to that given by attendants or parents. Open-ended questions proved inadequate, since few interviewees could answer them. However, a yes–no checklist, which most respondents answered, showed strong evidence of a bias in the form of acquiescence. Verbal and pictorial multiple choice questions proved to be the most useful question form. The authors conclude that the validity of answers given by individuals who are mentally retarded cannot be assumed; it must be demonstrated.

Risk and Human Rights

At 18 years of age, individuals begin to exercise such rights as voting and marrying, and can assume such privileges as obtaining a driver's license. Current legal guidelines vary from one state to another and often fail to meet the needs of individuals who are mentally retarded, becuase the legal system in most states views competence in all-or-none terms (Boggs, 1975). These individuals, on the other hand, vary one from another in their level of competence, and each person's level of competence may not be uniform in different aspects of functioning. Individuals with mental retardation would therefore be better served by a system which recognized partial incompetence and some forms of shared decision making.

In practice, decision-making responsibility is often divided between the individual who is mentally retarded, his or her family, and society, in the form of professionals representing agencies and courts. It is a difficult task to achieve a balance between the rights and responsibilities of the individual, his or her family, and society. As Wolf and Zarfas (1982) point out in discussing parental views on sterilization of their offspring who are retarded, novel approaches are needed to obtain a balance between various rights. They recognize that the rights of people who are mentally retarded to live as normally as possible include parenthood. However, they also acknowledge that the children they may bear have a right to a stimulating early environment, which their parents may not be able to provide. Moreover, the parents of adults with mental retardation have the right to an old age free from the responsibility of raising their grandchildren, a responsibility which may befall them if their children are discovered to be incapable of raising their children.

Unless parents are known to fall short of maintaining minimal standards in the care and protection they provide for their children, society rarely interferes in parental decision making. For children who are developmentally disabled, the work involved in providing child care, and the medical expenses, are often considerable and may not end at any given age, making these families more dependent on additional resources from the community. This dependence makes the families more vulnerable to interference in their decision making about their children by society's agents, usually well-intentioned professionals.

Best Interest Conflicts

Conflict between parents of children with mental retardation and the professionals who serve them has been documented around several issues. The reported areas of disagreement involve the process of diagnosis, provision of intervention and educational services, and deinstitutionalization.

Darling (1983) ascribes some of the conflict to differences in world views between parents and professionals, particularly physicians. The professional's clinical perspective is described as locating the source of problems within the victim's personality, and medicalizing all human problems. Clinicians are also reported to believe that professional dominance is necessary, and to accept the restriction imposed by the bureaucratic context of clinical work. Parents of handicapped children are described as being more likely than other parents to play an active role in their child's medical treatment, and to hold normalization as their prime motivating force. The concept of normalization is used here in the context of obtaining needed educational services.

A very frank parent describes another source of tension between parents and clinicians: "There is a certain animosity that is just there between parents and professionals that will always be there because you have these intervention programs, you can do this diagnosis, but you can't make our kids better" (Kupfer, 1985, p. 23). However, even when the professionals have enormous power to make children better—for instance, in the care of prematures in the neonatal intensive care unit—conflict is not eliminated. As Oster (1985) notes, "Five and a half years ago, when my son Nicholas was born prematurely, I felt more hostage than partner to a gang of powerful professionals who sustained his life and taught me rules of a strange new variety of motherhood" (p. 27).

Parents of individuals with mental retardation played a significant role in creating the atmosphere for deinstitutionalization, but have also had to struggle with many of the unintended effects. In a study evaluating the impact of New

York State's deinstitutionalization program, Willer and Intagliata (1984) reviewed records and interviewed deinstitutionalized individuals and their families. They state that, even at the height of institutionalization, only 10% of individuals with retardation were in institutions, yet the natural family has often been relegated to a secondary place in the process of deinstitutionalization. They report that the families of 70% of individuals placed in alternate settings out of the institution were never asked if they wanted their relative returned home, which 9% of the families would have chosen. Other families are totally opposed to deinstitutionalization, for a variety of reasons, and there have already been a number of court cases where parents have opposed the placement of their offspring out of institutions (Willer & Intagliata, 1984).

When professionals are urged to advocate the dignity of risk for children with mental retardation, parents may find that their anticipated rights to make decisions about how much risk is reasonable for their child are being interfered with. Though professionals have more knowledge about handicapping conditions, parents usually have more knowledge about the behavior and abilities of their own child, and about the specific dangers of the environment in which they live, critical information for risk assessment. The effort to enhance the autonomy of offspring who are mentally retarded should not abrogate the autonomy of their parents.

Overprotectiveness is a parental characteristic which professionals often try to mitigate. Though it exists, its definition is usually subjective. To know how much protection an individual needs requires information about the level of his or her cognitive and social functioning, and the dangers of the settings in which the individual lives (Adams, 1971). Professionals often live in better economic circumstances than their clients, and are unaware of the dangers and demands of the home and the neighborhood of the child whose parents they are counselling. To achieve realistic and reasonable risk assessment for particular conditions requires collaboration between the individual, his or her family, and society in gathering information and making a decision. Objective risk assessment also requires more extensive data on which to base the decisions.

Families have been, and continue to be, the primary caregivers to individuals with retardation. Their vast practical experience in evaluating risk has not been comprehensively studied. The parental opinions which have been most influential are those of the most educated and articulate parents, whose circumstances, values, and priorities may not invariably coincide with those of the majority of families. There is a need for more studies of the risks involved for given activities according to the age and retardation level of the individuals, and the nature of their environments. Clinical experience indicates that risk assessment in each case requires knowledge of the abilities of the individual, the nature of the dangers found in the community, and the availability and adequacy of a support network. The challenge is to allocate the power to make decisions about risk in a way that respects the autonomy of individuals who are mentally retarded, as well as that of their families. Professionals' opinion on how much risk is prudent is relevant only if it is based on data, not if it is solely a reflection of their own values.

REFERENCES

Adams, M. (1971). *Mental retardation and its social dimensions*. New York: Columbia University Press.

Albin, J.B. (1977). The treatment of pica (scavenging) behavior in the retarded: A critical analysis and implications for research. *Mental Retardation, 15*, 14–17.

Bates, P., & Wehman, P. (1977). Behavior Management with the mentally retarded: An empirical analysis of the research. *Mental Retardation 15*, 9–12.

Beauchamp, T.L., & Childress, J.C. (1983). *The principles of biomedical ethics*. New York: Oxford University Press.

Berggreen, S.M. (1972). Accidents and surgical emergencies in a population of mentally retarded children. *Acta Paediatrica Scandinavica, 62*, 289–296.

Birenbaum, A., & Seiffer, S. (1976). *Resettling retarded adults in a managed community*. New York: Praeger.

Boggs, E.M. (1975). Legal, legislative and bureaucratic factors affecting planned and unplanned change in the delivery of services to the mentally retarded. In M.J. Begab & S.A. Richardson (Eds.), *The mentally retarded and society: A social science perspective*. (pp. 441–468). Baltimore, MD: University Park Press.

Carey, W.B. (1972). Clinical implications of infant temperament measurements. *The Journal of Pediatrics, 81*, 823–828.

Chinn, P.C., Drew, C.J., & Logan, D.R. (1979). *Mental retardation: A life cycle approach*. St. Louis, MO: C.V. Mosby.

Christie, R., Bay, C., Kaufman, I.A., Bakay, B., & Nyhan, W.L. (1982). Lesch-Nyhan disease: Clinical experience with nineteen patients. *Developmental Medicine and Child Neurology, 24*, 293–306.

Committee on Research and Committee on Accident and Poison Prevention of the American Academy of Pediatrics. (1983). Reducing the toll of injuries in childhood. *Pediatrics, 72*, 736–737.

Danford, D.E., & Huber, A.M., (1982). Pica among mentally retarded adults. *American Journal of Mental Deficiency, 87*, 141–146.

Darling, R.B. (1983). Parent-professional interaction: The roots of misunderstanding. In M. Seligman (Ed.), *The family with a handicapped child: Understanding and treatment* (pp. 95–121). Orlando, FL: Grune & Stratton.

Diamond, L.S., Lynn, D., & Sigman, B. (1981). Orthopedic disorders in patients with Down's syndrome. *Orthopedic Clinics of North America, 12*, 57–71.

Doll, E. (1965). *Vineland Social Maturity Scale: Condensed manual of direction*. Circle Pines, MN: American Guidance Service, Inc.

Forman, M.A., Hetznecker, W.H., & Dunn, J.M. (1983). Disorders related to vegetative functions. In R.E. Behrman & V.C. Vaughan (Eds.), *Nelson Textbook of Pediatrics* (pp. 73–75). Philadelphia, PA: Saunders.

Gallagher, S.S., Finison, K., Guyer, B., & Goodenough, S. (1984). The incidence of injuries among 87,000 Massachusetts children and adolescents: Results of the 1980–81 statewide childhood injury prevention program surveillance system. *American Journal of Public Health, 74*, 1340–1346.

Guyer, B., & Gallagher, S.S. (1985). An approach to the epidemiology of childhood injuries. *The Pediatric Clinics of North America, 32*, 5–16.

Hall, J.E., Morris, H.L., & Barker, H.R. (1973). Sexual knowledge and attitudes of mentally retarded adolescents. *American Journal of Mental Deficiency, 77,* 706–709.

Hayes, C.S. (1973). Risk-taking by retarded and nonretarded children. *Psychological Reports, 32,* 738.

Jedrysek, E. (1985). *Mentally retarded children evaluated using the Behavior Screening Questionnaire.* Unpublished manuscript.

Koller, H., Richardson, S., Katz, M., & McLaren, J. (1982). Behavior disturbance in childhood and the early adult years in populations who were and were not mentally retarded. *Journal of Preventive Psychiatry, 1,* 453–468.

Krishef, C.H., & DiNitto, D. (1981). Alcohol abuse among mentally retarded individuals. *Mental Retardation, 19,* 151–155.

Kupfer, F. (1985). Severely and/or multiply disabled children. In *Equals in this partnership: Parents of disabled and at-risk infants and toddlers speak to professionals* (pp. 18–25). Washington, DC: National Center for Clinical Infant Programs.

Lakin, K.C., Hill, B.K., Hauber, F.A., Bruininks, R.H., & Heal, L.W. (1983). New admissions and readmissions to a national sample of public residential facilities. *American Journal of Mental Deficiency, 88,* 13–20.

MacEachron, A.E., & Janicki, M.P. (1983). Self-preservation ability and residential fire emergencies. *American Journal of Mental Deficiency, 88,* 157–163.

Matheny, A.P., Brown, A.M., & Wilson, R.S. (1971). Behavioral antecedents of accidental injuries in early childhood: A study of twins. *The Journal of Pediatrics, 79,* 122–124.

Meyer, R.J., Roelofs, H.A., Bluestone, J., & Redmond, S. (1963). Accidental injury to the preschool child: A study of some child, family and environmental associations with injury requiring hospitalization. *The Journal of Pediatrics, 63,* 95–105.

Nihira, L., & Nihira, K. (1975). Jeopardy in community placement. *American Journal of Mental Deficiency, 79,* 538–544.

Oster, A. (1985). Keynote address. In *Equals in this partnership: Parents of disabled and at-risk infants and toddlers speak to professionals.* Washington, DC: National Center for Clinical Infant Programs.

Perske, R. (1972). The dignity of risk. In W. Wolfensberger (Ed.), *Normalization,* (pp. 194–200). Toronto, Canada: Leonard Crainford.

Pueschel, S.M., Herndon, J.H., Gelch, M.M., Senft, K.E., Scola, P.H., & Goldberg, M.J. (1984). Symptomatic atlantoaxial subluxation in persons with Down syndrome. *Journal of Pediatric Orthopedics, 4,* 682–8.

Rapoport, A. (1979). Balancing safety with adventure. In S. Doxiadis, J. Thyrwhitt & S. Nakou (Eds.), *The Child in the world of tomorrow; A window into the future* (pp. 479–489). New York: Pergamon Press.

Richman, N., Stevenson, J.E., & Graham, P.J. (1975). Prevalence of behaviour problems in 3-year-old children: An epidemiologic study in a London borough. *Journal of Child Psychology and Psychiatry, 16,* 277–278.

Rusch, F.R. (1979). Toward the validation of social/vocational survival skills. *Mental Retardation, 17,* 143–145.

Sibert, J.R., & Newcombe, R.G. (1977). Accidental ingestion of poisons and child personality. *Postgraduate Medical Journal, 53,* 254–256.

Sigelman, C.K., Budd, E.C., Winer, J.L., Schoenrock, C.J., & Martin, P.W. (1982). Evaluating alternative techniques of questioning mentally retarded persons. *American Journal of Mental Deficiency, 86,* 511–518.

Singh, N., & Millichamp, J. (1985). Pharmacological treatment of self-injurious behavior in mentally retarded persons. *Journal of Autism and Developmental Disorders, 15,* 257–267.

Stephenson, J.B.P. (1980). Prader-Willi syndrome: Neonatal presentation and later development. *Developmental Medicine and Child Neurology, 22,* 792–794.

Tavormina, J.B., Henggeler, S.W., & Gayton, W.F. (1976). Age trends in parental assessment of the behavior problems of their retarded children. *Mental Retardation, 14,* 38–39.

Willer, B., & Intagliata, J. (1984). *Promises and realities for mentally retarded citizens: Life in the community.* Baltimore, MD: University Park Press.

Williams, C.E. (1973). Accidents in mentally retarded children. *Developmental Medicine and Child Neurology, 15,* 660–662.

Wolf, L., & Zarfas, D.E. (1982). Parents' attitudes toward sterilization of their mentally retarded children. *American Journal of Mental Deficiency, 87,* 122–129.

5

The Relationship of Residential Environment Differences to Adaptive Behavior of Mentally Retarded Individuals: A Review and Critique of Research

Janell I. Haney and Laird W. Heal
University of Illinois at Urbana-Champaign

Comparative empirical investigations seeking to clarify the relationship between residential environment factors and adaptive behavior outcomes in mentally retarded individuals are reviewed. In general, the reviewed articles support an association but not a causal relationship between normalized environments and adaptive skill improvement. The findings on maladaptive behavior are equivocal. The research is critiqued in light of a number of methodological concerns, and several recommendations are presented.

Landesman-Dwyer (1981) reports that she perused a total of 500 papers pertinent to residential care of mentally retarded people prior to writing her review of the subject. In addition, at least nine other reviews of the residential alternative issue have been published within the past decade. Most of the previous reviews examine the effects of either institutionalization (Birenbaum & Seiffer, 1976; Scheerenberger, 1976; Zigler & Balla, 1977) or deinstitutionalization (Craig & McCarver, 1984; Heal, Sigelman, & Switzky, 1978; McCarver & Craig, 1974; Pilewski & Heal, 1980). Others focus on specific aspects of the problem. For example, Balla (1976) and Baroff (1980) examine the relationship between facility size and quality of care. Landesman-Dwyer (1981), who most closely approached the topic of the present review, studied evidence regarding factors that contribute to successful "living in the community." However, her review had the purpose of highlighting unexpected findings in the literature at large, whereas the present review seeks to present a more comprehensive and detailed examination of studies within a single area: that of the effect of residential environment on adaptive behavior of mentally retarded individuals.

REVIEW OF THE LITERATURE

This literature review includes all relevant comparison studies obtained from perusal of the *Psychological Abstracts* from January 1970 to September 1984, and the subsequent examination of the reference section of each review and empirical article obtained in this fashion, continuing through reference sections until no new references were found. A total of 20 articles were obtained and categorized according to the environmental factors examined: setting type, type of care, normalization, and combined environmental factors. Each of these areas will be reviewed separately. Internal validity will be discussed immediately following each study or set of similar studies because of both its centrality to interpretation of these results and its variation from study to study. Other methodological concerns are to some extent relevant to virtually all of the investigations reviewed, and will be addressed in the last section.

Setting Type

Most of the studies that have investigated the influence of residential environment on adaptive behavior have examined setting type, and the primary target of investigation has been the institution. Five areas of investigation can be identified: (a) community versus institutional residence; (b) home versus institutional residence; (c) group home and community living arrangement versus institutional residence; (d) foster care (sometimes called family care or home care), board and care, and convalescent facility versus institutional residence; and (e) various community alternatives.

Comparison of community residence with institutional residence. Two studies compared community and institutional residence: one examined language behavior, and the other studied maladaptive behavior of residents.

In the first, Sievers and Essa (1961) used a static group posttest-only comparison to examine language behavior in institutionalized and community-placed mentally retarded individuals. Neither setting was described. A total of 74 subjects were randomly selected from the Columbus State School population for the institutional sample. Community subjects were 74 children within the same MA range as the institutionalized subjects, and were randomly selected from the Council for Retarded Children in Columbus, Ohio. The mean IQ for all subjects was 39.89; the age range was from 6 years, 11 months to 16 years, 11 months. Results of a single administration of the Differential Language Facility Test, an instrument developed by Sievers and Essa, indicated that the community residents scored significantly higher ($p<.01$) than the institutional residents on the overall test as well as on those subtests relating to meaningful verbal responses to test stimuli. Although community residents had a significantly higher mean IQ score than institutional residents and this difference may have had an impact on the results, the correlation between IQ and Differential Language Facility Test overall score was reported to be nonsignificant (actual r value not reported).

In the second study, Eyman, Borthwick, and Miller (1981) compared changes in maladaptive behavior among community- and institution-placed individuals through use of a static group pretest-posttest comparison. Community placements included family care, board and care (group homes and residential schools), convalescent hospitals, and family homes in California. Institutional placement consisted of a California state institution. The 426 subjects included all clients who were accepted for service by a certain regional center in California between 1974 and 1976, and who were available for a follow-up 2 years following intake. The mean age of the subjects was 12 years; retardation level ranged from profound to mild. Subject placement decisions were made by the regional center. Maladaptive behavior was assessed through direct care staff and social worker ratings on a shortened form of Part II of the Adaptive Behavior Scale (ABS; Nihira, Foster, Shellhaas, & Leland, 1974), both at the time of intake and following 2 years of service. Interrater reliabilities of .70 or more were obtained on all behaviors included in the analysis. Internal consistency reliability for the total score was .85. The results indicated that maladaptive behavior did not change over time, either overall or for community versus institution residence. Maladaptive behavior did differ for placement (less maladaptive behavior for community than for institutional placements). Profoundly mentally retarded subjects exhibited the most maladaptive behavior in the community but the least maladaptive behavior in the institution.

These first two studies indicate that community versus institutional residence was not associated with a difference in maladaptive behavior improvement but was associated with higher language development of mentally retarded children. Although this in itself is valuable preliminary information, no stronger statements may be made because the lack of random assignment of subjects to placements in these studies suggests that a difference in subject characteristics is a plausible explanation of the observed differences. This concern is greater in the Sievers and Essa (1961) study because of the absence of a pretest to assess pretreatment similarity and the initial IQ differences between the two groups in this study.

Comparison of home residence with institution residence.   Five additional investigations were more specific in examining home versus institutional residence differences in subjects' adaptive behavior. In particular, three investigations studied language and two investigated general development.

In the first of the language studies, Lyle (1960) used a posttest-only static group comparison to examine the speech and language of subjects living at home and subjects attending what were described as day schools. Neither environment was described. Subjects in the institution sample numbered 77, and subjects in the home sample totaled 117. The age range was 20 to 54 years. Subject selection procedures were not described. Ad hoc scales based on the Analytical Scale of Language Achievement (Williams, McFarland, & Little, 1937) included the following areas: word naming, word comprehension, word definition, speech sound, language complexity, speech clarity, speech frequency, and verbal intelligence. Speech clarity and frequency were evaluated on the basis of teacher ratings. Verbal intelligence was tested via the Minnesota Preschool Scale (Form A; Goodenough, Maurer, & Van Wagener, 1940), and the remaining areas were assessed by an experimenter. Subjects were each assessed once. The results indicated that subjects living at home performed significantly (p level not reported) better on all but the speech clarity and frequency measures. Moreover, these subjects also performed significantly better on these two measures when the influence of the characteristics of those subjects with Down's syndrome (which was found in a greater proportion in the home sample) was partialled out.

Nineteen years later, McNutt and Leri (1979) used a static group posttest-only design to compare institutionalized and noninstitutionalized individuals' spoken language structure and communication subskills. Institutionalized individuals lived in cottages or dormitories with "house parents," and noninstitutionalized individuals lived with their parents. Both groups attended classes that ranged from self-help to vocational training. Only individuals who had intelligible speech were selected as subjects. From this group, individuals were randomly selected and then chosen to participate if they met two criteria: (a) speech that included more than one-word utterances, and (b) ability to respond correctly to various questions. Subjects ranged in age from 8 years, 2 months to 17 years, 5 months, and in IQ from 30 to 65. Assessment consisted of a single administration of the Illinois Test of Psycholinguistic Abilities (ITPA) and collection of a single language sample to which the Length-Complexity Index and frequency counts of 11 grammatical categories were applied. Noninstitutionalized subjects scored significantly ($p<.012$) higher on the ITPA. Analyses of subtest means showed significantly (p's$<.042$) better performance by noninstitutionalized subjects on auditory reception, verbal expression, and auditory closure; significantly ($p<.048$) better performance by institutionalized subjects on auditory sequential memory; and nonsignificant differences on the remainder of the subtests. There were no significant differences on the length complexity and frequency count measures obtained from the language sample.

To summarize, both Lyle's (1960) and McNutt and Leri's (1979) results suggest that home residence was associated with better language performance in mentally retarded adults than was institutional residence. However, McNutt and Leri's (1979) study suggests that language is a multifaceted behavior in that each setting type was associated with strengths in different areas of language skill for mentally retarded children. No causal statements may be made because of the likelihood of subject selection factors as a possible explanation for the observed differences.

In a third language study, Schlanger (1954) attempted to remove selection as a concern and to equalize groups through matching. In this investigation, verbal output of institutionalized and home-reared children was compared in a prematched control group design. The home-reared subjects were 21 children selected from those receiving speech therapy and attending special classes in the Madison, Wisconsin, school system. The two groups of subjects were matched on sex, CA, MA, IQ, and consonant articulation proficiency. The mean IQ was 59, and the mean age was 12 years. Assessment consisted of analysis of spontaneous conversation for mean sentence length and words spoken per minute. Home-reared children scored significantly (p's $<.03$) higher than institutionalized children on both of the measures.

Although matching may appear beneficial in ruling out selection as a threat to internal validity in Schlanger's (1954) study, random assignment of the matched subjects to residence type is necessary for confidence in establishing a causal relationship between residential environment and verbal output. To the extent that home-reared children may have higher IQ scores than institution-reared children, selecting children with matching IQ scores may have resulted in the choice of individuals with extreme scores who would consequently regress toward their respective group means regardless of treatment—a spontaneous increase for home-reared subjects and a decrease for institution-reared subjects.

In the first of the studies including examination of development, Francis (1971) compared the developmental level of home-reared and institution-reared children with Down's syndrome. All subjects were under 4 years of age and had an MA under 2 years. No information concerning either subject selection or assignment was given. In addition, the home and institution environments were not described. Developmental level was assessed through 50-minute observations of behavior in the children's usual day settings. From this information, subjects were placed into one of six stages based on Woodward's (1959) test, which is derived from Piaget's scheme. Behaviors included diffuse movements of various body parts; self-oriented behavior such as chewing or rubbing; postures such as hand clasping; object-oriented behaviors such as waving, throwing, or tapping of objects; movement; and visual attention such as watching objects or other people.

The results indicated that behaviors that usually decrease with age were more prevalent in institution-reared subjects than in home-reared subjects. These results were obtained whether comparison was made on the basis of CA or developmental level, a finding that suggests that the differences were not a function of the retardation level of the institution-reared subjects. Further examination of the results indicated some environmental factors that may play a role in the persistence of immature behavior in the institutional setting: decreased availability of toys, increased use of physical restraint, and decreased social contact. Additionally, Francis suggested that social contact was influenced by ability and opportunity for locomotion. Examination of the effect of altering the environment was undertaken by comparing periods of time during institutional observations when two of the previously mentioned potential environmental factors—physical restraint and social contact—varied naturally. Francis (1971) found that diffuse movements and self-oriented behaviors (which increase with age) increased when social contact was present and when physical restraint was absent. However, it should be noted that physical restraint was absent during only four observations.

Stedman and Eichorn (1964) similarly looked at the comparative effects of hospital residence and home residence on developmental scores, but they used a prematched control group comparison. The hospital environment included toys, an adult–child ratio of no less than 1:5, and a nursery-type decor. The home residences were not described. Subjects were 20 toddlers with Down's syndrome who ranged in age from 17 to 37 months. A total of 10 subjects for hospital residence at Sonoma State Hospital had been located and placed through county and community agency referral of healthy children with Down's syndrome who were born after a specified date. Another 10 age-matched, home-reared subjects were later located through the Help for Retarded Children Associations in the San Francisco Bay area. Assessment occurred within a 120-day time frame and consisted of ratings on (a) the Infant Scale of Mental Development (a revision of Bayley's 1933 California First-Year Scale), (b) the Infant Motor Scale of Development (a revision of Bayley's 1936 California Infant Scale of Motor Development), and (c) the Vineland Social Maturity Scale. Home-reared subjects scored significantly higher than hospital-reared subjects on both the mental and social scales (p's$<.02$).

Both of these studies indicate that a greater degree of developmental maturity was associated with home-rearing as compared to institution-rearing of infants. Although preliminary information regarding relationships is provided, causal statements must await experiments which exercise better control over variables extraneous to the experimental manipulation.

Comparison of group home and community living arrangement residence with institution residence.   A third set of three studies compared group home and community living arrangement with institutional residences on various adaptive skills of the residents.

In an initial study, Schroeder and Henes (1978) used a prematched control group design to compare self-help, communication, socialization, and occupation skills in deinstitutionalized group home residents and in institutionalized individuals awaiting community residence vacancies in their county. The 38 subjects ranged in CA from 20 to 54 years and in MA from 4 to 7 years. The 19 community-placed subjects were those who had been placed in one of four group homes in the county from which they had come. The institution subjects were 19 individuals chosen randomly from those whose home counties had no group home vacancies. These subjects were matched with the community-placed subjects in terms of chronological and mental age. Assessment was comprised of administration of the Progress Assessment Chart (Gunzburg, 1969) on two different occasions: once within 2 years after relocation, and again a year later. Subjects did not differ at the initial testing. However, at posttesting the group home subjects scored significantly ($p<.005$) higher, indicating an association between group home living and greater improvement in adaptive skills.

Also using a prematched control group design, Conroy, Efthimiou, and Lemanowicz (1982) compared adaptive behavior change in institutional residents and community living arrangement residents. Neither environment was described. All 70 individuals who had been placed in community living arrangements from the institution were included as subjects. The "best available matches" for these subjects based on sex, retardation level, CA, length of institutionalization, prerelocation personal self-sufficiency score, and IQ were included in the institutional sample. The 140 subjects obtained in this fashion had a mean age of 36 years and a mean IQ of 28. There were between-group differences in medical needs, and analyses additionally indicated that there were (a) no significant between-group differences in IQ or age, and (b) significant differences in favor of the institutional group in terms of ambulation, vision, hearing, and seizures. Assessment was undertaken prior to relocation as well as 1 year following the change in placement. This assessment consisted of administration of Conroy et al.'s (1982) extension of the UCLA Neuropsychiatric Research Groups' Behavior Development Survey, which was a shortened form of the ABS. This instrument was administered to clients by the staff teams most familiar with them. High interrater reliability (.94) had previously been obtained on the adaptive behavior portion of this instrument, and good test-retest reliability had previously been obtained on the maladaptive portion. However, for the maladaptive section interrater reliability has been found to be inadequate and small behavior changes have been undetected. Results indicated no significant differences prior to relocation. Following relocation, community living arrangement residents scored significantly higher on adaptive behavior ($p=.009$). Maladaptive behavior did not change following relocation for community living arrangement dwellers but may have increased somewhat for those remaining in the institution.

In a more sophisticated study, Close (1977) used a pretest-posttest control group design with random assignment of subjects to groups to examine self-care and social skills in previously institutionalized individuals who had been placed in the community and individuals who remained in the institution. Institutional treatment was described as consisting of the "normal" treatment given by the state institution. Community placement consisted of placement in a community vocational program and a group home. The group home was a six-bedroom house in a residential neighborhood. Training programs in the group home were developed through task analytic procedures, and included sequential training techniques. Behavior management included contingency management and overcorrection. The 15 subjects ranged in age from 21 to 39 years and in social quotient from 10 to 28. Subjects were selected for the study on the basis of the following criteria: (a) having been admitted to the institution from Lane County, Oregon, with parents also residing in Lane county; (b) having severe or profound retardation; (c) being ambulatory without prostheses; (d) possessing sufficient self-feeding skills to eat with a spoon; (e) exhibiting a monthly average of less than one uncontrolled seizure; and (f) being at least 18 years of age. The 15 individuals who met these criteria were randomly assigned to either community placement or continuance in the institution. Progress from the beginning to the end of the 1-year period was assessed with the Developmental Record (Hutton & Talkington, 1974), which was administered by an experimenter blind to subject assignment, and the Community Living Observation System (Taylor & Close, 1976). The mean observer reliability on the latter instrument was .94. Although the groups did not differ at pretesting, the community placement group performed significantly better on both measures at posttesting (p's < .05).

These three investigations indicate that group home and community living arrangement residence in comparison with institutional residence is associated with greater adaptive behavior improvement for adults. The final, experimental study supports *attribution* of the significantly greater adaptive behavior in the group home residents to the placement difference, but the provision of a day program for the group home residences makes this difference difficult to interpret.

Comparison of foster (family or home care), board-and-care, and convalescent home residence with institution residence.   A fourth set of investigations compared foster care, board and care, and convalescent homes to institutions in terms of bringing about adaptive behavior change in residents. Evaluation of outcomes included study of both self-help and general adaptive skills.

Using a static group posttest-only comparison, Eyman, Silverstein, and McLain (1975) compared standard state hospital care and foster care with regard to the residents' self-help skills. Subjects in standard care remained in the living unit in which they resided, except for occasional recreational activities. Foster care was not described. Subjects were the 630 admitted Pacific State Hospital patients who were available for follow-up, whether they were residing at the institution or in foster care. Most of the subjects were profoundly mentally retarded, particularly within the standard care condition. Subjects who were completely toilet-trained were excluded from the toileting analysis, and ambulatory subjects were omitted from the ambulation analysis. Both ambulation and toileting assessments were included in ward personnel rating of 70 items determined to be critical to community placement. Both measures had been previously determined to be both valid and reliable. The results indicated that there were no significant differences between the institution and foster care groups.

In a broader investigation, Eyman, Silverstein, McLain, and Miller (1977) used spaced posttests to evaluate adaptive behavior changes in static groups exposed to varying residential environments and programming. Residents of two state institutions (one in California and one in Colorado), as well as residents in

California convalescent hospitals, foster care homes, and board and care homes, were compared. The Characteristic of the Treatment Environment (McLain, Silverstein, Hubbell, & Brownlee, 1977) and Residential Management Surveys (McLain, Silverstein, Hubbell, & Brownlee, 1975) were administered, and programming information as well as community program descriptions, based on the previous work of Bjaanes and Butler (1974) and O'Connor (1976) were obtained. Subjects, who spanned all levels of retardation and ranged in age from 1 to over 70 years, included all residents of the facilities. Administration of the ABS occurred yearly over a 3-year period in California and over a 2-year period in Colorado. The results indicated that residents of foster homes and board and care homes exhibited more positive adaptive behavior change than those in other settings. However, these facilities also contained residents who initially scored higher. Although the relationships between environmental measures and behavior change were reported to be modest, it was also noted that most of these relationships were significant (p level not reported). Environmental measures accounted for more of the variance than programming in most cases, but this may have been a result of the fact that the environmental measures were more clearly defined and more reliable.

While only one of these two studies supported the hypothesis that community facilities would surpass institutions in association with positive adaptive behavior change, subject, setting, and assessment variations may have accounted for the differing results. Given the lack of detail in description of these three factors, particularly in relation to the settings, it is difficult to determine the precise reason for the differential outcomes.

Comparison of various community alternatives. Two final investigations compared the impact of various community residential alternatives on general adaptive behavior of the residents.

Using a static group posttest-only comparison, Willer and Intagliata (1982) investigated the relationship of residential environment differences to adaptive behavior facilitation. Residential type included foster family care and group homes. Foster family care was provided for groups of two to three people by families. Group home care was provided to groups of about 10 people, either by staff who worked in shifts or, occasionally, by "house parents." Subjects were 338 individuals relocated from five institutions in New York state. Subjects averaged 46 years of age. IQ data were not given, although all subjects were reported to be mentally retarded. Subjects were included only if they were at least 13 years old at the time of relocation, had been institutionalized for a minimum of a year, and had been in the community placement a minimum of 2 years prior to the study. No additional subject selection information was given. Assessment consisted of care provider ratings on the Devereux Behavior Rating Scale (Spivack, Haines, & Spotts, 1967) and a retrospective problem list that included self-care, "adaptive behavior" (behavior problems), and community living skills. Care providers were asked to note areas on the problem list that were problems at the time of initial placement, and whether these continued to be problems. Both forms of assessment were given only once. The results indicated that, compared to family care residents, group home residents received significantly (p<.01) higher ratings of improvement in community living skills, but significantly (p<.01) lower ratings of improvement in adaptive behavior. The Devereux ratings similarly showed significantly more behavior problems for group home residents when retardation level was controlled. There was no difference in self-care improvement.

In a subsequent study, Willer and Intagliata (1984) also used a static group posttest-only comparison to investigate several residential alternatives' effects on community adjustment. Residential alternatives included group homes, foster care homes, natural homes, and residential care settings for the elderly (health care and board and care facilities). Subjects were selected from five developmental centers in New York state chosen so as to be representative in size and location (rural or urban). Subjects included only those who had been institutionalized a minimum of 1 year, whose release occurred between 1973 and 1976, and who were a minimum of 13 years of age at release. Follow-up questionnaires were sent to primary care providers a minimum of 2 years following relocation. A total of 464 (57.5% of those sent) were completed and returned by primary care providers, and 158 (36% of the total returned) were completed and returned by guardians. Those who were placed in their natural homes were the most severely handicapped and exhibited the greatest degree of behavioral deficit. These subjects improved the least in functioning and showed no improvement in behavior problems. Foster care residents improved in self-care skills, as well as some community living skills, and showed a decrease in behavior problems. Group home residents exhibited the most improvement in community living skills, but had high rates of maladaptive behavior. Little change in self-care and community living skills was found in either health care or board and care facilities, which generally do not focus on training of new skills. In addition, residents in board and care facilities exhibited about as many behavior problems as those in group homes, while residents in health care facilities exhibited more behavior problems than residents of any other setting.

These investigations are consistent in suggesting that group homes are associated with more adaptive skill improvement but greater rates of maladaptive behavior than foster care and other community residences for mentally retarded adolescents and adults. Additionally, the findings of the Willer and Intagliata (1984) investigation suggest that different types of subjects are placed in different settings, making setting comparison difficult. A concern in both studies is the retrospective nature of the pre- and post-placement questionnaires. This factor brings the validity of the assessment into question. A concern in the second study is the inclusion of data of only those who chose to respond to the questionnaire, particularly in light of the low return rate.

Summary. In general, community placement appears to be associated with greater adaptive skill improvement as compared to institutional placement. These results are borne out by comparisons between institutions and both natural homes and community placements such as group homes and community living arrangements (Close, 1977; Conroy et al., 1982; Francis, 1971; Lyle, 1960; McNutt & Leri, 1979; Schlanger, 1954; Schroeder & Henes, 1978; Sievers & Essa, 1961; Stedman & Eichorn, 1964). The comparisons of foster care and institutions are equivocal (Eyman et al., 1975, 1977). Within the community, comparisons with reference to adaptive skills favor group homes and community living arrangements (Willer & Intagliata, 1982, 1984). However, different results are obtained in examination of maladaptive behavior. For this class of behaviors, no difference in improvement was noted in community-institution comparison (Eyman, Borthwick, & Miller, 1981). Within the community, only foster care residence was associated with maladaptive behavior improvement (Willer & Intagliata, 1984). Only one investigation of setting type was a true experiment (Close, 1977), and that investigation suggested that group home plus vocational placement leads to greater adaptive behavior improvement than institutional placement.

Type of Care

In addition to setting type, a second environmental variable that has been explored in terms of its impact on adaptive behavior is the type of care offered by various residential environments. Four investigations of this type were located.

King and Raynes' (1968) study examined institutional care regime effects on social abilities through use of a static group posttest-only comparison. The comparison included three types of facilities in England: (a) a "regimented," "unstimulating" hospital ward; (b) an "individualized," "enriched" hostel; and (c) a voluntary home that included elements of both the hospital and hostel facilities. Subjects were the 18 children in one of the hospital wards, the 16 children in the hostel, and the 22 children in one of the voluntary home units. The method of selecting the hospital ward, hostel, and home unit were not described. Subjects were placed prior to the beginning of the study. The average age of the groups ranged from 11 years, 5 months to 12 years, 2 months; the mean IQ scores of the groups ranged from 31 to 37. Procedures such as mealtimes, toileting, and bathing were observed, although only feeding and verbal skills were reported. In both of these areas, home and hostel children performed significantly better (p's$<.02$) than ward children.

Tizard (1964) used a pretest-posttest control group design with random assignment to groups to compare the effects of two forms of child care on language, community living skills, and maladaptive behavior. Child care on the experimental unit consisted of the individualized, child-centered care found in residential nurseries for "normal" preschool children. Child care for a second group consisted of the standard hospital care at Fountain Hospital in London.

Children were selected from the hospital population on the basis of being ambulatory, moderately mentally retarded, and nonpsychotic. The experimental unit was to be composed of both boys and girls. About eight children were to be over 8 years of age, and two were to be less than 5 years of age. Mental ages were to be between 3 and 4 years for eight of the experimental subjects, and under 2 years for four of these subjects. A total of 32 children were selected and paired with these considerations in mind, and with matching based on sex, age, IQ, and, to the extent possible, diagnosis. One child from each of the pairs was selected for the experimental unit on the basis of lots. Speech and language (using Lyle's 1959 test) were assessed prior to, 1 year following, and 2 years following relocation. The results indicated a significant increase in verbal MA (14 months on the average) for the experimental group, and a smaller increase (6 months on the average) for the hospital group. Speech testing at the end of the study indicated that (a) 75% of the experimental group and 50% of the control group could name at least two-thirds of 50 common objects, and (b) 100% of the experimental group and 63% of the control group could respond to simple commands. Anecdotal information indicated that experimental children also exhibited better performance in regard to motor skills, domestic and self-care skills, and adjustment.

The Eyman et al. (1975) study, discussed previously, also compared standard and special hospital care using a static group posttest-only design. Special treatment involved either sensori-motor training, school instruction, or compensatory education. Nonambulatory subjects who received sensori-motor training scored significantly higher on ambulation than those who did not ($p<.05$). On toilet training, the gains of subjects in sensori-motor training and school programs were significantly greater (p value not reported) than the gain of the others.

Bjaanes and Butler's (1974) investigation included examination of residential environments in terms of resulting resident behavior characteristics and time-use patterns with a static group posttest-only design. All board and care facilities and two desirably located foster care facilities in a metropolitan area were selected for study. Board and care facilities provided minimal restriction of client movement. Foster care facility staff required that subjects remain within the facility most of the time and provided potentially closer supervision. The 190 potential subjects ranged in age from 20 to 55 years and in IQ from 48 to 76. Observation consisted of four 2- or 3-hour sessions that occurred at various points during the day. Subject selection for observation was random. Recording included characteristics of each activity performed by subjects. The results indicated that there were significant differences in behavior characteristics and time use patterns that could not be accounted for in terms of sex, facility location, or facility type (p level not reported). These differences appeared to be a function of the residential environment. For example, the less restricted, community-mobile board and care subjects showed less reliance on others than foster care subjects. In addition, residents of the foster care facility with the greatest staff structuring spent the least time in isolated passive leisure and personal activities.

In summary, the first of the three investigations regarding type of care (King & Raynes, 1968) suggests that stimulating, individualized environments are associated with improvements in children's self-care, verbal, and motor skills. Moreover, the use of random assignment in Tizard's (1964) study makes that demonstration of improvement particularly convincing. The final study (Bjaanes & Butler, 1974), which involved adults, indicates that less restrictiveness and subsequent community exposure is associated with decreased reliance on others and that greater structure is associated with decreased isolated and passive activity.

Normalization

The third environmental variable that has been subjected to analysis is that of normalization. This environmental feature has been considered in two relatively recent papers.

Eyman, Demaine, and Lei (1979) examined the relationship between residential facilities' PASS 3 (Wolfensberger & Glenn, 1975) scores and adaptive behavior changes through use of path analysis. The residential facilities consisted primarily of foster care and board and care homes located in southern California. A total of 245 developmentally disabled individuals, ranging in age from birth to 18 years and in retardation level from profound to mild, served as subjects. Subject selection was not described. Placement occurred prior to initiation of the study. Assessment of adaptive behavior through case worker ratings on the 1974 version of the ABS was undertaken yearly over a 4-year period. The results indicated that a number of the PASS factors (i.e., normalization and research policies, facility blend, service location and availability, and facility comfort and functionality) each appeared to be significantly related to positive adaptive behavior change (no p level reported).

Using a pretest-posttest control group design with random assignment to groups, MacEachron (1983) compared the adaptive behavior of residents who moved from old institutional buildings to new, more normalized residences on the institution's grounds with that of residents who remained in the old institutional buildings. Institutional settings housed an average of 54 or 55 people, whereas the more normalized settings, which consisted of cottages, housed between 8 and 16 residents. Examination of normalization variables showed the cottage settings to be more normalizing than the institutional settings in terms of physical environment (i.e., size, home-like design and appurtenances, and resident freedom of use) as well as social environment (i.e., resident-oriented resident management practices and programming, but not staff–client ratios). A total of 289 of the 1,700 institution residents (mean IQ=23; mean age=32 years) were found to meet certain unspecified selection criteria and were chosen to serve as subjects for the experiment. These 289 subjects were divided into 15 groups judged by the institution's clinical team to be homogenous in terms of programming needs (e.g., toileting, dressing, and communication skills) and intellectual category (i.e., profound and severe or moderate and mild) as defined by Grossman (1973). Within each group, subjects were separated by sex and were randomly assigned to either the institution or the cottages. Adaptive behavior was evaluated through administration of the ABS 1 year following relocation. Within each of the 15 groups, cottage residents scored higher on the ABS than institution residents. In 7 of 15 cases, this difference was significant (p's<.05). The strongest correlations between adaptive behavior in individuals and environmental variables were with (a) increased residential freedom of use (.57), (b) more resident-oriented resident management practices (.59), and (c) program participation (.56). Although IQ was found to be the best single predictor of adaptive behavior, an analysis of covariance with IQ as the covariate showed the treatment facility effect to be significant even when IQ was controlled ($p < .02$).

Together, these two investigations suggest that many aspects of what is defined as a "more normalizing" environment are associated with improved adaptive behavior. The MacEachron (1983) study's random assignment of subjects provides support for attribution of the improvement in the residents' adaptive behavior skills to normalization variables.

Combined Environmental Factors

Hull and Thompson (1980) included examination of the degree to which various residential variables are associated with adaptive behavior improvement using a static group posttest-only comparison. Facilities included foster homes, community residences, independent living facilities, and other community residences in Manitoba, Canada. Residential environment characteristics such as size, disability groups, staff attitudes, cost, type of facility, normalization, and community characteristics were assessed. Environmental normalization was evaluated via a 172-item rating instrument similar but not identical to PASS (Wolfensberger & Glenn, 1975) and having an interrater reliability ranging from 86 to 96%. A total of 369 individuals, ranging in age from 18 to 73 years and having IQs ranging from the low 20s to over 90, served as subjects. Subject selection was not described; subject placement occurred prior to the investigation. Assessment of adaptive behavior was undertaken through interviewing the "most knowledgeable informant" residing with the resident. Adaptive behavior was rated through use of a revised version of the Adaptive Functioning Index (Marlett, 1977a,b) and four behavior problem measures adapted from the ABS. The results indicated that seven of the environmental factors and four of the individual factors were highly correlated with adaptive behavior (multiple $R=.75$). The seven environmental factors included activities promoting social integration, appearance, transportation, community resources, social protection, resident-staff interaction, and quality of the physical setting. The four individual factors included IQ, resident satisfaction with the residence, resident independence, and problem behavior. Again, the caution concerning subject selection applies to these results and disallows causal statements.

CRITIQUE AND RECOMMENDATIONS

The methodological concerns raised through investigation of the studies in this area confirm those of Heal and Fujiura (1984) in their recent review of the methodological status of the residential alternative literature. These concerns include design, independent variable selection, subject selection, assessment, longitudinal impact, and social validity issues.

The majority of the investigations comparing residential environment impact on adaptive behavior of mentally retarded individuals have used quasi-experimental designs such as static group comparisons rather than true experimental designs. Although such designs suffice to lay the groundwork for further study by suggesting hypotheses to be tested, they do not, in and of themselves, provide an adequate basis for explanation, prediction, and intervention.

The majority of the reviewed investigations defined the independent variable in terms of setting type. Because standards vary from country to country, from state to state, and from administrator to administrator, comparison is difficult. A related issue is the need to separate out or control for the effects of day program influences on adaptive behavior over and above the influence of setting type.

Selection of the subject sample is a third concern. Samples are often selected on the basis of their placement prior to the study and may differ in critical ways from the population that they purportedly represent.

Assessment is an issue in that there is a predominance of rating-derived as opposed to observationally-derived measures of adaptive behavior in this literature. Although few direct tests of adaptive behavior are commercially available (see Meyers, Nihira, & Zetlin, 1979), use of observational as well as rating measures is important to confirmation of the validity of the assessment. Experimenter bias is likely to result from the common practice of using staff or parents as raters (only 3 of the 20 papers reported even one form of reliability assessment). This issue is critical with measures that have not been examined for validity and reliability previously.

Differential improvement over 1- or even 2-year periods is not necessarily an indication of long-term impact, particularly when the period of assessment immediately follows relocation, and the novelty of the new situation becomes an explanatory variable for at least some portion of the results.

None of the reviewed investigations considered the issue of social validity in anything more than a tangential fashion. Consideration of four relevant areas is recommended: (a) whether the target behaviors are indeed important to such potential subject needs and desires as meeting physical requirements or blending in with others in the community, (b) whether the target behaviors are of importance in terms of society's values, (c) whether the treatments being implemented are socially acceptable, and (d) whether improvements result in behavior that approximates societal or community norms. These forms of social validation have been discussed in detail elsewhere (e.g., Kazdin, 1982; Wolfe, 1978).

A concern less important to the actual conduct of the studies, but crucial to their replication, is the brevity and occasional absence of description of independent variables. Similar deficiencies are apparent, but not quite so striking, in the descriptions of subjects and of assessment.

A final issue relates to the focus on residential setting type as an independent variable. An increased emphasis on component analysis of operationally defined variables such as size, staff–client ratio, staff education and training, number and type of behavioral and instructional programs, frequency and type of staff-client interaction, environmental prostheses, and proximity to various community resources would serve not only to alleviate definitional confusion but also to answer fundamental questions. Given the need for a multiplicity of residential alternatives to accommodate varied individual needs, examination of environmental elements is more likely to yield important information than is the search for the single best residential alternative. Perception of the residential service system as a fluid, malleable tool for enhancing adaptation suggests the exciting possibility of establishing or altering environments to fit individuals, as well as the usual process of placing individuals in the existing environment best matched to their needs.

SUMMARY

The literature relating to residential environment impact on adaptive behavior of mentally retarded individuals has been reviewed and critiqued. Generally, the findings indicate an association between community residence and adaptive skill improvement, with little differentiation in setting types in terms of maladaptive behavior outcomes. This finding was supported by the remaining (program-oriented) investigations, which collectively suggest an association between normalizing environments and adaptive behavior improvement. Unfortunately, very little may be stated concerning causal relationships due to the rarity of true experimental designs. In addition to employment of true experiments, recommendations for future research include improved definition of independent variables; representative population sampling; unbiased and reliable observational assessment; longitudinal assessment; social validation of target behaviors, treatment acceptability, and behavior improvement; replicability; and component analysis using operational definitions.

REFERENCES

Balla, D.A. (1976). Relationship of institution size to quality of care: A review of the literature. *American Journal of Mental Deficiency, 81*, 117–124.

Baroff, G.S. (1980). On "size" and the quality of residential care: A second look. *Mental Retardation, 18,* 113–117.

Bayley, N. (1933). *The California First Year Mental Scale.* Berkeley, CA: University of California Press.

Bayley, N. (1936). *The California Infant Scale of Motor Development.* Berkeley, CA: University of California Press.

Birenbaum, A., & Seiffer, S. (1976). *Resettling retarded adults in a managed community.* New York: Praeger.

Bjaanes, A.T., & Butler, E.W. (1974). Environmental variation in community care facilities for mentally retarded persons. *American Journal of Mental Deficiency, 78,* 429–439.

Close, D. (1977). Community living for severely and profoundly retarded adults: A group home study. *Education and Training of the Mentally Retarded, 12,* 256–262.

Conroy, J., Efthimiou, J., & Lemanowicz, J. (1982). A matched comparison of the developmental growth of institutionalized and deinstitutionalized mentally retarded clients. *American Journal of Mental Deficiency, 86,* 581–587.

Craig, E.M., & McCarver, R.B. (1984). Community placement and adjustment of deinstitutionalized clients: Issues and findings. In N.R. Ellis & N.W. Bray (Eds.), *International review of research in mental retardation.* (pp. 95–122). Orlando, FL: Academic Press.

Eyman, R.K., Borthwick, S.A., & Miller, C. (1981). Trends in maladaptive behavior of mentally retarded persons placed in community and institutional settings. *American Journal of Mental Deficiency, 85,* 473–477.

Eyman, R.K., Demaine, G.C., & Lei, T. (1979). Relationship between community environments and resident changes in adaptive behavior: A path model. *American Journal of Mental Deficiency, 83,* 330–338.

Eyman, R.K., Silverstein, A.B., & McLain, R. (1975). Effect of treatment programs on the acquisition of basic skills. *American Journal of Mental Deficiency, 79,* 573–582.

Eyman, R.K., Silverstein, A.B., McLain, R., & Miller, C. (1977). Effects of residential settings on development. In P. Mittler (Ed.), *Research to practice in mental retardation: Care and intervention* (Vol. I, pp. 305–314). Baltimore, MD: University Park Press.

Francis, S.H. (1971). The effects of own-home and institution-rearing on the behavioural development of normal and Mongol children. *Journal of Child Psychology and Child Psychiatry, 12,* 173–190.

Goodenough, F., Maurer, K.M., & Van Wagener, M.J. (1940). *Minnesota pre-school scale manual.* Minneapolis, MN: Educational Test Bureau, Educational Publishers Inc.

Grossman, H.J. (Ed.). (1983). *Classification in mental retardation.* Washington, DC: American Association on Mental Deficiency.

Gunzberg, H.C. (1969). *P-A-C manual* (3rd ed.). Birmingham, England: SEFA Publications, Ltd.

Heal, L.W., & Fujiura, G.T. (1984). Methodological considerations in research on residential alternatives for developmentally disabled persons. In N.R. Ellis & N.W. Bray (Eds.), *International review of research in mental retardation* (pp. 205–244). Orlando, FL: Academic Press.

Heal, L.W., Sigelman, C.K., & Switzky, H.N. (1978). Research on community residential alternatives for the mentally retarded. In N.R. Ellis (Ed.), *International review of research in mental retardation* (Vol. 9, pp. 209–249). New York: Academic Press.

Hull, J.T., & Thompson, J.C. (1980). Predicting adaptive functioning of mentally retarded persons in community settings. *American Journal of Mental Deficiency, 85,* 253–261.

Hutton, W., & Talkington, L. (1974). *Developmental record.* Corvallis, OR: Continuing Education Publications.

Kazdin, A.E. (1982). *Single-case research designs: Methods for clinical and applied settings.* London: Oxford University Press.

King, R.D., & Raynes, N.V. (1968). Patterns of institutional care for the severely subnormal. *American Journal of Mental Deficiency, 72,* 700–709.

Landesman-Dwyer, S. (1981). Living in the community. *American Journal of Mental Deficiency, 86*, 223–234.

Lyle, J.G. (1960). The effect of an institution environment upon the verbal development of imbecile children—II. Speech and language. *Journal of Mental Deficiency Research, 4*, 1–13.

MacEachron, A.E. (1983). Institutional reform and adaptive functioning of mentally retarded persons: A field experiment. *American Journal of Mental Deficiency, 88*, 2–12

Marlett, N.J. (1977a). *Adaptive Functioning Index rehabilitation programs manual*. Calgary: The Vocational and Rehabilitation Research Institute.

Marlett, N.J. (1977b). *Adaptive Functioning Index standardization manual*. Calgary, Canada: The Vocational and Rehabilitation Research Institute.

McCarver, R.B., & Craig, E.M. (1974). Placement of the retarded in the community: Prognosis and outcome. In N.R. Ellis (Ed.), *International review of research in mental retardation* (Vol. 7, pp. 650–655). New York: Academic Press.

McLain, R.E., Silverstein, A.B., Hubbell, M., & Brownlee, L. (1975). The characterization of residential environments within a hospital for the mentally retarded. *Mental Retardation, 13*, 24–27.

McLain, R.E., Silverstein, A.B., Hubbell, M., & Brownlee, L. (1977). Comparison of the residential environment of a state-hospital for retarded clients with those of various types of community facilities. *Journal of Community Psychology, 5*, 282–289.

McNutt, J.C., & Leri, S.M. (1979). Language differences between institutionalized and noninstitutionalized retarded children. *American Journal of Mental Deficiency, 83*, 339–345.

Meyers, C.E., Nihira, K., & Zetlin, A. (1979). The measurement of adaptive behavior. In N.R. Ellis (Ed.), *Handbook of mental deficiency, psychological theory and research* (2nd ed., pp. 431–481). Hillsdale, NJ: Erlbaum.

Nihira, K., Foster, R., Shellhaas, M., & Leland, H. (1974). *American Association on Mental Deficiency Adaptive Behavior Scale*. Washington, D.C.: American Association on Mental Deficiency.

O'Connor, G. (1976). *Home is a good place: A national perspective of community residential facilities for developmentally disabled persons*. Washington, DC: American Association of Mental Deficiency.

Pilewski, M.E., & Heal, L.W. (1980). Empirical support for deinstitutionalization. In A.R. Novak & L.W. Heal (Eds.), *Integration of developmentally disabled into the community* (pp. 21–34). Baltimore, MD: Paul H. Brookes.

Schlanger, R. (1954). Environmental influences on verbal output of mentally retarded children. *Journal of Speech and Hearing Disorders, 19*, 339–343.

Scheerenberger, R.C. (1976). *Deinstitutionalization and institutional reform*. Springfield, IL: Charles C. Thomas.

Schroeder, S.R., & Henes, C. (1978). Assessment of progress of institutionalized and deinstitutionalized retarded adults: A matched-control comparison. *Mental Retardation, 16*, 147–148.

Sievers, D., & Essa, S. (1961). Language development in institutionalized and community mentally retarded children. *American Journal of Mental Deficiency, 66*, 413–420.

Spivack, A., Haines, P.E., & Spotts, J. (1967). *Devereux Adolescent Behavior Rating Scale Manual*. Devon, PA: The Devereux Foundation.

Stedman, D., & Eichorn, D. (1964). A comparative study of growth and developmental trends of institutionalized and noninstitutionalized mongoloid children. *American Journal of Mental Deficiency, 69*, 391–401.

Taylor, V., & Close, D.W. (1976). *Community Living Observational System*. Eugene, OR: Rehabilitation Research and Training Center in Mental Retardation, University of Oregon.

Tizard, J. (1964). *Community services for the mentally handicapped*. London: Oxford University Press.

Willer, B., & Intagliata, J. (1982). Comparison of family-care and group homes as alternatives to institutions. *American Journal of Mental Deficiency, 86*, 586–595.

Willer, B., & Intagliata, J. (1984). *Promises and realities for mentally retarded citizens: Life in the community.* Baltimore, MD: University Park Press.

Williams, H.M., McFarland, M.L., & Little, M.F. (1937). Development of language and vocabulary in young children. University of Iowa Study: *Study in Child Welfare,* Vol. XIII, no. 2.

Wolf, M.M. (1978). Social validity: The case for subjective measurement or how applied behavior analysis is finding its heart. *Journal of Applied Behavior Analysis, 11,* 203–214.

Wolfensberger, W., & Glenn, L. (1975). *PASS 3 field manual.* Toronto, Canada: National Institute on Mental Retardation.

Woodward, M. (1959). The behaviour of idiots interpreted by Piaget's theory of sensori-motor development. *British Journal of Educational Psychology, 29,* 60–71.

Zigler, E., & Balla, D.A. (1977). Impact of institutional experience on the behavior and development of retarded persons. *American Journal of Mental Deficiency, 82,* 1–11.

6

Health Status and Community Placement of People Who Are Profoundly Retarded and Multiply Disabled

Wayne P. Silverman, Ellen Johnson Silver, Robert A. Lubin, Warren B. Zigman
New York State Institute for Basic Research in Developmental Disabilities

Matthew P. Janicki and John W. Jacobson*
New York State Office of Mental Retardation and Developmental Disabilities

Health problems and service utilization patterns of 115 profoundly retarded, nonambulatory, and multiply disabled people residing at a large, service-intensive facility were examined using a specially designed survey instrument. Data also were obtained for 23 individuals with similar intellectual and functional impairments identified a priori as the most disabled residents of small, community facilities in New York City. Results indicated that, in most respects, the groups overlapped considerably in patterns of respiratory, neuromuscular, and seizure disorders. Residents of the larger facility received more services from nurses and physicians, but these services appeared to be related to chronic disorders or to nonmedical considerations, rather than to a greater need for acute interventions. Although results suggested that profoundly disabled and

* The authors thank Dr. D. Jody, Dr. S. Sklower, Ms. M. Grebbin and Ms. C. Graham for their valuable assistance in developing the Health Status Indicator Survey (HSI), as well as the directors and staff of participating programs for all their help. This project was supported in part by a grant from the New York State Advisory Council on Mental Retardation and Developmental Disabilities. Points of view or opinions stated do not necessarily represent the official position of the funding agency or of the New York State Office of Mental Retardation and Developmental Disabilities. Reprints and copies of the HSI can be obtained from W. Silverman, New York State Institute for Basic Research in Developmental Disabilities, 1050 Forest Hill Road, Staten Island, NY 10314.

medically fragile people can be served in community-based residential programs, the long-term effects of living in such programs remain to be determined for this select population.

Profoundly mentally retarded and physically disabled people are likely to be admitted to small, community-based residential facilities at accelerated rates. Best-Sigford, Bruininks, Lakin, Hill, and Heal (1982) reported that, while before 1960 people with IQs above 50 accounted for two thirds of all discharges from residential institutions that served people who are mentally retarded, people with IQs under 50 make up two thirds of all current discharges. In addition, Bruininks, Kudla, Hauber, Hill, and Wieck (1981) noted, based upon examination of data from several national surveys, that people admitted to community residences will be more severely and multiply handicapped than those people admitted previously. Although some profoundly retarded people already live in community programs (Best-Sigford et al., 1982; Landesman-Dwyer & Sulzbacher, 1981), many more people expected to be placed during the current phases of deinstitutionalization may have serious health problems (Bruininks et al., 1981). Mayeda & Sutter (1981) discussed the importance of the availability of skilled nursing care for these individuals. This is in marked contrast to the earlier phases of the deinstitutionalization movement in many states, in which the overwhelming majority of people leaving institutions were mildly or moderately retarded, exhibited fewer concomitant physical problems, and required less intensive support for independent or group living. Obviously, the degree of cognitive impairment and associated physical problems which are exhibited by profoundly mentally retarded people will be determinants of their community adjustment and service requirements.

Profoundly mentally retarded people exhibit more physical disorders and higher mortality rates than mentally retarded people who are less intellectually impaired (Epple, Tesiny, Rettig, & MacEachron, 1982; Richards, 1976). Investigators have noted that compared with other mentally retarded people, those with profound mental retardation are more likely to exhibit central nervous system pathology (Tarjan, Dingman & Miller, 1960), difficulties in ambulation or arm-hand use (O'Connor, Justice, & Payne, 1970), and deviations in height and weight (Kugel & Mohr, 1963).

Among people who are profoundly mentally retarded, pneumonia and other respiratory infections account for a greater proportion of deaths compared to more capable persons. For instance, Chaney, Eyman, and Miller (1979) reported that, at Pacific State Hospital, 75% of the profoundly retarded people who died between 1944 and 1975 succumbed to some form of respiratory disease, compared to 58% of their sample of less retarded people. Similar data were reported by Epple et al. (1982) for a study sample in New York. In contrast, risks of death from cerebrovascular, cardiovascular, and neoplastic disease are less for people with profound mental retardation, perhaps because these problems most commonly occur at ages beyond their life expectancy (Cleland, Powell, & Talkington, 1971; Richards, 1976).

Even among profoundly retarded people, the age specific death rates for nonambulatory people are higher than those found for people who exhibit some ambulation skills (Eyman & Miller, 1978; Miller, 1975; Miller & Eyman, 1978). This may be related to an increased incidence of respiratory infection, as nonambulatory status predisposes the individual to inadequate ventilation and to aspiration of fluids (Chaney et al., 1979). Seizure disorders may further add to the risk of respiratory infection among profoundly retarded people by producing a tendency to aspirate fluids during periods of impaired consciousness (Chaney et al., 1979). However, even among profoundly retarded people without a history of seizures or musculoskeletal impairment, there is an increased risk of mortality associated with respiratory problems, and some of these people appear to have a decreased ability to cough or swallow that may lead to respiratory infection (Richards, 1976).

Currently, there exists an urgent need to know more about the physical characteristics and health care needs of people who are profoundly retarded. While the consequences of mainstreaming and deinstitutionalization often have been measured in terms of personal and social development (e.g., Conroy, Efthimiou, & Lemanowicz, 1982) the health care and status of mentally retarded people in community residential programs have not been intensively studied. This omission is critical for profoundly mentally retarded people with multiple disabilities, whose health status may be especially dependent upon ready access to appropriate and comprehensive health services (Garrard, 1982). An inadequate or inaccessible health service system could, by increasing the morbidity and mortality risks to this population, obviate the value of community-based care as an alternative to institutional care.

This chapter reports on an investigation of several aspects of the health status and service needs of profoundly retarded, physically disabled people who either resided in small community programs at the time of the study or were expected to move from a large developmental disabilities specialty hospital to the community within the near future. Since the hospital residents were considered to be representative of the most profoundly developmentally disabled people, accessibility of appropriate medical care was expected to be among the principal factors determining the success of their eventual placement into small community facilities. Data therefore were gathered to describe the health status characteristics of the hospital residents, and to determine whether any people with profound mental retardation already living in community settings exhibited comparable health problems and received equivalent medical services. The existence of such people within community-based facilities would suggest that, at a minimum, community placement of hospital residents is feasible. Further, if specialty hospital clients were receiving any specific services not presently delivered to community residents, the need for service development could be documented.

METHOD

Sample

Hospital residents. The primary participants in this investigation were 115 profoundly mentally retarded and physically disabled people who resided at a large developmental disabilities specialty hospital. This specialty hospital, located in New York City, was a transitional treatment setting that provided residential as well as intensive habilitative services to 151 developmentally disabled people who also required substantial medical care. The specialty hospital was more comparable to a skilled nursing facility than to an acute care hospital setting.

The hospital residents participating in this study had been transferred from another large facility and were awaiting placement in small community-based programs. With few exceptions, these individuals were nonambulatory, and were considered to be among the most disabled people receiving developmental services in New York State (Silver, Silverman, & Lubin, 1984). Data obtained from the Developmental Disabilities Information System (Janicki & Jacobson, 1982), a statewide computerized data base containing information on all people receiving services from the New York State Office of Mental Retardation and Developmental Disabilities (OMRDD), were used to provide a preliminary description of the functional characteristics of the people in the sample. These data are summarized in Table 1.

Community residents. In order to select community programs for the study, two sources of information were used. The first of these was the Developmental Disabilities Information System (DDIS). A profile of characteristics of people residing at the hospital was developed, and the DDIS data base was searched in order to locate facilities in New York City which provided services to people with similar disability profiles. Second, in order to verify that programs selected for participation through the DDIS were indeed serving the most disabled people living in community programs in New York City, regional administrators who were familiar with this resident population were asked to propose candidates for the study. Using converging information from these two sources, 14 foster family care homes and 15 intermediate care facilities for the developmentally disabled (ICF/DD programs) were identified as serving profoundly and multiply disabled people. However, only five of the ICF/DD programs and none of the foster care homes served a majority of residents who were nonambulatory. The 23 residents of these five programs constituted our community sample. These five ICF/DD programs consisted of three 3-resident programs, one 4-resident program, and one 10-resident program. Although a small number of residents living in these programs were less intellectually impaired or displayed some ambulation and self-care skills, Table 1 shows considerable overlap between the hospital and community residents, and that some community residents were comparable to the most impaired hospital residents.

As indicated in Table 1, the community residents did not constitute a matched control group. Further, our method of selection of ICF/DDs was not intended to be a random sampling of facilities serving this client population. However, the purpose of the present study was not to describe the characteristics of people residing in community residences, and these methodological considerations are not relevant to the present aims. If hospital client characteristics and service needs are comparable to those of community residents in even a small number of ICF/DDs, the feasibility of establishing residential services for the profoundly retarded multiply handicapped people presently living at the specialty hospital will be demonstrated.

Instruments

The Health Status Indicator (HSI), a 15-page survey instrument composed of 102 multiple choice items, was used to collect information about medical problems experienced by residents and the health care they received during the 6-month period preceding the current investigation. Items included in the HSI provide an

Table 1

Demographic and Functional Characteristics of Health Status Survey Participants

Variable	Hospital Sample	Community Sample
Age (years)		
Mean	25	19
Range	16–37	10–32
Gender		
Male	36%	61%
Female	24%	39%
Mobility		
Walks	2%	10%
Operates wheelchair	4%	5%
Wheelchair, needs help	95%	85%
Receptive Language		
Does not demonstrate understanding	77%	55%
Expressive Language		
Does not speak or sign	96%	65%
Eating		
Completely dependent on others	82%	25%
Toileting		
Completely dependent on others	95%	70%
Multiple disability		
Cerebral palsy and/or epilepsy	68%	85%

assessment of resident health with respect to specific body systems (respiration, cardiovascular, neurological, dental, musculoskeletal). In addition, information included in a standard physical examination is collected (e.g., age, gender, height, weight), along with descriptions of special diets, incidence of infections, accidents and injuries, and medications. The HSI also provides a description of the care or treatment that an individual receives relevant to their physical condition. Survey items include both objective and subjective measures of health status (e.g., "During the past 6 months, how often did this person receive oxygen?"; "How would you rate this person's respiratory condition?"). Except for recording of residents' physical attributes (e.g., height), items required multiple choice responses. Additional information regarding the development and characteristics of the HSI has been presented elsewhere (Silverman, Silver, Lubin, & Zigman, 1983), and the instrument currently is undergoing refinement.

While the HSI provided an assessment of a wide range of health and service characteristics, the present report focuses on items evaluating respiratory, neurological, and musculoskeletal functioning. These areas seemed critical for anticipating survival of profoundly retarded individuals. Data on numbers of eye, ear, throat, gastrointestinal, skin, and urinary infections, as well as other signs of acute problems experienced by residents (i.e., vomiting, diarrhea, fever, constipation, frequent urination, infected sputum), also were obtained. Finally, the type and frequency of health-related treatment received from program staff or medical consultants also was examined.

Data Collection

HSI surveys were completed between May and September 1981. Data were collected for people living at the specialty hospital by interviewing their primary nurses. For the ICF/DD sample, questionnaires were sent to the individual programs, and residence managers designated the appropriate respondents. Whether interview or self-administered survey, people providing information were instructed to refer to a resident's medical record in order to answer the questions. Data were obtained for 112 hospital residents and all 23 people living in ICF/DD programs.

RESULTS

Respiratory problems

As shown in Table 2, all respiratory problems which occurred among hsopital residents during the survey period also were found among some persons living in the community. The apparent differences in the presence of breathing difficulty and secretion problems between hospital and community residents were not statistically significant. [Fisher's exact test of the association of the variables setting (Hospital vs. Community) and Health Problem (presence vs. absence)].

Table 2

Percentage of People Exhibiting Respiratory Problems and
their Related Service Use

Characteristic	Hospital Sample	Community Sample
Breathing Difficulty	5%	-
Once a week or more		
Weekly or less	13%	9%
Never	82%	90%
Secretion Problems	5%	4%
Once a week or more		
Weekly or less	12%	4%
Never	83%	91%
Colds	48%	39%
None		
One	29%	39%
Two or more	23%	22%
Wheezing (episodes)	87%	83%
None		
One	7%	17%
Two or more	6%	-
Pneumonia (once or more)	6%	4%
Cyanotic Episodes (one or more)	6%	4%
Oxygen Administration		
Once a week or more	4%	-
Weekly or less	4%	4%
Never	93%	96%
Respirator Use (once or more)	1%	-
Manual Suctioning (For Secretions)		
Yes	12%	-
No	5%	9%
Not applicable (no problems)	84%	91%
Chest Physical Therapy (for secretions)		
Yes	13%	4%
No	4%	4%
Not applicable (no problems	84%	91%

Note. Totals may not equal 100%, due to rounding.

While the percentages of hospital and community residents receiving services for respiratory problems were comparable, two findings were noteworthy. First, a small number of hospital residents received manual suctioning to relieve problems with secretions. In contrast, no community resident received this service. Second, the breathing of one hospital resident was assisted through the use of a respirator. Again, this service was not provided in the community during the period assessed.

Musculoskeletal condition

The likelihood of having some impairment in the use of one's limbs did not differ between the two groups, as shown in Table 3. However, when data were analyzed separately for arm and leg use, it appeared that degree of impairment did vary. A greater proportion of the hospital residents were completely unable, as opposed to at least partially able, to use their arms, Fisher's exact probability = .044 (2 tailed). Comparable percentages of the two groups also had some leg impairment, but hospital residents more frequently had no ability to use their legs, χ^2 (1) = 4.39, $p<.05$.

Table 3
Percentage of People Exhibiting Musculoskeletal Problems
and their Related Service Use

Characteristic	Hospital Sample	Community Sample
Impaired Limb Use		
No limbs impaired	6%	13%
Arms only	1%	-
Legs only	14%	26%
Arms and legs impaired	79%	61%
Arm Use		
Full use	21%	39%
Limited Use	55%	57%
No use	24%	4%
Leg Use		
Full use	7%	13%
Limited use	45%	65%
No use	48%	22%
Reasons for Impaired Limb Use		
Contractures only	75%	57%
Other problems[a] only	4%	17%
Contractures and other(s)	16%	13%
Not applicable (full use of limbs)	6%	13%
Physical Therapy for Contractures		
Once a day or more	81%	57%
Serveral times a week	6%	4%
Once a week	2%	-
Never	2%	9%
Not applicable (no contractures)	9%	30%
Fractures (one or more)	1%	4%
Hot/swollen joints (one or more episodes)	5%	9%

Note. Totals may not equal 100%, due to rounding.
[a]Paralysis, malformation, and/or missing part(s).

Reduced ability to use one's limbs generally was attributed to contractures, and services related to this condition also were examined. Among people with contractures, most individuals received physical therapy on a daily basis, regardless of their setting. Finally, no differences were found with respect to episodes of joint inflammation or occurrences of bone fractures, both of which may be indicators of skeletal fragility.

Seizure disorders

Data presented in Table 4 indicated that hospital and community residents did not differ with respect to having some history of seizure disorders, or in experiencing seizure episodes during the 6-month survey period. Further, most people having seizures during the survey period experienced grand mal seizures, irrespective of setting.

Among people experiencing seizures, community residents tended to exhibit multiple types of seizure episodes, while hospital residents tended to experience a single class of seizures, Fisher's exact probability = .04 (2-tailed). In addition, community residents who experienced seizure episodes during the 6-month period were likely to have them daily, while hospital residents experienced seizure episodes on a less than daily basis, Fisher's exact probability = .0008 (2-tailed).

Multiple conditions

Respiratory problems may occur more frequently and become more serious among profoundly retarded people who are nonambulatory or who have seizure

Table 4
Types and Frequency of Seizure Disorders
Among Study Participants

Characteristic	Hospital Sample	Community Sample
Occurence of seizures		
None, has never had seisures	52%	65%
Has history, but none during survey period	23%	8%
Grand mal only	15%	-
Petit mal, complex partial, and/or simple partial seizure	7%	9%
Grand mal and another type of seizure	4%	17%
Frequency of seizures		
Daily	-	17%
Weekly	5%	4%
Monthly or less	20%	4%
No seizures	75%	74%

Note. Totals may not equal 100%, due to rounding.

disorders (Chaney et al., 1979). Therefore, combinations of these physical problems also were examined. For this comparison, "respiratory problem" was operationally defined as the occurrence of one or more of the following during the survey period: (a) difficulty breathing or problems with secretions at least once a month, (b) two or more colds or episodes of wheezing, (c) one or more cyanotic episodes, (d) occurrence of pneumonia, (e) regular use of respiratory medication, and (f) administration of oxygen or use of a respirator. Whether or not residents had impaired use of their legs or had any history of seizure episodes were used as operational definitions of problems in these areas.

As shown in Table 5, combinations of respiratory, musculoskeletal, and seizure disorders were distributed similarly among hospital and community residents. Comparable percentages of hospital and community residents (34% and 39%, respectively) exhibited at least one indication of respiratory difficulty, and most individuals with respiratory problems also displayed one or more predisposing or complicating disorders (seizures or nonambulatory status). In addition, similar percentages of both groups exhibited all three disorders, and hospital and community residents did not differ in exhibiting one or more predisposing conditions, even when respiratory problems did not occur.

Infections and acute signs

A variety of acute infections and related signs of illness were evaluated, as shown in Table 6. Similar percentages of hospital and community residents experienced at least one episode of infection of some type. Further, people in the hospital and the community experienced a comparable number of episodes of infection (Ms = 1.4, 1.7, SDs = 23, 2.7, respectively). Community residents, however, were more likely to experience at least two different types of infection, $\chi^2 (2)$ = 10.2, $p<.01$. Indeed, all community residents who experienced more

Table 5

Percentage of People Exhibiting Combinations
of Respiratory Problems, Impaired Leg Use,
and Seizure Disorders

Characteristic	Hospital Sample	Community Sample
None	2%	4%
Respiratory only	-	4%
Impaired leg use only	33%	39%
Seizures only	1%	-
Respiratory and impaired leg use	16%	17%
Respiratory and seizures	4%	4%
Impaired leg use and seizures	30%	17%
All	15%	13%

Note. Totals may not equal 100%, due to rounding.

Table 6
Percentage of People Exhibiting Episodes of Infection
and Acute Signs
of Illness

Characteristic	Hospital Sample	Community Sample
Acute Infections		
Ear	6%	30%
Eye	18%	9%
Throat	8%	13%
Gastrointestinal	3%	26%
Urinary	4%	4%
Skin	23%	8%
Other Acute Conditions		
Fever	45%	39%
Constipation	49%	56%
Diarrhea	4%	48%
Vomiting	23%	35%
Increased urination	-	9%
Infected sputum	5%	4%
Services for Infection		
Repeated Physician Visits[a]	23%	44%
Hospitalization[b]	3%	-

[a]More than once in 10 days during a single episode of infection.
[b]For hospital residents, moved from a residential to medical unit.

than one episode of infection also experienced at least two distinct types. In contrast, about two thirds of the hospital residents who experienced more than one infection had repeated instances of the same type.

More community than hospital residents had either ear or gastrointestinal infections, χ^2s (1) = 9.5 and 13.3, respectively, p's<.01. As also indicated in Table 6, the groups differed in experiencing episodes of diarrhea, χ^2 (1) = 30.3, p<.01, and instances of increased urination, Fisher's exact probability = .028 (1-tailed). While no other group differences were significant, three hospital residents were "hospitalized" (i.e., moved to a medical unit) for treatment of infection(s) during this period. No resident of a community program was admitted to a hospital for treatment of an acute infection.

Habilitative and nursing services

As Table 7 indicates, all habilitative and nursing services used within the hospital also were provided to some extent within the community programs. While more hospital than community residents were treated by licensed practical nurses (LPNs), Fisher's exact probability = .03 (2-tailed), and nurse practitioners, χ^2

Table 7
Health and Therapy Services Provided to Hospitals
and Community Residents

Service	Hospital Sample	Community Sample
Nursing		
Licensed Practical Nurse		
Daily	99%	52%
Weekly or less	-	35%
Never	1%	13%
Registered Nurse		
Daily	100%	52%
Weekly or less	-	48%
Nurse Practitioner		
Daily	49%	9%
Weekly or less	-	9%
Never	51%	83%
Habilitative		
Physical Therapist		
Daily	86%	61%
Weekly or less	13%	30%
Never	1%	9%
Occupational Therapist		
Daily	81%	22%
Weekly or less	11%	39%
Never	9%	39%
Physicians and Specialized Care		
Dental services (one or more visits)		
Dental Hygienist	52%	36%
General Practioner (dentist)	88%	82%
Dental Specialist	4%	5%
Primary Physician		
Daily	94%	-
Weekly or less	6%	92%
Never	-	8%
Medical Specialist		
One or more visits	84%	62%

Note. Totals may not equal 100%, due to rounding.

(1) = 6.5, $p<.01$, all residents received care from registered nurses (RNs). All hospital residents received daily nursing care, but only 57% of the community residents received nursing services on a daily basis, Fisher's exact probability = .0002 (2-tailed).

While more hospital than community residents also received occupational therapy, χ^2 (1) = 11.5, $p<.01$, comparable percentages of the groups received physical therapy during the survey period. In addition, all residents received at least one of these two services during the survey period. However, a greater proportion of the hospital residents (88% vs. 66% of the community residents) received some type of habilitative services daily, χ^2 (1) = 7.4, $p<.01$.

Physicians and specialized care

Table 7 provides data regarding physician and dental services. Individual dental services did not vary by setting. In addition, similar proportions of hospital and community residents saw their primary physician at least once during the survey period. However, the majority of hospital residents saw a primary physician daily, whereas the community residents saw them less often, χ^2 (2) = 97.5, $p<.01$.

A comparable number of hospital and community residents received some type of specialized medical care at least once during the survey period. When the actual numbers of specialists seen by each person were compared, however, analysis indicated that community residents saw a greater number of different types of specialists compared to hospital residents (Ms = 3.0 and 2.1, respectively) t (131) = 2.16, $p<.05$. Specialized services provided to the two groups are summarized in Table 8.

In both groups, services of otolaryngologists, eye specialists, neurologists, and orthopedists were most often used, and no differences were found between hospital and community residents. However, community residents more often saw gastroenterologists, as well as gynecologists or urologists, during the survey period, χ^2s (1) = 6.98 and 9.25, respectively, p's$<.01$. In addition, while specialists involved in acute care (e.g., surgery, internal medicine) were not often seen by residents of either setting, more community residents received services from internists, Fisher's exact probability = .016 (2-tailed). Further,

Table 8
Percentages of Residents Receiving Services from
Selected Medical Specialists

Specialist	Hospital Sample	Community Sample
Allergist	20%	4%
Endocrinologist	-	17%
Eye Specialist	40%	39%
Gastroenterologist	13%	39%
Gynecologist/Urologist	3%	22%
Internist	2%	17%
Neurologist	33%	52%
Orthopedist	35%	52%
Otolaryngologist	49%	44%
Lung Specialist	11%	9%
Surgeon	5%	9%

several community residents, but no hospital residents, were seen by endo-crinologists, Fisher's exact probability = .0013 (2-tailed). No hospital resident received medical care from a type of specialist that was not also seen by some community residents.

DISCUSSION

The present investigation was intended to determine whether profoundly men-tally retarded, nonambulatory, multiply disabled people currently residing in a specialty hospital and awaiting placement were more physically impaired than the most disabled people already residing in small community programs. If found, greater levels of impairment and service usage of specialty hospital resi-dents could be predictive of problems they might encounter following communi-ty placement.

It has been suggested, for example, that the relationship between level of functioning and increased mortality is due, in part, to greater incidence of respi-ratory infection among persons who are profoundly impaired (Richards, 1976). In the present study, however, respiratory disorders did not appear to be charac-teristic of the majority of either the hospital residents awaiting placement or the people already living in the community. Indeed, 66% of the hospital residents and 61% of the community residents in these samples, determined a priori to represent the most seriously impaired members of their respective populations, did not exhibit any respiratory problems during the period of the study. While risk of respiratory problems is high, the status of their respiratory conditions has not presented insurmountable obstacles to placement for the community residents we studied, and, therefore, we would not expect such problems to prevent the majority of hospital residents from moving to community-based residences.

Our findings consistently showed group overlap in both physical disorders and service use. Some community residents exhibited each of the respiratory disorders that occurred among hospital residents, including severe problems such as pneumonia. Community residents also had limb contractures, and experienced seizures during the 6-month period at least as frequently as did hospital residents. Some community residents had multiple impairments and presumably shared with hospital residents a similar high risk with respect to serious medical prob-lems.

Nearly all of the medical services received by hospital residents also were used to some extent by residents of community programs. Although no commu-nity resident required manual suctioning or use of respirators during the period assessed, these services may have been available if needed. Indeed, several community residents received chest physical therapy for secretions, and at least one person was administered oxygen, suggesting that many critical services were available within some community programs. While hospital residents received more frequent health and therapy services from some staff, this difference is not necessarily indicative of greater acute service need, and therefore may not reflect morbidity. For example, primary physicians at the hospital may examine residents who are not acutely ill in the course of rounds, and greater service use may to some extent reflect administrative procedures.

We have not yet considered the relative effects of different types of programs or service provision on the health and behavior of profoundly disabled persons, and descriptions of clients' problems and service use patterns do not necessarily address the issue of whether treatment provided at the hospital and within ICF/DDs would be equally successful in maintaining or improving clients' status over time. However, data relevant to acute infections indirectly address this issue. Community residents were more likely than hospital residents to have gastrointestinal and urinary disturbances, as well as ear infections. If there is an equivalent predisposition towards manifesting such infections in both residential populations, this could indicate that the higher intensity of health services delivered at the hospital was more effective in preventing these types of problems. While this notion is quite speculative, hospital residents could face increased risk of infection-related problems and complications if they were transferred to small community residences.

It is likely that no existing community program provided all services that might be needed by every hospital resident. However, our data indicated that most medical care currently provided to hospital residents could be made accessible within small community settings. Although health risks due to chronic and predisposing conditions constantly must be anticipated if the risk to life is to be minimized, it has been noted that relatively simple preventive measures, such as positioning or special feeding procedures, can be instituted to allow drainage of secretions and control aspirations (Polednak, 1975). Further, because the incidence of acute or emergency situations appeared to be low, we would expect that the majority of specialty hospital residents, representing the most impaired among New York's developmentally disabled population, would not evidence significantly higher morbidity and mortality if they were moved to the community. Indeed, six of the most seriously disabled hospital residents were moved to an ICF/DD program in September 1981, and all of them were surviving at the time of this report (October 1984).

Interpretation of these data must be qualified, nevertheless. All participating programs were located proximate to the extensive health service network in New York City. Because such extensive networks of services may not exist within nonurban locations, the number of potential sites for residential facilities for this group may be constrained to a greater degree than for less physically impaired populations. Further, it is possible that providing intensive medical care equivalent to the specialty hospital situation could result, necessarily, in a community setting which does not reflect the concepts of "normalization," and would thus defeat a major purpose of community-based care. We therefore need to examine program characteristics and relate them to changes in both health and adaptive competence of the residents. If there are no environmental or service differences, or no differences in programs' effects on residents, other factors (e.g., proximity to family, cost, etc.) may best determine which residential program meet the needs of people who are profoundly retarded and multiply disabled.

REFERENCES

Best-Sigford, B., Bruininks, R.H., Lakin, K.C., Hill, B.K., & Heal, L.W. (1982). Resident release patterns in a national sample of public residential facilities. *American Journal of Mental Deficiency, 87,* 130–140.

Bruininks, R.H., Kudla, M.J., Hauber, F.A., Hill, B.K., & Wieck, C.A. (1981). Recent growth and status of community residential alternatives. In R. Bruininks, C. Meyers, B. Sigford, & K. Lakin (Eds.), *Deinstitutionalization and community adjustment of mentally retarded people* (pp. 14–27). Washington, DC: American Association on Mental Deficiency.

Chaney, R.H., Eyman, R.K., & Miller, C.R. (1979). Comparison of respiratory mortality in the profoundly mentally retarded and in the less retarded. *Journal of Mental Deficiency Research, 23,* 1–7.

Cleland, C., Powell, H., & Talkington, L. (1971). Death of the profoundly retarded. *Mental Retardation, 9,* 36.

Conroy, J., Efthimiou, J., & Lemanowicz, J. (1982). A matched comparison of the developmental growth of institutionalized and deinstitutionalized mentally retarded clients. *American Journal of Mental Deficiency, 86,* 581–587.

Epple, W.A., Tesiny, E.P., Rettig, J.H., & MacEachron, A.E. (1982). *Mortality in New York State developmental centers:* Final report. Albany, NY: New York State Office of Mental Retardation and Developmental Disabilities.

Eyman, R.K., & Miller, C.R. (1978). A demographic overview of severe and profound mental retardation. In C. Meyers (Ed.), *Quality of life in severely and profoundly mentally retarded people: Research foundation for improvement* (pp. ix–ixii). Washington, DC: American Association on Mental Deficiency.

Garrard, S.D. (1982). Health services for mentally retarded people in community residences: Problems and questions. *American Journal of Public Health, 72,* 1226–1228.

Janicki, M.P., & Jacobson, J.W. (1982). The character of developmental disabilities in New York State: Preliminary observations. *International Journal of Rehabilitation Research, 12,* 191–202.

Kugel, R.B., & Mohr, J. (1963). Mental retardation and physical growth. *American Journal of Mental Deficiency, 68,* 41–48.

Landesman-Dwyer, S., & Sulzbacher, F.M. (1981). Residential placement and adaptation of severely and profoundly retarded individuals. In R. Bruininks, C. Meyers, B. Sigford, & K. Lakin (Eds.), *Deinstitutionalization and community adjustment of mentally retarded people* (pp. 182–184). Washington, DC: American Association on Mental Deficiency.

Mayeda, T., & Sutter, P. (1981). Deinstitutionalization: phase II. In R. Bruininks, C. Meyers, B. Sigford, & K. Lakin (Eds.), *Deinstitutionalization and community adjustment of mentally retarded people* (pp. 375–381). Washington, DC: American Association of Mental Deficiency.

Miller, C.R. (1975). Deinstitutionalization and mortality trends for the profoundly mentally retarded. In C. Cleland & L. Talkington (Eds.), *Research with the profoundly retarded: A conference proceeding* (pp. 1–8). Austin, TX: Western Research Conference and the Brown Schools.

Miller, C.R., & Eyman, R.K. (1978). Hospital and community mortality rates among the retarded. *Journal of Mental Deficiency Research, 22,* 137–145.

O'Connor, G., Justice, R.S., & Payne, D. (1970). Statistical expectations of physical handicaps of institutionalized retardates. *American Journal of Mental Deficiency, 74,* 541–547.

Polednak, A.P. (1975). Respiratory disease mortality in an institutionalized mentally retarded population. *Journal of Mental Deficiency Research, 74,* 541–547.

Richards, B.W. (1976). Health and longevity. In J. Wortis (Ed.), *Mental retardation and developmental disabilities: An annual review (Vol. VIII)* (pp. 168–187). New York: Brunner/Mazel Publishers.

Silver, E.J., Silverman, W., & Lubin, R. (1984). Community living for severely and profoundly retarded persons. In J.M. Berg (Ed.), *Perspectives and progress in mental retardation* (pp. 363–371). Baltimore, MD: University Park Press.

Silverman, W., Silver, E.J., Lubin, R., & Zigman, W. (1983). *Health status of profoundly retarded persons in a specialty hospital and in small community programs.* (Technical Report No. 83-1). New York: New York State Office of Mental Retardation and Developmental Disabilities, Institute for Basic Research in Developmental Disabilities.

Tarjan, G., Dingman, H.F., & Miller, C.R. (1960). Statistical expectations of selected handicaps in the mentally retarded. *American Journal of Mental Deficiency, 65,* 335–341.

7

Intermediate Care Facilities for the Mentally Retarded and the Problems of Emerging Social Policy

Parnel Wickham-Searl

Syracuse University

Many of the federal policies emerging from the 1960s and 1970s concerning disabilities promoted community-based services as alternatives to institutions as well as standards for quality programs. The policy for Intermediate Care Facilities for the Mentally Retarded (ICFs/MR), however, manifests the problems of these policies. Reflecting its Medicaid heritage, ICF/MR has been a costly program that perpetuates institutional forms of services. The implementation of the ICF/MR policy by the federal government and by the states documents these problems: jurisdictional disputes between state and federal administrators, expansive costs, and the perpetuation of substandard conditions in institutional settings. Efforts to reform the ICF/MR policy appeared in the Community and Family Living Amendments of 1983. Originally, the proposed bill was intended to transfer Medicaid funding from institutions to community services. Recent compromises in the bill, however, preserved funding for some institutions. These revisions to the proposed amendments recall the dilemmas of Medicaid and the ICF/MR policy. But despite concessions, the Community and Family Living Amendments may provide a new direction for public policy for disabled citizens.

The introduction of the Community and Family Living Amendments in 1983 (S. 2053) culminated more than two decades of public policy developments concerning individuals with developmental disabilities. As an attempt to reform the federal policy for Intermediate Care Facilities for the Mentally Retarded (ICFs/MR) (Social Security Amendments of 1971), the Community and Family Living Amendments proposed fiscal incentives for states to direct services away from large institutional settings into community settings. Although the proposed Amendments were not enacted in 1983, revisions were already underway in 1984. The substance of those revisions reflected three issues confronting policy-makers concerned with providing services to people with developmental disabilities. First, public policy for people with developmental disabilities has generally reinforced an institutional bias in service delivery, although increasingly in the 1960s and 1970s federal policy turned to community-based alternatives. The second problem concerns economic motives which have continued to influence social policy decisions. Third, jurisdictional conflicts between federal and state governments often create dilemmas in policy implementation. These three problems are apparent in the ICF/MR policy and Congress' efforts to reform the ICF/MR policy through the Community and Family Living Amendments.

The chapter focuses first on the legislative history of the ICF/MR policy to explain, in part, the policy's reliance on institutional models of care. The next section introduces the specific policy-making activities which accompanied the enactment of the ICF/MR legislation in 1971. The chapter goes on to describe the policy-making environment in the area of developmental disabilities in the late 1960s and 1970s. This analysis of the policy environment points out some of the discrepancies between federal policies promoting community care and the ICF/MR policy's perpetuation of institutional services. Following this analysis, an overview of ICF/MR policy implementation by the federal government and the states after the law's enactment is presented. This overview clearly shows the policy's institutional bias and the program's escalating jurisdictional disputes. In conclusion, the chapter shifts its perspective from the ICF/MR policy to the Community and Family Living Amendments, summarizing the major forces pressing for reform and the impediments to change within the context of current policy-making.

The research methodology selected relied on printed documents and interviews with individuals participating in or knowledgeable about ICF/MR policy-making. The documents that were analyzed included formal federal policy statements, such as Presidential statements, Congressional hearings, the Federal Register, the Congressional Record, and other reports and accounts of governmental policy-making. Nongovernmental documents that were analyzed included reports prepared by universities, such as economic and demographic studies, newspaper and journal articles, and analytical studies.

Individuals were selected for interviews on the basis of their knowledge of the issues surrounding the development of the ICF/MR policy. Individuals included representatives of consumer organizations, representatives of professional organizations, government employees, members of Congress, and university personnel. Most of the interviews were conducted by telephone due to the geographical dispersion of respondents. In general, interviews were unstructured, although certain specific topics were introduced to some individuals who were known to possess a unique or informative perspective.

THE SOCIAL SECURITY HERITAGE OF THE ICF/MR POLICY

The history of the ICF/MR policy corresponds with two important strands of social thinking and policy-making. The first of these strands has to do with the

Social Security heritage, and the second strand has to do with policy-making regarding mental disabilities in the 1960s. The Social Security heritage of the ICF/MR policy strongly influenced the content of that policy. Not until later in the 1970s did the ICF/MR program begin to reflect other federal policies concerning mental retardation and developmental disabilities. A minor amendment to Medicaid (Social Security Amendment of 1965), the ICF/MR legislation in many ways incorporated the contradictions of that important piece of social legislation. This section describes those contradictions in a review of Social Security policy developments from the early 1960s.

Medicaid, passed in 1965, was one of a pair of laws deriving from the Great Society having to do with health care. Its companion policy, Medicare, provided health care benefits to elderly citizens within the context of a nationalized health program. Medicaid, on the other hand, was designed to provide health care benefits to poor and disabled individuals within the context of established welfare programs.

There were other important differences between Medicare and Medicaid. While Medicare was basically a new contributory health insurance program for elderly people, Medicaid revised already existing health and welfare programs which were implemented by state governments. An extension of the Kerr-Mills Act of 1960, Medicaid increased the availability of health services for poor and disabled citizens through greater federal support of states' welfare efforts.

In 1960, Senator Kerr from Oklahoma and Representative Mills from Arkansas proposed the Social Security Amendment (P.L. 86-778) which bears their names, to extend already existing federal cost-sharing of medical benefits to certain categories of needy individuals. Under the Kerr-Mills Act, the federal government was to share the costs of these benefits with the states, but the states were authorized to determine the extent of the benefits and the limitations of the program.

The Kerr-Mills program brought numerous problems in implementation. Many viewed the program as a windfall for states:

> Kerr-Mills was perhaps less a means of increasing aid to the elderly than it was a means for shifting the burden of that aid from others to the federal government. The many counties in the United States subsidizing medical relief could look upon Kerr-Mills as a golden egg of additional state support. (Stevens & Stevens, 1974, p. 30)

Furthermore, costs of providing services to states rose dramatically, and services varied considerably across the country. Another important problem concerned the institutional bias of the Kerr-Mills Act. Although promoting the concept of noninstitutional services, the program, through its generous funding of in-hospital and nursing home care, actually supported such forms of care with fiscal incentives. Indeed, in 1965, after the program had been implemented for 5 years, the total vendor payments amounted to $1.4 billion, $1.0 billion of which went for nursing home or in-hospital care. Vendor payments for nursing home care alone rose from $47 million in 1960 to $449 million in 1965 (Stevens & Stevens, 1974).

Congress introduced the Medicaid program in 1965 to correct some of these problems of the Kerr-Mills Act. But although Congress hoped to counteract the windfall effect by requiring states to develop new programs rather than replace state money with federal, the problem remained:

> The states, smelling easy federal money under the new Title, began putting on the pressure for implementation. Even as Title XIX was going through Congress, Pennsylvania had a bill in its legislature designed to obtain maximum funds for that state. . . . Other states, too, saw Medicaid as a vehicle for accelerating already accepted welfare developments. (Stevens & Stevens, 1974, p. 79)

In 1965, the Department of Health, Education, and Welfare (HEW) estimated that the Medicaid program cost the federal government $950 million a year, but, within 1 year, the estimate had grown to $3 billion (Stevens & Stevens, 1974). Alarmed, Congress searched for ways to contain the program.

While problems of rising costs dominated the policy environment, another important issue emerged: the provision of services in nursing homes and other out-of-hospital settings. In an attempt to establish standards of quality, the federal government engaged the states in disputes over the issue of authority; many states resented federal intrusion into what they considered was a state-operated program. Eventually, a compromise was reached in 1967, whereby the federal government accepted state standards and certification procedures for reimbursement purposes, with certain specific staffing provisos required (Markus, 1972).

Still concerned with problems in the nursing home industry, Congress attempted to modify the laws to promote more accountability, as well as to save costs. Additional amendments to the Social Security Act were passed in 1967 to legislate standards for care, to issue professional requirements, and to provide another level of care to reduce costs. That new level, known as Intermediate Care, reimbursed services beyond simply room and board, but avoided the large expenses of skilled nursing. Congress recognized that not all elderly people needing care required the intensity of skilled nursing:

> At the present time old-age assistance recipients whose primary need is for care in an institution other than a skilled nursing home are frequently classified as in need of 'skilled nursing home' care and placed in such institutions because of the decided financial advantage to a State under present matching formulas. . . . Thus, the Federal and State governments often may pay upwards of $300 a month for skilled nursing home care for a patient who could be adequately taken care of in another type of institution for $150 or $200 a month. (S. Rep. 744, 1967, pp. 188–189)

Implementation of the 1967 Amendments produced the same obstacles as previous efforts of reform: standards for ICFs were embroiled in controversy. Congress accused states of converting skilled nursing homes to ICFs apparently to escape the more stringent requirements of skilled nursing care. Some states were actually charging more for ICFs than they were for skilled nursing facilities, and other states attempted to use ICF funds for purposes other than that for which they were intended (specifically, in fact, for institutions for mentally retarded individuals). Indeed, a report published by the General Accounting Office (GAO) documented that states were converting mental retardation institutions to skilled nursing facilities in order to access the funding. California alone claimed $14.2 million for mentally retarded residents in institutions between September 1968 and August 1969. The GAO reported:

> Our review of Medicaid claims by the State of California for the care of individuals in State institutions for the mentally retarded showed that claims were being made on behalf of most of these individuals simply because they were in institutions certified by the State as skilled nursing homes rather than because they were in need of such care. . . . A substantial portion of claims made by the State of California . . . are questionable because most individuals in the State institutions for the mentally retarded did not need, and did not receive, skilled nursing care. (General Accounting Office, 1970, p. 11)

In order to counter these costly trends and to impose more effective rules, a new amendment to the Social Security Act was introduced in Congress in 1970. After several revisions, the new bill proposed that HEW should determine standards for ICFs, and that the ICF program should be moved from Title XI, where it was originally placed, to Title XIX, Medicaid. The move to Medicaid, Congress felt, would enable HEW to supervise the program more closely, thus controlling quality as well as costs. Furthermore, Congress proposed to extend the definition of eligible recipients in the ICF program to mentally retarded persons living in public institutions which qualify as ICFs. ICFs for mentally retarded individuals would provide active treatment and rehabilitiation in addition to room and board in order to qualify for funding.

Although the original bill of 1970 died when the 91st Congress adjourned, it was revitalized again as H.R. 1 in May, 1971. While H.R. 1 became bogged down in controversy once more, the Senators from Oklahoma—Bellmon and Harris—introduced a minor amendment on December 4, 1971 (Senate, Congressional Record, 1971). Congress enacted the legislation quietly on December 28, 1971. The new law, P.L. 92-223, provided death benefits for families of servicemen killed overseas, and included three riders: one restricted eligibility for the work incentive (WIN) program for recipients of aid to families with dependent children (AFDC); another transferred the ICF program to Medicaid; and the third rider expanded the definition of ICFs to public institutions for mentally retarded individuals. Members of Congress debated the WIN amendment, but apparently ignored the ICF/MR amendment altogether.

THE POLITICAL ENVIRONMENT OF P.L. 92-223

Congressional efforts to reform Social Security programs addressed two major problems: the first problem had to do with the unexpectedly high costs of providing Social Security programs, and the second problem had to do with the quality of services provided. From the early 1960s, legislators struggled to contain costs while at the same time attempting to standardize quality services through federal regulations. Members of Congress probably intended to improve services in the nation's mental retardation institutions by passing P.L. 92-223. By stipulating that recipients of ICF/MR funds must provide active treatment and rehabilitation in addition to room and board in ICF/MR-certified facilities, Congress was probably trying to control conditions that were notoriously disreputable (Blatt & Kaplan, 1966; Blatt, Ozolins, & McNally, 1979). It seems unlikely, however, that Congress considered the costs involved with P.L. 92-223, because, by broadening the definition of ICFs to include mentally retarded individuals in public institutions, costs to the federal government were certain to rise.

To fully understand the factors which contributed to the passage of P.L. 92-223, one must look beyond Congress. Other policy-makers in the early 1970s included administrators of state departments of welfare as well as consumer advocates. Motivated primarily by the attraction of federal resources, a few state officials seized the opportunity to convert public institutions for mentally retarded persons to ICFs in order to supplant state funds with federal funds. At the same time, certain consumer advocates wanted to attract federal funds to state institutions in order to improve facilities known to be unsafe, unsanitary, and often inhumane.

The State of Oklahoma figures prominently in the policy-making activities of the period. The state's influence on federal welfare policy can be traced to the Kerr-Mills Act, as well as to Senator Bellmon's and Senator Harris' 1971 ICF/MR Amendment. Furthermore, Oklahoma was a leader in promoting other welfare legislation in the nation. The Welfare Director of Oklahoma, Lloyd Rader, is described by many as a powerful force behind Oklahoma's welfare initiatives. In addition to supervising his state's welfare department, Mr. Rader controlled the state's three public institutions for mentally retarded people. The Oklahoma Welfare Director's influence extended to both Congress and HEW as well. Rader's own publicity pamphlet, quoted in a Gannett News Service Special Report, described him thus:

> Oklahoma programs became models for other states. Successive governors asked [him] to stay on. He is known to most of Washington's officialdom as the dean of welfare directors, mainstay of the American Public Welfare Association, consultant to congressional committees. (Gallagher, Hanchette, & Sherwood, 1982, p. 28)

Rader's power in Washington is touched with irony, for, while he commanded respect in Washington, scandal tainted those human services offered back home in Oklahoma. The Gannett News Service, running a series of articles in 1981 and 1982, exposed abusive conditions at the state's juvenile detention centers and its mental retardation facilities. But, despite the notorious reputation of Oklahoma's institutions, Lloyd Rader apparently earned great respect among public officials and administrators.

Along with other state administrators, he proposed to shift the ICF program to Medicaid in order to extend federal benefits to mentally retarded people in public institutions. Many members of Congress may have thought that this minor piece of legislation was a small price to pay for other, more significant, political favors. In any event, the Welfare Director from Oklahoma, Lloyd Rader, is described by people as the most influential person behind P.L. 92-223, as the "person who wrote the legislation."

If the ICF/MR legislation seemed fairly insignificant in the overall scheme of federal policy, it was extremely important to the group of public administrators which included state welfare directors as well as to consumer advocates. Not only did the legislation legally qualify mental retardation institutions for the Medicaid largess, but it mandated improvements in these institutions also. Whatever their motivation, the diverse advocates of the legislation joined forces to ensure the passage of P.L. 92-223. By doing so, they extended previous patterns of Social Security programs, including the perpetuation of institutional forms of care, expansive costs, and conflicts between state and federal administrators over regulatory authority.

PUBLIC POLICY AND DEINSTITUTIONALIZATION

The decades of the 1960s and 1970s brought notable changes in other federal policies and a growing public awareness of issues concerning people with developmental disabilities. One of these issues had to do with the deinstitutionalization of people through the provision of services in communities rather than in large institutions (General Accounting Office, 1977; Kugel & Shearer, 1976). One of the first mental health policy statements of the period appeared in 1960, when the Joint Commission on Mental Illness and Mental Health published its report, "Action for Mental Illness." A forerunner of the concept behind the Community Mental Health Centers, the report advocated for new models of providing service in socially integrated communities rather than solely in isolated institutions.

Similarly, a report was issued by the President's Panel on Mental Retardation in 1962. The Panel, too, recommended that services for people with mental retardation be located in communities:

> Bringing the provisions of services as close as possible to the local community is a basic tenet on which the Panel's recommendations rest. This would be consistent with the general movement of health and mental health services in this direction, in

itself an important and key movement in developing new services of [*sic*] the retarded. (p. 141)

President John F. Kennedy reiterated this position in his statement of February 5, 1963:

Services to both the mentally ill and to the mentally retarded must be community based and provide a range of services to meet community needs. . . . We must move from the outmoded use of distant custodial institutions to the concept of community-centered agencies. . . . (Cited in Senate Subcomm. on Health, 1963)

A major piece of legislation to come out of this growing federal commitment to people with mental disabilities was the Mental Retardation Facilities and Community Mental Health Centers Construction Act of 1963 (P. L. 88-164). Following the recommendations of the Joint Commission on Mental Illness and Mental Health, Congress authorized funds for the construction of community-based facilities to serve people with psychiatric disabilities. Congress' intention regarding the mental retardation facilities was somewhat more ambiguous. Funds were authorized to stimulate construction of mental retardation facilities, both residential and day program. But, in a report submitted by the Secretary of HEW in 1969, it was apparent that a significant amount of the funds allocated under the Mental Retardation Facilities and Community Mental Health Centers Construction Act went to the construction of large public mental retardation institutions. For example, one such facility in Arizona housed a total of 1,240 residents, one facility in Connecticut housed 1,954 residents, one in Florida housed 1,500 residents, one in New Hampshire housed 1,076, and one in Oklahoma was built for 996 residents (Dept. of Health, Education, and Welfare, Secretary's Committee on Mental Retardation, 1969). Thus, in this case, the policy's implementation tended to support institutional services. Indeed, it is important to note that, within this period of emerging federal leadership, at no time did proponents of community-based services abandon institutional forms of service. Rather, policy-makers advocated for a dual service system: community-based programs to complement existing institutional models of care.

However, Congress continued to authorize funds for construction and staffing of mental health facilities located in communities. The list of the legislation passed in the 1960s which promoted services in the community includes, for example, the Mental Retardation Facilities and Community Mental Health Centers Construction Act Amendments of 1965 (P.L. 89-105), the Vocational Rehabilitation Act Amendments of 1965 (P.L. 89-333), and the Mental Retardation Amendments of 1967 (P.L. 90-170). Along with the legislation for ICFs/MR, one of the first acts of Congress for disabled individuals in the 1970s was the Developmental Disabilities Services and Facilities Construction Amendments of 1970 (P.L. 91-517). This law broadened the definition of disabilities to encompass individuals with complex needs, and attempted to strengthen federal oversight in existing programs.

Also in 1970, the President's Task Force on the Mentally Handicapped issued its report, entitled "Action Against Mental Disability." Stressing a renewed commitment to community-based care rather than institutional care, the Task Force recommended expanding Medicaid and Medicare coverage to individuals with mental disabilities.

One of the most direct attacks on institutional care for people with mental retardation was issued by President Richard Nixon, in his statement on November 16, 1971:

> . . . I invite all Americans to join me in commitment to two major national goals:
> • To reduce by half the occurence of mental retardation in the United States before the end of this century;
> • To enable one-third of the more than 200,000 retarded persons in public institutions to return to useful lives in the community. (Nixon, 1971)

President Nixon's statement reaffirmed the federal commitment to community-based services from which federal policies would continue to emerge in the 1970s. In addition to acts of Congress, these policies increasingly included decisions of federal courts in suits concerning the rights of individuals committed to institutions for both mentally ill and mentally retarded people.

In *Wyatt v. Stickney* (1972), for example, the U.S. District Court in Montgomery, Alabama ruled that the psychiatrically disabled and mentally retarded residents of Alabama's institutions had a right to treatment in the least restrictive setting. The "least restrictive setting" concept, initiated with this decision, heavily influenced later policy decisions. The concept suggests service alternatives that permit personal independence and social integration (Turnbull, 1981). Furthermore, rights to such services as education and treatment were upheld in a variety of federal court decisions, including, for example, *Welsch v. Likens* (1974), *New York State Association for Retarded Children v. Carey* (1975), and *Halderman v. Pennhurst State School and Hospital* (1977). Some of these decisions also reaffirmed the federal policy of service provision in the least restrictive setting (*Dixon v. Weinberger*, 1975).

Other policies instituted by Congress assured that more federally assisted services would reach disabled individuals already living in communities. The Social Security Act Amendments of 1972 (P.L. 93-66), for example, established the Supplemental Security Income program (SSI) to ensure that aged and disabled people receive equitable shares of federally subsidized income maintenance. (Another amendment of 1976 authorized SSI payments to individuals living in small community residences.) The Rehabilitiation Act of 1973 (P.L. 93-112) promoted services especially for individuals who were severely handicapped or who had been institutionalized at one time. This Act, by focusing on the needs of people previously institutionalized or at risk of institutionalization, established priorities in public policy for this previously neglected population. And in addition, the Rehabilitation Act of 1973 ensured the civil rights of individuals with disabilities, and provided protection from discrimination.

In the Rehabilitation Act Amendments of 1974 (P.L. 93-516), Congress reaffirmed the public commitment to full, meaningful social integration of handicapped individuals in community living, work, and service programs. Similarly, President Ford, in 1974, reiterated the national goal of returning mentally retarded individuals from institutions to productive community living. Congress followed up this statement with the Social Services Amendments of 1974 (P.L. 93-647), which confirmed the need for Social Security program participants to become as independent as possible, to live in community environments, and to prevent restrictive, institutional forms of care. At the same time, the Community Mental Health Centers Amendments of 1975 (P.L. 94-63) reinforced Congress' commitment to individuals in communities.

One landmark piece of legislation in the mid-'70s, the Developmentally Disabled Assistance and Bill of Rights Act of 1975 (P.L. 94-103), attempted to promote better standards for care in institutions receiving federal funds, while, at the same time, attempting to prevent inappropriate placement of individuals in institutions, and supported increased alternatives to institutions in community settings. Another Congressional Act passed in 1975, the Education for All Handicapped Children Act (P.L. 94-142), ensured that all children, regardless of where they lived, were eligible for education services.

Thus, federal policy as it emerged in the 1970s continued to promote services in the community and to prevent institutionalization. Policies began to focus on those individuals particularly susceptible to institutionalization—severely handicapped people—and promoted the concept of "least restrictive settings;" that is, providing services in settings which are most conducive to the person's independence and full social integration. But while public policy espoused the shift of services from institutions to communities, at no time did policy-makers attempt to discard altogether the nation's institutions. Federal policy implicitly concluded that institutions would continue to be inhabited by some individuals, who, most likely, would be the most severely handicapped.

While the policies of the early 1970s promoted the civil rights of individuals with developmental disabilities, including severely handicapped individuals, a shift in emphasis occurred in the late 1970s and early 1980s. The election of President Ronald Reagan in 1980 initiated a transition from social responsibility to fiscal conservatism. No longer were policies to be formulated on the basis of social need without regard to economic impact. Although, as noted in the ICF/MR policy environment, the costs of social policies had previously attracted the attention of members of Congress as well as administrators, by the 1980s this interest in program costs began to replace the concern for social justice.

One of the first major pieces of legislation to come from the Reagan administration was the Omnibus Reconciliation Act of 1981 (P.L. 97-35). This Act was one of President Reagan's first initiatives to deal with the nation's spiraling health costs. The Act's amendments to Medicaid permitted the Secretary of Health and Human Services (formerly HEW) to waive certain federal requirements in order to enable states to provide personal care and other services (but not room and board) for those individuals who would ordinarily be eligible for institutional services regulated by Medicaid. The new law specified that service providers must document that each recipient would otherwise be institutionalized in a Medicaid-funded facility, and that individualized plans must be maintained for each individual. Furthermore, states must document that alternative care costs no more per capita than institutionalization.

Federal regulations to implement the so-called Medicaid Home and Community-based Care Waiver Authority (known as the Medicaid Waiver) appeared in the Federal Register on October 1, 1981. The summary preceding the regulations repeats the original intent of the legislation:

> This rule amends current Medicaid regulations to permit States to offer, under a Secretarial waiver, a wide array of home and community-based services that an individual may need in order to avoid institutionalization. Before enactment, little coverage under Medicaid was available for noninstitutional long-term care services. Conversely, institutional long-term care services represent a significant part of the budgets of State Medicaid programs. (p. 48532) (Federal Register, 1981, p. 48532)

Although the Medicaid Waiver supports the process of deinstitutionalization by providing incentives for the development of community-based services, there is no question that the enactment of the Medicaid Waiver was motivated by a President and a Congress whose priority was to trim health and welfare costs (Bovbjerg & Holahan, 1982).

Thus, the policy of the ICF/MR legislation remained ambiguous and contradictory. Patterns in deinstitutionalization continued into the 1980s, but the motivation for shifting resources to community settings was increasingly economic. At the same time, policy-makers most likely never fully intended to replace institutions with community programs. On the contrary, most policies supported a dual service system of institutions and community-based services. The ICF/MR policy conformed to these patterns.

POLICY IMPLEMENTATION AND THE FEDERAL ICF/MR REGULATIONS

At about the same time that federal policies for mental disabilities were gaining momentum in the mid 1970s, the regulations for ICFs/MR were being written by HEW. The regulations focused on standards for active treatment and rehabilitation, safety, and sanitary conditions, reflecting the Department's mandate to improve conditions in institutions receiving federal funds. These standards were initially modeled after those of the Joint Commission on the Accreditation of Hospitals (JCAH). Relying on a medical model of treatment, the standards have often been criticized for promoting concepts having to do with illness and disease in mentally retarded individuals who are not, as a group, characterized by either illness or disease.

Criticized also by state administrators for their inflexibility and complexity, the standards have often been blamed for the ICF/MR program's escalating costs. Taking a defensive posture, the Department of Health and Human Services (HHS) continues to modify the ICF/MR regulations in an effort to hold states more accountable. Under the present administration, however, HHS is reconsidering its regulations less publicly.

One of the more notable accomplishments of the initial regulations of HEW was an early provision that permitted states to apply different standards to facilities housing 15 and fewer residents than the standards which applied to those housing over 15 individuals. By doing so, HEW permitted smaller, community-based residential facilities to quality for reimbursement under the ICF/MR program. The final regulations, issued on January 17, 1974, specified the variances allowed for smaller facilities.

The final regulations established a 3-year date for compliance by the states. The leniency of the HEW compliance dates was one aspect of a familiar pattern of implementation of the ICF/MR program. Table 1 presents the sequence of regulations, together with the major provisions of each revised set. The compliance date extensions given to states became a familiar pattern in the ICF/MR program. On the one hand, it may be said that HEW was responsive to the criticisms of its proposed regulations; thus, the Department heeded requests from states for more time to implement the massive changes required by the federal government. On the other hand, HEW proceeded with extreme caution into its new role as overseer of ICF/MR programs. Previously, these services for mentally retarded people had been operated and monitored solely by the states or locally. States' complaints of federal intrusion into what they considered their exclusive territory provoked antagonisms with federal administrators. In an introduction to new regulations published on June 3, 1977, HEW reported:

> Many comments objected to the introduction of Federal determinations into a process which by statute is interpreted as a State function and authority. HEW agrees, in essence, with the comments that the authority for determining whether institutions meet the requirements for participation in Medicaid rests with the State. (Federal Register, 1977, p. 28700)

With this dichotomy, then, between the rights of states to implement the Medicaid program, and the need for the federal government to provide oversight to the program, the ICF/MR program became entangled in regulatory issues which continue to this day. In general, due to the history of the Medicaid program and the issue of states' rights, states have gained control of the ICF/MR program from the outset, while the federal government still tries to exert a measure of authority.

Federal–state jurisdictional disputes complicated the implementation of the ICF/MR program. Within the context of the policy's institutionally biased heritage, these disputes resulted in unintended and contradictory outcomes of

Table 1
Chronological Sequence of Federal ICF/MR Regulations

Date	Content Summary	Reference in Rederal Register
March 5, 1973	Original proposed regulations for ICFs and ICFs/MR: eligibility, state plans, standards administration	Vol. 38, no. 42, pp. 5874-5985
Jan. 17, 1974	Original final regulations: modification of original regulations reflecting criticisms; compliance target of 3 years: March 18, 1977	Vol. 39, no. 12, pp. 2223-2235
Jan. 18, 1977	Proposed regulations: postpones compliance—March 18, 1978 for staffing standards, March 18, 1980 for environmental standards	Vol. 42, no. 12, pp. 3325-3328
March 18, 1977	Final regulations: postpones compliance from March 18, 1977 to July 18, 1977	Vol. 42, no. 53, pp. 15063-15064
June 3, 1977	Final regulations: postpones compliance—July 18, 1978 for staffing standards, July 18, 1980 for environmental standards; creates variances	Vol. 42, no. 107, pp. 28700-28704
Jan. 6, 1981	Final regulations: postpones compliance from July 18, 1980 to July 18, 1982	Vol. 46, no. 3, pp. 1268-1270
Aug. 24, 1981	Proposed regulations: phase-out provisions; "negotiates revisions": in state plans	Vol. 46, no. 163, pp. 42698-42701
Aug. 26, 1982	Final regulations: phase-out provisions and negotiated revisions; maximum target for compliance: 5 years	Vol. 47, no. 166, pp. 37547-37550

state-implemented ICF/MR programs. Costs increased out of proportion with other Medicaid programs, federal standards were compromised, and the institutional bias prevailed.

According to data furnished by the Health Care Financing Administration (HCFA), the ICF/MR program cost the federal government $98 million in 1973 for 29,000 recipients. Ten years later, in 1983, it was projected that the program would cost the federal government $2,151 million for 132,000 recipients (Smith, 1984). Indeed, the figure projected for 1984 rose to nearly $2.5 billion, about

$16,000 per client (Heckler, 1984). HHS claims that Medicaid is now the major source of funding for individuals living in mental retardation institutions. Furthermore, ICF/MR payments constituted 12% of all Medicaid payments in 1983, up from 1.9% in 1973, making it the fastest growing category in the Medicaid program (Heckler, 1984).

An irony exists in this influx of federal funds to institutions, for, while reimbursements to institutions grew out of proportion to other Medicaid-funded programs, the population in the nation's institutions declined. In 1972, for example, there were 173,775 individuals residing in public residential facilities, and, by 1982, 10 years later, there were 119,335 individuals living in the facilities (Senate Subcomm. on Health, 1984). By the mid-1980s, it is estimated that there will be only 95,000 people living in institutions (National Association of State Mental Retardation Program Directors, 1980). Thus, the increase in expenditures in the nation's institutions coincided with a decrease in the populations of the institutions. More money was being spent on institutions with fewer residents.

These patterns are confirmed by the National Association of State Mental Retardation Program Directors (NASMRPD) in the publication, *Trends in Capital Expenditures* (1980). Commissioned by the President's Committee on Mental Retardation, the study attempted to determine the effects of the emerging policies of deinstitutionalization on the ICF/MR program. To summarize, the report produced the following findings:

1. States committed most of their capital outlays for institutional renovation and construction as opposed to community facilities.
2. In particular, five states accounted for nearly three fourths of capital construction for institutions.
3. Of those states responding, 67% claimed that capital outlays were intended to make improvements in institutions in order to meet ICF/MR standards.
4. States reported potential losses of millions of dollars if they failed to meet ICF/MR standards.
5. The increase in facility renovation occured simultaneously with a steady decrease in the number of residents in those facilities.

Based on these findings, the NASMRPD study implicates the ICF/MR program in the development of costly state institutions for mentally retarded people. The conclusions acknowledge that the ICF/MR policy provides fiscal incentives to states to invest capital resources in large facilities rather than smaller, community-based facilities, a pattern which continues in spite of a policy context of deinstitutionalization.

Federal funds contribute to the perpetuation of institutional forms of care in other ways as well. Although the movement of people from institutions to community settings has increased markedly over the last decade, the ICF/MR program has not supported this movement. In the period from 1977 to 1984, 82% of the federal funds reimbursed for ICF/MR services went to large institutions; only

18% of the reimbursements went to community services (Braddock, Howes, & Hemp, 1984). In addition, further examination reveals that some states claim community-based ICF/MR status for facilities actually located in clusters or on the grounds of large facilities. In New York State, for example, at least five "small group residences" are located on the grounds of the state's large institutions (New York State Office of Mental Retardation and Developmental Disabilities, 1984). By stretching its definition of small ICF/MR facilities, New York, like other states, projects numbers of small homes that on closer inspection contradict the federal intention.

Furthermore, some states began to reclassify already-existing small group homes as ICFs/MR in order to capture the Medicaid dollars. An internal audit in New York State, for example, revealed that the state was converting former community residences to ICFs/MR without regard for the individual needs of the residents (New York State Commission on Quality of Care, 1980). Furthermore, HCFA reviewed small ICFs/MR in New York State, prompted by concerns for the state's reclassification of residents from community residences to ICFs/MR without substantiating individual needs. In this same report, HCFA described the substandard conditions which existed in these small facilities classified as ICFs/MR (General Accounting Office, 1982). But, despite the inflated and contradictory reports of small ICF/MR facilities, the data indicate that the numbers of small community-based ICFs/MR are growing as institutions depopulate. There *is* a trend toward federally supported small ICFs/MR, but the figures also show that the trend toward federally supported large institutions is much greater (Braddock, Howes, & Hemp, 1984).

The Kennedy Institute, in a study conducted in 1982, documented that, of the total 119,208 individuals served in ICFs/MR in 1981, less than 5% were living in smaller facilities. In addition, the study noted that 86% of those living in ICFs/MR were living in public facilities. Ninety-nine percent of those individuals living in public facilities were in larger ICFs/MR. In summary, the report concluded that, while 53% of the total number of ICFs/MR were smaller, only 4% of ICF/MR residents actually lived in the smaller facilities (Wells & Robertson, 1982).

Thus, despite the evolution of public policy committed to services in least restrictive settings, the federal ICF/MR program clearly supports primarily large, public residential facilities for mentally retarded citizens. Assuming, then, that institutions have been recipients of massive amounts of federal funding, one question remains: how successful has the ICF/MR program been in upgrading conditions in these settings?

Most observers agree that the ICF/MR program has had a positive impact on institutions (Smith, 1984). Buildings have been refurbished, living areas promote greater privacy, safety conditions are improved, and sanitation is better.

However, reports from various observers around the country indicate that the substantive problems linked with public residential facilities for mentally retarded people still exist. Taylor et al. (1981), for example, document deficiencies in institutions in 24 states, deficiencies that often were singled out in federal reports and were still in need of correction. The authors point out that federal surveying agencies typically accept an institution's *plan* for compliance, or permit waivers of certain regulations: ''In every ICF/MR survey report reviewed—in the most comprehensive and the least adequate, surveyors accepted strikingly inadequate and empty plans of correction as complying with the standards'' (Taylor et al., 1981, p. 79).

Other reports document that states fail to meet HHS' published regulations. For example, Congressional hearings and judicial proceedings reveal the inability or unwillingness of states to comply with federal standards. In Connecticut, litigation concerning the Mansfield Training School implicated ICF/MR policies along with the State of Connecticut in providing inadequate care. At a Congressional hearing which explored some of the problems associated with Mansfield, the testimony referred to the failure of the institution to meet the ICF/MR standards. One state official acknowledged his state's inability to bring the institution into compliance, despite the infusion of federal funds and a significant increase in personnel (Senate Subcomm. on the Handicapped, 1981). Independent observers at Mansfield corroborated the evidence that the institution failed to comply with federal standards: there was a paucity of active treatment and a failure to keep adequate records (Carl, 1982; Jones, 1982). In Oklahoma's institutions, others reported similar conditions, although the state received $19 million in federal funds in 1981 to upgrade its institutions through the ICF/MR program (Gallagher, Hanchette, & Sherwood, 1982).

New York State, too, attempted to obtain Medicaid reimbursement for substandard ICF/MR facilities. In 1982, the General Accounting Office informed the Secretary of Health and Human Services that New York State continued to certify institutions as ICFs/MR in spite of the fact that they failed to meet federal standards:

> With few exceptions, the 150 ICFs/MR having 15 clients or fewer initially certified by New York State had major deficiencies. Health Care Financing Administration Region II officials found that, when the State recertified these facilities, 67 still had major deficiencies, according to HCFA. (General Accounting Office, 1982, p. 1)

In an attempt to continue the flow of Medicaid dollars to New York State facilities, HCFA and New York officials reached an agreement:

> So that Federal funds will be disbursed only to New York ICFs/MR which meet program standards for adequate care, HCFA Region II and New York State officials have agreed that in the future ICFs/MR will not receive state Medicaid certification unless they meet at least 13 [of a total] of 116 specific standards. (General Accounting Office, 1982, p. 1)

Thus, the Federal government recognized deficiencies in New York's ICFs/MR, but compromised the standards in order to continue the funding stream. Although such practice was probably common in the period prior to the GAO paper, the Federal government now reports it is taking a tougher position. In her testimony before the Senate Subcommittee on the Handicapped, HHS Secretary Margaret Heckler reported on recently conducted inspections of 17 of the country's ICFs/MR. Her findings include:

> The majority of institutions did not meet requirements concerning provision of active treatment, a requirement added to the law to avoid creating merely another custodial program. . . . Some were not meeting sanitation and physical environment standards. Deficiencies relating to heating, ventilation, cleanliness, and general maintenance were common. Some facilities were seriously deficient in their dispensing and/or monitoring of drugs administered to clients. . . . Many facilities also failed our requirements for food and nutrition services. . . . Some facilities were found to have Life Safety Code . . . deficiencies. . . . *All* of the 17 facilities inspected were substandard. Nine had *major* health and safety deficiencies. (Heckler, 1984, pp. 5–7)

The response of HHS to these deficiencies, as described by Secretary Heckler, was to require state plans for corrections and to intensify surveillance. While this approach to correcting deficiencies is reminiscent of previous federal efforts to gain control of the ICF/MR program, the current plan has not yet been fully implemented.

THE COMMUNITY AND FAMILY LIVING AMENDMENTS

Two problems in the ICF/MR program, as noted previously, provide an impetus for reform: the perpetuation of institutional forms of care, and the persistently substandard conditions in these institutions. Congress responded to these problems with the Community and Family Living Amendments of 1983, S. 2053. Introduced by Senator John H. Chafee of Rhode Island, S. 2053 proposed to amend the Medicaid legislation to redirect reimbursements for services to severely handicapped people from institutional settings to community settings. Major provisions of the bill included the following:

- Within a specified number of years, all large and mid-size ICFs/MR would be required to phase out their federally supported programs.
- The federal government would provide financial incentives for each individual moving from an institution to a community-based residence.
- States could expand eligibility for reimbursed services to individuals who, although not eligible for Medicaid by present standards, incur high personal costs for services.
- Additional Medicaid-reimbursed services could be provided under the bill.

Proponents of the bill supported the Community and Family Living Amendments for reasons of social justice for individuals who live in large mental retardation institutions (Operation Real Rights, 1983). Their position is voiced by Burton Blatt, who wrote:

> We must evacuate the institutions for the mentally retarded. There is not time any more for new task forces and new evaluation teams. The time is long past for such nonsense. Joint accreditation commissions do no good. We need to empty the institutions. The quicker we accomplish that goal the quicker we will be able to repair the damage done to generations of innocent inmates. The quicker we get about converting our ideologies and resources to a community model, the quicker we will learn how to forget what we perpetuated in the name of humanity. (Blatt, Ozolins, & McNally, 1979, p. 143)

Those who supported the Community and Family Living Amendments of 1983 included certain parents, consumer advocates, and service providers who recognized the need for an individualized approach to human services. They advocated for normalized approaches to serving disabled individuals in socially integrated settings. The failures of the nation's institutions, they claimed, created systems of isolation and neglect. The proponents reported that institutional forms of service deny citizens their civil rights and fail to provide needed programs. Furthermore, advocates for the bill cited the cost savings that would accompany services in small community-based settings rather than in institutions (Operation Real Rights, 1983; Senate Subcomm. on Health, 1984).

Opponents of the Community and Family Living Amendments of 1983 included many state and local administrators as well as parents who favored institutional forms of care. These critics maintained that the bill would fail to stem rising Medicaid costs, because of the proposed increase in eligible recipients along with the need for new construction of community-based facilities. Furthermore, opponents claimed that the bill would create management and fiscal difficulties for states which had invested heavily in institutional facilities. Perhaps most important, many of those opposed to the Community and Family Living Amendments of 1983 advocated for the maintenance of institutional care for those individuals most severely impaired (Senate Subcomm. on Health, 1984). Peter Kinzler, representing the Parents' Network of the Northern Virginia Training Center, stated:

> We are generally very satisfied with the care our children are receiving in today's institutions, which more accurately deserve the name "training centers." While we are well aware of the need for more community living arrangements—and fully support additional funds for their creation—we believe they are needed to supplement, not replace, institutional care. What is needed is a continuum of care so that retarded citizens can receive the most appropriate care to fit their needs. (Subcomm. on Health, 1984, p. 270)

The controversies accompanying S. 2053 dramatize the problems inherent in the ICF/MR policy: the tensions between state administrators and federal officials, the dichotomous service systems that continue to support institutions while promoting community-based services, and the seemingly uncontrollable costs of Medicaid programs. The extent of the controversy reflects the bill's radical departure from past Medicaid policies. Indeed, the Community and Family Living Amendments of 1983 attempted to reverse decades of public policy and human service practice which relied extensively on institutional forms of care for developmentally disabled individuals.

In another effort, Senator Chafee introduced a revision of the Community and Family Living Amendments, S. 873, in April 1985. The new bill upholds the intent of S. 2053 to transfer fiscal incentives from institutions to community settings, but its revisions respond to the concerns of S. 2053's critics. Some of the major changes in S. 873 include:

• Provisions to maintain a diminished flow of Medicaid funds to institutional facilities.
• An extension of the time within which states must comply with the legislation.
• A restriction on the previously proposed eligibility criteria for participating individuals.
• The addition of a program which would enable developmentally disabled people to live more independently in community settings.

The first three of these modifications represent concessions to the opponents of S. 2053. The new bill proposes to limit the cost of the program by restricting eligibility, and it maintains federal support for states' institutional services. As though to reinforce the original thrust of the Amendments, and to counter anticipated criticism from original advocates, however, S. 873 adds another program to support independent living. Most likely the combination of revisions will attract supporters for the bill who represent both advocates and critics of S. 2053.

It seems likely that, within the next decade, public policy will break with past practice to the extent that more developmentally disabled citizens will find services in community-based settings rather than in large public institutions. The Community and Family Living Amendments may be the vehicle to reverse decades of health and welfare programs that promote costly systems of institutional care.

REFERENCES

Blatt, B., & Kaplan, F. (1966). *Christmas in purgatory: A photographic essay on mental retardation.* Boston, MA: Allyn & Bacon.

Blatt, B., Ozolins, A., & McNally, J. (1979). *The family papers: A return to purgatory.* New York: Longman.

Bovbjerg, R.R., & Holahan, J. (1982). *Medicaid in the Reagan era: Federal policy and state choices.* Washington, DC: Urban Institute Press.

Braddock, D., Howes, R., & Hemp, R. (1984). *A summary of mental retardation and developmental disabilities expenditures in the United States: FY 1977–1984 (Preliminary working data).*

Public Policy Monograph Series, Monograph #3. Chicago, IL: Institute for the Study of Developmental Disabilities, the University of Illinois at Chicago.

Carl, R.L., Jr. (1982, April 15). *Report to the Connecticut Association for Retarded Citizens on the visit to Mansfield Training School, the Seasons, Mystic Aural, and Seaside.*

Community Mental Health Centers Amendments of 1975, Pub. L. No. 94-63, §301, 89 Stat. 308 (1975) (repealed 1981).

42 Fed. Reg. 28,700-28,704 (1977).

46 Fed. Reg. 48,532-48,542 (1981).

Dept. of Health, Education, and Welfare. Secretary's Comm. on Mental Retardation. (1969). *Mental retardation construction program: Research centers, university-affiliated facilities, community facilities.* Washington, DC: Government Printing Office.

Developmental Disabilities Services and Facilities Construction Amendments of 1970, Pub. L. No. 91-517, 84 Stat. 1316 (1970) (amended 1975).

Developmentally Disabled Assistance and Bill of Rights Act of 1975, 42 U.S.C. § 6001 (1982).

Dixon v. Weinberger, 405 F. Supp. 974 (1975).

Education for All Handicapped Children Act of 1975, 42 U.S.C. § 1401 (1982).

Gallagher, B., Hanchette, J., & Sherwood, C. (1982). *Oklahoma shame: A Gannett News Service special report.* Washington, DC: Gannett News Service.

General Accounting Office. (1970). *Report to the Congress: Questionable claims under the Medicaid program for the care of the mentally retarded in California.* Washington, DC: Government Printing Office.

General Accounting Office. (1977). *Report to the Congress: Returning the disabled to the community: Government needs to do more.* Washington, DC: Government Printing Office.

General Accounting Office. (1982, April 16). Correspondence to the Secretary of the Dept. of Health and Human Services.

Halderman V. Pennhurst State School and Hospital. 446 F. Supp. 1255, (1977).

Heckler, M.M. (1984, July 31). Statement before the Senate Subcomm. on the Handicapped, Comm. on Labor and Human Resources, and the Subcomm. on Labor/HHS/Education Comm. on Appropriations.

Jones, W.E. (1982, April 29). *Report of visit to the Mansfield Training School, November 23 and 24, 1981.*

Kugel, R., & Shearer, A. (Eds.). (1976). *Changing patterns in residential services for the mentally retarded* (rev. ed.). Washington, DC: President's Committee on Mental Retardation.

Markus, G.R. (1972). *Nursing homes and the Congress: A brief history of developments and issues.* Washington, DC: Library of Congress.

Mental Retardation Amendments of 1967, Pub. L. No. 90-170, 81 Stat. 527 (1967) (amended 1975).

Mental Retardation Facilities and Community Mental Health Centers Construction Act Amendments of 1965, Pub. L. No. 89-105, 79 Stat. 427 (1965) (amended 1975).

Mental Retardation Facilities and Community Mental Health Centers Construction Act of 1963, Pub. L. No. 88-164, 89 Stat. 486 (1963) (amended 1975).

National Association of State Mental Retardation Program Directors. (1980). *Trends in capital expenditures for mental retardation facilities: A state-by-state survey.* Arlington, VA: National Association of State Mental Retardation Program Directors.

New York State Association for Retarded Children v. Carey. 393 F. Supp. 715 (E.D.N.Y. 1975).

New York State Commission on Quality of Care. (1980). *Converting community residences into Intermediate Care Facilities for the Mentally Retarded: Some cautionary notes.* Albany, NY: Commission on Quality of Care.

New York State Office of Mental Retardation and Developmental Disabilities. (1984). *OMRDD Program/Capital Plan 1985–1990.* Albany, NY: OMRDD.

Nixon, R.M. (1971, November 16). Statement by the President. *Weekly Compilation of Presidential Documents, 7,* 1530.

Omnibus Reconciliation Act of 1981, § 2176, 42 U.S.C. § 1396a (1982).

Operation Real Rights (1983). *Community living*. Philadelphia, PA: Operation Real Rights.

President's Panel on Mental Retardation. (1962). *A proposed program for national action to combat mental retardation*. Washington, DC: U.S. Government Printing Office.

Rehabilitation Act Amendments of 1974, 29 U.S.C. § 701 (1982).

Rehabilitation Act of 1973, 29 U.S.C. §§ 31-41c, § 701 (1982).

S. 2053, 98th. Cong., 1st Sess., 129 Cong. Rec. S.15480.

S. 873, 99th Cong., 1st Sess., 131 Cong. Rec. S. 3999.

Senate. 117 Cong. Rec. 44,720-44,721 (1971).

S. Rept. 744 to Accompany H.R. 12808, 90th Cong., 1st Sess..

Senate Subcomm. on Health, Comm. on Finance. (1984). *Hearing: Community and Family Living Amendments of 1983*. Washington, DC: U.S. Government Printing Office.

Senate Subcomm. on Health, Comm. on Labor and Public Welfare. (1963). *Hearings on S. 755 and 756*. Washington, DC: U.S. Government Printing Office.

Senate Subcomm. on the Handicapped, Comm. on Labor and Human Resources. (1981). *Hearings on oversight on the effects of deinstitutionalization of mentally retarded citizens*. 97th Cong., 1st Sess..

Smith, M.F. (1984). *S. 2053 and the transfer of mentally retarded persons from larger institutions to small community living arrangements*. Washington, DC: Library of Congress.

Social Security Act, Amendments of 1972, § 210, 42 U.S.C. § 1382 (1982).

Social Security Amendments of 1960, § 601a, 42 U.S.C. §§301-306 (1982).

Social Security Amendments of 1965, §§1901-1905, 42 U.S.C. §§301-306, §§1381-1385 (1982).

Social Security Amendments of 1967, 42 U.S.C. §§ 401-428 (1982).

Social Security Amendments of 1971, 42 U.S.C. § 1396d (1982).

Social Services Amendments of 1974, Pub. L. No. 93-647, § 2, 88 Stat. 2337 (1975) (amended 1980).

Stevens, R., & Stevens, R. (1974). *Welfare medicine in America: A case study of Medicaid*. New York: The Free Press.

Taylor, S.J., Brown, K., McCord, W., Giambetti, A., Searl, S., Mlinarcik, S., Atkinson, T., & Lichter, S. (1981). *Title XIX and deinstitutionalization: The issue for the 80's*. Syracuse, NY: Center on Human Policy.

Turnbull, H.R., III (Ed.). (1981). *The least restrictive alternative: Principles and practices*. Washington, DC: American Association on Mental Deficiency.

Vocational Rehabilitation Act Amendments of 1965, Pub. L. No. 89-333, 79 Stat. 1282 (1965) (repealed 1973).

Wells, A., & Robertson, T.M. (1982). *A census of Intermediate Care Facilities for the Mentally Retarded*. Baltimore, MD: The John F. Kennedy Institute, Johns Hopkins Medical Institutions.

Welsch v. Likens, 373 F. Supp. 487 (1974).

Wyatt v. Stickney, 344 F. Supp. 391 (1972).

8

The Availability Of Community Resources To Group Homes In New York City

Carole R. Gothelf
Hunter College

The data presented in this chapter were part of a larger survey on the availability and use of community resources by small community-based residences for individuals with developmental disabilities in New York City. Variables considered were the availability of needed resources, obstacles to the use of community resources, and satisfaction with the neighborhood in which the residence was located. The Utilization of Community Resources Schedule was given to the residence administrator of each of 155 participating residences in a structured interview. Results indicated that needed resources were generally available for use in the community. Public transportation, neighborhood schools, competitive employment, and private medical and dental care were considered the least available and least adequate resources. The respondents were generally satisfied with their immediate neighborhoods. Characteristics identified as less than satisfactory were: freedom from petty crime, proximity to recreational facilities, and ease of recruiting staff from the neighborhood.

In 1982, there were 58,000 people with developmental disabilities living in approximately 6,300 small group homes in various types of communities—urban, rural, and suburban; large and small—throughout the United States (Jacobson & Janicki, 1982). How well each home satisfies the needs of its residents depends to some degree on the community in which it is located, the characteristics of the residents, and the success of its professional staff in addressing the unique challenges of its particular setting and population (Heal, Sigelman, & Switzky, 1978; Landesman-Dwyer, Schunkit, Keller & Brown, 1977).

An important component of successful community living is a flexible network of community resources consisting of educational, social, vocational, medical, commercial, and recreational resources. Persons with developmental disabilities must use the resources of the general community in ordinary ways: living in ordinary housing, shopping in neighborhood stores, traveling on public transportation, working at meaningful jobs, attending neighborhood schools, and participating in cultural and recreational activities (Close, O'Connor, & Peterson, 1981).

Sherman, Frenkel, and Newman (1984) point out that the use of this network of community resources is a form of participation in the local neighborhood. While the use of community resources does not necessarily involve socialization with other community members, it does demonstrate a community orientation. The degree to which these resources are used by the residents may be seen as a partial measure of integration into the community. Baker, Seltzer, and Seltzer (1977) assert that one of the basic differences between a group home and an institution is that, in a group home, all resources that may be required by the residents should be provided by and used in the community.

Gollay, Freedman, Wyngaarden, and Kurtz (1978) were early investigators of community integration. They assessed the community experiences of deinstitutionalized, mentally retarded individuals, and identified those factors that affected community adjustment. Caregivers' estimates of the resources provided in the community were positively associated with their ratings of higher resident activity level in the community, fewer problems in adjusting to community living, more independence in the living environment, and fewer unmet needs. These findings are supported by Jacobson, Silver, and Schwartz (1982), who found resource provision from within the community to represent a potential source of adaptive change for occupants, as well as by the earlier study of Edgarton and Bercovici (1976), who reported that retarded people who successfully adjusted to the community were those who interacted in their communities in normal ways.

In a national study of group homes, O'Connor (1976) found that 90% of the respondents reported one or more community resources to be unavailable or inadequate, while nearly half reported four or more such resources to be unavailable or inadequate. Resources frequently judged inadequate included transportation, as well as social, educational, and vocational programs. Gollay et al. (1978) also found that many communities provided inadequate choices for competitive employment rather than sheltered employment. In addition, the community did not provide the level or breadth of social and recreational services required to meet the resident's needs. These findings were supported by Bostwick (1980), who, in a subsequent national study, assessed the adequacy of services, and found that services commonly identified as unavailable (transportation, friendship and social programs, and community employment) were those frequently considered to be vital to community integration.

Bostwick (1980) and O'Connor (1976) assert that locally oriented studies are an important aspect of the validation of the principles supporting the deinstitutionalization movement. They may serve to uncover factors that can be modified to help individuals requiring long-term residential support to live more comfortably within the community.

This chapter describes the community-based residences of New York City (by borough), in relation to the availability of needed community resources. It addresses satisfaction with the location of the group homes and discusses issues related to living in New York City.

METHOD

Settings

The unit of analysis of this study is a "center" which is regarded as a community-based residence regardless of type (Intermediate Care Facility for the Mentally Retarded, Supervised Community Residence, Supportive Community Residence) or auspice (state, voluntary). Community-based residences are considered to be homes or apartments located within a neighborhood setting serving 15 or fewer children or adults with developmental disabilities.

At the time this study was conducted, there were 49 state and voluntary agencies sponsoring small community-based residences in New York City (New York City County Service Group, 1983). Forty of these agencies agreed to participate in this study. The 155 cooperating centers, representing 85% of the 183 available centers in New York City located throughout the 5 boroughs, comprised 330 living units, serving 1,569 residents between October 1982 and January 1983. According to the State Operations Manual (1981), a living unit comprises sleeping, dining, and activity areas. Each center represented one or more living units in the same apartment building or neighborhood, supervised by the same administrator.

The nine voluntary agencies that did not participate in the study operated a total of 18 centers. Of the centers operated by the 40 agencies granting permission, six centers did not meet the criteria (two served more than 15 people, and four were located on the grounds of a developmental center). The residence managers of three centers did not wish to participate, and one residence manager was newly hired and did not have the information needed to complete the interview.

Centers began providing residential care as early as 1957, although 86% of the centers initiated their services between 1977 and 1982. Forty-one percent of the participating centers were located in neighborhoods considered by the respondents to be low income. Fifty-three percent and 6%, respectively, were located in neighborhoods considered by the respondents to be middle and high-income. Only 3% of the centers were located in business or commercial areas as opposed to residential neighborhoods.

Most of the residents of the participating centers were male (59%). Twenty-two percent of the residents were 21 years of age or younger, 48% were between the ages of 22 and 35, and the remaining 30% were 36 years or older. The respondents indicated that 21% of the residents were diagnosed as mildly retarded, 23% as moderately retarded, 31% as severely retarded, and 25% as profoundly retarded.

According to the respondents, 62% of the residents lived in a large institutional setting prior to residing in a community group home. Sixty-six percent of the respondents reported that their centers trained the residents to use community resources, and 65% of the centers conducted in-service training programs for staff on the use of community resources.

Instrument and Procedure

The Utilization of Community Resources Schedule (UCRS) is an interview schedule that was constructed for this research. The UCRS has three sections. The first section, Facility Identification, obtains an overall picture of the residence and the community in which it is located. This includes such information as auspice (state or voluntary), type of neighborhood (residential or commercial), degree of satisfaction with the neighborhood, size of facility (number of residents), etc. The second section, Resident Identification, obtains specific information about the residents, such as age, sex, level of retardation, other handicapping conditions, prior residence, and specific characteristics of adaptive behavior. The third section, Program Identification, obtains information about the facility's program, including where the residents work, type of day program, where they obtain medical and dental care, food and clothing, recreation and leisure activities, etc.

The UCRS was designed to secure descriptive data from the residence administrator of each center. According to the literature (Bostwick, 1980; O'Connor, 1976), it is the residence administrator who has the responsibility for working with the residents as well as for locating and using community resources. In addition to any other responsibilities of his or her job, each residence administrator interviewed was responsible for working with the residents to obtain and use community resources.

The UCRS was given to the residence administrator of each center during a structured interview that lasted approximately 25 minutes. Of the 155 interviews conducted, 131 took place at the participating residence. The remaining 24 were conducted over the telephone to accommodate the time constraints of the residence administrators.

RESULTS AND DISCUSSION

Availability of Needed Resources

The centers' need for available community resources was reflected in the percentage of activities identified by the respondents as either needed and available, needed but not available, or not needed. Interviewees were presented with a list of activities identified as typical parts of day-to-day community life. They were asked to indicate whether the activities listed were needed, and, if they were needed, whether they were available for use within the community. Most resources identified as needed were generally available for use within the community (see Table 1).

Table 2 presents the percentage of centers reporting the availability of needed community resources within each of the five boroughs. Resources reported as needed by the respondents were generally available to them regardless of the borough in which they were located.

In contrast to previous studies (Bostwick, 1980; Gollay et al., 1978; O'Connor, 1976), this New York City survey finds that public transportation was reported as needed by and available for 75% of the respondents. One reason for this difference may be that New York City has the most extensive mass transportation system of any American city (First National City Bank, 1972). Further-

Table 1
Percentages of 155 Centers Reporting Community Resources

Resources	Needed and Available	Needed But Not Available	Not Needed
Have paid jobs in the community	5	43	52
Use community parks and playgrounds	89	10	1
Visit museums	86	2	12
Attend concerts	88	6	6
Use community libraries	48	9	43
Participants in community events, e.g., dances	59	28	13
Go to movies or other entertainment in community	90	4	6
Attend sporting events	84	5	11
Visit in the homes of neighbors	37	36	27
Eat in neighborhood restaurants	90	3	7
Shop in neighborhood stores	95	3	2
Use public transportation	75	7	18
Attend religious center	74	10	16
Attend neighborhood school	9	14	77
Keep money in local bank	69	7	24
Use local pharmacy	83	7	10
Use dry cleaners or laundromat	77	3	20
Use local recreational facilities, e.g., bowling alley, skating rink	73	14	13
Use local hair dresser or barber	81	8	11

Note: From "Variations in resource provision forcommunity residences serving persons with developmental disabilities" by C. R. Gothelf, (1985), *Education and Training of the Mentally Retarded, 20*(2). Copyright 1985. Adapted by permission.

more, New York City continued the development of this system while many other cities abandoned urban mass transit in favor of highway construction.

While mass transit can meet the journey-to-work requirements, it has not succeeded in overcoming obstacles to personal mobility (First National City Bank, 1972). Public transportation was reported by the respondents as an available community resource, but one to which the residents have difficulty obtaining access. Problems with public transportation may reinforce dependency on staff, private car services, and agency cars for transportation, and may also limit the opportunity to become more integrated into the mass transportation network and to "rub elbows" with society at large.

Distance from services was cited as an obstacle to the use of community resources, in part due to the structure of the mass transit network, which focuses on getting people into and out of Manhattan (Koller, 1980). The public transportation system serves a limited travel function within the outer boroughs. Multiple fares, lengthy waiting times, and the need to combine subway and bus travel in order to reach one's destination serve to limit the ease of mass transit use.

Employment and education are major ways in which citizens participate in community life and build social ties (Moreau, Novak, & Sigelman, 1980). Educational services within the community were reported as needed and available by 9% of the respondents. In three out of 20 centers located in the Bronx (15%), the respondents expressed need for education in a neighborhood school, and all three respondents reported its availability. In eight of the 37 centers located in Queens (22%), respondents expressed the need for education in a neighborhood school, while only one of the eight (13%) found it available.

These data are interesting in light of the difference in the level of educational attainment reported in recent census data (Bureau of the Census, 1980a). That is, 29% of the Bronx residents over 25 years of age received 8 or fewer years of education, as compared to 21% in Queens, while 20% of the over-25 residents of the Bronx reported 1 or more years of college, as compared to 29% in Queens. The level of educational attainment for persons over 25 years of age is higher, and the availability of needed public education for people living in community group homes is lower, in Queens than in the Bronx. Additional research examining the relationship between the level of educational attainment in a community and the availability of public education to the developmentally disabled living in community group homes may be fruitful.

Only 5% of the respondents stated that paid jobs in the community were needed and available. Respondents from Manhattan centers reported the highest percentage (33%) of jobs available to them within the community, perhaps because Manhattan accounts for about two-thirds of employment city-wide, and more than half of the city's manufacturing jobs (Ehrenhalt, 1982). Bronx respondents stating need for jobs in the community reported none available to them (0%). The Bronx has the lowest median family income and the highest percentage of population on welfare of the five boroughs (Koller, 1980).

Table 2

Percentage of Centers within each Borough Reporting the Availability of Needed Community Resources

Resources	Manhattan			Brooklyn			Bronx			Staten Island			Queens			Total		
	N^n	N^a	%	N^n	N^a	%	N^n	N^a	%	N^n	N^a	%	N^n	N^a	%	N^n	N^a	%
Have paid jobs in the community	12	4	33	31	2	6	8	0	0	7	1	14	16	1	6	74	8	11
Use community parks and playgrounds	27	25	93	56	48	86	20	18	90	14	14	100	36	33	92	153	138	90
Visit museums	22	20	91	52	51	98	17	17	100	14	14	100	32	32	100	137	134	98
Attend concerts	24	21	88	55	52	95	18	18	100	14	14	100	34	31	91	145	136	94
Use community libraries	13	11	85	37	33	89	6	5	83	8	6	75	25	20	80	89	75	84
Participate in community events, e.g., dances	24	18	53	39	74	15	10	67	13	5	38	30	20	67	135	92	68	
Go to movies or other entertainment in community	26	23	88	55	54	98	17	17	100	14	13	93	33	32	97	145	139	96
Attend sport events	24	20	83	49	46	94	18	18	100	14	13	93	33	33	100	138	130	94
Visit in the homes of neighbors	16	7	44	49	26	53	14	8	57	9	3	26	14	54	114	58	51	

	N^n	N^n	%	N^n	N^n	%	N^n	N^n	%	N^n	N^n	%	N^n	N^n	%	N^n	N^n	%
Eat in neighborhood restaurants	24	22	92	55	54	98	18	18	100	14	13	93	34	33	97	145	140	97
Shop in neighborhood stores	25	23	92	56	56	100	20	19	95	14	13	93	36	36	100	151	147	97
Use public transportation	24	23	96	45	42	93	16	14	88	12	11	92	30	26	87	116	91	
Attend religious center	22	18	82	48	46	96	16	12	75	14	10	71	30	28	93	130	114	88
Attend neighborhood school	3	1	33	17	7	41	3	3	100	4	2	50	8	1	13	35	14	40
Keep money in local bank	21	16	76	43	43	100	13	11	87	13	10	77	28	27	96	118	107	91
Use local pharmacy	25	21	84	52	51	98	16	13	81	14	11	79	33	33	100	140	129	92
Use dry cleaners or laundromat	25	22	92	43	43	100	14	14	88	12	11	92	9	29	100	124	119	96
Use local recreational facilities, e.g., bowling alley, skating rink	22	16	73	55	45	82	19	15	79	14	12	86	33	25	76	143	113	79
Use local hair dresser or barber	23	21	91	49	46	94	19	16	84	12	11	92	34	31	91	137	125	91

N^n = Number of centers reporting need for resource.

N^n = Number of centers reporting availablility of needed resource.

% = Percentage of centers reporting availability of needed resource.

Job distribution in New York City has been changing for over two decades (Ehrenhalt, 1982; First National City Bank, 1972). The largest increases were in the professional, managerial, technical, clerical, and sales groups, while the greatest occupational losses have been in unskilled or semi-skilled jobs, due in part to the exodus of industry from New York City (Rogers, 1971). The greatest losses were experienced in the outer boroughs (Gerard, 1982; Hess, 1982), and, since the majority of the citizens with developmental disabilities included in this study (82%) resided in the outer boroughs, the center's location has probably contributed to limited job opportunities.

Respondents were asked to list four available community resources to which the residents had difficulty obtaining access, and four obstacles to the full use of available community resources. The items for each question were combined to reflect similar services or obstacles, and were tallied and rank ordered.

Private medical and dental services were reported by the respondents as available community services to which the residents have difficulty obtaining access. In previous studies (Bostwick, 1980; Gollay et al., 1978; O'Connor, 1976), medical and dental services were identified as the most adequate and

Table 3

Available Community Resources Which Respondents stated
Were Difficult for the Residents to Obtain

Resources	Number of Responses	Percentage
Indoor recreational facilities	35	41
Private medical services	25	29
Private dental services	23	27
Public transportation	20	24
Local stores	12	14
Adult education	10	12
Dental health services	10	12
House of worship	9	11
Swimming	6	7
Hair dresser/barber	4	5
Public education	4	5
Restaurants	4	5
Community events	4	5
Competitive employment	3	34
Movies	3	4
Parks	3	4
Religious education	3	34
After school program	3	4
Senior citizens programs	2	2
Improved housing	1	1

Number of centers responding = 85.

Table 4

Obstacles to the Full Use of Available Community Resources as
Stated by Respondents

Obstacles	Number of Responses	Percentage
Shortage of staff	57	42
Lack of funds	41	30
Behavior of residents	39	28
Safety	33	24
Attitude of community members	29	21
Distance from services	28	20
Poor public transportation	24	18
Residents' level of functioning	18	13
Inaccessible due to wheelchairs	14	10
Agency policies	13	9
Staff lacks skill in utilizing community	12	9
Lack of appropriate programs	11	8
Disinterest or lack of NAC	9	7
Little time for leisure	8	6
Medicaid	8	6
State vouchers	7	5
Residents are cheated by merchants	7	5
Residents don't want to go out	7	5
Inappropriate neighborhood	7	5
Special arrangements	3	2
Residents lack skill in negotiating community	3	2
Unreliable private transportation	2	1
Health of residents	2	1
High functioning don't want to go out with low functioning residents	2	1

Number of centers responding = 137.

available community resources. However, these researchers were not specific as to whether the medical and dental services were provided by private practitioners or by community clinics. The respondents in the present study showed a preference for obtaining medical and dental services for the residents of their facilities from local, private medical practitioners. An obstacle to the full use of available community services was the reported reluctance of private medical practitioners to accept Medicaid. This finding raises the question of the adequacy and willingness of New York City's private service system to augment the developmental disabilities services system (Rowitz, 1981). In order to reach this goal, efforts should be made to provide specialized training and orientation to prospective health providers (Janicki, Castellani, & Lubin, 1982).

Shortage of staff, lack of funds, neighborhood safety, attitudes of community members, and behavior of the residents were reported by the respondents as obstacles to the full use of available community resources. Despite their compliance with ICF/MR guidelines, respondents pointed to the inadequacy of staffing ratios. Absenteeism, or the necessity of dealing with sudden emergencies, may strain the abilities of the staff to conduct the programs in a normalized manner, resulting in a reversion to an institutional model where large numbers of people are shepherded to and from activities.

The economics of providing services to people who are developmentally disabled is intimately tied to the economy of the larger society (Bogdan, Biklen, Blatt, & Taylor, 1981). In an economic environment of scarcity and limited resources, the needs of the people with developmental disabilities must be weighed along with all the other requirements of society. The limits of a service delivery system should not, however, be viewed as an obstacle to normalization but as part of the normalization process: everyone is restricted in his or her opportunities both by the choices of the marketplace and the availability of funds.

Safety when traveling in the community was cited by 24% of the respondents as an obstacle to the use of community resources. Clearly, the overall issue of safety is a problem for everyone living in New York City. According to the United States Federal Bureau of Investigation (1981), New York City was ranked fifth among large cities in total crimes per 100,000 people, and third in terms of violent crimes. However, violent crimes decreased by 5% from 1981 to 1982, and by 9% from 1982 to 1983. ("New York City Finds 9% Drop in Major Crime," 1984).

Negative attitudes of community members towards their neighbors with developmental disabilities have been studied extensively (Gottlieb, 1975; Heal et al., 1978; Kastner, Reppucci, & Pezzoli, 1979; Sigelman, 1976; Walbridge & Conroy, 1981; Walbridge, Whaley, & Conroy, 1981). In the present study, 21% of those responding cited attitudes of community members as an obstacle to the use of community resources. According to Moreau et al. (1980), in order for social integration to occur, members of the community must be willing to accept or at least tolerate people with developmental disablties in their midst. Although this study indicates the presence of stigmatizing attitudes in the community, there is no evidence about the extent to which these attitudes translate into opposition.

Finally, resident behavior was reported by 28% of the respondents as an obstacle to the full use of community resources. Maladaptive behavior, however, was reported as being present in the majority of the residents in only 29% of the centers (Gothelf, 1984), with stereotypic behavior the most prevalent maladaptive behavior. Whereas stereotypic behavior is not harmful to others, it is stigmatizing and may serve as a barrier to the integration of individuals in a community setting.

Satisfaction with the Neighborhood

The residence administrators' satisfaction with the centers' immediate neighborhoods is presented in Table 5. According to Stucky and Newbrough (1981), the quality of the neighborhood can enhance the efforts of an individual with developmental disabilities to function adequately. Throughout the city, the respondents were generally satisfied with their immediate neighborhoods. Consistently identified problems were: freedom from petty crime, proximity to neighborhood recreational facilities, and ease of recruiting professional staff and volunteers from within the neighborhood.

Freedom from petty crime is a problem for everyone in most large urban areas (United States Federal Bureau of Investigation, 1981) and it is reasonable to expect centers in New York City to be confronted by it. In 1982, over 1 million petty crimes were reported in New York City (State Reports of Complaints and Arrests, 1982). The city-wide average is 150 petty crimes per 1,000 persons. However, Manhattan reported twice the city-wide average, with 300 petty crimes per 1,000 residents, while Staten Island reported an average of only 60 petty crimes per 1,000 residents, illustrating the disparate character of the different boroughs.

Proximity to neighborhood recreational facilities may be related to the difficulty in getting to and from the facility. While not all available recreational facilities are in close proximity to the centers, the difficulty in getting to less proximate recreational facilities is compounded by the difficulty in using mass transit. The distance from the bus stop or subway is not the problem, since most community group homes studied by Jacobson (1983) were located less than one fourth mile from a bus stop or subway. The New York City mass transit system is primarily oriented towards transporting people in and out of Manhattan (First National City Bank, 1972). In proportion to its size, Manhattan is the best-served borough in terms of number of subway stations, track route miles and bus routes, while Staten Island is the poorest served (Heller, 1984).

Although the respondents would like to employ neighborhood people, they are unable to satisfy this desire. It may be assumed that familiarity of local staff and volunteers with the residents and the center would have a positive effect on the living environment by creating a liaison between the centers and the neighborhood. The difficulties encountered may be a result of the lack of qualified and interested neighbors, or of the hiring policies of the sponsoring agency, including the methods of recruiting personnel.

The respondents from Manhattan centers expressed the most satisfaction with the proximity of shopping facilities, reflecting the mixed residential and commercial environment of Manhattan. Manhattan also has the most uniformly dense population of the five boroughs, with almost 65,000 people per square mile (Bureau of the Census, 1980b). Jacobson (1983), in his study of group homes, found that, in Manhattan, all examined resources were within one half mile of the facilities.

Respondents from Brooklyn centers were dissatisfied with their immediate

Table 5

Reported Level of Satisfaction* with Immediate Neighborhoods as Locations for Centers, by Borough

Items	Manhattan (N = 28)			Brooklyn (N = 56)			Bronx (N = 20)			Richmond (N = 14)			Queens (N = 37)			Total (N = 155)		
	N	$\bar{X}$	SD	N	$\bar{X}$	SD	N	$\bar{X}$	SD	N	$\bar{X}$	SD	N	$\bar{X}$	SD	N	$\bar{X}$	SD
Flow of traffic in relation to pedestrian safety	28	2.60	1.19	56	2.80	.98	20	2.50	1.05	14	2.07	.91	37	2.00	1.00	155	2.47	1.07
Quality of public services (e.g., garbage removal, street maintenance)	28	2.64	1.33	56	2.58	.94	20	2.60	1.31	14	2.21	.97	37	1.91	1.06	155	2.40	1.13
Freedom from petty crime (e.g., vandalism, graffiti)	28	3.00	1.33	56	3.44	1.24	20	3.00	.79	14	2.71	1.26	37	2.59	1.23	155	3.03	1.24
Freedom from serious crime (e.g., mugging, theft)	28	3.04	1.35	56	3.50	1.14	20	2.90	1.02	14	2.36	1.08	37	2.51	1.26	155	3.00	1.25
Degree of police cooperation with your program	27	2.15	.99	55	2.55	.89	20	2.20	.95	14	2.07	.83	37	2.19	1.22	153	2.20	.99
Proximity of neighborhood shopping facilities	28	2.07	1.36	56	2.30	1.13	20	2.10	.85	14	2.71	1.20	37	2.22	1.08	155	2.25	1.14

Measure	N	Mean	SD	N	Mean	SD	N	Mean	SD	N	Mean	SD	N	Mean	SD	N	Mean	SD
Accessibility of neighborhood shopping facilities	28	2.18	1.28	56	2.46	1.14	20	2.20	.83	14	2.79	1.25	37	2.14	.98	155	2.33	1.11
Proximity of public transportation	28	1.71	1.12	55	2.22	.94	20	1.75	.79	13	2.15	.90	37	2.05	.97	153	2.02	.97
Quality of public transportation	28	2.46	1.20	55	3.13	1.16	20	2.75	1.21	13	3.15	1.07	37	2.51	1.02	153	2.81	1.16
Accessibility to public transportation	28	2.18	1.33	55	2.67	1.12	20	2.15	.99	13	2.62	.77	37	2.70	1.27	153	2.52	1.17
Attitude of neighbors toward your facility	28	2.36	1.03	55	2.33	.82	20	2.15	.87	14	2.36	.84	37	2.62	1.06	154	2.38	.93
Proximity of neighborhood recreational facilities	28	1.75	1.24	56	3.30	1.04	20	2.65	.88	14	3.21	1.25	37	3.00	1.03	155	3.04	1.09
Accessibility of neighborhood recreational facilities	28	2.64	1.25	56	3.14	1.00	20	2.65	.88	14	3.21	1.05	37	2.81	1.10	155	2.92	1.07
Availability of program support or supplemental services (e.g., medical, dental)	28	2.43	.92	55	2.56	1.05	20	2.75	1.21	14	2.57	.65	36	2.14	.87	153	2.46	.99
Ease of recruiting professional staff	18	3.44	1.15	36	3.31	1.12	11	2.45	1.29	7	3.29	.76	29	3.00	1.07	101	3.15	1.13
Ease of recruiting non-professional staff	18	3.44	1.04	40	2.75	.74	13	2.23	1.01	8	3.25	.46	30	2.80	1.00	109	2.85	.94
Ease of recruiting volunteers	15	3.27	1.49	33	3.27	1.04	7	3.43	.53	7	3.14	1.07	26	3.31	1.01	88	3.28	1.07

*Level of satisfaction was computed on a scale from: 1 - Totally satisfactory; 2 - Fairly satisfactory; 3 - Satisfactory

neighborhoods, due to the existence of both petty and serious crime, the poor quality of public transportation, and the distance from, as well as the accessibility of, neighborhood recreational facilities. When compared with other boroughs, Brooklyn respondents were the least satisfied with their neighborhoods. In 1982, approximately 210 crimes per 1,000 persons were committed in Brooklyn (State Reports of Complaints and Arrests, 1982). Although Manhattan had more than twice the number of crimes per person, Manhattan respondents did not report crime as a major area of dissatisfaction, although it was reported as such in Brooklyn. Fifty-three percent of the Brooklyn respondents, more than in any other borough, reported that their centers were located in low income neighborhoods (Gothelf, 1984). The low income neighborhoods in Brooklyn where centers were located were often isolated industrial areas or residential communities with few resources available to them. Although Brooklyn has more miles of subway track routes (84.06) than Manhattan (71.06), Brooklyn is far larger (70 square miles versus 22 square miles for Manhattan), contributing to the isolation of many neighborhoods and the difficulties in obtaining access to various resources within the borough.

The Bronx respondents reported the highest level of satisfaction of all the boroughs, with their proximity to public transportation, ease of recruiting professional and nonprofessional staff, and attitudes of neighbors towards the centers. Although it would seem that the attitudes of neighbors towards the centers would contribute to the ease of recruiting staff from the neighborhood, Bronx respondents were least satisfied with ease of recruiting volunteers from the neighborhood. The discrepancy between the recruiting of paid staff and volunteers may reflect both the agencies' policies towards volunteers and an economy where volunteering in leisure time is not done.

The Staten Island respondents reported the most satisfaction of all the boroughs with the degree of police cooperation with their programs and the freedom from serious crime (only 60 serious crimes per 1,000 people: Statistical Reports of Complaints and Arrests, 1982). The level of satisfaction expressed may be a reflection of Staten Island's suburban qualities. Staten Island has the most suburban character of the boroughs; it has a population density of only 6,000 people per square mile (Bureau of the Census, 1980b). However, it is also possible that the suburban nature and the relative newness of many of the communities on Staten Island may contribute to the items found unsatisfactory: quality of public transportation, proximity to and accessibility of neighborhood recreational facilities, and recruiting paid and volunteer staff.

The Queens respondents were the most satisfied with the quality of public services, freedom from petty crime, accessibility of recreation facilities, flow of traffic in relation to pedestrian safety, and the availability of program support or supplemental services. The respondents in Queens were more generally satisfied with the availability of resources than any other borough. In contrast to many neighborhoods in other boroughs, the Queens neighborhoods in which the centers were located were uniformly stable and cohesive. Until the incorporation of the City of New York in 1898, Queens consisted of independent villages within the four townships of Flushing, New Town, Jamaica, and the Rockaways. These areas still retain their independent nature and neighborhood identity, reflected in the ability to identify the postal areas by the original township names (Oates, 1984).

CONCLUSIONS

Support for community-based programs has been predicated on the belief that resources should be obtained through the community in order to maintain people in the least restrictive settings. While obstacles exist, most resources identified by the respondents as needed were generally available for use within the community. Resources considered to be unavailable (paid jobs in the community and neighborhood schools) were among services considered in the literature (Moreau et al., 1980) to be essential for the successful integration of individuals with developmental disabilities into the community. In addition, respondents expressed dissatisfaction with the apparently available, but not really accessible, resource of public transportation. These concerns remain consistent with the national studies conducted in the late 1970s (Bostwick, 1980; Gollay et al., 1978; O'Connor, 1976). While these problems may be seen as general problems of all urban communities, the developmental disabilities service system must be able to respond to these problems in ways that enable a local community to satisfy its own requirements.

The respondents expressed dissatisfaction with available medical and dental services. This differed from the results reported in the earlier national studies. This may reflect dissatisfaction with the quality of medical and dental services provided to individuals with developmental disabilities in the metropolitan area, or it may reflect a change in the quality of these generic services since the previous national studies.

The need for accessible resources is universal. Variations among neighborhoods exist in all urban areas. The focus of service providers must be on coping with the exigencies of a particular locality in order to achieve the promise of community living. Replication of this study in other communities would provide a perspective on the degree to which the availability of needed community resources, as well as satisfaction with neighborhoods depends on the nature of the community.

REFERENCES

Baker, B.L., Seltzer, G.B., & Seltzer, M.M. (1977). *As close as possible: Community residents for retarded adults.* Boston, MA: Little, Brown & Co.

Bogdan, R., Biklen, D., Blatt, B., & Taylor, S.J. (1981). Handicap prejudice and social research. In

H.G. Haywood & J.R. Newbrough (Eds.), *Living environments for developmentally retarded persons* (pp. 235–247). Baltimore, MD: University Park Press.

Bostwick, D.H. (1980). The utilization of community services by the staff and residents of group homes for the mentally retarded. *Dissertation Abstracts International, 41,* 105A–2054, (University Microfilms International No. AAD80–24842).

Bureau of the Census (1980a). *1980 Census of Population: Social and Economic Characteristics* (New York State Vol. PC 80–1–C34). Washington, DC: Author.

Bureau of the Census (1980b). *1980 Census of Population: Number of Inhabitants* (New York State Vol. PC 80–1–A34). Washington, DC: Author.

Close, D.W., O'Connor, G., & Peterson, S.L. (1981). Utilization of habilitation services by developmentally disabled persons in community residential facilities. In H.C. Haywood & J.R. Newbrough (Eds.), *Living environments for developmentally retarded persons* (pp. 155–167). Baltimore, MD: University Park Press.

Edgerton, R.B. & Bercovici, S.M. (1976). The cloak of competence—years later. *American Journal of Mental Deficiency, 80,* 485–497.

Ehrenhalt, S.M. (1982). The outlook for the New York City labor market. In *Proceedings of the New York City Council on Economic Education: Challenges of the changing economy of New York City. Foundations for growth: Some positives for the city* (pp. 2–33). New York: The New York City Council on Economic Education.

First National City Bank (1972). *Profile of a city.* New York: McGraw Hill.

Gerard, K.N. (1982). New York City's economy: Development policy and outlook. In *Proceedings of the New York City Council on Economic Education: Challenges of the changing economy of New York City. Foundations for growth: Some positives for the city.* (pp. 34–38). New York: The New York City Council on Economic Education.

Gollay, E., Freedman, R., Wyngaarden, M., & Kurtz, N. (1978). *Coming back: The community experiences of deinstitutionalized mentally retarded people.* Cambridge, MA: Abt Books.

Gothelf, C.R. (1984). Availability and use of community resources by small community group homes for the developmentally disabled in New York City. *Dissertation Abstracts International, 45,* 08. (University Microfilms International No. 84–25589).

Gothelf, C.R. (1985). Variations in resource provision for community residences serving persons with developmental disabilities. *Education and Training of the Mentally Retarded. 20,* pp. 130–138.

Gottlieb, J. (1975). Public, peer, and professional attitudes toward mentally retarded persons. In M.J. Begab & S.A. Richardson (Eds.), *The mentally retarded and society: A social science perspective* (pp. 99–125). Baltimore, MD: University Park Press.

Heal, L.W., Sigelman, C.K., & Switzky, H.N. (1978). Research on community residential alternatives for the mentally retarded. In N.R. Ellis (Ed.), *International review of research in mental retardation* (Vol. 9) (pp. 209–249). New York: Academic Press.

Heller, M. (1984, January 16). *Personal communication.* New York: Transit Authority Agency Liaison, (Transit Authority Facts and Figures).

Hess, R.L. (1982). Initiatives for the outer boroughs. In *Proceedings of the New York City Council on Economic Education: Challenges of the changing economy of New York City. Foundations for growth: some positives for the city* (pp. 63–65). New York: The New York City Council on Economic Education.

Jacobson, J.W. (1983, November 23). *Personal communication.* Albany, NY: Bureau of Program Research and Planning, OMRDD, (Demographic Questionnaire data).

Jacobson, J.W., & Janicki, M.P.C. (1982). *Variation in occupant characteristics within a community residence system.* (LARP TR82–12). Albany, NY: New York State Office of Mental Retardation and Developmental Disabilities.

Jacobson, J.W., Silver, E.J., & Schwartz, A.A. (1982). *Service provision in New York's group homes* (LARP TR82–6). Albany, NY: New York State Office of Mental Retardation and Developmental Disabilities.

Janicki, M.P., Castellani, P.J., & Lubin, R.A. (1982). *A perspective on the scope and structure of New York's community residence system* (LARP TR 82–5). Albany, NY: New York State Office of Mental Retardation and Developmental Disabilities.

Kastner, L.S., Repucci, N.D., & Pezzoli, J.J. (1979). Assessing community attitudes toward mentally retarded persons. *American Journal of Mental Deficiency, 84,* 137–144.

Koller, E. (1980). Mainstreaming in turbulent waters. In H.J. Cohen & D. Kligler (Eds.), *Urban community care for the developmentally disabled* (pp. 78–121). Springfield, IL: Charles C. Thomas.

Landesman-Dwyer, J.J., Schunkit, J.J., Keller, L.S., & Brown, T.R. (1977). A prospective study of client needs relative to community placement. In P. Mittler (Ed.). *Research to practice in mental retardation: Vol. 1. Care and intervention* (pp. 337–388). Baltimore, MD: University Park Press.

Moreau, F.A., Novack, A.R., & Sigelman, C.K. (1980). Physical and social integration of developmentally disabled individuals into the community. In A.R. Novack & L.W. Heal (Eds.), *Integration of developmentally disabled individuals into the community.* (pp. 91–103). Baltimore, MD: Paul H. Brooks.

New York City County Service Group. (1983, January). *New York City residential services directory.* New York: Author.

New York City Finds 9% drop in major crime. (1984, March 1). *New York Times,* pp. A1, B10.

Oates, D. (1984), January 16. *Personal communication.* Long Island City, NY: Queens Chamber of Commerce.

O'Connor, G. (1976), *Home is a good place: A national perspective of community residential facilities for developmentally disabled persons* (Monograph No. 2). Washington, DC: American Association on Mental Deficiency.

Rogers, D. (1971). *The management of big cities: Interest groups and social change strategies* Beverly Hills, CA: Sage Publications.

Rowitz, L. (1981). Service paths prior to clinic use by mentally retarded people: A retrospective study. In R.H. Bruininks, C.E. Meyers, B.B. Sigford, & K.C. Lakin (Eds.), *Deinstitutionalization and community adjustment of mentally retarded people.* Washington, DC: American Association on Mental Deficiency.

Sherman, S., Frenkel, E., & Newman, E. (1984). Foster family care for older persons who are mentally retarded. *Mental Retardation, 6,* 302–308.

Sigelman, C.K. (1976). A Machiavelli for planners: Community attitudes and selection of a group home site. *Mental Retardation, 14,* 26–29.

State of New York Office of Mental Retardation and Developmental Disabilities (1982). *Update 83: The 1983–84 update of the comprehensive plan for services to mentally retarded and developmentally disabled persons in New York State.* Albany, NY: Author.

State Operations Manual (1981). *Interpretive guidelines and survey procedures for the application of the standards for intermediate care facilities for the mentally retarded (ICFs/MR) as they apply to facilities serving is or fewer persons* (Section 3152; Appendix J). Washington, DC: Department of Health and Human Services, Health Care Financing Administration.

Statistical reports of complaints and arrests: Crime comparison report. (1982). Crime analysis section, New York City Police Department.

Stucky, P.E. & Newbrough, J.R. (1981). Mental health of retarded persons: Social ecological considerations. In H.C. Haywood & J.R. Newbrough (Eds.), *Living environments for developmentally retarded persons.* (pp. 31–56). Baltimore, MD: University Park Press.

United States Federal Bureau of Investigation. (1981). *Uniform crime reports for the United States.* Washington, DC: U.S. Government Printing Office.

Walbridge, R.H., Conroy, J.W. (1981). *Evaluation of the court-ordered deinstitutionalization of the Pennhurst Center. Changes in community attitudes.* (Contract No. 130–81–0022). Washington, DC: Office of Human Development.

Walbridge, R.H., Whaley, A.M. & Conroy, J.W. (1981). *Evaluation of the court-ordered deinstitutionalization of the Pennhurst Center. Models of change in community attitudes.* (Contract No. 130–81–0022). Washington, DC: Office of Human Development.

9

Families' Perspectives on Respite Services for People with a Developmental Disability*

Bernice Schultz, Betsy Edinger, & Meg Morse
Transitional Living Services of Onondaga County, Inc., Syracuse, New York

Respite services, a vital support to families, provide occasional, short-term substitute care as relief to parents or other family caregivers of developmentally disabled persons living at home. The service may occur in-home or out-of-home, depending on the service model and the arrangement between the family and the sponsoring agency. This paper reports on a study which draws upon the experiences, opinions, and recommendations of families who volunteered to be interviewed on their use of respite. Their perspectives provide insights into the need for respite, the types of respite preferred by families, and the impact of respite as a total family support. Major principles underlying a successful respite program, and factors which contribute to a successful respite system, are presented.

The traditional concept of respite has been that of occasional, short-term care of a person with a disability living at home; the focus has been on relief for the primary caregiver. The service may take place in or out of the home, depending on the arrangement between the sponsoring agency and the family. Within the system which serves people with a developmental disability, respite is slowly being re-defined in the broader context of family supports, focusing attention upon both the needs of the caregiver and the needs of the person with a disability. There is a growing recognition that systematic, planned support plays a major role in the maintenance of natural families (Appolloni & Triest, 1983; Salisbury

---

* Funds for this study were made available through a grant to Transitional Living Services of Onondaga County, Inc. under Chapter 548 of the New York State Laws of 1982, and through a grant to the Syracuse Developmental Services Office from the SSI Disabled Children's Program.

& Griggs, 1983). This enlightened view emphasizes respite as a ''service designed to facilitate the normalization of the families of the developmentally disabled'' (Cohen & Warren, 1985, p. 34).

One reported benefit to the family using respite services is a reduction in tension and stress, including physical strain (Appolloni & Triest, 1983; Joyce, Singer, & Isralowitz, 1983). Cohen states that ''families report their satisfaction with life, hopefulness about the future, and ability to cope with a disabled child in the home improved with the use of respite services'' (1980, p. 65A).

Another benefit which may accrue to a family from planned respite services is the prevention or delay of out-of-home placement (Appolloni & Triest, 1983; Cohen, 1980; Joyce, Singer, & Isralowitz, 1983). Families often ''lack the resources in their own support network to provide them with the assistance they need'' (Edinger, Schultz, & Morse, 1984, p. 24). Some families forfeit vacations, holidays, and family outings, frequently for years on end (Ptacek, et al., 1982). Others lack the time to participate in school and outside activities with their other sons and daughters (Rimstidt, 1983). Social isolation, and the lack of acceptance of the disabled individual in age-appropriate roles, have been reported to increase as the child grows older (Suelzle & Keenan, 1981). These circumstances can erode the well-being of the family caring for a person with a disability.

Respite services provide support by allowing family members to pursue other activities (Joyce, Singer, & Isralowitz, 1983; Salisbury & Griggs, 1983). In addition, opportunities for new experiences provided during respite may help the person with a disability achieve more independence and self-confidence (Appolloni & Triest, 1983), the results of which contribute towards easing the demands placed on caregivers.

A report (New York State Office of Mental Retardation and Developmental Disabilities, 1984) discussing the statewide effort in New York to look at the ways respite is used, states that as many as 80% of all developmentally disabled persons live at home with their families (p. 1). In recognition of the need for respite services among these families, a demonstration project by the Office of Mental Retardation and Developmental Disabilities (OMRDD) was authorized by legislative mandate (Chapter 548 of the Laws of 1982) to consider critical factors related to respite service provision.

In conjunction with this statewide examination of the respite service system, a study (Edinger, Schultz, & Morse, 1984) was conducted using interviews with families in a five-county region of Central New York, to give them a way to voice their opinions about the respite services they use.

The families interviewed used one or more of the following respite services:

1. A sitter-companion service which offers short-term, overnight, and day as well as evening respite care for the child or adult with a disability within his or her own home. Arrangements for respite are made by the parent through direct contact with the agency coordinator, who links the family with an appropriate

sitter-companion. Although a stipend is paid by the family to the sitter, it is modest, and families tend to view the sitters as volunteers. The agency offers a limited number of stipends to assist families for whom payment would pose an undue hardship or for whom service would be inaccessible. This is one of two respite services provided by a parent-organized and-governed nonprofit agency serving families in one of the five counties represented in the study. Eleven of the 39 families interviewed used this service.

2. Homemaker services, a second in-home, short-term respite service, is provided through the sponsorship of a public agency which subcontracts with a variety of vendors in the region. Coordination of this service delivery is the responsibility of the case manager assigned to the family. Homemakers are typically paid at or near minimum wage. There is no charge to the families. Twelve of the 39 families interviewed used this service.

3. An out-of-home respite service, Host Family, matches natural families of sons or daughters with a disability with another (host) family in the community. The purpose of the service is to build new friendships for the person with a disability while the parents are receiving respite. The length of each visit with the host (provider) may vary, and is dependent on the arrangements made by the people involved. Most host families provide service on a voluntary basis, although a stipend is available to cover recreational expenses. This service is the second of two organized and governed by parents. Of the 39 families interviewed, five used this service.

4. Respite provided in community residences is a second out-of-home respite service. It is generally regarded as temporary, overnight care, occurring most often as a weekend visit, although the length of stay may vary according to the family situation and the availability of space in the designated residence. Three agencies in the region provide this type of respite. Two are private, nonprofit agencies; one is a public sector regional provider. The private agencies serve adults only in their respective counties; these agencies charge a fee for service. The public agency serves children and adults at no charge.

Other models of respite available in the five-county region include service at the regional developmental center, in Family Care homes, or by a parent cooperative exchange. One family in the study used respite in a Family Care home. No data were obtained from families using the other services.

Research has been reported (Gardner, 1977; Heal & Daniels, 1978; Intagliata, Willer, & Cooley, 1979; Mayeda & Wai, 1976; Murphy & Datel, 1976) which indicates that persons with developmental disabilities living at home cost society less than those in community residences and state institutions. Our interviews provided an opportunity to learn more about families caring for a person with a developmental disability: the need for respite in people's lives, families' preferences for types of service, and areas of service which need to be developed. Recommendations for the establishment of both a successful respite program and a successful system of respite services will be presented.

Table 1
Family Use of Respite Services

Type of Service	# Using	Average Use per Month
Homemaker	12	13.8 hours
Sitter-companion	11	16.2 hours
Family care	1	—
Host family	5	16.2 hours
Community residence	17	.22.2 hours

METHOD

Sample

Letters were sent to all families using respite services in a five-county region of Central New York by individual agencies providing these services (N = 214). This approach was used to protect the confidentiality of the agencies' clients. Families were asked if they would be willing to be interviewed about their use of respite services. A stamped envelope with our address printed on it was included for families to return a positive response.

Forty-three families volunteered to be a part of the study (20% response), although four families later dropped out due to scheduling problems. The 39 remaining families use one or more of a variety of respite services provided through the public or private sectors (see Table 1). There are other types of respite services available (e.g., respite in the developmental center) that are not included in this study. No families volunteered to be interviewed on these other services. As a further note, prior to the beginning of the interview process, three of the families had stopped using respite service due to the inability of the particular service to meet their needs. They were interviewed and their perspectives and comments are included in the analysis.

Of the 39 families who volunteered to be interviewed, 41 people with disabilities were involved (two families each had two members with a disability); 32 of these families used one type of respite service only. Seven others used more than one service (for example, a community residence and in-home respite).

The family caregiving situations varied: 33 were natural parents; 3 were extended family (e.g., brother, sister, or grandmother); 1 was a foster mother; and 2 were Family/Personal Care providers.[1] Seventy-four percent of these

---

[1] Although we recognize the variety of possible caregivers, for the sake of brevity in this paper, respondents will be referred to as "parents."

families were two-parent households. Thirty-two of the respondents estimated their yearly income: 12 were under $10,000; 4 between $10,000 and $20,000; and 16 over $20,000. Women caregivers were respondents in all instances. Three interviews were conducted with another family member present (e.g., husband or daughter). Their comments were included in the analysis.

The persons with a disability range in age from 1 to 51 years; 85% were under the age of 25. There were 18 males and 23 females, 95% of whom were Caucasian; one person was Asian and one person was Black. The primary disability of 32 people was mental retardation, ranging from mild to profound. Secondary disabilities included cerebral palsy, vision and hearing impairments, and psychiatric disabilities. People with disabilities other than mental retardation included one person described as learning disabled, one person described as having cerebral palsy, two people described as being hearing impaired, two people described as autistic, one person described as having epilepsy and cerebral palsy, and two people described as having medical disabilities.

Design

A Family Interview Guide was developed, with questions based on recommendations derived from preliminary interviews conducted with parents, service providers from private and public agencies, and policy-makers. Based on a semi-structured format, the guide was the main tool used in gathering data.

The interview was divided into five different content areas, involving a total of 44 open-ended questions. The areas were as follows:

1. The Introduction set the stage for the interview. Since most people have not participated in this type of research, it was important to give them a general idea of what to expect and how the information will be used.
2. The Background Information section established a context for understanding the impact of respite services on the particular family. The discussion of such topics as skill level of the disabled member, his or her daily schedule, the family's lifestyle, and their network of supports provided an in-depth look at why they needed respite and how they used it.
3. The section on Respite Services reflected both the issues in the OMRDD guidelines and the interest of local service providers in evaluating the effectiveness of their programs. The emphasis was on process, program, and staffing considerations.
4. The Knowledge of Services Available section addressed the relationship between the awareness of the existence of a service and the use of that service.
5. The Summary provided closure to the interview. The family was encouraged to re-emphasize points they felt were most important. They were also given an opportunity to make recommendations and raise issues not previously covered.

The interviews were done in families' homes or at a place of their convenience over a 4-month period, October 1983 through January 1984. The preference was to tape each session for the purpose of capturing the detail of the conversation; permission was granted to tape the sessions in all but one instance. The length of the sessions varied from 25 minutes to 3 hours, with an average time of 1 hour, 18 minutes.

Two staff members hired through a grant to study respite services conducted the interviews individually. Both people were experienced in interviewing techniques and procedures. Prior to the start of the interviews with families, the interviewers came to an agreement on the purpose and meaning of each question in the Guide.

ANALYSIS

The analysis underwent a series of phases: discovery, coding, refining, and "retrospective examination" (Stainbeck & Stainbeck, 1984; Taylor & Bogdan, 1984). The discovery phase began during the interviewing process. Certain themes came up consistently during the individual interviews. The two researchers compared their interview experiences, keeping notes on consistent themes to be used in the analysis. When the interviews were completed, they were re-read several times, to identify additional possible themes.

Coding categories were developed based on the identified themes. These were reviewed for possible overlap, and collapsed when necessary. Approximately 70 categories and subcategories were used. For example, "the impact of respite" is a major category. It was divided into the subcategories of "effect on the parents," "effect on other family members," and "effect on the individual with a disability." Within these subcategories, further divisions were made as seemed appropriate. The data were then sorted by category, including both positive and negative examples about respite experiences.

The data were reviewed and coding categories refined to fit the data collected, and a determination was made about whether the data supported the previously identified themes. The results presented in this chapter reflect major trends running throughout the interviews. On occasion, a point is included which was made by one or a few parents and which provided a particular insight into a major issue concerning respite.

RESULTS AND DISCUSSION

Why Families Say They Need Respite
Parents needed occasional relief from their caregiving responsibilities, and time to spend with other family members. They also needed time for such everyday occurrences as shopping, appointments, an evening out, or simply time to relax

and "enjoy the peace and quiet." Sometimes, respite was needed on special occasions or in emergency situations. In addition, parents sought the social and learning opportunities that respite services offered their child. They frequently described their children as "lonely," a situation which created pressure on families to fulfill a variety of roles almost entirely by themselves.

Parents did not want to abuse or "take advantage" of the system. They turned to respite services for help because they had few alternatives. They often lacked the resources within their own support network to provide them with the assistance they need. Three-fourths of the parents interviewed relied solely upon their immediate or extended family, where "extended family" was generally taken to mean grandparents. Parents were reluctant to ask grandparents for help because of their age. Siblings were frequently too young to provide care, or they were grown and out of the home. The families who said they relied solely on their immediate or extended family for caregiving support were providing the care for the disabled child themselves. In one-third of these families, one parent had all of the caregiving responsibility; these were either single parents or elderly couples in which one had a severe health problem.

About one-fourth of the parents interviewed said they had resources for care besides their own family. Some asked for help from neighbors and friends, but almost half of these families said they would ask them only in an emergency or on occasion. In some cases, they did not feel comfortable asking for help because they had not had the time or freedom to develop and maintain the kind of relationship which would promote this kind of sharing between families. Some parents we interviewed tried to use existing services such as daycare or nursery schools. Many were refused, or told, after a short time, "We can't handle your child."

All of the parents interviewed believed respite is an important resource for themselves, their family member with a disability, and the entire family.

The Impact of Respite on Families

According to families, respite offers emotional support, a break in the 24-hour ongoing care, a chance to spend quality time with spouses and other children, an opportunity for social and learning experiences for the disabled person, and a chance to develop a supportive relationship with the respite provider.

Without respite support, a majority of the families (56%) we interviewed said they would seriously consider placing their disabled child out-of-home. Even though the parents felt they could give their child the best care, they and other family members reported becoming tired and strained if they did not get an occasional break. Without this break, they felt they were in the position of having to choose "the lesser of two evils," the evils being either institutionalization or a tense, worn-out family. Respite offered them a way to resolve this dilemma. Families felt that the occasional relief respite afforded them reduced their tension and stress, and institutionalization was no longer actively under consideration. "The best thing about respite is that it's made it so I can keep Mary Anne at home."

Respite care was a resource families feel they can trust because the providers are interested in working with disabled individuals and are qualified to do so. The availability of trained respite providers meant that many parents experienced for the first time the feeling that they can trust their son or daughter to someone else's care. "Respite has been helpful just being able to get out. But, it's more having someone there who you can trust . . . you can leave without feeling guilty and you can really relax."

Respite not only offered families a relief in caregiving responsibilities, it also offered a chance to develop and nurture their relationships with each other— parents with their other children, husbands with wives. Parents spoke of how respite "changed our whole outlook and what goes on within the family." One woman who cared for her disabled brother-in-law spent the time during respite with her daughter: "She thinks we are spending too much time with him . . . she says we're not a family anymore. We need the time to spend with her to let her know that it's not that we are abandoning her, but we've had to add this responsibility to our family."

Couples whose son or daughter needed constant supervision often alternate caregiving responsibilities; consequently, they have very little time together. They used respite to have some time alone because they feel "a husband and a wife need to get out once in awhile just to keep their own relationship going."

Respite not only had an impact on individuals but also on the functioning and well-being of the family as a whole. This is of particular importance, because these families get most of their support, both caregiving and emotional, from each other.

Besides helping the family to continue as a supportive group, respite had other "intangible" effects as well. For example, parents said they feel "renewed energy" as a result of getting a break from "the same situation day in and day out." Parents also said "it helps mentally knowing the support is there." Without respite as an option, parents spoke of "feeling totally trapped," because they had few resources for care of their child when they needed it, especially in unexpected or crisis situations. Respite services provided "someplace to turn when there was nothing else."

Many families also developed supportive relationships with the people providing respite. The host family, the in-home sitter, or the staff person in a community residence became a source of encouragement, advice, or just a listening ear. Parents said these providers lifted their spirits by their generosity and willingness to help. "I almost can't believe there are people as good as these. . . They should be saints. . . Respite has given me faith in other people."

Not only did respite care result in the kind of impact on families just described, it also had significant impact on the individual receiving care. It provided disabled people of all ages with valuable opportunities for social and learning experiences. For example, one mother of a 2-year-old boy found it difficult to take him anywhere, because he reacted poorly to changes in the environment. "If we changed the furniture in the livingroom around, he would cry and scream for days." But, after receiving respite from another family, he was exposed to new situations on a regular basis, and his mother was then able to take him many places.

Parents of older children especially appreciated the social and learning opportunities that respite provided. This differs from the statement of Joyce, Singer, and Isralowitz, (1983) in which they discuss the need for respite for older versus younger disabled individuals:

> It is assumed that parents who have had to cope with the care of disabled children/adults for longer periods of time have already developed resources to deal with the care of their child. While respite care services are helpful to these families, they do not have the same impact as they do for families with younger children who have not yet developed stable care options. (p. 155)

These older parents were concerned about their disabled child's future without them; the respite experience helped parents feel they were taking steps toward encouraging their child to be more independent. "I used to worry all the time about what would happen to him when I'm gone. But since I've been in contact with the respite program, I feel he is beginning to adjust to life without me. I am doing something about the future, so I feel much more comfortable."

Respite was often the only opportunity the disabled person had for friendships outside the family. One mother whose daughter used respite in a community residence pointed out, "It's the only place she has where she has her own friends, not mine." Parents felt that these friendships relieved the isolation and boredom their child often felt, and added a necessary dimension to the child's life.

Respite had other effects on the disabled son or daughter which benefited the parents as well. For example, many parents remarked on the positive changes they saw in their child's behavior once they started receiving respite. Much of this improvement in behavior occurred because the respite provider was often a role model whom the disabled child wanted to emulate. Reinforcement of behaviors and skills taught at home also occurred, especially in respite in the community residence, where staff worked with residents on skill development. One mother said, "It's helped my daughter to see I'm not the only one who has these expectations."

Family Preferences for Types of Respite Service

Family preferences for types of respite service were based on data from a section of the interview focused on different models of service and the reasons why parents would or would not use a particular model. There was also an opportunity for parents to offer their ideas on how to provide respite. From this information, we can draw some conclusions about what respite models ought to be developed based on parents' expressed needs.

It is important to keep in mind some of the general comments and attitudes expressed by parents. For example, they had a tendency to prefer a familiar model of service, and were sometimes reluctant to say they would use an option about which they knew little. In addition, some parents found it difficult to talk about choices or preferences, saying, "I just take what I can get."

We asked parents if they would use respite provided (a) in their own home, (b) in someone else's home, (c) in an agency residence, (d) in a developmental center, (e) in a cooperative arrangement (taking turns caring for each other's children), (f) at a special respite center, or (g) in another way. Parents could select as many options as they liked. Some parents chose a variety of models. while others preferred just one.

All 39 people interviewed provided some response to these questions (see Table 2). In some instances, they immediately stated their choice, saying they would not use anything else. Therefore, the interviewer did not ask about other models of service. Depending on the question, the number of responses ranged from 82% to 100% of the entire sample (or 32 to 39 people).

Respite provided in the parents' own home would be used by 62% (or 24 out of 39 people) in our sample. It was the preference of parents whose children were young or had severe physical disabilities. Those parents caring for a physically disabled child often designed their homes for their child's safety and mobility. They were concerned that environments outside their home would not be safe for their child.

There were other factors involved in parents' preference for in-home respite. Many said it was simply "easier" for short-term needs such as time to do errands, keep appointments, or spend an evening out. Some felt they "have more control over the situation" when the respite is given in their own home. Lack of transportation is another factor which made parents prefer in-home rather than out-of-home respite.

Table 2
Family Preferences for Types of Respite Service

Service provided	# Responding	# Responding Positively	% Responding Positively
Parents' own home	39	24	62%
Someone else's home	34	22	65%
Agency residences	36	23	64%
Developmental center	38	3	8%
Cooperative arrangement	33	4	12%
Special respite center	32	17	53%

Families who did not feel in-home respite met their needs were primarily those who relied on other family members for short-term care, or those who used respite as an opportunity for the disabled person to have new experiences and friendships. There were also some families who did not want "strangers coming into my home."

Respite provided in someone else's home would also be used by a majority of families (65% of those who responded to the question, or 22 out of 34 people). These parents liked the benefits of the new friendships and learning opportunities that out-of-home respite offered their child. They also liked using the "natural" environment of a home which makes respite "seem more like a visit." In addition, there were parents whose choice of respite services was not made in order to enable them to go out, but who preferred to stay home and get things done around the house or relax for a few hours.

Some parents did not choose this option. Parents of young children or those with severe physical disabilities did not feel comfortable taking their child out of their home for care. Lack of transportation meant that some people could not get to out-of-home respite. There were also two attitudinal barriers which prevented some parents from choosing this option. Some said they would feel guilty asking for help from another family, "like I was sending him to somebody else, because I couldn't handle it. It just doesn't sound right." Others said it was hard "to really know" and "trust" other people.

Respite provided in a community residence would also be used by a majority of families (64% of those who responded to the question, or 23 out of 36 people). Some of the reasons why they liked this option were similar to the previous model discussed: the disabled child had the opportunity for new experiences and friendships, and parents preferred the small, "home-like" environment for respite. In addition, some parents considered the group situation in the community residence an important learning experience. Other factors involved in parents' preferences were the presence of professional staff and the hope that "my son might be able to live there rather than in an institution when we're gone."

The families who would not choose this option included those with young children or children whose needs required a lot of attention and special equipment. "It's just not set up to handle a person with severe medical needs," said one mother.

In addition, some parents said they would worry about the adjustment of their child. Given the high demand for respite in the community residence, other parents were reluctant to request this service. Parents of children whose disability was not mental retardation (e.g., who have cerebral palsy or a hearing impairment) did not feel this was an appropriate option for them. A small percentage of families had never heard of this type of respite, and said they would need to "know more about it" before saying they would consider it.

Respite provided in a developmental center was not considered an option by most families. Only 3 out of 28 families (or 8%) said they would use it, and two of these said they would "only when we have no other choice." "It's better than sticking him out in the snow. . . There are things you do (in an emergency) you wouldn't do otherwise." Their comments reflected what one mother said: "It's really not a place for people to be." In particular, they cited "the cold and institutional environment." Some said that the thought of using respite there "goes against a parent's instincts." Most parents questioned how "so many people in one place can be taken care of properly." Several parents used respite there in the past, but would not use it again. One parent reported that her child was physically harmed while there. The other two were described by their parents as being "generally traumatized" by the experience.

Respite provided by cooperative exchange was also not considered an option by most families. There were only 4 out of 33 families (12% of those who responded to the question) who said it would be one of their choices. As a matter of interest, 3 of these families were single-parent households. These parents thought that this arrangement would offer "shared experiences," not only for their child, but for themselves: "Just to know somebody else has got the same problem; a chance to exchange ideas on how to cope and expand your own support network." Futhermore, they felt that other families with a disabled family member would be "sensitive" and "understanding" of their child. And they would like to do something in return for the respite they received.

However, most families did not see this as an alternative: "We need respite, not more work." There were a variety of reasons why parents found a cooperative arrangement difficult. Some, who were caring for an individual with more complex needs, did not see how they could possibly care for someone else. Older parents said they "simply don't have the energy anymore." A few said they would worry about having the responsibility for someone else. People living in rural areas thought transportation would be too difficult to arrange.

Respite provided at a "special respite center" was emphasized by over half of the parents (53% of those who responded to the question, or 17 out of 32 people) as an important option to develop. This number might have been larger, but a number of people (16%) said they "would have to see it first." Likewise, some of the people who said they would use it qualified their answers with the statement: "If it were like a group home; small and home-like."

Parents liked this option for many of the same reasons they would choose respite in a community residence (e.g., the learning and social experiences it could offer). The main difference they saw was that it would be more accessible than a community residence because it would be used exclusively for respite.

Other suggestions parents had for respite were: identifying existing daycare, nursery, and recreation programs that could provide respite with the help of appropriately trained staff; letting families choose their own respite providers and reimburse the cost through Medicaid or other funding; and having someone live in and help care in exchange for room and board.

Areas of Service Which Need to be Developed

This section reflects the gaps in the service system which parents said are of a priority nature and are critically in need of development.

The needs parents expressed, ordered from the greatest (20) to the least (5) number of responses, are as follows:

Expansion of respite services parents are currently using. Many parents would rather have more care from the service they were already receiving than become involved in a new respite service. They would like to be able to "count on" their present service for a certain amount of time on a regular basis.

Development of options to be used in an emergency or on short notice. Most of the families felt they had nowhere to turn in an emergency or on short notice. While each of the existing services responded to this need on occasion, families who received emergency respite realized it was not available systemically, and considered themselves "lucky" to have received it.

Development of options to provide respite for extended periods of time. A vacation was not considered a possibility for many families caring for a person with a disability. They were reluctant to request this amount of time needed from volunteers; those who use homemaker services could not "save up" their time in order to take a vacation. Even if parents could do this, they worried, "What would we do for the rest of the year?" Extended respite in a community residence was limited, because of the already high demand for the few available beds. In addition, respite in a community residence was often unavailable to disabled people, because they were not in a day program during the week.

The developmental center was the only remaining option parents were aware of, and the majority of people interviewed did not feel comfortable using it, even for short periods of time.

Development of services for after school, workshop, and day training/day activity hours. This recommendation was of particular importance to mothers who had difficulty finding someone to care for their disabled child on a regular basis. Some mothers said that the lack of this kind of support discouraged them from seeking employment.

Development of respite as a part of other community services. Parents suggested the expansion of generic services in parks and recreation programs, teen centers, nursery schools, and other community facilities for the provision of respite. One possibility for expansion, they suggested, was to support a particular program with staff who were trained to work with disabled people. They preferred this type of respite because they were looking for ways to provide their child with social and recreational experiences outside both the family circle and the programs that were established for disabled people only.

CONCLUSIONS

We have learned a great deal from the families who took the time to tell us about themselves and the services they used. As a result of the discussions with the families, we offer the following recommendations for the establishment of both a successful respite program and a successful system of respite services.

Principles Underlying a Successful Respite Program

Create a personal service.   Parents often find it difficult to entrust the care of their child to someone else. Having a responsive and personal service can alleviate many of their concerns. One fundamental element in the design of a more responsive service is the establishment of a coordinator of service who can play a pivotal role in developing familiarity with families and providers. Parents need to talk directly with someone who has the authority to make arrangements or to answer questions about the service.

Ask for a minimum of paperwork to be completed.   Forms should be designed to yield information relevant only to the provision of respite. Assistance in completing the forms would help families when needed.

Develop respite as a separate service while maintaining a link to the larger system.   Some parents will not consider asking for help from the social service system despite their need for respite. Others feel that their respite needs are not given priority attention. Parents in our study liked the uniqueness of the agencies that were designed to offer respite only.

Incorporate mechanisms for parental involvement into the design of a system.   Direct parent involvement encourages parents to exercise control over the services they use. Their involvement adds a valuable perspective on what works and what does not. There are several ways a service can foster parental empowerment: (a) having a coordinator allows parents to negotiate changes directly and choose staff they feel best meet their needs, (b) establishing a parent board or including parents on existing boards makes them a part of the decision-making process, (c) and setting aside time for them to orient providers to the specific person and situation enables parents to develop more confidence in the quality of care. Support groups and get-togethers at picnics or parties also help parents become familiar and involved with a service.

Introduce families to the program, possibly with a dinner or overnight, if it is a community residence. This is another way for parents to become familiar with the service and to establish a relationship with the people who offer it. Parents point to an orientation as one of the important ways to relieve some of their concerns about leaving their son or daughter.

Recruit and maintain quality providers. Direct care staff have a great deal of influence on how a family feels about a service. Parents consistently said that certain qualities in a provider are more important than formal training. It is essential to possess such qualities as "common sense" and "an interest in working with people who have a disability." Most parents believed that a person who had experience or exposure to disabled people is more likely to be sensitive and comfortable with their child.

Parents caring for severely disabled persons often want a provider trained in lifting, feeding, nonverbal communication, giving medication, and handling seizure episodes. Some parents prefer professional staff because they can offer assistance in developing their child's skills and behaviors.

The qualities and skills mentioned are not necessarily mutually exclusive. However, a provider who does not have formal training can be just as successful as one who does. Services require people with a variety of skills and qualities in order to meet the needs of each family.

Besides these qualities and skills, there are other considerations relevant to staffing issues. In general, parents prefer having the same provider for each respite visit. They feel it is important for staff to get acquainted with their child and learn about his or her needs. It is also important that a program offer support to the direct care staff. This might be accomplished by offering continued training, involving them in policy and service decisions, providing a mechanism for feedback and support (for example, through team meetings or frequent contact with the coordinator), and recognizing the importance of their role through such mechanisms as pay increases or formalizing their role as a respite provider.

Consider environmental factors on two levels. First, parents want respite options which offer the most "natural" surroundings and "normal experiences" for their children. Since they live in the community, they want respite to take place in the community. Second, when respite is given in a place other than the parents' own homes, it must be accessible and properly equipped for the disabled person's safety and comfort.

Develop a plan to make the service accessible to families. Families need to know a service exists before they can use it. Many families in our study were unaware of most respite options available. Since respite is considered a relatively new service, planned and extensive public relations on an ongoing basis will bring that information to the community.

Sufficient resources are required to meet the demand for service. This includes planned respite on a regular basis and the ability to respond to emergency or crisis situations.

It is advantageous that a service be conveniently located in close proximity to the families who want to use it. If it is not located conveniently, assistance should be given to help families arrange for transportation.

Guidelines for using a service should be thoroughly explained to parents. Parents in our study were often unclear about how much service they might have or in what way they could use it. Frequently, they worried about "overusing" a service; thus, they did not request it as much as they may have needed it.

Cost of service prevents some people from using it. A sliding fee scale, or similar mechanism, would assist families who need help paying for service. There are also families who can afford to pay a reasonable amount for service and would like to do so. This factor can be taken into consideration when developing a fee schedule.

Incorporate flexibility into the program design to respond to the differing and changing needs of families. Depending on a particular family's support network and lifestyle, its need for service may differ from others. This need may be more or less compelling at any given point in time.

It is crucial that a service be responsive to changing circumstances. Having sufficient resources (for example, staff, space, or funds), and a coordinator who is aware of each family's needs, are ways to make a service more flexible. Furthermore, respite provision seems to be hindered when there are "a lot of rules and regulations." Strict allowance of hours which have to be used within a narrow time frame often forces families to request service for a time that is less useful to them than it might be at another time. The result is that families then find they do not have the hours if something occurs later, when they do need respite.

Principles Underlying a Successful System of Respite Services

Establish a central coordinating mechanism for referral and program development. A person or team in charge of coordinating and developing a variety of respite options would enhance the current system. Additionally, a forum established for all agencies to work together would increase their own understanding of the nature of the various options available. Families, consumers, and direct care staff, as well as agency representatives, are important to include because of the different perspectives they offer. The forum could be a resource for encouraging and assisting the development of new programs. It would also provide an opportunity for sharing new ideas and for mutual problem-solving.

Develop a continuum of respite options to meet the needs of every age level and disability. While respite is a vital caregiving support, it also offers the person with a disability unique social and developmental opportunities. A range of respite options, including in-home and out-of-home services, is necessary to meet the differing needs of families and their children with a disability. A system of services must also take into consideration the changing circumstances within a particular family. For example, most parents prefer in-home respite when their children are younger; they begin to seek out-of-home opportunities for them as their children grow older. As parents' support networks change, they may require more or less respite. Parents of older children need ways to help their children make the transition into more independent living situations. These needs must be considered and addressed within the system.

Public and private agencies must be given incentives for developing and providing services. It is important to support existing, successful models of service and to encourage the implementation of new alternatives such as emergency and crisis respite. It is also important to keep in mind that parents want local, community-based models of service.

Provide a stable funding source for each respite option. There were cases we studied where parents found they could not use a service on a consistent basis, because the availability of its funding was unpredictable. Thus, they were reluctant to depend on the service for ongoing support. In short, parents need a service they can rely on over time. Funding respite is a way to encourage the private sector to develop more options. A financial commitment over the long term allows for such development.

Coordinate public relations efforts to inform families of the various respite options. Families feel it is important that information about respite services be placed in schools, at work and day programs, in clinics, and in doctors' offices.

Design and support a transportation network. Lack of transportation affects people's choice and use of a service. It is a particular problem for families who live in rural areas, for families who do not have their own means of transportation, for families whose son or daughter is difficult to transport, or for those families who have to travel a long distance to receive respite (some families travel 40 miles per round trip). Methods and ways to share resources need to be developed to assist families in this area.

This paper has attempted to shed some light on the perceptions and feelings of parents on their use of respite services. There are still many unanswered questions about service provision which require further study. For example, would the creation of a statewide system of respite services be useful? Could it be maintained? Should parents receive direct subsidy to make their own respite arrangements? Are certain models of respite care more cost-effective than others? How can the service delivery system identify and assist families who are presently receiving no respite services? The answers to these and other questions must come from consumers, direct care staff, administrators, policy-makers, and the unserved population.

REFERENCES

Apolloni, A.H., & Triest, G. (1983). Respite services in California. *Mental Retardation, 21,* 240–243.

Cohen, S. (1980). *Demonstrating model continua of respite care and parent training for families of persons with developmental disabilities.* Unpublished manuscript. The Special Education Development Center, New York, New York.

Cohen, S., & Warren, R.D. (1985). *Respite care.* New York: Pro-Ed, Inc.

Edinger, B., Schultz, B., & Morse, M. (1983). *A research plan to study respite services for people with a developmental disability.* Unpublished manuscript. Respite Project of Central New York, Syracuse, New York.

Edinger, B., Schultz, B., & Morse, M. (1984). *Family interviews.* Unpublished manuscript. Respite Project of Central New York, Syracuse, New York.

Gardner, J.M. (1977). Community residential alternatives for the developmentally disabled. *Mental Retardation, 15,* 3–8.

Heal, I.W., & Daniels, B.S. (1978, May). *A cost effectiveness analysis of residential facilities for selected developmentally disabled citizens of three northern Wisconsin counties.* Paper presented at the 102nd Annual Meeting of the American Association on Mental Deficiency, Denver, Colorado.

Intagliata, J.C., Willer, B.A., & Cooley, F.B. (1979). Cost comparison of institutional and community-based alternatives for mentally retarded persons. *Mental Retardation, 17,* 154–156.

Joyce, K., Singer, M., & Isralowitz, R. (1983). Impact of respite care on parents' perception of quality of life. *Mental Retardation, 24,* 153–156.

Mayeda, T., & Wai, F. (1976). *The cost of long-term developmental disability care.* Washington, DC: Department of Health, Education and Welfare.

Murphy, J.G., & Datel, W.E. (1976). A cost-benefit analysis of community versus institutional living. *Hospital and Community Psychiatry, 27,* 165–170.

New York State Office of Mental Retardation and Developmental Disabilities. (1982). *Respite demonstration projects: requests for proposals.* Albany, NY: Author.

New York State Office of Mental Retardation and Developmental Disabilities. (1984). *Respite services for developmentally disabled individuals in New York State.* Albany, NY: Author.

Ptacek, L.J., Sommers, P.A., Graves, J., Lukowicz, P., Keena, E., Haglund, J., & Nycz, G. (1982). Respite care for families of children with severe handicaps: an evaluation study of parent satisfaction. *Journal of Community Psychology, 10,* 222–227.

Rimstidt, S. (1983, December). When respite care does not exist. *The Exceptional Parent,* 45–48.

Salisbury, C., & Griggs, P.A. (1983). Developing respite care services for families of handicapped persons. *The Journal of The Association for Persons With Severe Handicaps, 8,* 50–57.

Stainbeck, S., & Stainbeck, W. (1984). Methodological considerations in qualitative research. *The Journal of The Association for Persons With Severe Handicaps, 9,* 296–303.

Suelzle, M., & Keenan, V. (1981). Changes in family support networks over the life cycle of mentally retarded persons. *American Journal of Mental Deficiency, 86,* 267–274.

Taylor, S., & Bogdan, R., (1984). *Introduction to qualitative research methods.* New York: John Wiley & Sons.

10

The Community Resources Training Program: A Collaborative Program Between the University of North Carolina at Charlotte and Goodwill Industries of the Southern Piedmont

Patricia K. Keul, Fred Spooner, Teresa A. Grossi, and Harold W. Heller*

University of North Carolina at Charlotte

Although many people with mental retardation have been released from institutional placement nationally, community resources have not kept pace with the needs of this deinstitutionalized population. The Charlotte-Mecklenburg metropolitan area in North Carolina is typical of an urban area in which community services have been sorely lacking for people with mental retardation. The Community Resources Training Program is a newly developed service program which assists in instructing people with mental retardation to access their community through (a) teaching independent living skills, (b) involving parents and family members in the instructional program, and (c) training people with mental retardation to use community resources. In this chapter, community funding and administration of the program, population served, training philosophy and instructional methods, and recommendations for replication are discussed.

During the past decade, there has been an extension of the limits to community integration for people who are mentally retarded. Within this short time, the

---

* The authors would like to acknowledge the assistance of Phyllis Griffin, Pat Geiser, Kelli Wilson, and Laura Bushnell in the preparation of this manuscript. Dr. David W. Test is also thanked for editing a previous version of this manuscript. Patricia Keul was Project Coordinator of the CRT Program in 1981–1983 and currently serves as a consultant from UNCC to the project at GWISP, Teresa Grossi is the present coordinator of the CRT program at GWISP, Fred Spooner has a secondary affiliation with the Human Development Research and Training Institute at Western Carolina Center, Morganton, NC, and Harold W. Heller is Dean of the College of Education and Allied Professions. A copy of the Assessment of Independent Living Skills (AILS) instrument is available from the first author upon request.

deinstitutionalization movement and the development of community services have resulted in the return of approximately 60,000 people with mental retardation from institutions to their communities in the United States (Conroy & Bradley, 1985). The principle of normalization (Wolfensberger, 1972) has had a profound impact on several areas of service, including: (a) relocating services to the community, (b) reducing the number of individuals served by large segregated programs and increasing the number served by smaller and more appropriately staffed community programs, (c) integrating individuals physically into the community and thus increasing the probability of their social interaction with the normal population, (d) developing programs that encourage independence and autonomy, and (e) hiring trained and competent staff to implement appropriate programs (Laurendeau, Blanchet, & Coshan, 1984). Similarly, innovative vocational programs, such as work stations in industry and supported employment models (Goodall, Wehman, & Cleveland, 1983; Wehman, Hill, Goodall, Cleveland, Brooke, & Pentecost, 1982) have demonstrated that people with severe mental retardation can secure and maintain competitive employment for nontrivial wages in integrated work sites (Bellamy, Sheehan, Horner, & Boles, 1980; Wehman, 1981).

Despite these advances, the majority of adults with mental retardation continue to lead a life-style that is socially segregated; their access to the community is restricted and their opportunities to exercise independence and self-initiative are severely limited. People who work in segregated, adult-service programs for handicapped individuals and live in restricted, nonintegrated residences within the community cannot be said to have achieved community integration. Although these people reside and work in the community, the programs with which they are affiliated (e.g., group homes and sheltered workshops) have a tendency to segregate them from the population at large (Crapps, Langone, & Swaim, 1985; Halpren, Close, & Nelson, 1985).

While the policy of deinstitutionalization commands remarkable support among professionals and lay people, field experience has shown that community resources have not kept pace with the needs of the deinstitutionalized population. Because there has been little research on the variables which affect community integration, our lack of readiness to provide training and other services within the community may be attributed to a lack of information (Gollay, 1977).

One way of achieving integration is through direct interaction of the individual with people and services in his or her community. In addition, the identification of social and family support systems is essential in achieving integration. Generally, people having social and family support systems make easier transitions to the community than people without such support systems. This finding is corroborated by Edgerton and Bercovici (1976) and Kerman and Koegel (1980), who found social support systems to be an important factor in the success of community integration and competitive employment.

The environment has a substantial influence on the individual's efforts to integrate with his or her community (DeJung & Hughes, 1980). By reducing certain physical, social, and psychological barriers, many of the limitations experienced by individuals with mental retardation can be reduced. Lewis and Lewis (1977) noted several reasons for controlling variables in the environment: (a) negative aspects of the community environment may be detrimental to the growth and development of individuals, (b) positive aspects of the community environment can support individual growth and development, and (c) professionals are helpless in their attempts to serve individuals when environmental factors do not change to keep pace with individual change.

Another factor important in achieving community integration is the ability of the individual to function within the community. Schalock and Harper (1978) discovered that deficits in money management, apartment cleanliness, social behavior, and meal preparation were associated with the return of residents from community programs to more restrictive institutional settings. A 5-year follow-up of the deinstitutionalized individuals from the Schalock and Harper study revealed that the skill areas of personal maintenance, communication, community utilization, clothing care and use, and food preparation were more important to successful independent living than those previously thought to be good predictors (Schalock, Harper, & Carver, 1981) such as tested intelligence and functional academics (money, banking, and time concepts).

PROGRAM SETTING

The Charlotte-Mecklenburg metropolitan area (population 1.03 million for a seven county region [Clay, Orr, & Stuart, 1982]) is typical of many communities in its range of services for adults with mental retardation. The predominate adult services are sheltered workshops or adult developmental activity programs (ADAP), both of which are segregated from the general labor force. In 1983, Goodwill Industries of the Southern Piedmont (GWISP) initiated the first work station in industry—a janitorial crew of handicapped workers—and in July, 1984, a small supported-employment program was begun at GWISP. Other than these two employment programs, independent community integration is not a focus of the adult services in the Charlotte-Mecklenburg community. While 11 group home residences for people with mental retardation serve approximately 60 clients, the waiting list for these services contains close to 200 names. The ADAPs and sheltered workshops all have large waiting lists of people in need of some adult services.

Clearly, there was a need to improve the range of services to individuals with retardation who reside in the community. In October, 1981, the College of Education and Allied Professions at the University of North Carolina at Charlotte (UNCC) responded to this need by initiating the Community Resources Training (CRT) Program, a service delivery model designed to teach independent living skills through the use of community resources. During the past 3 years, 141 adults with mental retardation were served by the program. The program was federally funded its first year, and acquired state funding its second year of operation.[1]

The Community Resources Training program entered its third year of service delivery in 1983, and came under the administration of GWISP of Charlotte, N. C. in January, 1984, with funding from the Mecklenburg County Commission and United Way. The CRT program is now administered by GWISP, with consultative and research assistance provided by UNCC.

PROGRAM MODEL

CRT is a service delivery model which addresses the problem of community integration of adults with mental retardation through a three part process: (a) training independent living skills, (b) involving parents and family members in the instructional program, and (c) teaching people with mental retardation to use community resources. The project also provides case management services to maintain contact with the client after he or she has completed the CRT program.

Without the CRT program's intervention, many people with moderate and severe retardation would not receive vocational training from GWISP, because GWISP has traditionally focused on training higher functioning people. Based upon individual needs, some clients are enrolled in the CRT program as a prerequisite to vocational training, while others receive these services in conjunction with vocational training or concurrently with their placement in competitive employment through GWISP'S supported employment program.

The CRT program has met the overwhelming need for a service that would help adults with mental retardation to gain access to the community. The absence of such a service often meant that these adults would return to an institutional environment or live at poverty level incomes due to their lack of skills in coping with their community. This chapter will provide demographic data on the population which the program has served, describe the CRT program's training philosophy and instructional methods, and give recommendations for the replication of the program in other locations.

POPULATION SERVED

The population which the CRT program served over the past 3 years is comprised of 141 adults (ages 18 and older) who reside in the Charlotte-Mecklenburg metropolitan area. The client population included slightly more females (79) than males (62), and there were considerably more white (91) than black (50) clients served by the program. The disability range of the population was from mild to

---

[1] Project LEAR (Leisure Education and Recreation) was one of the original 25 special recreation programs funded through Title III, Section 316, by the Office of Special Education, Rehabilitative Services Administration in 1981, Harold W. Heller, Principal Investigator.

severe, with slightly more individuals with mild mental retardation (52) receiving service than those with moderate (34) or severe (49) retardation. Six clients manifested a dual-diagnosis, mental retardation and mental illness. These disability levels were established with the American Association on Mental Deficiency's guidelines (Grossman, 1977).

The CRT program served clients from high, middle, and low income brackets; however, the largest proportion of clients were those living at or near the poverty level. Thirty-three percent of the client population had annual incomes of under $5,000, while an additional 20% had annual incomes under $10,000. At these income levels, CRT clients and their families can only provide the essentials of daily life (i.e., food, clothing, and shelter) and are unable to pay for necessary education and vocational programs.

Thirty-two CRT clients had a history of prior institutionalization. In many cases, it was impossible to determine the number of years spent in an institution, because of the advanced age of many of these clients. Family members were often absent or elderly and were unable to supply information on the length of time the client had resided in an institutional setting. Approximately 80% of the clients who were deinstitutionalized received no services from the community prior to their referral to the CRT program.

The majority of client referrals to the CRT program came from human service agencies within the municipal locality (e.g., Center for Human Development, Association for Retarded Citizens, Area Mental Health Authority). The largest CRT population group (67 clients) was between the ages of 18 to 25 years. Younger clients and their families were more frequent users of the human service agencies, in part because of the access these clients had to public education, which led them to seek adult services upon graduation from special education. Among the 74 clients between the ages of 26 to 55 years; educational backgrounds often reflected a lack of special education services because of the limited availability of such services during childhood. Of these 74 clients, 34 were aged 26 to 35 years, 20 were aged 36 to 45 years, 11 were aged 46 to 55 years, and 9 were over 56 years of age.

A particular focus of the CRT service system is to assist individuals who, prior to enrollment in the CRT program, received no other instructional services from the community; that is, people who were "lost" to community agencies. Forty-two CRT clients had received no other agency services prior to enrollment in the CRT program. This unserved client population was older, ranging in age from 35 to 65 years, and their families were unaware of available services in the community for their family member with retardation. These families, for the most part, did not know where or how to obtain services for their relatives, and often were unaware of their relative's need for services.

Clients resided in one of five living arrangements in the community: (a) living with family members, (b) living in nursing or rest homes, (c) living in group homes, (d) living alone, or (e) married and living with their spouses. Ninety-two (65%) of the clients were living with family members, a living arrangement which often placed a large burden on elderly parents or adult siblings of the client. For this reason, the CRT program received most of its referrals from agencies and families who were not able to secure a group home residence for these clients. Only 15 (11%) of the clients served by the CRT program resided in group homes. Two married clients were served by the CRT program. In one case, the spouse was not mentally retarded, while, in the other case, the spouse functioned in the mildly retarded range. Spouses provided assistance to their mates with mental retardation in achieving their CRT goals. Thirteen clients lived alone.

Among the 19 clients who resided in nursing or rest homes, 10 clients were under the age of 55 years. These clients were placed in nursing or rest homes because of a lack of adequate group home placements for people with retardation. People with mental retardation over the age of 55 are more likely to be placed in restrictive environments such as institutions, rest homes, or nursing homes (Seltzer, Seltzer, & Sherwood, 1982). Premature and inappropriate placement of adults with mental retardation in nursing homes is not cost effective for the community. The cost to clients and their families is substantial. The quality of life for a young to middle-aged adult with mental retardation in a nursing home surrounded by elderly and severely ill individuals was found to greatly reduce access to age appropriate activities (Seltzer et al., 1982). In many cases, educational and vocational services, as well as regular recreation activities, do not exist in these facilities.

Employment status of the CRT client population was defined by engagement in full- or part-time competitive work. Only five CRT clients were employed, and all of these clients held low paying, unskilled, service-related jobs (e.g., food and janitorial service). Sheltered employment in vocational workshops and ADAP services was counted as a separate category from that of competitive employment. Fourty-five clients (32%) were receiving vocational training in a sheltered workshop, while only 13 (9%) were served by day programs. Seventeen clients were still enrolled in public school special education programs, and most of these attended Metro Center, a self-contained public school for students with moderate to severe mental retardation, while five clients attended a compensatory course for adults with mental retardation at Central Piedmont Community College. Fourteen clients received other ancillary services besides the CRT program. These services included mental health counseling and intervention from a variety of social service agencies (e.g., case worker support and child and family welfare). Forty-two clients were receiving no training or day services.

CRT PROGRAM DESCRIPTION

Training Philosophy

The CRT program represents a new focus in service delivery for adults with mental retardation. The core of the training program is built around skills and environments which foster self-direction and initiative in each person. Rather than providing instruction to clients in a traditional classroom setting or in the confines of a central location, CRT instructors go to the homes of the clients to deliver instruction on a one-to-one basis. Because independent living skills and the appropriate use of community resources are the primary areas of focus within the program, clients are taught to function more independently within their home and neighborhood environment. From the home, the CRT instructor and client venture into the community for specific instruction at various community locations. The client's leisure or discretionary time becomes the vehicle through which he or she is taught the independent living skills which are necessary for successful community integration (e.g., handling money, using public transportation, grooming, using the telephone and newspaper). The CRT program uses many community resources—shopping malls, restaurants, museums, banks, and public transportation systems have all been used successfully as training environments.

Independent living can be defined as self-reliance and control of one's own living circumstances (DeJung, 1979). Training functional skills in the environment in which the skills are to be used (e.g., Brown, Branston, Hamre-Nietupski, Pumpian, Certo, & Gruenewald, 1979; Brown, Branston-McClean, Baumgart, Vincent, Falvey, & Schroeder, 1979; Brown, Nietupski, & Hamre-Nietupski, 1976; Wilcox & Bellamy, 1982) is the unifying premise of the CRT program. Research, such as that conducted by Keith and Lange (1974), indicates that, when skills are trained in one environment (e.g., the institution) and are expected to generalize to another (e.g., the community), as much as 40% of instructional training in certain independent living skills programs (e.g., self-feeding, grooming, dressing) is lost within 3 to 26 months after institutional release. Although these data are not striking, based on what we now know about the phenomenon of skill generalization—that is, skill generalization has not been an expected outcome of training for persons with mental retardation (Baer, Wolf, & Risley, 1968; Stokes & Baer, 1977)—a more critical barrier to successful community integration for the adult who is mentally retarded is a lack of appropriate training in skills necessary for community integration.

The intent of the CRT program is to provide the missing link for older people with mental retardation who may have the potential for competitive or sheltered employment but have never been taught the vocational or social skills necessary for successful employment.

Instructional Content: The Assessment of Independent Living Skills (AILS)

The instructional content used by the CRT program is based upon the Assessment of Independent Living Skills (AILS) developed by the CRT program and UNCC's College of Education and Allied Professions (Keul, Spooner, Test, Heller, & Grossi, 1985). The AILS was designed to assess the use of community resources by adults who are mentally retarded. The scale includes eight skill areas: (a) socialization skills, (b) public behavior skills, (c) grooming skills, (d) use of time and money management, (e) use of transportation, (f) use of informational resources, (g) use of leisure resources, and (h) use of community resources. Each skill area is sub-divided into competencies which represent a range of tasks ranked by degree of difficulty.

Each of the eight skill areas of the AILS has 10 descriptive statements, arranged hierarchically from minimal performance of a given skill to a high level of total independence with that skill. To administer the AILS, a trained interviewer asks questions of a person who knows the client's behavior well. The usual respondents are parents or other relatives with whom the client lives, or vocational or day program staff. The interviewer asks the first question in the Social Skills area, and, if the response is that the client demonstrates independence in performing the skill, the response area is marked as being passed with complete independence (i.e., a score of 1 out of 4, see Client Progress on Goals section below). The interviewer continues asking questions in this area, and each question is scored accordingly. The sum total performance on Social Skills is recorded as an area score. This process is repeated until all eight areas have been covered.

The result is a profile of client skills in all eight areas. The CRT instructors then focus on questions in which total independence was not demonstrated, and choose to develop the most appropriate skills for the individual's educational program. In most cases, it is the first question in each area where total independence is not demonstrated. Although the questions are arranged developmentally for most people, individual variance is sometimes reflected on the AILS such that a client's profile may show gaps in which higher level skills exist, but lower level performance of skills is not demonstrated. For example, due to a client's previous experience or education, the client may not independently discriminate when to bathe (skill 3.2 in grooming), yet demonstrate the appropriate selection of clothing when dressing (skill 3.5 in grooming). In this case, the lower level goal is vital to good grooming; thus, the goal for this client would be to provide instruction in the skills necessary to close the gap.

Part I of the AILS is an initial diagnostic instrument to determine the baseline skill level of each client in each of the eight skill areas. Part II provides specific, concrete behaviors which are indicators of those skills. Part I is used for determining needs and setting priorities for the client's program goals, while Part II is used for developing specific, individual, instructional activities.

Validating the AILS.   Concurrent validity of the AILS was assessed in 1983 by correlating Part I area scores with domain scores on the Adaptive Behavior Scale (Nihira, Foster, Shellhaas, & Leland, 1974). The Pearson product-moment correlation coefficients ranged from +.32 to +.72 for the 1983 client population. Total scores on each section of the instrument, obtained by summing area scores of the ABS, had a correlation of +.77.

The degree of relationship between the two instruments in this sample was considered an indication that the AILS measured much the same skills as the

ABS, but that 41% of the variance in the AILS scores was not accounted for by variance in the ABS scores. Since the AILS was supposedly measuring functional independence, while the ABS measured a full range of behaviors, that variance unaccounted for could have been due to the different goals of the two instruments.

Another analysis is the correlation between AILS area scores and ABS domain scores which are purported to measure similar constructs. For example, both scales have categories for socialization. The correlation between the two socialization scores was +.58. The correlations between the ABS domains "Numbers and Time" and "Economic Activity" with the AILS "Time and Money Skills" were +.53 and +.68, respectively. Of particular interest was the ABS domain "Independent Functioning", since the AILS emphasized independence in demonstrating community access skills. In fact, the highest correlation in the entire matrix of 99 correlations was +.92, the correlation between "Independent Functioning" and the total AILS score.

Part I of the instrument, taken as a whole, describes and measures behaviors related to the level of independent functioning of adults with mental retardation. The high, positive correlation with another accepted scale demonstrates that the AILS was sensitive to differences in behaviors, which indicate varying levels of skill. All eight areas appeared to be positively related to the total score; however, the last three areas, (information resources, transportation skills, and community resources) had highly different distributions from that of the total, so any interpretation of correlations in those areas is questionable.

A Sample Instructional Session

Each client is evaluated upon enrollment in the CRT program to determine a beginning level of community living skills. An Individual Program Plan (IPP) for each client, based on the AILS scores, and program objectives, are evaluated quarterly to determine progress towards meeting the specific goals. A sample IPP is presented in Table 1.

The IPP consists of Goals (Terminal Objectives) as specified by Part I of the AILS, together with the enabling objectives in Part II of the AILS corresponding to each terminal objective. The IPP details the methods and materials used to instruct the client, and provides space for quarterly evaluations of client progress.

Throughout their time together, the CRT instructor encourages the client to talk about his or her lifestyle and personal interests. This anecdotal information is helpful in planning instructional activities that match the interests of the client. CRT clients are expected to contribute their own ideas for planning and participating in instructional sessions. Each instructional session begins with the CRT instructor and client reviewing the client's IPP goals together, in order to make choices concerning the session's activities and the community resources for the session.

Although the specific goals set for each client are the main focus of instruc-

Table 1

CRT IPP III (Midterm and Final Evaluation)

Client: _____Client /1: _____Instructor: _____Date: _____

Goal (Terminal Objective): Client Exhibits Appropriate Behavior When Waiting in Line in a Public Place.

Objectives (Enabling)	Instructional Methods and Materials Quarterly*			
	1	2	3	4
2.2.1 Client finds correct line and takes his/her place at the end	2.2.1.1	Discuss and role play appropriate behavior in the clients home.		
	2.2.1.1	Review discussion while traveling to the resource selected.		
	2.2.1.3	Model behavior for the client.		
2.2.2 Client uses appropriate conduct while standing in line in a public place. (stand erect, stands in his//her own space, keeps hands to self, socializes only with people he/she knows, speaks in a proper tone of voice.	2.2.2.1	Shape and verbally reinforce the behavior (if necessary use edible reinforcers and fade these over time)		
	2.2.2.2	Practice the behavior in a variety of settings		
	2.2.2.3	Instruct parents to follow-up and reinforce the behavior.		

Key: 1-activities demonstrated inependently; 2-activities demonstrated with verbal prompts; 3-activities after demonstration and verbal prompts; 4-activities not demonstrated.

tional sessions, every opportunity is used to explore all skill areas and their relationship to one another. For example, Goal 4.5 in money management consists of the identification and counting of groups of coins and bills and the transaction of simple purchases with exact change. Selection of a store, in close proximity to the client's home, is the first step, followed by the determination of a means of transportation. In most cases, the client and instructor will walk to the store in order to insure that the client is not dependent on someone else to provide transportation. While Charlotte has a city bus service, the transit system does not serve the neighborhood of many CRT clients. Appropriate grooming, public behavior skills, and social skills must also be demonstrated by the client as she or he makes a purchase. Many times, these excursions into the community provide systematic opportunities to teach a client skills related to the targeted goals. For example, a visit to the neighborhood store to make a purchase (money skills), could also lead to a chance encounter with neighbors and friends, providing an opportunity to work on social skills, such as appropriate conversation etiquette.

There are two full-time instructors in the CRT program. Each instructor maintains a caseload of 20 clients and up to 10 clients in case management. A total of no less than 60 clients can be served by the CRT program each year. Instructors are responsible for conducting weekly sessions with the client, and for involving parents and family members in the instructional goals. The instructional sessions for each client last 60 to 90 minutes. Client instruction is primarily one-to-one, but on occasion (e.g., when social behavior is the primary goal for a client), up to three clients may be grouped for an instructional session. Emphasis is placed upon teaching clients how to use community resources in their neighborhoods, thereby increasing the likelihood that these resources will be used by the clients on their own.

Client Progress on Goals

Client progress on individual goals is presented in Table 2, arranged by goal area, goal number, and the percentage of goals achieved each year, as well as the total percentage of goals achieved over the 3 years of the CRT program. Progress on individual goals for each instructional session is assessed on a four point scale: (a) activities demonstrated independently earned a score of 1, (b) activities demonstrated with verbal prompts earned a score of 2, (c) activities demonstrated with verbal prompts and demonstration earned a score of 3, and (d) activities not demonstrated earned a score of 4. Mastery on individual goals is achieved when a client earns a score of 1 (i.e., activities demonstrated independently) during four consecutive instructional sessions. Thus, only goals which were achieved at the independent mastery level were included in the data in Table 2.

Public Behavior (skills necessary to access public facilities and secure assistance or services) and Social Skills (appropriate social interaction skills) were the areas of greatest goal achievement by the CRT clients. Overall, 57% of Public Behavior, 52% of Social Skills, and 50% of Community Resources goals were achieved by CRT clients. The areas of Time and Money Management, Transportation, and Leisure Skills demonstrated goal mastery levels between 41% and 46%. Mastery of goals in the area of Grooming was demonstrated by 39% of clients who attempted these goals, while only 32% of clients who worked on goals in the area of Information Resources achieved these goals.

Although not reflected in Table 2, client progress other than mastery was also documented. Approximately 75% of the clients who did not achieve mastery did achieve a higher level score (i.e., from a baseline score of 4 to 3, or from 3 to 2) during their tenure in the program. In most cases, clients worked on three goals during each quarter, which were continued in the next quarter if mastery was not achieved.

Client progress was influenced by many variables external to the control of CRT instructors. Often, instructional sessions had to be forfeited to attend to case

Table 2
CRT 1982–1984
Percentage of Goals Achieved

Goal Area	Goal #	1982 % Achieved	1983 % Achieved	1984 % Achieved	82–84 Total %	Goal area	Goal #	1982 % Achieved	1983 % Achieved	1984 % Achieved	82–84 Total %
Social Skills	1.1	100	57	100	75	Public behavior	2.1	50	100	—	60
	1.2	50	0	100	29		2.2	80	50	0	60
	1.3	7	0	0	50		2.3	80	0	0	57
	1.4	60	42	0	44		2.4	9	100	—	15
	1.5	75	54	33	52		2.5	43	0	0	43
	1.6	32	50	71	44		2.6	57	100	100	44
	1.7	66	0	100	66		2.7	66	33	0	50
	1.8	46	0	67	43		2.8	14	60	0	27
	1.9	—	0	—	0		2.9	—	—	—	
	1.10	100	75	100	89		2.10	0	50	43	31
Combined		58	41	56	52	Combined		59	55	29	57
Grooming	3.1	0	20	—	17	Time and money management	4.1	86	33	0	70
	3.2	60	50	0	50		4.2	33	100	0	43
	3.3	60	0	0	43		4.3	38	50	25	39
	3.4	0	100	100	33		4.4	50	50	50	50
	3.5	64	0	50	57		4.5	50	42	36	42
	3.6	100	—	—	100		4.6	75	67	100	75
	3.7	86	100	—	88		4.7	0	0	0	0
	3.8	50	78	0	53		4.8	20	67	50	43
	3.9	20	—	50	29		4.9	100	—	—	100
	3.10	0	100	33	0		4.10	0	—	50	33

Goal Area	Goal #	1982 % Achieved	1983 % Achieved	1984 % Achieved	82–84 Total %	Goal area	Goal #	1982 % Achieved	1983 % Achieved	1984 % Achieved	82–84 Total %
Combined		52	52	33	39	Combined		49	47	39	46
Transportation	5.1	50	—	—	50	Leisure skills	6.1	50	—	100	67
	5.2	0	100	33	—		6.2	0	0	30	—
	5.3	0	—	43	25		6.3	25	50	30	
	5.4	25	—	38	50		6.4	17	—	38	
	5.5	33	83	39	—		6.5	25	50	58	
	5.6	33	50	42	50		6.6	55	64	100	
	5.7	33	—	100	43		6.7	50	20	100	44
	5.8	40	—	100	43		6.8	—	0	—	44
	5.9	—	0	100	67		6.9	—	—	—	—
	5.10	—	100	75	50		6.10	—	100	100	
Combined		36	24	56	41	Combined		39	31	62	43
Information resources	7.1	0	—	—	0	Community resources	8.1	60	100	66	64
	7.2	—	—	—	—		8.2	0	0	100	33
	7.3	25	0	20	21		8.3	0	100	50	42
	7.4	0	0	50	11		8.4	—	—	—	—
	7.5	83	0	50	50		8.5	0	—	—	0
	7.6	33	—	100	43		8.6	13	—	—	13
	7.7	43	—	20	33		8.7	56	—	33	50
	7.8	—	—	33	100		8.8	—	—	50	
	7.9	—	—	100	—		8.9	—	—	—	—
	7.10	—	—	—	—		8.10	50	100	73	71
Combined		35	0	36	32	Combined		34	86	65	50

management or crisis situations. For example, many indigent clients experienced difficulty in maintaining subsistence from day to day (i.e., securing clothing, shelter, and food). The CRT instructor was, in many cases, the only advocate the client could call on to assist him or her to track down an errant SSI check or find emergency medical care. When these issues arose, the CRT instructor used the experience to teach the client how to solve the problem for himself or herself. Clients were taught how to seek appropriate assistance, as well as which agencies provided the services they needed.

Another variable influencing client progress was the support of parents and family members in conducting follow-up training between instructional sessions. Parents and family members were also important in determining goals for clients. If the family expressed resistance to goals suggested by the CRT instructor, progress on these goals was invariably poor. CRT instructors learned to steer away from goals when family members expressed resistance.

The goal area which met with the most resistance was the area of Transportation. Parents who did not use the city bus system were reluctant to allow their offspring with mental retardation to ride the bus. This resistance was also predictably demonstrated along economic lines. That is, low income families who depended on the transit system readily agreed to bus training, while middle income, nonusers of the transit system were the most reluctant.

Parents demonstrated more support and follow-up activities in the areas of Public Behavior and Social Skills, in part because they valued these skills as prerequisite to vocational success and group home or independent living. Skill areas which required academic skills (i.e., Time and Money Management and Information Resources) were the most difficult to teach during weekly instructional sessions, and for families to follow up due to their lack of experience in teaching academic skills.

Most of the clients who worked on Grooming were either living alone or were of low economic status and living with family members. Follow-up by low income families who themselves did not demonstrate consistent grooming skills was negligible. It was also difficult to sustain the good grooming for clients who lived alone, although many of these clients did achieve mastery when the CRT instructor was successful in developing intrinsic reinforcers in these clients (such as pride in their appearance and a sense of self-esteem). A trip to the local beauty or barber shop often worked wonders in inspiring these clients to improve their grooming habits. Assisting the client to purchase grooming supplies (combs, shampoo, deodorant, make-up, etc.), and teaching the proper use of grooming aids, also promoted the maintenance of grooming habits.

While the main barometer of the program's success is measured by client mastery of individual goals, case management services were representative of the success of the CRT program. This assistance included referral to vocational or day programs, mental health or social services, and assistance to families, when appropriate, to secure legal guardianship for their offspring with mental retardation. Assistance was also provided to secure placement in group homes or a space on the waiting list for a group home for CRT clients. In a few cases, clients were helped to secure their own apartments.

PROGRAM IMPLEMENTATION: DIFFICULTIES AND REPLICATION

The primary difficulty encountered by the CRT program was securing a permanent funding base beyond the initial federal grant, which was intended as pilot money to later be supplemented by in-kind money from local community funding agencies. Funding was further complicated by a lack of understanding from community funding agencies about the use of the community as a major resource and training site. The concept of training independent living skills in the community was a radical departure from facility-based services which were familiar and currently receiving money from local funding agencies. In a similar fashion, the concept of supported employment has experienced resistance from local communities who have traditionally depended on sheltered workshops and ADAPs to serve adults with severe mental handicaps (Bellamy et al., 1980). Recent federal initiatives have focused on discretionary grant programs to develop pilot programs as well as mechanisms to allocate more local and state funding resources to supported employment and independent living skills training programs.

The CRT program experienced resistance from some service providers and families who were not confident of the ability of adults with mental retardation to learn to use community resources independently. Often, the expectations and attitudes of parents and service providers do not reflect the great progress which has been demonstrated in training programs and vocational services for adults with mental retardation during the last decade (Moon & Beale, 1985). Other service providers and families supported the concept of the CRT program, but were reluctant to lobby for local fiscal support because they were afraid that local funds used to support the CRT program would threaten funds needed for new group homes and day programs.

These problems were overcome through a public relations campaign by the CRT program to present the concept of the program as well as demonstrate the program's success with individual clients. First, the CRT program was presented to the governing boards or directors of each of the human service agencies in Charlotte-Mecklenburg who served populations of adults with mental retardation. In this way, human service agencies became familiar with the CRT program, enabling them to refer their own clients (or clients they were unable to serve) to the CRT program. The public relations campaign was then extended to the general public through the use of feature articles in all the daily newspapers and local weekly newspapers, as well as through radio and television interview spots on both public and commercial stations. This part of the campaign was targeted to a population and their families who received no services from human service agencies, yet were in need of the CRT program's services.

The second year of the CRT program was funded by a State of North Carolina Council on Developmental Disabilities grant. During this time, the CRT staff worked to secure permanent funding from the local community. Each time the funding base changed, service delivery was interrupted for several weeks while the program staff revised policies, procedures, and record-keeping standards to meet the demands of the new funding agency.

Replication of the CRT program would be easier and more efficient if the concept of CRT was supported by community service providers, families, and advocates before external or local funding was secured. A base of support among various service providers and advocates in the community can be developed by educating them about the merits of the CRT program and through involving them in the process of securing an administrative base and funding for the program. Through this base of support among the various service providers and advocates in the community, the program could address any resistance which may be experienced before the program was funded and implemented.

Administration of the CRT program by GWISP was accomplished to establish the CRT program in an existing local agency. The CRT staff interested GWISP in the merger by demonstrating the success of the program with clients traditionally unsuccessful in the services GWISP provided to date. This merger enabled the program to (a) reduce its operating budget and (b) request local fiscal support not available to the program as a pilot project administered by UNCC. In addition, merger with GWISP provided a location more central to the city and the clients the program serves.

After the first operating months of the CRT program, client referrals were not a problem. Even those service providers who were reluctant, at first, to support local funding for the CRT program referred clients to the program. The CRT program's in-home training was valued by service providers who were unable to provide this service delivery for their clients. CRT staff also provided important feedback to agencies about client skill generalization regarding skills initially taught by another service provider and in turn used in the community in the company of CRT instructors. In addition, the CRT program became popular with agencies because of the referral and case management services the program offered clients and their families. Families of older clients often resisted the services of agencies out of fear of the unknown, or because they had experienced poor treatment from agencies many years ago. Several referrals to the CRT program were middle-aged adults with mental retardation who lived with an elderly, sick parent. Agencies or concerned relatives would refer these individuals to the CRT program to help the family to secure legal guardianship, group home residence, or day placements, as well as to provide independent living skills training for the client.

Service providers also referred clients to the CRT program to complement the prevocational and vocational training clients received in sheltered employment and training programs. The community access skills (i.e., bus riding, handling money, social skills) taught by the CRT program are concurrent skills for competitive employment. Replication of the CRT program in conjunction with vocational training or supported employment programs is suggested to best use the strengths of both of these program models.

Staff selection, training, and staff management were critical to the program's success. After some early experimentation with part time positions and, in some cases, volunteers, the project staff was reduced in number, but all positions were converted to paid full time jobs. Paid staff were more committed to the program and full time positions produced the best client/staff ratio. Because of the reduction in staff size, part time clerical support was all that was required to support the program's clerical needs. The merger with GWISP also reduced the staff position needed to administer and manage the project staff and overall program operation to a half time position.

Management and supervision of the CRT staff required that the program develop new strategies to insure staff accountability. Daily reports on client progress, contacts with parents, and communication with ancillary agencies were required of each staff member. Since the CRT instructors used their own cars to travel to appointments with clients, mileage reimbursement forms were submitted each week and were checked against client contacts reports for accuracy.

Because the CRT instructors spend most of their worktime with clients in the community, they occasionally experienced frustration due to their lack of daily contact with their fellow instructors. Weekly staff meetings provided a forum for the CRT instructors to discuss problems with individual clients and solicit assistance from their peers and the program coordinator. Also, weekly staff meetings in the CRT office were necessary to maintain contact with the staff and provide necessary information, additional in-service training, or feedback on client progress to the entire staff. In addition to weekly staff meetings, the CRT instructors and coordinators would often arrange to meet for lunch later in the week to discuss problems with clients between appointments in the community.

Replication of the CRT program by various communities should not be difficult once the concept of the model and funding for the program are supported by the local community. Success with the CRT program is not dependent on a large metropolitan area. Smaller cities and towns may demonstrate even greater success with the model due to the close proximity of even limited community resources. Rural communities may, however, find the CRT model less appropriate where great distance separates the population from available resources. Locating the CRT program in an existing service agency will enable the program to run on a relatively modest operating budget.

FUTURE DIRECTIONS AND RESEARCH

Future plans for the CRT program involve continued development of the AILS, as well as continued field-based research. The next steps in the validation of the

AILS include: (a) administering the revised instrument to another group of people with mental retardation, (b) replicating the validity analysis described previously, (c) assessing reliability, and (d) evaluating the utility of the instrument by comparing AILS scores with global ratings of independent functioning given by educators, parents, or peers.

Future field-based research will focus on empirically validating training procedures (e.g., using public telephones) as well as surveying families of clients to measure attitudes toward such concepts as deinstitutionalization, independent living skills training, community placements, and community support systems for parents and their disabled children. Research is also planned to examine which community resources are most often used by clients independently, and why these resources are used more frequently than others.

As the CRT program gains experience in providing community resources training for populations of adults with mental retardation, the practical application of this service delivery model will be disseminated. Dissemination of the research and program outcomes will be a continuing goal of the CRT program, to encourage the replication of the CRT service delivery system nationally.

REFERENCES

Baer, D.M., Wolf, M.M., & Risley, T.R. (1968). Some current dimensions of applied behavior analysis. *Journal of Applied Behavior Analysis, 1*, 91–97.

Bellamy, G., Sheehan, M., Horner, R., & Boles, S. (1980). Community programs for severely handicapped adults: An analysis. *Journal of the Association for the Severely Handicapped, 5*, 307–323.

Brown, L., Branston, M., Hamre-Nietupski, S., Pumpian, I., Certo, N., & Gruenewald, L. (1979). A strategy for developing chronological age appropriate and functional curriculum for severely handicapped adolescents and young adults. *Journal of Special Education, 13*, 81–90.

Brown, L., Branston-McClean, M., Baumgart, D., Vincent, L., Falvey, M., & Schroeder, J. (1979). Using the characteristics of current and subsequent least restrictive environments in the development of curricular content for severely handicapped students. *AAESPH Review, 4*, 409–424.

Brown, L., Nietupski, J., & Hamre-Nietupski, S. (1976). The criterion of ultimate functioning and public school services for severely handicapped students. In M.A. Thomas (Ed.), *Hey, don't forget about me: Education's investment in severely, profoundly, and multiply handicapped*, (pp. 2–15). Reston, VA: Council for Exceptional Children.

Clay, J.W., Orr, D.M., & Stuart, A.W. (1982). *North Carolina urban economic atlases*. Charlotte, NC: Urban institute and Department of Geography and Earth Sciences, University of North Carolina at Charlotte.

Conroy, J.W., & Bradley, V.J. (1985). *The Pennhurst longitudinal study: A report of five years of research and analysis*. Philadelphia, PA: Temple University, Developmental Disabilities Center.

Crapps, J.M., Langone, J., & Swaim, S. (1985). Quantity and quality of participation in community environments by mentally retarded adults. *Education and Training of the Mentally Retarded, 20*, 123–129.

DeJung, G. (1979). Independent living: From social movement to analytic paradigm. *Archives of Physical Medicine, 60*, 435–446.

DeJung, G., & Hughes, J. (1980). *Report of the Surbridge Conference on independent living services.* Medical Rehabilitation Research and Training Center. Boston, MA: Tufts-New England Medical Center.

Edgerton, R.B., & Bercovici, S.M. (1976). The cloak of competence: Years later. *American Journal of Mental Deficiency, 80,* 485–497.

Gollay, E. (1977). Deinstitutionalized mentally retarded people: A closer look. *Education and Training of the Mentally Retarded, 12,* 137–144.

Goodall, P.A., Wehman, P., & Cleveland, P. (1983). Job placement for mentally retarded individuals. *Education and Training of the Mentally Retarded, 18,* 271–278.

Grossman, H.J. (Ed.). (1977). *Manual on terminology and classification in mental retardation.* Washington, DC: American Association on Mental Deficiency.

Halpren, A.S., Close, D.W., & Nelson, D.J. (1985). *On my own: The impact of semi-independent living programs for adults with mental retardation.* Prepublication copy, University of Oregon, Eugene, OR.

Keith, K.D., & Lange, B.M. (1974). Maintenance of behavior change in an institution-wide training program. *Mental Retardation, 12,* 34–37.

Kerman, K.T., & Koegel, P. (1980). Employment experiences of community-based mildly retarded adults. In R.B. Edgerton (Ed.), *Lives in progress: Mildly retarded adults in a large city* (pp. 9–26). Washington, DC: American Association on Mental Deficiency.

Keul, P.K., Spooner, F., Test, D.W., Heller, H.W., & Grossi, T. (1985). *Assessment of Independent Living Skills* (AILS). Unpublished manuscript, University of North Carolina at Charlotte, College of Education and Allied Professions, Charlotte, NC.

Laurendeau, M.C., Blanchet, A., & Coshan, M. (1984). Studying the effects of deinstitutionalization programs on mentally handicapped persons. *The Canadian Journal on Mental Retardation, 34,* 33–41.

Lewis, M., & Lewis, J. (1977). The counselors impact on community environments. *Personnel and Guidance Journal, 55,* 356–358.

Moon, M.S., & Beale, A.V. (1985). *Helping Your child with severe developmental disabilities receive vocational training and employment: Guidelines for parents.* Unpublished manuscript, Virginia Commonwealth University, Rehabilitation, Research, and Training Center, Richmond, VA.

Nihira, K., Foster, R., Shellhaas, M., & Leland, H. (1974). *AAMD Adaptive Behavior Scale* (revised ed.). Washington, DC: American Association on Mental Deficiency.

Schalock, R.L., & Harper, R.S. (1978). Placement from community-based MR programs: How well do clients do? *American Journal of Mental Deficiency, 83,* 240–247.

Schalock, R.L., Harper, R.S., & Carver, G. (1981). Independent living placement: Five years later. *American Journal of Mental Deficiency, 86,* 170–177.

Seltzer, M.M., Seltzer, G.B., & Sherwood, C.C. (1982). Comparison of community adjustment of older versus younger mentally retarded adults. *American Journal of Mental Deficiency, 87,* 9–13.

Stokes, T.F., & Baer, D.M. (1977). An implicit technology of generalization. *Journal of Applied Behavior Analysis, 10,* 349–367.

Wehman, P. (1981). *Competitive employment: New horizons for severely disabled individuals.* Baltimore, MD: Paul H. Brookes.

Wehman, P., Hill, M., Goodall, P., Cleveland, P., Brooke, V., & Pentecost, J.H. (1982). Job placement and follow-up of moderately and severely handicapped individuals after three years. *Journal of the Association for the Severely Handicapped, 7*(2), 5–16.

Wilcox, B., & Bellamy, G.T. (1982). *Design of high school programs for severely handicapped students.* Baltimore, MD: Paul H. Brookes Publishing Co.

Wolfensberger, W.W. (1972). *The principle of normalization in human services.* Toronto, Canada: National Institute on Mental Retardation.

11

Parental Adequacy and Sterilization of Mentally Retarded People*

Perry Sirota and Diane Hoffman
Queen's University

Historically, the argument in favor of sterilization of mentally retarded people was based on eugenic grounds. However, more recently, it has shifted to a concern for the offspring of mentally retarded parents. A sample of research addressing parental adequacy of mentally retarded individuals was critically evaluated, and revealed serious methodological flaws and premature conclusions. Furthermore, the assessment of competence for parental decision-making presents numerous problems. The paper concludes with the suggestion that selective sterilization of people who are mentally retarded may reflect a societal prejudice towards this group.

HISTORICAL PERSPECTIVE

Over the past two decades, the concept of normalization (Wolfensberger, 1972) has had tremendous impact on the field of mental retardation. Recognizing that ". . . deviancy in handicapped people has been fostered by differential treatment, labeling, and segregation, this principle advocates providing retarded persons with conditions which are as much like normal conditions as possible to foster culturally normative behavior" (Roos, 1981, p. xxi). As a result, educational mainstreaming, employment opportunities, and community living have largely been secured by mildly mentally retarded people. Their fundamental involvement in more intimate areas, such as sexuality, marriage, and parenthood, however, has progressed at a much slower rate (Haavik & Menninger,

* Order of authorship was determined randomly. Requests for reprints should be addressed to Diane Hoffman, Department of Psychology, Queen's University, Kingston, Ontario. K7L-3N6. We would like to thank Dr. Patricia Minnes for reading the manuscript and providing valuable comments and direction.

202

1981). Child rearing by people who are mentally retarded, in particular, has been a long-standing controversial issue (Ainsworth, Wagner, & Strauss, 1945). Several forms of control have been employed to prevent the mentally retarded person from bearing children; the most severe and irreversible procedure is nontherapeutic sterilization.

The grounds for using sterilization as a contraceptive measure have changed over the years. Originally, the argument was predicated on "the elitism of social Darwinism and totally erroneous assumptions about the genetic transmission of mental retardation [which] resulted in something called the eugenics movement" (Baker, 1983, p. 3). Although the concept of selective breeding to improve the human race has existed for a long time, it was Sir Francis Galton who proposed the term "eugenics" and essentially established it as a "science" (Murray, 1983). There are two ways in which eugenics can be accomplished. Positive eugenics refers to the encouragement of procreation in those individuals with favorable or desirable qualities, whereas negative eugenics involves discouraging the procreation of individuals with undesirable characteristics (Haavik & Menninger, 1981). Proponents of the eugenics movement believed that the physical and behavioral characteristics associated with mental retardation, as well as mental illness, epilepsy, and criminality, were for the most part inherited. Negative eugenics were emphasized, and various procedures, including sterilization, were invoked to prevent these individuals from having children (Law Reform Commission of Canada, 1979).

In addition to Galton's influence, two other events facilitated the incorporation of eugenic sterilization into law (Paul, 1973). The rediscovery of the laws of heredity of Gregor Mendel provided "a scientific basis for eliminating defective genes and improving human genetic stock" (Haavik & Menninger, 1981, p. 106). Second, the development of medically safe surgical procedures for sterilization, such as vasectomy and tubal ligation, provided more acceptable methods than castration and hysterectomy (in men and women, respectively). These latter procedures were not favored by legislators because of potential side effects and complications (Haavik & Menninger, 1981; Macklin & Gaylin, 1981).

The first involuntary sterilization statute in North America was enacted in the state of Indiana in 1907 (Dickens, 1982). Although it was declared unconstitutional and was eventually revised in the 1920s, similar statutes were adopted in other states during the 1920s. While many of these laws were challenged in the courts, Virginia's compulsory sterilization act of 1924 was upheld as constitutional in the infamous United States Supreme Court case of *Buck v. Bell* (1927). This is the first and only case to reach the Supreme Court considering the constitutionality of a sterilization law for mentally retarded people (Haavik & Menninger, 1981). Following this decision, 20 states enacted eugenic sterilization laws. The number of reported sterilizations increased substantially during the 1930s, with approximately 28,000 mentally retarded individuals sterilized in the United States (Robitscher, 1973).

Eugenic laws also existed in two Canadian provinces. Amendments of Alberta's 1928 sterilization legislation included mentally retarded persons. In 1933, British Columbia enacted the Sexual Sterilization Act which also applied to mentally retarded individuals. Both of these laws remained intact despite "vigorous and uncompromising condemnation from expert geneticists" (Dickens, 1982, p. 304) until they were repealed in 1972 and 1973, respectively.

The Alberta legislation was proposed to prevent "the transmission of any mental disability or deficiency to offspring, or a mental injury either to such persons or to the progeny" (Law Reform Commission of Canada, 1979, p. 27). Before the legislation was repealed, 2,822 sterilizations had been approved, and in the final year alone, 55 individuals were sterilized (Gibson, 1974). In contrast, the provisions of the British Columbia legislation were narrower and the law was used less frequently (Law Reform Commission of Canada, 1979).

RATIONALES FOR STERILIZATION

Scientific research examining the causes of mental retardation has largely discredited the social and biological fallacies inherent in the eugenic legislation (Baker, 1983; Dickens, 1982). First, the risk of a mentally retarded individual giving birth to a child who is mentally retarded is only about 10% (Lubs & Maes, 1977); however, if both parents are mentally retarded and have previously given birth to a retarded child, the risk increases to approximately 40% (Reed & Reed, 1965). Furthermore, Macklin and Gaylin (1981) reviewed a number of studies which suggest that 80% or more of mentally retarded individuals are born of parents of normal intelligence. Second, mental retardation is caused by a number of other factors which are not of genetic origin. Environmental variables, such as nutrition, injury, infection, and environmental deprivation occurring at pre-, peri-, and post-natal periods, contribute to the etiology of mental retardation (McCormack, 1979). Thus, sterilization is unlikely to significantly affect the epidemiology of mental retardation.

As a result, the eugenic rationale underlying sterilization has largely been dismissed. Recent court decisions favoring sterilization of mentally retarded individuals have been based upon three other rationales: A consideration of genetics, the good of the state, and the capacity for parenthood (Macklin & Gaylin, 1981). The genetic rationale applies to a very small proportion of individuals in which the likelihood of the birth of a genetically damaged child can be established with a high degree of certainty. The second rationale considers the burden to the state if it must provide special services for the care of the disabled child, and support services for parents unable to cope or provide adequate care for their child. These additional burdens on society are primarily financial, and as such do not justify sterilization. As Macklin and Gaylin (1981) point out, "fundamental rights cannot justifiably be abrogated merely because respecting them involves expense" (p. 92).

The third rationale considers the ability of the person who is mentally retarded to function as a parent. This rationale appears at first to be a compelling and persuasive argument in favor of sterilization. It has been raised with respect to the well-being of the mentally retarded individual, with respect to societal concerns, and finally with respect to the well-being of the potential children born to mentally retarded parents (Law Reform Commission of Canada, 1979).

The benefit to the mentally retarded individual, it is argued, is that sterilization prevents the person from being placed in a situation (i.e., parenthood) where he or she would likely be unable to cope (Murdock, 1974). Furthermore, these individuals would now be able to engage in "heterosexual contact without the burden of pregnancy and parenthood" (Vining & Freeman, 1978, p. 850), and this would, in turn, facilitate their participation in the "moral community" (Macklin & Gaylin, 1981). The underlying assumption, however, is that people who are mentally retarded are unable to care for a child and "ought not be given the responsibility of raising a child" (Gaylin, 1976, p. 15). It has also been argued that sterilizations by hysterectomy be performed in order to terminate menses when this becomes a burden to either the woman who is mentally retarded or her caretakers (Freeman & Vining, 1980; Vining & Freeman, 1978).

The benefit to society represents a similar argument proposed by those in favor of eugenics. It has been suggested that the inadequacies of the parents will impair the cognitive and social development of their children; these children will, as a result of poor parenting, be prone to crime and other social problems. Thus, it is argued that the state has "the right to protect itself from being swamped by mental illness, mental retardation, crime, poverty and other social ills, and the high financial costs of these conditions" (Law Reform Commission of Canada, 1979, p. 32).

Finally, involuntary sterilization has been proposed as a protection for the unborn children whose upbringing and future may be qualitatively uncertain because of parental inadequacy (Krishef, 1972). This argument rests mainly on the assumption that mildly retarded individuals are incapable of parenting children, and that, in order to prevent potential children from being abused and neglected, mentally retarded individuals should be sterilized.

PARENTAL CAPACITY

Judicial standards for making decisions about involuntary sterilization have been explicated in two court cases: The Washington Supreme Court case of *In re Hayes* (1980), and the New Jersey case of *In re Grady* (1981). In both of these cases, the court insisted that, if a person was to be sterilized, the petitioner must provide convincing evidence which supports a number of criteria (Melton & Scott, 1984). One of these criteria, perhaps the most controversial, raises the issue of parental capacity and states that "the nature and extent of the individual's disability, as determined by empirical evidence and not solely on the basis of standardized tests, renders him or her permanently incapable of caring for a child, even with reasonable assistance" (*In re Hayes,* 1980, p. 641). This issue has become the focal point, and indeed can be considered the most significant and pervasive underlying argument favoring compulsory sterilization.

Justification to sterilize mentally retarded people must be based on empirical evidence demonstrating in a convincing manner that this group of people make inadequate parents. Clearly, because the consequences of such a finding are serious in terms of sterilizing mentally retarded people, the research should be rigorously controlled and unequivocal. We will critically review a small sample of the empirical research conducted during the last 40 years. Although most authors conclude that mentally retarded individuals are inadequate parents, it will be argued that this assertion is not in fact supported by the empirical evidence.

Empirical Research on Parental Adequacy of People who are Mentally Retarded.

Given the current trend in legislation prohibiting sterilization (Dowben & Heartwell, 1979), it could be argued that a review of studies linking parents who are mentally retarded with child abuse and neglect is unnecessary. There are problems, however, with such a contention. First, it appears that there has been a dearth of empirical research in the last 10 years on the association between parents who are mentally retarded and child abuse, perhaps due to the practice of removing children from these parents at birth (Crain & Millor, 1978). Second, the hypothesized relationship between mental retardation and child abuse is assumed by many to be factual, and, furthermore, pregnancy and parenthood are commonly viewed as a burden to the person who is mentally retarded. These views are often discussed without reference to the relevant research (Donovan, 1982; Perrin, Sands, Tinker, Dominguez, Dingle, & Thomas, 1976; Vining & Freeman, 1978). For example, Vining & Freeman (1978) argued in favor of sterilization for "trainable individuals when it would permit normalization and heterosexual contact without the burden of pregnancy and parenthood" (p. 850). Third, it is reported that there is a general acceptance of sterilization by the parents of adolescent mentally retarded girls. For example, Passer, Rauh, Chamberlain, McGrath, and Burket (1984) reported that 46% of the parents they surveyed had considered sterilization, while 85% favored legislation permitting sterilization under certain situations. The two most common reasons given for these opinions were prevention of pregnancy and elimination of menstruation.

These factors may underlie reports of a potentially high incidence of voluntary sterilizations (Shaman, 1978). Further, it has been suggested that involuntary sterilizations are being performed on 9- to 18-year-old females who are retarded, yet are not being documented due to a conspiracy of silence between parents and the physicians who perform these procedures (Dowben & Heartwell, 1979), making reliable estimates of the incidence of sterilizations very difficult. Thus, there is a need to review the empirical research in order to determine whether there is validity to the generalization that people who are mentally retarded are not adequate parents.

Based on their review of the literature, Schilling, Schinke, Blythe, and Barth (1982) noted that all but one of 14 studies found mentally retarded people were either unsatisfactory parents or overrepresented in samples of abusing or neglecting parents. For example, Ainsworth et al. (1945) followed 50 retarded people discharged from an institution for at least 10 years. Based on a five-point scale, they rated 30% as poor housekeepers and mothers. More recently, Berry and Shapiro (1975) investigated 10 mentally retarded couples with children. Child care was viewed as poor and probably unacceptable by middle class standards. Most of the parents required substantial help from support agencies, and it was thought that the parents could not cope without the assistance of these agencies. In Northern Ireland, Scally (1973) surveyed the parenting standards of parents who were considered mentally retarded, taken from the total sample of mentally retarded people in the country known at the time. He found that over 50% of the male parents and 90% of the female parents were rated as making "less than adequate contributions to the running of the home and to the welfare of the children" (p. 192). Additionally, over 60% of the children of these mentally retarded parents required outside state intervention.

There are numerous problems with these reports. First, there is an absence of reliability data for the assessment of parental competency. Indeed, it has been argued in general that assessments of parental adequacy have very low reliability (Melton & Scott, 1984). Second, a potentially large bias exists when researchers rate people whom they know in advance to be mentally retarded, especially if their bias is that they cannot make good parents. Third, the mentally retarded people were not compared to control groups matched for socioeconomic status (SES) or family support (i.e., relatives and friends). Fourth, in the Scally (1973) survey, parental intelligence was not reported, and evaluations of parenting ability were based on case reports, not first hand observations by the author. Fifth, there is the bias that middle class standards are the basis against which comparisons should be made. In the absence of controls, Berry and Shapiro (1975) concluded that retarded people, who tend to be overrepresented in lower SES groups (Schilling et al. 1982; Melton & Scott, 1984), were inadequate relative to middle class standards. Clearly, middle class standards are not the only standards in our society.

The Berry and Shapiro (1975) study reflects a prejudice against low SES people who can not usually afford to "live up to" middle class standards. It is likely that many researchers who share this bias would find unacceptable the parenting styles and quality of homes of most low SES people, independent of IQ. Additionally, mentally retarded people can not usually afford the extra hired help that many middle class people can afford, and thus turn to social service agencies to supplement their parenting efforts. This does not mean that they are less adequate than people who do not take advantage of social services. It is ironic that services are provided to compensate for the impoverished circumstances of many people, especially those who may have been institutionalized for many years and do not have existing social support networks. After being encouraged to take advantage of social services, these people are then penalized and labeled as inadequate parents because they cannot cope without these same services.

Another strategy to relate parenting ability with intelligence has been to focus on samples of known child abusers and assess the proportion who are mentally retarded. For example, Smith (1975) found that 50% of a sample of 125 physically abusive mothers were borderline normality or below. Their IQ scores were found to be significantly lower than a nonabusive control group. Oliver (1977) reported that 30% of a smaller group of severely abusive parents had borderline or moderate mental subnormality. Hyman (1977), however, found a nonsignificant trend of low IQ in a sample of abusive parents, relative to the population at large.

Again, these studies are open to major criticisms. The Smith (1975) study used a middle class control group, the Hyman (1977) study was not controlled, and the Oliver (1977) study did not specify the assessment device used to determine IQ. More importantly, there may be reasons other than parenting skills which account for the overrepresentation of mentally retarded people in samples of abusive parents. First, they are already under the scrutiny of social service agencies, thus increasing the probability that a problem will be reported (Hertz, 1978–79). According to Grant (1980), "once a person is declared incompetent his or her life is subject to a scrutiny that many 'normal' people could not pass" (p. 70). In addition, neighbors may be more likely to report a case of alleged abuse if they assume the abusing parents are retarded.

In a related study, Borgman (1969) reported on 50 women referred for testing by child care workers. Most women found in the study to have WAIS IQ scores below 60 were previously judged as inadequate parents. A potentially large bias exists with this study. Some women were referred because of child neglect to determine the appropriateness of sterilization, while others were referred for employment counselling. The researchers knew in advance that these women were less intelligent, and it is likely that they were assumed to be incompetent as parents and workers in advance of any actual investigation.

It has also been reported that mentally retarded parents are less loving towards their children than normal parents. Robinson (1978) questioned mildly retarded mothers and found them to have more controlling and punitive attitudes than a control group of college educated mothers. Apart from the obvious problems with an educated control group most likely overrepresented by middle class individuals, this study says little about parenting skills or actual parenting practice. Indeed, it may only be reflecting differences in social desirability between groups.

The literature cited in this review suggests that some mentally retarded individuals are not adequate parents, but, due to problems with these studies, it is uncertain whether IQ per se is related to parental inadequacy. When control groups are included in studies, they are not matched for income, education, and extra-family support, nor do they take into account the fact that many of the mentally retarded people in their studies were previously institutionalized, and that a number of their problems may be due to general deprivation and lack of experience. Indeed, Floor, Baxter, Rosen, and Zisfein (1975) noted that institutions do not provide good family models, or allow for the development of responsibility or the acquisition of sexual information. They asserted that "the individual is often perceived as an institutional entity, to be guided and protected by personnel who often deal with him in a manner suggesting that he will remain in an institution the rest of his life. . ." (p. 33).

Assessment of Intelligence and Parental Ability

The equivocal nature of previous research makes it difficult to arrive at a decision concerning involuntary sterilization based on the parental competency argument. Perhaps, for this reason, it is advised within the judicial guidelines proposed in the court case of *In re Hayes* (1980) that parental competence be assessed before a decision is made. A number of issues arise when an assessment of this nature is attempted. Four issues will be discussed in detail, namely, limitations of stardardized IQ tests, individualized assessment, development of effective parenting standards, and predictive assessment.

Limitations of IQ tests. There are many problems with the label mental retardation. As described by Macklin and Gaylin (1981), one of the major objections to using IQ tests in defining mental retardation, especially for individuals who are mildly mentally retarded, refers to the causes of mental retardation. In a small proportion of mentally retarded individuals, a physiological defect can be ascertained which is associated with low IQ score. However, in approximately 90% of the people who are mildly retarded according to IQ (scores of 55 to 69), there is no evidence that the mental retardation was caused by an organic or physiological defect. Those who object to the use of IQ tests to measure the abilities of these individuals argue that, in a culturally heterogenous society, such as the United States and Canada, it is difficult to determine or define normality. If the tested individual is not a full participant in the primary culture, then he or she is likely to perform less well than a person reared in the dominant culture. Dickens (1982) has argued that the present classification scheme for individuals who are mildly mentally retarded is essentially dynamic and arbitrary, in that both individual and social (or environmental) forces, including training and life experiences, can influence a person's IQ score.

The limitations of IQ scores are only beginning to be accepted by the courts.

Payne (1977–78) described custody cases where low parental IQ was acknowledged by the court as a major factor in terminating parental rights. The landmark case was *In re McDonald* (1972), where an Iowa Supreme Court found that a parent's low IQ justified the involuntary termination of the relationship between a young married couple and their twin daughters (Galliher, 1973). According to Payne (1977–78), the court's numerous references to the parents' low IQ scores suggested that "the court treated the fact of a low score on a certain standardized test as creating a strong presumption of incapacity to be an adequate parent" (Payne, 1977–78, p. 805).

Individualized Assessment.   It is recognized that, within the subcategories of the mental retardation classification scheme, individuals vary widely in their abilities. Since these categories do not represent homogenous groups (Czukar, 1983), individualized assessment is clearly of paramount importance. This is in agreement with the criteria proposed for *In re Hayes* (1980) which stated that parental incapacity cannot be determined solely on the basis of psychometric tests. This caution is supported by empirical research which to date has not demonstrated a relationship between parental IQ and parental competence (Czukar, 1983; Haavik & Menninger, 1981).

As mentioned previously, the individual's social background, including life experiences and training, are important influences on the person's IQ score and adaptive behavior. These factors may also play a heightened role in determining the individual's ability to care for a child. A recent case report described two mentally retarded individuals who were married and had allegedly abused or neglected their two children (Crain & Millor, 1978). The father had spent most of his life in a state hospital (from ages 7 to 27) and then lived for 2 years in a group home before he was married. It is unlikely that this individual had much opportunity to experience or learn the essentials of marriage or child-rearing.

Parenting Standards.   In considering sterilization, the overreliance on test scores must be avoided, and, as a result, the assessment of parental competence is at best a difficult accomplishment, especially given the absence of good parenting standards. The minimum requirement is that the individual is independently capable of caring for him or herself (Melton & Scott, 1984). The legal system in neglect proceedings has, in general, recognized four skills as essential for adequate parenting, namely, love and affection, housekeeping skills, fulfilling the child's physical needs, and providing intellectual stimulation for the child (Hertz, 1978–79). Other commentators have suggested six specific, albeit vague, criteria for parental incompetence: "1) lack of language, 2) pervasive reality distortion, 3) persistent malevolence toward a child, 4) inconsistency in value system, 5) inability to communicate essential survival information or to act as a model for a child and, 6) inability to establish interpersonal relationships" (Macklin & Gaylin, 1981, p. 95–96).

One issue that arises when standards for minimally acceptable parenting are applied to mentally retarded individuals for decision-making purposes is that the six criteria suggested have been challenged because they are likely to be more stringent than those applied to nonretarded parents. Clearly, it is unjust to enforce these criteria only for people who are mentally retarded. Indeed, this procedure violates the premise of equal protection under the law. Any law whose purpose is to prevent children from exposure to inadequate parenting "that limits itself to mentally retarded persons is underinclusive . . . [in that] other people have a substantial likelihood of being poor parents, yet they are not covered by the sterilization laws" (Haavik & Menninger, 1981, p. 132). Thus, professionals should exercise great caution in setting standards for adequate parenting.

Predictive Assessment. Mildly retarded individuals are capable of learning new skills; they continue to develop cognitively, emotionally and socially, albeit more slowly than the person of average intelligence. Thus, in assessment it must be determined with reasonable accuracy whether the individual will be able to learn new skills aimed at caring for a child, and be able to cope, given support services. Due to a lack of data in the area, our ability to make longterm predictions regarding parental care is very limited (Goldstein, Freud, & Solnit, 1973), thus reducing our capability to assess parenthood capacity, in general.

In custody cases, before children are removed, most courts ensure that the parents have had an opportunity to participate in educational programs whenever they are feasible (Baker, 1983; Hertz, 1978–79). Feasibility is determined, not by availability, but rather by the likelihood of improving the situation, (Hertz, 1978–79). The candidate for sterilization deserves the same consideration. Indeed, there is empirical research which demonstrates that mentally retarded people are capable of acquiring child-care skills from rehabilitative treatment programs (Hertz, 1978–79). Some programs aimed at enhancing effective parenting exist in the United States, and it has been demonstrated that these programs improve parenting ability, especially in conjunction with educational programs for the children (Czukar, 1983).

In sum, a number of problems exist when attempting to assess intelligence and parenting capacity in mentally retarded individuals. Traditional testing is used in an overly broad way, without consideration for the limits of these devices with this population. Not only is there an absence of standardized criteria which define effective parenting, but, in addition, the possibility of mentally retarded parents acquiring these skills has, for the most part, been ignored. Moreover, if objective criteria did exist, there is little justification for applying them exclusively to mentally retarded individuals.

Attitudes Concerning Sterilization of People who are Mentally Retarded

Mentally retarded individuals have received considerable attention regarding their capacity to parent children. One solution for their potential inadequacy has been sterilization. It is interesting that other groups of parents known to be at high risk for child abuse, such as alcoholics and previous child abusers, are not under similar scrutiny for sterilization. If society were both truly concerned about preventing child neglect and abuse, and were to become consistent in its treatment of offenders and potential offenders, it would impose sterilization on all people at risk for child abuse and neglect. This would include all known child abusers who are likely to abuse again, as well as people who have been abused in the past, given the high number of child abusers who were themselves abused as children (Kempe & Kempe, 1978).

Clearly, this notion is untenable, and would be considered repugnant by most members of our society. This suggests that there is something intrinsic to the concept of mental retardation which justifies the differential treatment which people so labelled receive with respect to sterilization. If many groups abuse, and only one is put forward for sterilization, there must be some factor other than abuse per se which distinguishes that particular group. It is our position that this difference is accounted for by a common societal bias against the retarded which associates intelligence with humanness (Roos, 1975), and low intelligence or retardation with sub-humanness (Wolfensberger, 1969). It is also possible that earlier notions of eugenics are still operating, and that arguments for child protection are no more than carefully placed masks to make a repugnant goal appear more acceptable.

It may also be the case that people who are mentally retarded are considered for sterilization because of the assumption that they will not be bothered by such an event, while the normally intelligent child abuser, alcoholic, or neglecting parent will be severely traumatized by such an action. Most people would probably view sterilization of intelligent neglectful parents as inhuman. It therefore seems consistent with Wolfensberger's argument that the retarded are viewed as sub-human. Roos (1975) found many older references (e.g., Popenoe, 1928) suggesting that a prevailing view at one time was that mentally retarded people readily accept sterilization. This is in contrast to the literature with nonretarded people cited by Roos (1975) which clearly points to a deleterious effect of sterilization, especially with young women who had less than three children (Wolf, 1965).

Perhaps the reason mentally retarded people are assumed to not care about being sterilized is that they were not asked. Indeed, Roos (1975) suggests that most retarded people can understand the meaning of parenthood and sterilization, and that they do not accept sterilization as uncaringly as was once assumed.

In a study in which well-adjusted mentally retarded people living in the community were questioned on the matter, Edgerton (1965) found that sterilization was perceived negatively. In a related investigation, mentally retarded people reported that they perceived sterilization as a sign of reduced or degraded status (Sabagh & Edgerton, 1962). Roos (1975) argues that retarded people, who have very high needs for intimacy due to loneliness, are denied these opportunities. He concludes by reasserting that retarded people are in fact sensitive to the effects of sterilization, and that "[the] psychological impact . . . is likely to be particularly damaging. . . [when] the procedure is a result of coercion and when the retarded person has not previously had children" (p. 54). In this context, the 308 people under 18 years of age who were sterilized in Ontario in 1976 (Mecredy-Williams, 1979) are likely to have suffered a great deal, especially when they reach a point where child rearing becomes an important need.

It is again ironic that society has been so sensitive to the needs of potential children brought up in neglectful abusing homes by retarded parents, yet so insensitive in considering the implications of such an action to the sterilized person. While there is rarely any weight given to the feelings of the retarded person being sterilized, in one paper the authors suggest that, since "sterilization of an adult retardate can be emotionally disturbing . . . [the] ideal solution would be sterilization of the child before puberty" (Green & Paul, 1974, p. 122). This appears to be a very misguided form of sensitivity.

SUMMARY

The original justification to sterilize people who are mentally retarded for eugenic purposes has been replaced by arguments based on parental competency which argue that sterilization is in the best interests of the potential children of mentally retarded individuals. The results of empirical research evaluating the parental abilities of mentally retarded people are equivocal due to sampling problems and biases. Moreover, the assessment of intelligence and parental ability of people in this population presents numerous problems. Even if some mentally retarded people are actually inadequate parents, this is not sufficient justification for sterilizing all members of this group. The same treatment of other people at risk for child neglect and abuse would be considered repugnant and inhuman.

REFERENCES

Ainsworth, M., Wagner, E., & Strauss, A. (1945). Children of our children. *American Journal of Mental Deficiency, 49,* 277–241.

Baker, J.D. (1983, October). *Love, marriage and the baby carriage.* Paper presented at the Conference of the Mentally Handicapped Parent, Chatham, Ontario.

Berry, J., & Shapiro, A. (1975). Married mentally handicapped patients in the community. *Proceedings of the Royal Society of Medicine, 68,* 27–38.

Borgman, R.D. (1969). Intelligence and maternal inadequacy. *Child Welfare, 48,* 301–304.

Buck v. Bell, 274 U.S. 200 (1927).

Crain, L.S. & Millor, G.K. (1978). Forgotten children: Maltreated children of mentally retarded parents. *Pediatrics, 61,* 130–132.

Czukar, G. (1983). Legal aspects of parenthood for mentally retarded persons. *Canadian Journal of Community Mental Health, 2,* 57–69.

Dickens, B.M. (1982). Retardation and sterilization. *International Journal of Law and Psychiatry, 5,* 295–318.

Donovan, P. (1982). Fertility-related state laws enacted in 1981. *Family Planning Perspectives, 14,* 63–67.

Dowben, C., & Heartwell, S.F. (1979). Legal implications of sterilization of the mentally retarded. *American Journal of Diseases of the Child, 133,* 697–699.

Edgerton, R.B. (1967). *The cloak of competence.* Berkeley, CA: University of California Press.

Floor, L., Baxter, D., Rosen, M., & Zisfein, L. (1975). A survey of marriages among previously institutionalized retardates. *Mental Retardation, 13,* 33–37.

Freeman, J.M., & Vining, E.P.G. (1980). Sterilization and the retarded female: Another perspective. *Pediatrics, 66,* 651.

Galliher, K. (1973). Termination of the parent-child relationship: Should parental I.Q. be an important factor? *Law and the Social Order, 4,* 855–879.

Gaylin, W. (1976). Sterilizing the retarded child. *Hastings Center Report, April,* 15.

Gibson, D. (1974). Involuntary Sterilization of the mentally retarded: A western Canadian phenomenon. *Canadian Psychiatric Association Journal, 19,* 59–64.

Goldstein, J., Freud, A., & Solnit, A.J. (1973). *Beyond the best interests of the child.* New York: The Free Press.

In re Grady, 85 N.J. 235, 426 A.2d 467 (1981).

Grant, C.J. (1980). Parents with defined intellectual limitations. In *Sterilization and mental handicap: Proceedings of a symposium.* Toronto, Canada: National Institute on Mental Retardation.

Green, B., & Paul, R. (1974). Parenthood and the mentally retarded. *University of Toronto Law Journal, 24,* 117–125.

Haavik, S.F., & Menninger, K.A. (1981). *Sexuality, law, and the developmentally disabled person.* Baltimore, MD: Brookes Publishing Co.

In re Hayes, 93 Wash. 228, 608 P.2d 635 (1980).

Hertz, R. (1978–79). Note: Retarded parents in neglect proceedings: The erroneous assumption of parental inadequacy. *Stanford Law Review, 31,* 785–805.

Hyman, C.A. (1977). A report on the psychological test results of battering parents. *British Journal of Social and Clinical Psychology, 16,* 221–224.

Kempe, R.S., & Kempe, C.H. (1978). *Child abuse.* Cambridge, MA: Harvard University Press.

Krishef, C.H. (1972). State laws on marriage and sterilization of the mentally retarded. *Mental Retardation, 10.*

Law Reform Commission of Canada. (1979). *Sterilization,* (Working Paper 24), Ottawa, Ontario: Minister of Supply and Services.

Lubs, M.L.E., & Maes, J.A. (1977). Recurrence risk in mental retardation. In P. Mittler (Ed.), *Research to practice in mental retardation* (Vol. 3). Baltimore, MD: University Park Press.

Macklin, R., & Gaylin, W. (1981). (Eds.). *Mental retardation and sterilization: A problem of competency and paternalism.* New York: Plenum Press.

McCormack, M.K. (1979). (Ed.). *Prevention of mental retardation and other developmental disabilities.* New York: Marcel Dekker.

In re McDonald, Iowa 201 N.W. 2d 447 (1972).

Mecredy-Williams, B. (1979). Marriage law and the mentally retarded. *Canadian Journal of Family Law, 2,* 63–80.

Melton, G.B., & Scott, E.S. (1984). Evaluations of mentally retarded persons for sterilization: Contributions and limitations of psychological consultation. *Professional Psychology, 15,* 34–48.

Murdock, C. (1974). Sterilization of the mentally retarded: A problem or a solution? *California Law Review, 62,* 917–924.

Murray, D.J. (1983). *A history of western psychology.* Englewood Cliffs, NJ: Prentice-Hall.

Oliver, J. (1977). Some studies of families in which children suffer maltreatment. In A.W. Franklin (Ed.), *The challenge of child abuse*. New York: Grune and Stratton.

Passer, A., Rauh, J., Chamberlain, A., McGrath, M., & Burket, R. (1984). Issues in fertility control for mentally retarded female adolescents. 11. Parental attitudes towards sterilization. *Pediatrics, 73,* 451–454.

Paul, J. (1973). State eugenic history: A brief overview. In J. Robitscher (Ed.), *Eugenic sterilization*. Springfield, IL: Charles C. Thomas.

Payne, A.T. (1977–1978). The law and the problem parent: Custody and parental rights of homosexual, mentally retarded, mentally ill and incarcerated parents. *Journal of Family Law, 16,* 797–818.

Perrin, J.C., Sands, C.R., Tinker, D.E., Dominguez, B.C., Dingle, J.T., & Thomas, M.J. (1976). A considered approach to sterilization of mentally retarded youth. *American Journal of Diseases of the Child, 130,* 288–290.

Popenoe, P. (1928). Eugenic sterilization in California, XI. Attitudes of patients towards the operation. *Journal of Social Hygiene, 14,* 280–285.

Reed, E.W., & Reed, S.C. (1965). *Mental retardation: A family study*. Philadelphia, PA: Saunders.

Robinson, L.H. (1978). Parental attitudes of retarded young mothers. *Child Psychiatry and Human Development, 8,* 131–144.

Robitscher, J. (Ed.). (1973). *Eugenic sterilization*. Springfield, IL: Charles C. Thomas.

Roos, P. (1975). Psychological impact of sterilization on the individual. *Law and Psychology Review, 1,* 45–56.

Roos, P. (1981). Introduction. In R. Macklin & W. Gaylin (Eds.), *Mental retardation and sterilization: A problem of competency and paternalism*. New York: Plenum Press.

Sabagh, G., & Edgerton, R.B. (1962). Sterilized mental defectives look at eugenic sterilization. *Eugenic Quarterly, 4,* 213–222.

Scally, B.G. (1973). Marriage and mental handicap: Some observations in Northern Ireland. In F. de la Cruz & G. LaVeck (Eds.), *Human sexuality and the mentally retarded*. New York: Bruner/Mazel Publishers.

Schilling, R.F., Schinke, S.P., Blythe, B.J., & Barth, R.P. (1982). Child maltreatment and mentally retarded parents: Is there a relationship. *Mental Retardation, 20,* 201–209.

Shaman, J.M. (1978). Persons who are mentally retarded: Their right to marry and have children. *Family Law Quarterly, 12,* 61–84.

Smith, S.M. (1975). *The battered child syndrome*. Reading, MA: Butterworth Publishers.

Vining, E.P.G., & Freeman, J.M. (1978). Sterilization and the retarded female: Is advocacy depriving individuals of their rights? *Pediatrics, 62,* 850–853.

Wolf, R.C. (1965). Can new laws solve the legal and psychiatric problems of voluntary sterilization? *The Journal of Urology, 93,* 402–406.

Wolfensberger, W. (1969). The origin and nature of our institutional models. In R.B. Kugel & W. Wolfensberger (Eds.), *Changing patterns in residential services for the mentally retarded*. Washington, DC: The President's Committee on Mental Retardation, U.S. Government Printing Office.

Wolfensberger, W. (1972). *The principle of normalization in human services*. Toronto, Canada: National Institute on Mental Retardation.

12

The Role of the Small Institution in the Community Services Continuum

Kevin K. Walsh and Philip McCallion
American Institute—The Training School at Vineland

A brief history and selected characteristics of institutions are reviewed, suggesting that the anti-institutional bias often held by proponents of community living arrangements may be unjustified. Historical approaches to the role of the institution are presented, showing that problems facing the field today are not new, nor are the proposed solutions. The assumptions underlying an anti-institutional position are examined in light of empirical evidence pertaining to the size of the facility, quality of care, orientation of the management, and effects on clients. Arguments are presented that the organization and management of institutions are equally, if not more, important than other variables in evaluating quality of residential environments. A case is made for the small institution's role in developing and sustaining transitional programs and specialized community services.

Community service options for developmentally disabled individuals have grown in number and importance since the 1960s and early 1970s. Concepts of de-institutionalization and normalization, along with legal decisions, legislation, and the social policy directives of governmental bodies, have guided, supported, and, in many cases, mandated increased community services. The notion of providing normalized services in community settings arose and gained strength because a number of scientific, philosophical, and social phenomena came to-gether in a culture that was ripe for change. By the mid-1960s, human rights issues had been highlighted by the civil rights movement; a Presidential commit-tee had been empaneled by a President whose sibling was retarded; inhumane conditions in institutions for mentally retarded people were exposed in the media; scientists were conducting research leading to new, effective methods for chang-ing behavior; and national advocacy groups engaged in political and legal action on behalf of a constituency that previously had no voice.

Much of the public and professional sentiment concerning the need for community services was manifest in attacks on the institutions that then served developmentally disabled people. Although often strident, most of these attacks were not without justification. Institutional facilities had grown old and bleak, and care practices had declined to the simple execution of custodial necessities. Staff in such facilities, themselves, had become institutionalized; "treatment" was often chemical or mechanical at best; and normalization was unknown. Exposés in the 1960s and 1970s that piqued the compassion of even the most indifferent observers were the first accounts informing most people about life in institutions. Blatt and Kaplan's photo-essay *Christmas in Purgatory* (1966) and the 1972 television report by Geraldo Rivera on the Willowbrook facility were two such notable presentations. These reports resulted in demands for immediate action toward providing humane care and treatment for institutionalized people.

Without doubt, the reorientation of the field that followed such disclosures was sorely needed. However, the fervor of early change agents may have galvanized public and professional opinion to such an extent that certain components of service systems for developmentally disabled people may have been unduly damaged. One such component, in our view, is the small institution. It is our goal, in this chapter, to argue in favor of a continued role for small institutions in the continuum of services for developmentally disabled individuals.

In this chapter, we will argue that problems of humanity, rights, and quality of care are not automatically avoided in small-group community living placements. We will examine the characteristics of institutions and argue that absolute size of a facility may be less important to quality services than are such things as management orientation, availability of programming, and resource allocation.

Finally, we will present a proposed role for the small institution as a transitional training site and a resource bank providing specific services needed to fully realize the objectives embodied in the concepts of normalization and deinstitutionalization.

DEFINITION OF TERMS

Words are often prisoners of current usage, and, during the last century, common usage of the term "institution" has changed often. Regardless of meaning, institutions are still with us. Braddock and Heller (1985), however, report that only "one eighth of the state operated institutions that existed in this country in 1965 have been closed" (p. 168). At the same time, the number of clients served in institutions has declined substantially. Rotegard, Bruininks, and Krantz (1984) reported reductions of as much as 40% in the numbers of institutionalized clients served between 1967 and 1982. Furthermore, one effect of the negative revelations about institutions has been to *increase* resources flowing into them. Therefore, institutions for developmentally disabled people in America are undergoing substantial changes: fewer institutions are serving fewer clients, with more resources (Griffith, 1985).

We propose definitions that take into account both size and orientation, realizing that, for any particular facility, the definition may not be fully accurate. We consider a *large institution* to have 1,000–2,000 beds or more, and to be centralized, less than homelike, and relatively not resident-oriented in care practices. A *small institution* (what is often called a *regional center*) has generally under 300 beds, is more homelike, and organized to serve a specific geographical area.

We consider these to be "working" definitions for this chapter only. Restraint must be exercised in their interpretation, since other factors contribute to the environment of any particular facility. Indeed, it is precisely to this point that this chapter is directed.

HISTORICAL PERSPECTIVE

Given the support community living arrangements have gained from professionals, advocacy groups, and governmental agencies, the future role of institutions for developmentally disabled individuals is questionable. History reveals that public, and to a lesser extent private, residential institutions have been fundamental in the care of mentally retarded individuals for over a century (Scheerenberger, 1983). In particular, examination of the earliest accounts of the institutional movement shows that the intent was not permanent custodial care of mentally retarded people. Rather, short-term remedial training, often vocational in nature, was envisioned, with return to the larger community (Scheerenberger, 1983).

Isaac Kerlin, an early proponent of institutions, initially expressed the sentiment that humane care was of the utmost importance. He described the position of *attendant* in an institution as a "sacred trust" (Kerlin, 1891). Kerlin, however, recognized that many individuals could be returned to the community and family. In his address to the second annual meeting of the Association of Medical Officers of American Institutions for Idiotic and Feeble-Minded Persons, now the American Association on Mental Deficiency (AAMD), Kerlin argued that vocational training was a means for institutionalized children to reenter a particular community (Kerlin, 1877).

The thinking of Kerlin and his contemporaries on the education and treatment of mentally retarded people in America was based on the work and philosophy of Édouard Seguin. Seguin, who arrived here from Europe in 1848, influenced the growing movement toward specialized facilities (Talbot, 1964) and was influential in the formation of the AAMD in 1876. Seguin's approach was an educational one, and decidedly not custodial in nature (Seguin, 1866). Under the direction of the leaders of this new association (Seguin was the first President), residential schools were established and principles of their operation were articulated. Crissey (1975) presents some of these principles:

The educational program was to proceed by small, sequential steps from basic skills to more formal education, and from play activities to useful work, and vocational skills. . . . There was to be intensive study of the children to discover the origins of their defects and thereby lay foundations for prevention. There was to be research on, and constant development of, new teaching approaches. . . . There was to be constant striving for interchange with the community—the child to remain at home during the early years, his education to be guided by advice from the institution, then trained by the institution's special methods, and then returned to home and community. For the few who have no home, a small auxiliary domicile, near the training school and the vocational center, would be available. (p. 802)

Imbued with the philosophies of Seguin, Hervey B. Wilbur began a private training program in his home in Massachusetts for one mentally retarded child, with a clear educational emphasis. Hervey Wilbur would later become the first superintendent of the first state funded residential school for mentally retarded children at Syracuse, New York. Scheerenberger (1983) notes that, throughout his career, Wilbur believed that institutions were less than appropriate for the teaching of mentally retarded children. Charles Bernstein, an early superintendent of the Rome State School in New York, likewise held the belief that large institutional environments were inimical to normal development. Indeed, Bernstein championed the development of placements that fostered individual independence in small community-living settings (Bernstein, 1920).

It is clear that, at the turn of the century, leaders of institutions were interested in small, homelike living arrangements for mentally retarded people. Kerlin (1877) proposed the following for developing conditions within the institution:

The appointments of the institutions should be home-like as possible; attractive and roomy, without extravagance. The general dormitories should be arranged to accomodate from four to sixteen or twenty, and there should be a few separate rooms for single cases requiring special care. (p. 24)

Kerlin's recommendations became a reality in the hands of S. Olin Garrison, founder and first director of the Vineland Training School, in the 1890s. Garrison developed what has become known as the "cottage plan," of which Eugene Doll (1976) wrote:

Although somewhat more expensive, this system enabled Garrison to reproduce family living as closely as possible—in contrast to what he called "institutional monotony". Garrison constantly urged the importance of making the children feel at home and stressed their right to privacy. . . . Equally important, the cottage system facilitated classification of the children for differential methods of care. It proved both popular with patrons and therapeutically efficacious. (p. 6)

Such descriptions of the institution bear little resemblance to the conditions later exposed by Burton Blatt or Geraldo Rivera. What happened to institutions between the turn of the century and the 1960s? Despite the positions of early leaders that mentally retarded people are best served either through education and training in the institution, with return to the community (e.g., Seguin, Wilbur, Kerlin), or that community placement alone is most appropriate (e.g., Bernstein), institutions grew larger and flourished. Scheerenberger (1983) concluded:

> In the final analysis, however, and in spite of varying philosophical postures, institutions continued to serve a population of individuals whose needs could not or were not met in the community, regardless of level of retardation. (p. 192)

Scheerenberger goes on to point out that family needs and finances, rather than functioning level of the individual, often played a significant role in the decision to institutionalize. For example, special education services were usually limited to urban centers, forcing parents in rural areas to seek institutional placement for educational reasons. The Eugenics movement, supported by pronouncements about the hereditary transmission of mental retardation (e.g., Goddard, 1912), and increasing public fear of the mentally retarded offender (e.g., Fernald, 1909), placed additional demands on parents to institutionalize their defective offspring.

The mental testing movement at the turn of the century provided tools with which to identify and classify those in need of care. As Crissey (1975) notes,

> For practical purposes, the intelligence test quickly became the primary and, in some cases, sole criterion for identifying and classifying retardation. Unfortunately, the initial research results were interpreted in light of the hereditary/genetic view of retardation, with social stratification as a result of inherited mental differences. The concept of the "fixed IQ" was in accord with the social mores of the time and was agreeably accepted. (p. 803)

The ideas of hereditary transmission of retardation, "criminal instincts," and the immutability of the IQ are presented here to document why institutions flourished. Placement in an institution was often thought to be for the good of the individual during the early part of the century. Of course, protection of society was also considered. As more individuals were identified, waiting lists grew and the size of institutions grew in proportion.

Under social, professional, economic, and other pressures, then, institutions grew large and overcrowded. They ceased to be centers for short term education and training, as envisioned by Seguin, Garrison, Wilbur, Kerlin, and their colleagues. Institutions have not lived up to the expectations of those who began them in the latter part of the last century.

We cannot change the past; but, in understanding it, we can correct problems for the future. Our intent here has been to show that, from laudable beginnings, social forces have altered the nature of institutions for developmentally disabled people. The very real problems facing institutions reflect very real societal issues.

CURRENT STATUS

Providing a basis for change, Wolfensberger (1972) presented an eloquent statement on the principle of normalization and laid the conceptual groundwork for recapturing the ideals of Seguin. Normalization, with its emphasis on services in the least restrictive setting, prompted the development of community services. Shortly after Wolfensberger published his work, the task of deinstitutionalizing mentally retarded people was undertaken with vigor (Bradley, 1978; Roos, McCann, & Addison, 1980).

Longitudinal follow-up data on a sub-group of mentally retarded adults deinstitutionalized in 1960–61 (Edgerton, Bollinger, & Herr, 1984) showed that these clients were more hopeful and independent despite ill health and stressful life events. Similarly, Alexander, Huganir, and Zigler (1985) report decreased wariness in people from smaller settings, especially when preinstitutional social deprivation is low. Other research shows similar positive effects in the area of vocational employment. For example, a 5-year follow-up study (Brickey, Campbell, & Browning, 1985) found better adjustment and family relations for clients placed in competitive employment than for those who remained in workshop settings.

The normalization philosophy has resulted in changed public policy of many states, associations, and related interest groups. For example, in 1981 the Executive Board of The Association for the Severely Handicapped (TASH) passed a resolution calling for ''a cessation of capital investment in institutional renovation and construction in large residential settings and a redirection of resources to integrated community services'' (The Association for the Severely Handicapped, 1981). Furthermore, legislation being sponsored at the federal level, and supported by groups such as TASH and the Association for Retarded Citizens (ARC) seeks to realize the goal of the TASH resolution by redirecting federal Medicaid funds over a fixed period of time from institutions to community and family settings [nb. See Chapter 7.]

It is our view, however, that deinstitutionalization should not simply represent a rejection of previous models of service. Rather, it should include serious attempts to explore all the options in meeting the needs of developmentally disabled people. A similar view has been espoused by Landesman-Dwyer (1981). Our work (McCallion, 1983) has shown us that it is possible, within a small institution, to develop an environment through a unit-based cottage system which provides services in a less restrictive manner.

We believe an additional goal should be added to deinstitutionalization; that is, using existing residential facilities as a catalyst for the regional development of community programs with administrative and professional support. This goal takes into account that institutions employ large numbers of individuals (e.g., administrators, professionals, direct care staff) with extensive knowledge of services for developmentally disabled people. In addition, the practical components of service systems (e.g., documentation, programming systems) are already available in the institution, and could be used to establish community services. Finally, we believe that a regional institution can prepare clients for community living. However, this may not always be the case.

The Pennsylvania League of Concerned Families of Retarded Children, a group of volunteer advocates representing families of some of the mentally retarded individuals who have been deinstitutionalized under federal mandate from the Pennhurst facility in Pennsylvania, in their 1985 report documents several concerns regarding the deinstitutionalization and community placement of Pennhurst residents. Abuses of psychotropic medications, poor staffing ratios in group homes, lack of behavior programs, reliance on commitment to mental hospitals, inadequate medical care, disregard for parental concerns, and a lack of commitment and monitoring on the part of administrative agencies are thought to be the outgrowth of a poorly organized community system. Since many mentally retarded clients have a variety of needs, community providers may ignore, or be unable to serve, the complex needs of their clients. For example, a study of service provision in group homes by Jacobson, Silver, and Schwartz (1984) found the delivery of professional services to be "uneven," depending on the type of group home placement (e.g., ICF vs. non-ICF, public vs. private, etc.), and the client characteristics. Deinstitutionalization may mean a reduction of quality services for some people.

Winokur and McCallion (1985) have documented this phenomenon in dental hygiene and care. They found that many community dentists will not accept developmentally disabled clients, and, if they do, may provide only the most cursory care. Similar issues in other domains have prompted the PLCFRC (Pennsylvania League of Concerned Families of Retarded Children, 1985) to state:

> We feel strongly that problem situations will continue to plague the process until philosophy is replaced by reality and the identified goal of the system is to meet the needs of the mentally retarded people—not implement change for change's sake. (p. 2)

We do not believe that it is the concept of deinstitutionalization per se that is at fault. Rather, it appears that deinstitutionalization is applied in unquestioning ways based upon assumptions about institutions which are reified in policy.

CHARACTERISTICS OF RESIDENTIAL PLACEMENTS

In a discussion of the complexities of conducting research on institutional effects, as well as the difficulty in developing social policy from such research findings, Zigler and Balla (1977) suggested that a strong position either for or against institutions was premature.

If there is a consistent theme to this 20 years of work on the effects of institu-tionalization on retarded persons, it is a continuing and increasing emphasis on the social-policy implications of our research. We are convinced that any comprehen-sive program or research must take into account not only the behavioral functioning of residents but the quality of life they experience, the extent to which they maintain contact with the community, and whether they are successfully discharged to community placement. We believe that only by means of such a multifaceted research program will it be eventually possible to determine empirically the optimal residential setting at the optimal cost. (p. 10)

Emerging from the work of Zigler and others (Cleland & Dingman, 1970; King, Raynes, & Tizard, 1971) was the view that institutions vary along a number of dimensions. Given that the history of mental retardation in America is largely a history of institutional practices, and realizing that the term *institution* can apply to facilities that are quite different, a brief examination of the literature is presented to evaluate the merit of the anti-institutional position.

Two variables in particular are thought to influence the effects of institutional living on residents: (a) size of the facility, and (b) quality of care. Both variables are complex. In terms of size, two institutions may have equal enrollments, however, one may house residents in large, 100-bed dormitories and employ large group dining halls with few, if any, programs available to residents. The other facility may use a cottage system with substantially smaller living units and meals served family style following a full day of programming in educational and vocational settings.

Quality of care poses similar problems, and may only be interpretable within a particular service system. As an example, a well-managed institution, devoted only to custodial maintenance of residents, may achieve this goal admirably. If quality care is viewed as including proactive habilitative programming, then the custodial services of this facility would, of course, not warrant a description of "quality."

Institutional Size and Quality of Care

The anti-institutional position assumes that institutions are inherently restrictive, nonnormal environments for humans to inhabit. A related assumption is that, the larger the institution, the more aberrant the environment. Large size is presumed to be closely associated with restrictive, or institutionally oriented care practices. In reviewing the research on the size variable, three classes (or sizes) of institu-tions are considered, in line with previous research (e.g., King et al., 1971; Zigler & Balla, 1977): (a) large institutions as defined above; (b) smaller institu-tions as defined above; and (c) group homes, hostels, or other small-group arrangements.

In a review of this area, Balla (1976) showed that, while institutional size and quality of care are related to the institutional classes noted above, within the groupings the relationship is unclear. This allows the possibility that certain group homes may be institutionally oriented or restrictive, while selected large facilities may be client-centered. To account for such findings, Zigler and Balla (1977) have suggested that moderator variables might be relevant.

One moderator variable is the *orientation* of the facility (King et al., 1971). These researchers developed a Resident Management Practices Inventory to place an institution on a continuum ranging from institution-oriented practices at one end (i.e., an impersonal, regimented approach for the convenience of staff) to resident-oriented practices at the other (i.e., personal space and belongings, private time, visitation, etc.). Using this inventory in various large and small settings, King et al. (1971) found the expected size-quality correlation. However, when orientation of the facility was taken into account, the relationship was no longer found. That is, the type of facility was more important than the absolute size in the determination of whether or not the facility was oriented toward the institution or the resident.

In a recent study on placement decisions, Hodapp and Zigler (1985) administered the Resident Management Inventory in two large institutions and seven smaller institutions. The authors report that the smaller institutions were generally less restrictive and more resident-oriented than the large institutions. It was noted that one of the small institutions had a scale score higher than that obtained by one of the large institutions. "This fact supports the argument that size alone is not a reliable indicator of care practices" (p. 122).

Other moderator variables affecting the size-quality relationship were reviewed by Baroff (1980), who pointed out that living unit size, clarity in staff–resident responsibilities, and level of caretaker–resident commitment, all account for some of the variance in the size-quality relationship. Raynes (1980) argues that the overall functioning level of resident groupings may be more important in determining characteristics of care than is size of the grouping.

In her review of the issues involved in community living, Landesman-Dwyer (1981) concluded that there may not be adequate data supporting many policy decisions. Similarly, we contend that many of the problems of institutions lie in their orientation and how they are managed. Institutions and the people in them experience problems when they go about their business in the wrong ways.

Roos (1970), for example, provided a description of the communication problems that exist in large institutions. Roos argues that grandiose organizational channels, set up on paper for "effective" communication, simply do not work. At best, Roos shows, information channels may work one way—down. In a similar vein, Shafter (1971) noted that routine practices of administrators "tend to dehumanize our so-called non-professional employees" (p. 3), with the results (turnover, lack of motivation, abuse, etc.) leading the institution into trouble. These practices may be negatively affected by the size of the facility, and, in turn, these practices affect the resident directly.

Size, Quality of Care, and Behavioral Effects on Clients

The anti-institutional position is that the impoverished conditions in institutions *must* affect those living within them. In particular, maladaptive behavior is usually directly attributed to the deprived environment. Empirical evidence suggests that reality is somewhat more complex [nb. See Chapter 5].

The research of Zigler and his colleagues on the effects of institutionalization on dimensions of personality illustrates that multiple variables are needed to explain behavior. Zigler and his colleagues have found that various personality characteristics, such as wariness, self-concept, and anxiety, in institutionalized mentally retarded individuals are related to variables in addition to size of the facility. or its orientation. Balla and Zigler (1979) concluded that effects of institutions on dimensions of personality are related to such factors as level of preinstitutional social deprivation, length of institutionalization, age at institutionalization, gender, and diagnosis.

In a recent investigation, MacEachron (1983) obtained adaptive behavior measures of institutionalized residents who were assigned either to existing older units (average size 54 beds) or to newly-designed residential units within a 1,700-bed institution. The newer living units were designed to be more normalizing, and consisted of an average of 122 beds divided into four wings. The administration of these newer units was divided between two teams, each responsible for half of a unit. MacEachron found a significant correlation between adaptive behavior and type of living unit ($r=.36$, $p<.05$). Noting that this study was conducted within a large, centralized institution, it was concluded that *what* is done is more important than *where* it is done.

Another area of research interest in community placements is changes in interpersonal social behavior and affiliation of clients. Normalization implies more than just homelike living quarters. It is important to inquire whether typical social behavior of clients is improved in small living settings.

Work conducted by Berkson and Landesman and their colleagues has examined such behavior in group home settings. While some of the social behavior can be attributed to the group home setting (Romer & Berkson, 1980), it appears that the relationships are complex, with variation in social behavior related to other variables, such as physical attractiveness, presence of more intelligent peers, sex of the client, and desire for affiliation (Romer & Berkson, 1980). Such studies are not controlled comparisons of social behavior between institutions and group homes. As Landesman-Dwyer, Berkson, and Romer (1979) conclude:

> Whether changes in the environmental setting can produce desirable social change and enhance the development of friendships remains to be determined. For now, we feel that ample evidence has accumulated demonstrating that the character of a group home can be measured and related to the social behavior of residents. (p. 579)

Comparisons with institutions aside, it is interesting to note that size variation within group homes may have differential effects. Landesman-Dwyer, Sackett, and Kleinman (1980) found that residents in *larger* group homes (home size ranged from 6 to 20 beds) actually engaged in more social behavior, maintained more intense friendships, and spent more time with friends and peers, than residents in the smaller group homes. These researchers also reported that staff–resident interaction was not related to size of the home, despite the increased staff to resident ratios existent in the smaller homes. They conclude that other variables, such as location of the home and nature of the functional groups, were more important than size of the home in observed behavior.

In light of the findings presented, it is apparent that the relationships among size, quality of care, and behavior are complex, depending on the operation of many moderating variables. Based on such findings we reject, at this time, the assumptions underlying the anti-institutional position.

Other writers (Crissey, 1975; Throne, 1979) reject the assumptions on conceptual grounds in addition to the empirical findings. Throne contends that "the distinction between institutions and communities is a false one. A human community is composed of people *and* their institutions" (p. 171). Throne argues that the important issue is not one of size, but one of the type of institution that best serves the client's needs. Crissey (1975) states essentially the same idea: "The issue is really not institutions versus community. The issue is where can the most suitable care be provided?" (p. 807). From a philosophical vantage point, Throne and Crissey seem to be saying that there are many variables relevant to meeting human needs, regardless of the setting.

A WORKING MODEL

We believe that the small institution (usually under 300 beds), regional in scope, fills a need in the continuum of services for developmentally disabled individuals between the large institution and community placements. The problems associated with large institutions and community residences alike may be avoided in such a model, which fosters the deinstitutionalization process and ensures that placements do not degenerate into custody only.

Drawing upon our own experience, the need for the regional resource center can be demonstrated. In reviewing the community resources that are available to developmentally disabled persons in New Jersey, the Developmental Disabilities Council (1983) identified the following major service gaps:

1. diagnosis, evaluation and information/referral services
2. development of group homes
3. provision of case management services
4. operation of vocationally-oriented day programs
5. providing training programs in daily-living skills
6. development of professional and paraprofessional staff

7. coordination and provision of transportation services
8. integration of developmentally disabled persons into leisure time and recreation activities

A survey of existing community programs by the Council revealed that they did not have the resources or personnel to deliver these programs.

Research reports (Downey, Castellani, & Tausig, 1985; Intagliata, Kraus, & Willer, 1980) indicate that this problem is not unique to New Jersey. Downey et al. (1985) report from their study of 12 counties in one northeastern state, identical problems including: "a lack of knowledge on the part of people with developmental disabilities and their families that the service existed, lack of information on other agencies' programs and resources, and a general lack of planning and interagency cooperation at the local level" (p. 21). Similarly, Intagliata et al. (1980) found that primary referers for service, families, and physicians were generally unaware of available services.

The needs identified are important, the resources to meet them are limited and are not well coordinated to be effective. This is the gap in the service continuum that the regional resource center may be able to fill.

In 1982, a conference of leaders in the field was held at Vineland to determine the components of a progressive service system for mentally retarded people. This conference identified three areas in which the regional center can provide leadership (Conference Proceedings, 1982), areas which close the gap between the large institution and the small community setting.

In the model developed, the major tasks of the regional center are: (a) to develop transitional living and vocational programs; (b) to develop and support specialized treatment programs, both within the facility and in the community; and (c) to develop the facility into a regional resource center. Central to success in these tasks is that the traditional boundaries of the institution, its "walls," become fluid. The institution is no longer viewed as a place; rather, it becomes an integrated set of services and programs for diverse groups of individuals. The distinction between the institution on the one hand, and the community on the other, is intentionally blurred.

Table 1 presents the services offered in a "fluid" residential facility, arrayed according to primary location (i.e., either the institution or the community setting). In practice, distinctions are not maintained; staff, clients, program structure, and processes are shared among all program locations. Field offices and extension programs, sharing common administrative and professional staff with the institutional programs, are set up as needed. The table shows that professional and consultation services are shared among all programs to encourage quality control and consistency of client programming. All of the cottages and treatment programs in the facility are considered transitional in nature. That is, residents may move within the facility through developmentally arranged programs and cottages, with the ultimate steps being completed in the community.

Table 1

Program and Service Listings for Main Components of a Regional Resource Center

Core Institution (Traditional Emphasis)	Regional Resource Center	Community (Special Program Emphasis)
Client Services and Programs	Diagnostic and Referral Services	Client Services and Programs
Transitional Residential Programs	Assessment Services	Community Living Arrangements
• structured cottage system	• professional diagnostic testing and	• group homes
• specialized treatment units	evaluation	• supervised apartments
• transitional programming	• specialized assessment services (e.g., deaf	• foster care arrangements
• respite services	retarded)	Specialized Treatment Programs
Educational Programs	• professional consultation	• specific treatment group homes (e.g.,
• special education school	Counseling Services	autistic, dual diagnosis)
• remedial instruction	• family counseling	• specialized day programs
• adult education	• genetic counseling and information	• parent training programs (at-home)
Vocational Programs	programs	consultation
• pre-vocational training	• adjustment counseling for clients, families,	Day Vocational Programs
• work activity training	staff	• work activity training

- sheltered employment
- competitive employment training
- work-study program

Programs for the Aged
- adult day care
- enrichment/movement programs
- skilled nuring care

Recreational Programs
- leisure skills training
- summer camp program
- religious programming

Ancillary Services
- medical specialties
- psychology/behavioral programs
- speech/hearing/language
- occupational therapy
- physical therapy

Volunteer Programs
- foster grandparents
- service club affiliation
- school/college volunteers

Educational and Resource Services

Cooperative Staff Educational Programs
- university, college, and community college affiliations
- high school and specialized school affiliations (e.g., nursing schools)
- specialized training (seminars, summer courses, workshops, lectures)

Research and Professional Activities
- professional association affiliations
- demonstrations projects
- papers, articles, books
- materials development
- speaker's bureau

- sheltered employment
- competitive employment training
- job placement
- specialized rehabilitation training

Early Intervention Programs
- genetic screening/counseling
- early identification services
- infant stimulation programs
- specialized day care/preschool

Field Services
- family counseling
- parent training
- diagnostic and referral services
- follow-up services (home visitation)

Ancillary Services
- medical specialties
- psychology/behavioral programs
- speech/hearing/language
- occupational therapy
- physical therapy
- remedial programs

The regional center is a 24-hour, full time facility serving long-term residents as well as meeting emergency or respite client needs on a short-term basis. Professionals from all disciplines move between the residential and community settings with experience and abilities to produce quality programming, while clients, at different times, find themselves in different locations, residentially and programmatically, depending on their needs at any given time.

Such a facility is life-span in its client services and inter-disciplinary in its methods, so that the center would offer services such as genetic screening and counseling to at-risk parents with infants or children at one end of the life-span, as well as geriatric nursing care to the aged mentally retarded clients at the other. The primary goal of the regional resource center is to provide quality services wherever the client may be—at home, in the community, or in the institution. Movement among the various day programming and living options is unencumbered and can be effected quickly, based on client need rather than availability of funding. All placements, day or residential and community or facility alike, provide proactive, habilitative programming suited to the needs of the clients, using an interdisciplinary, individualized program planning system. A fluid, process-oriented facility of this type bears little resemblance to traditional, closed, monolithic institutions.

We take the position that the residential bed size of the regional center is dependent upon the needs of the region in which it is located. Our assessment of our own region, for example, indicated that under 300 beds appeared to be the optimum size to operate a facility and yet maintain rates of admission and discharge (both approximately 40 clients per year) to ensure that movement is based upon needs of clients rather than the desire to fill beds. Processes to fully integrate our services throughout the region are still underway.

Transitional Programs

A large percentage of the institutionalized population now being considered for placement in the community were previously thought to be long-term institutional residents. It is unlikely that these mentally retarded individuals were given sufficient programming in community survival or independence skills. Many of these clients are arriving in group homes without the requisite skills, and the group home is unable to provide adequate training, due to resource shortages and lack of professional consultation. The quality of the client's life in such situations is being impaired. The regional center may alleviate this problem by offering specialized residences within the institution that closely approximate community living. These transitional cottage programs are able to provide intense community skill training employing all the resources of the core institution prior to actual placement in the community.

Cottages are arranged hierarchically along developmental lines. Several small, homelike cottages are used, and each is charged with the responsibility of providing programming for a specific set of skills. For example, entry level cottages concentrate on training basic self-help skills. Once residents attain these skills, they move to a cottage that focuses on adaptive daily living skills or independent functioning. Attaining these skills prompts resident movement to community skill cottages, which are the final step prior to community placement. The entire placement process, then, is transitional, with movement to less restrictive settings incumbent upon client skill attainment.

Vocational and educational programs are structured along the same developmental hierarchy, such that attainment of basic prevocational skills leads to placement in work activity or job placement programs, and then to trade training, until transfer to a community program or job placement is made concurrent with group home placement.

Taking this approach, the institution becomes the community return advocate for the client, assisting the client to make the choices necessary to determine the most suitable community placement and providing the training to ensure that the placement is successful. Few community service providers have the resources to deliver such integrated, interdisciplinary programs.

We view the institution living arrangement immediately preceding community placement as essential, and yet it is the most often overlooked. In our own setting, we have identified two small cottages (10 beds each) to serve as this final step before transition into the community. In these cottages, group home living is approximated. Community skills such as shopping, money management, banking skills, transportation, meal preparation, self-medication, and leisure time skills are taught to residents to prepare them for community living.

Integrated community homes continue the programming begun by the institution, expanding the clients' skills. The programs in the transitional cottages are as closely monitored as any others in the institution. Equipped with basic community skills in the institution, and supported by an interdisciplinary team in close communication with community program staff, the client should make a smooth transition with little chance of reinstitutionalization. It is this approach that fully embodies the century-old founding principles of the field (e.g., Crissey, 1975).

Specialized Treatment Programs

Taking advantage of technology and treatment advances, the regional center is able to offer a range of specialized programs targeted for specific diagnostic groups, in either residential programs or day programs such as vocational training and education. Traditional placement systems based simply on sex, age, and functioning level are avoided, in favor of more meaningful variables (observed behavioral characteristics, skill deficits, social functioning, etc.). In combination with a small-cottage plan, even the most difficult clients become manageable as staff members become expert in working with them intensively. Also, resources can be allocated in a more efficient and timely manner.

As the network of community-based services continues to expand, populations such as the elderly, medically involved, and multiply-handicapped will also be considered for placement. As identified in the PLCFRC (1985) report, there is a need to develop options within the community so that the only choices for a client not succeeding in community placement are not large doses of psychotropic medication, commitment to a mental hospital, or return to the institution.

Specialized community-living programs are possible for each subpopulation. However, support services such as physical therapy, occupational therapy, behavioral programming, specifically-designed day placement, intensive medical services, and dietary consultation are not always readily or easily available [nb. Refer, however, to Chapters 6 and 8]. The resources of the regional center could meet these needs.

Using the expertise available within the institution we have successfully set up a specialized treatment group home for clients diagnosed as exhibiting the Prader-Willi syndrome (Holm, Pipes, & Steffes, 1981). This syndrome, resulting from a genetic disorder, organic dysfunction, or both, involves central nervous system dysfunction (often mental retardation), various physical characteristics, extreme obesity, and serious behavior problems frequently centered around food, food purchase or preparation, and meals. In a nonspecialized group home, these clients, who are often only mildly retarded, cannot maintain diets and learn appropriate food-related behaviors. This had been the experience of the clients in our group home in previous placements. Intense behavior problems, food stealing and foraging, and uncontrolled weight gain was characteristic for all of the clients. In the prior placement, cooking and grocery shopping skills, as well as diet maintenance, were not taught. Rather, staff controlled all activities in these areas. In this group home clients prepare all meals, know their own as well as all other clients' diets, and so forth. Inspection of the rate of behavior incidents reported for 8-week periods following the opening of the home revealed a 42% reduction of behavior incidents over 8 months (Omrod, Rose, & Walsh, 1985). Over a 9-month period, an average weight loss of 8.25 pounds has been observed (range 1.75–16.50).

Much of the program development and monitoring is conducted with consultants (e.g., psychologist, dietician) supplied by the institution. Thus, diets, exercise, weight control, and the monitoring of special medical problems (e.g., diabetes) presented by this client group is being achieved within a community environment through a group home program which draws upon the technical and programmatic support available through the institution.

Regional Resource Center

For both deinstitutionalized clients and clients who have never been institutionalized, the residential facility may also have a continuing role as a resource center at the regional level. Based upon an ongoing needs assessment, the center can augment existing services and meet service gaps as identified. The resource center provides support systems, information services, and expertise not available through other community agencies.

The resource center, like the regional facility itself, is best thought of as a set of services and processes rather than a specific place. Its purposes are to make services available and to provide professional expertise, training, and research. Mutually beneficial links are formed with colleges, counseling centers, and professional associations. Information is gathered, organized, and presented. The regional center becomes a clearinghouse on the regional level for information on developmental disabilities. Many of the problems associated with the development of community services grow out of a lack of understanding in the community about developmental disabilities. Regional resource services can provide this knowledge while at the same time demystifying the institution and those it serves.

The institution is able to supply information and support to programs and services as needed (for example, if assessment services are needed for an influx of clients to a community day program from another facility, or a college program needs specialized presentations in a developmental disabilities course sequence). Potential client groups can be reached more efficiently, since the services of the center are known and locally available. Fears that often arise in the development of community programs are assuaged, and problems avoided, because people are reached with accurate information, and a reputation for quality services is recognized. Finally, staff members sense greater fulfillment in their jobs through the opportunity to influence services in a variety of areas.

SUMMARY AND CONCLUSIONS

In this chapter, we have questioned the pervasive thrust toward total community services based on an analysis of selected research evidence. We cannot accept the assumptions underlying the strong anti-institutional positions, empirically or philosophically. We are not building a case for large, needlessly restrictive institutions or the discarding of the concepts of normalization and deinstitutionalization, but wish to argue for a continued role of the small institution in achieving these ideals.

We believe that the small institution is in a favorable position to implement deinstitutionalization in a thoughtful and efficient manner. We have argued that concepts useful in building community services are valuable for rebuilding institutional services as well. We contend that the quality of services for developmentally disabled people rests on the elimination of boundaries between the institution and the community. Programs and services need to be evaluated on their quality and appropriateness for the client, and not on whether the administrative body is a community agency or an institution.

Restructuring institutions demands a shift in emphasis from relentless custody to transitional programming. Proactive, habilitative training must be unstintingly directed toward imparting skills needed by clients to move continuously to less restrictive settings, beginning with the most basic skills in the institution and ending in successful, continued community placement. In this way, the concepts of normalization and deinstitutionalization become key principles for service for all developmentally disabled clients and not only those on the verge of community return.

REFERENCES

Alexander, K.A., Huganir, L.S., & Zigler, E. (1985). Effects of different living settings on the performance of mentally retarded individuals. *American Journal of Mental Deficiency, 90,* 9–17.

Balla, D. (1976). Relationship of institution size to quality of care: A review of the literature. *American Journal of Mental Deficiency, 81,* 117–124.

Balla, D., & Zigler, E. (1979). Personality development in retarded persons. In N.R. Ellis (Ed.), *Handbook of mental deficiency: Psychological theory and research* (2nd ed., pp. 143–168). Hillsdale, NJ: Erlbaum.

Baroff, G.S. (1980). On ''size'' and the quality of residential care: A second look. *Mental Retardation, 18,* 113–117.

Bernstein, C. (1920). Colony and extra-institutional care for the feebleminded. *Mental Hygiene, 4,* 1–29.

Blatt, B. & Kaplan, F. (1966). *Christmas in purgatory.* Boston, MA: Allyn & Bacon.

Braddock, D. & Heller, T. (1985). The closure of mental retardation institutions I: Trends in the United States. *Mental Retardation, 23,* 168–176.

Bradley, V.J. (1978). *Deinstitutionalization of developmentally disabled persons.* Baltimore, MD: University Park Press.

Brickey, M.P., Campbell, K.M., & Browning, L.J. (1985). A five-year follow-up of sheltered workshop employees placed in competitive jobs. *Mental Retardation, 23,* 67–73.

Conference Proceedings, Professional Advisory Committee, The Training School at Vineland (1982). *Development of a model service facility for mentally retarded people.* Vineland, NJ: American Institute—The Training School at Vineland.

Cleland, C.C. & Dingman, H.F. (1970). Dimensions of institutional life: Social organization, possessions, time and space. In A.E. Baumeister & E. Butterfield (Eds.), *Residential facilities for the mentally retarded* (pp. 138–162). Chicago, IL: Aldine.

Crissey, M.S. (1975). Mental retardation: Past, present, and future. *American Psychologist, 30,* 800–808.

Developmental Disabilities Council, New Jersey (1983). *New Jersey state plan for services to persons with developmental disabilities, 1983 update.* Trenton, NJ: New Jersey Developmental Disabilities Council.

Doll, E.E. (1976). *Before the big time: The early history of the Training School at Vineland and its influence.* Centennial paper presented at annual meeting of AAMD.

Downey, N.A., Castellani, P.J., & Tausig, M.B. (1985). The provision of information and referral services in the community. *Mental Retardation, 23,* 21–25.

Edgerton, R.B., Bollinger, M., & Herr, B. (1984). The cloak of competence: After two decades. *American Journal of Mental Deficiency, 88,* 345–351.

Fernald, W. (1909). The imbecile with criminal instincts. *Journal of Psycho-Asthenics, 8,* 25–35.

Goddard, H. (1912). *The Kallikak family: A study in the heredity of feeblemindedness.* New York: Macmillan.

Griffith, R.G. (1985). Institutions: What is going on? *Mental Retardation, 23,* 105–107.

Hodapp, R.M. & Zigler, E. (1985). Placement decisions and their effects on the development of individuals with severe mental retardation. *Mental Retardation, 23,* 125–130.

Holm, V.A., Pipes, P.L., & Steffes, M.J. (Eds.). (1981). *The Prader-Willi syndrome.* Baltimore: University Park Press.

Intagliata, J., Kraus, S., & Willer, B. (1980). The impact of deinstitutionalization on a community based service system. *Mental Retardation, 18,* 305–307.

Jacobson, J.W., Silver, E.J., Schwartz, A.A. (1984). Service provision in New York's group homes. *Mental Retardation, 22,* 231–239.

Kerlin, I.N. (1877). The organization of establishments for the idiotic and imbecile classes. *Proceedings of the Association of Medical Officers of American Institutions for Idiotic and Feeble-Minded Persons* Media, PA: Lippincott (pp. 19–24).

Kerlin, I.N. (1891). *Manual of Elwyn: 1863–1891.* Philadelphia, PA: Lippincott.

King, R.E., Raynes, N.V., & Tizard, J. (1971). *Patterns of residential care: Sociological studies in institutions for handicapped children.* London: Routledge & Kegan Paul.

Landesman-Dwyer, S. (1981). Living in the community. *American Journal of Mental Deficiency, 86,* 223–234.

Landesman-Dwyer, S., Berkson, G., & Romer, D. (1979). Affiliation and friendship of mentally retarded residents in group homes. *American Journal of Mental Deficiency, 83,* 571–580.

Landesman-Dwyer, S., Sackett, G.P., & Kleinman, J.S. (1980). Relationship of size to resident and staff behavior in small community residences. *American Journal of Mental Deficiency, 85,* 6–17.

MacEachron, A.E. (1983). Institutional reform and adaptive behavior functioning of mentally retarded persons: A field experiment. *American Journal of Mental Deficiency, 88,* 2–12.

McCallion, P. (1983). *The neglected third point in deinstitutionalization: A refinement of Garrison's cottage plan.* Paper presented at annual meeting of AAMD, Region IX. Williamsburg, VA.

Omrod, S., Rose, J., & Walsh, K.K. (1985). *The Prader-Willi group home: A specialized treatment program.* Paper presented at annual meeting of AAMD, Region IX. Baltimore.

Pennsylvania League of Concerned Families of Retarded Citizens (1985). *Deinstitutionalization: The record speaks for itself in Pennsylvania.* Annual Report. Doylestown, PA: Author.

Raynes, N.V. (1980). The less you've got the less you get: Functional grouping, a cause for concern. *Mental Retardation, 18,* 217–220.

Romer, D., & Berkson, G. (1980). Social ecology of supervised communal facilities for mentally disabled adults: II. Predictors of affiliation. *American Journal of Mental Deficiency, 85,* 229–242.

Roos, P. (1970). Evolutionary changes of the residential facility. In A.E. Baumeister & E. Butterfield (Eds.), *Residential facilities for the mentally retarded* (pp. 29–58). Chicago, IL: Aldine.

Roos, P., McCann, B.M., & Addison, M.R. (1980). *Shaping the future: Community-based residential services and facilities for mentally retarded people.* Baltimore, MD: University Park Press.

Rotegard, L.L., Bruininks, R.H., & Krantz, G.C. (1984). State operated residential facilities for people with mental retardation July 1, 1978–June 30, 1982. *Mental Retardation, 22,* 69–74.

Shafter, A.J. (1971). A philosophy of administration: A revisit. *Mental Retardation, 9,* 3–5.

Scheerenberger, R.C. (1983). *A history of mental retardation.* Baltimore, MD: Brookes.

Seguin, E. (1866). *Idiocy and its treatment by the physiological method.* New York: William Wood.

Talbot, M.E. (1964). *Édouard Seguin: A study of an educational approach to the treatment of mentally defective children.* New York: Teachers College Press.

The Association for the Severely Handicapped (1981). *TASH Newsletter.* Falls Church, VA: Author.

Throne, J.M. (1979). Deinstitutionalization: Too wide a swath. *Mental Retardation, 17,* 171–175.

Winokur, D., & McCallion, P. (1985). *A total approach to dental care for persons with developmental disabilities.* Paper presented at the annual meeting of AAMD, Philadelphia.

Wolfensberger, W. (1972). *The principle of normalization in human services.* Toronto, Canada: National Institute on Mental Retardation.

Zigler, E., & Balla, D.A. (1977). Impact of institutional experience on the behavior and development of retarded persons. *American Journal of Mental Deficiency, 82,* 1–11.

13

The Community Imperative and Human Values

Burton Blatt
Syracuse University

THE PARADOX OF COMMUNITIZATION

It's difficult to discuss institutions for people who are mentally retarded without engaging in controversy. After all, and to twist a phrase, the Willowbrooks and Pennhursts of the world are infamous for being infamous. On the other hand, one of the persistent criticisms of the *deinstitutionalization movement* has been the valid assertion that the effectiveness of the *communitization movement* has not been documented well. However, the ineffectiveness of the institution has been more than adequately documented. Then why can't sufficient examinations of community placements be achieved in order to settle the question? Good question, but there is an explanation if not exactly an answer.

Within our inability to develop an adequate data base to speak to that question lies a paradox, one that may not only puzzle us but offer illumination. We can discuss the paradox in terms of another question (possibly, paradoxes are best discussed by indirection): Has there been a conclusive demonstration of the effectiveness of living in one's natural home? Some may think this is a silly question. After all, the overwhelming majority of people in our society live in their natural homes. What does it mean to document the effectiveness of one's home? That's exactly the point. Some homes are good; some aren't so good. Some homes are good on so-called objective criteria, but, nevertheless, there are people who don't like to live in them. And there are other homes which are not good as measured against objective criteria, but there are people who seem to prefer living there. It is virtually impossible to implement a serious study of the effectiveness of ordinary homes, or ordinary communities, or one's society.

Of course, there are many informed people who write compelling papers on home life in America (or elsewhere), or the American Culture (or the American Dilemma). There are people who describe home life in America, or in certain segments of our culture—who discuss it and even try to do something about it. But where is there adequate *documentation* to speak to the hypothesis that home life in America is effective or ineffective? It is simply not a fair question. It is too large, and it is connected to an almost infinite array of other unanswerable questions. Hence the paradox.

To the degree that mentally retarded people live in ordinary homes and ordinary neighborhoods, it becomes less and less possible to document the effectiveness of those environments. Of course, one can describe a home, or even a neighborhood, but no one—and no group and no field—can speak to whether a culture or normal environment is good or bad. By the very fact that there is such a thing as a normal environment, or ordinary homes, the question has been answered. That is what the people want. That is the regularity.

Social scientists are infinitely better at describing, analyzing, and discussing variations from the norm than the norm itself. The only way to judge an ordinary home or normal environment on objective grounds with practical meaning would be to judge that home or environment using institutional criteria. Who wants that? And what good would it do? Put another way, we will know that deinstitutionalization works when mentally retarded people "disappear" in the environment. In the end, that is the true test.

INSTITUTIONS AND FREEDOM

The institutionalization controversy has been argued in two ways: as a developmental issue, and as a freedom issue. If the advocates for deinstitutionalization made any serious strategic blunder during the past decade or two, it may have been their insistent, almost perverse, devotion to the clinical, the developmental, argument. Consequently, there have been debates at our national and regional AAMD meetings, there have been more or less scientific studies published in our professional and scientific journals and in books such as the one of which this chapter is a part, and there have been polemics published in our newspapers and newsletters affirming or denying that the institution is a better place for people or that the segregated school is a better place for children, that the group home is better or that the mainstreamed class is better. It is possible that the more important argument could have been made with regard to the "freedom" issue— the belief that people are entitled to live free in a natural setting, irrespective of what particular environment most enhances their reading capability or vocational aptitude. As I have discussed and written elsewhere (Blatt, 1981), Abraham Lincoln did not emancipate the slaves in order to promote their school capability or vocational viability. The slaves were freed because people deserve to live free, unless, of course, they are dangerous to themselves or others; there are even people—persuasive people, like Tom Szasz (1964)—who are not at all sanguine about enchaining (institutionalizing) those who are "merely" dangerous to themselves.

The question of freedom is a favorite for discussion in our religious and philosophical literature, as well as a preoccupation of poets and novelists. Virtually every great thinker and leader has said something about the concept of freedom—everyone including Lincoln and Dostoevsky, Moses and Robert Frost. At once, the concept of freedom is both maddening and elusive for the individual to understand, but either simple or impossible to achieve. That is, if one denies authority, he or she is free; if one accepts tyranny, he or she is imprisoned. It will, of course, be dangerous to deny certain authority, but such denial always confirms one's freedom. Indeed, in the ultimate sense, if one wishes it to be, freedom is the final option. Hence, lives are laid down in its defense, and untold sacrifices are made to insure its continuance. Almost no one makes a genuine sacrifice to increase a grade of reading. That would be silly, even lunatic. People die for freedom, while nobody willingly dies to read a little better, or, by definition, to be happier. If we thought about it more seriously, most people might regard freedom as the most precious gift which can be conferred on a human being. In a way, a person needs to be free to maintain a personal sense of humanness. In a way, the concept of freedom is irrevocably connected to the definition of humanity. In a way, for many people, freedom is a more precious gift than life itself—possibly for most people.

Let's attempt to lay by the heels the issues surrounding the controversy over institutionalization versus communitization and special classes versus mainstreaming. This should lead the reader to the real debate—on freedom, and the current and future society. As I wrote in a series of questions I once asked and answered myself (Blatt, 1975), simply stated, the controversy is between those who believe that children with special needs—indeed, all children and all people—should live in ordinary communities and attend ordinary schools in ordinary classes, and others who contend that children with special needs are best served in specialized programs, which are supervised by specially trained administrators, who employ specially trained teachers, who use special methods and unique facilities and equipment.

The quintessential debate is between those who believe that freedom is a more precious right than treatment, as contrasted with those who might be willing to sacrifice physical integration to foster educational benefits. Yet there doesn't seem to be any compelling research in support of either approach. Probably, the most that can be claimed is that some children fare better in separate class programs, while others do better in ordinary programs. Such research, sometimes called "efficacy studies," leads to the conclusion that current segregated programs—essentially, special classes and special schools—are of no more benefit to the mentally retarded (or, for that matter, to handicapped children in general) than other types of class organizations and arrangements (Blatt, 1956, 1963, 1971).

WHAT IS THE PROBLEM?

Then what is the controversy; what is the problem? There is no single problem, with a single debate surrounding the communitization issue. There are problems. There are debates. There are assertions, facts, polemics, and preferred solutions. The controversy is grounded more in preferences, prejudices, and inclinations than in facts. It's powered more by a sense of shared values than an understanding of common data. It endures more out of certain fears (and loves) than demographics and research findings. There is no prepotent problem. And, consequently, there is neither a single nor simple answer. There are no better answers than those which one debater gives to another or accepts from another.

There are problems and there are solutions. There are levels of integration that some would call segregation, and there are levels of segregation that others would call integration. There is no black or white, as there are no clear-cut dichotomies or other subdivisions and boundaries to the issues. Notwithstanding, there are competing values. There are ideological differences between those who believe that the state was created to serve human beings—to free them—and those who believe that people must be organized to serve the state. There are those who claim that the state must be kept responsible to care for people who have social, intellectual, and other kinds of "deviancies." On the other hand, there are those who assert the right of *any* human being to do exactly as he or she pleases, to live exactly as he or she wishes, just so long as he or she isn't dangerous to other people or to himself or herself. There are those who believe that their freedom is more precious to them than their lives, and who might even appreciate the concept of anarchy. And there are those who believe that human beings must be controlled, and who might even appreciate the concept of the totalitarian state.

But most of us, most of the people, have values that fall somewhere between these polarities. Most of us have some sympathy for the idea that people are better off with their "own kind." And many of us believe that the world is enriched as we engage in relationships with those who are different; many of us would endorse Hungerford's (1950) vision of a world which is enriched *because of* the differences among us. And of course, there are people who argue on one side or the other of this debate because of certain selfish interests. The plain fact is that segregated schools, segregated classes and institutions, require that architects design them, contractors build them, people administer them, teachers and other professionals work in them, and bankers finance them. Especially, we are familiar with the irony that, while specialization incurs certain sacrifices which the specialist must make, there nevertheless are certain benefits which accrue to the specialist. So, what are your values? What are your selfish interests? Answer those questions, and you'll get close to the real problem embedded in this controversy.

Segregation is always more expensive than integration, both in terms of real dollars and insofar as the preservation and enhancement of human resources are concerned. I also assert that most people want to live with their families and friends in ordinary communities, and that most children want to go to ordinary schools. Nothing I know of that's segregated can be good for other than acute periods in a person's life. That is, it's reasonable to be in a hospital when you're sick, but it's not reasonable to live in the hospital. It's certainly justified to be alone when you want to be alone, but being alone too long makes people despondent, drives them crazy, and sometimes turns them into monsters. That's the lesson to be learned from Mary Shelley's *Frankenstein*. Another lesson to be learned is that people can be alone when in a crowd, and at peace when away from everything but their inner visions.

DEINSTITUTIONALIZATION ARGUMENTS

Insofar as institutionalization is concerned, here too there is a seemingly unremitting debate. There are those who argue vigorously against deinstitutionalization, contending that:

1. The idea of deinstitutionalization is not grounded in an empirical base.
2. Deinstitutionalization is a slogan of the anti-establishment.
3. There are people so profoundly retarded that they can't benefit from any sort of educational programming, that they are custodial.
4. The community is not prepared to integrate severely and profoundly handicapped people.
5. There are both good and bad institutions and good and bad communities, with neither type of setting inherently good or bad.
6. Institutions are more efficient than less expensive ways to provide services to people with severe handicaps.

Let's look closer at these criticisms of deinstitutionalization of the mentally retarded:

1. The idea that deinstitutionalization is not grounded in an empirical base is probably true. However, while there is no evidence that humane normal environments lead to greater human development, there should be sufficient face evidence that humane normal environments foster human normal environments.
2. The contention that deinstitutionalization is little more than a slogan of the anti-establishment is puzzling when, to this date, thousands of people are unnecessarily institutionalized—such estimates made by federal judges, state commissioners, and even people who debate the issue in support of continuing practice of institutionalization.
3. The idea that people are so profoundly retarded that they can't benefit from any educational programming denies the real lesson to be learned from the *The Wild Boy of Aveyron:* namely, that all human beings can learn. It denies the lesson to be learned from *Emile:* that all people are noble. It also denies the lessons to be learned from the lives of Helen Keller and Ann Sullivan and thousands and thousands of other documented cases of individuals who have changed remarkably when placed in nurturing environments.
4. The idea that the community is not now prepared to accept the profoundly retarded, and probably never will, leaves us with moral paralysis. Does this mean that we are to perpetuate injustice? If it does, then the 13,000,000

people who died in the ovens of Auschwitz and Buchenwald deserved to die there. They too were incarcerated legally and dealt with according to the legal codes of Nazi Germany. If a parent wants to send a normal child to an orphanage, should a parent be given that privilege? If a parent kills a child, is that the parent's right (because the parent wishes to do it) or the parent's crime (irrespective of whether the parent wants the child in the home, or to live)? The idea that there are good and bad institutions and good and bad community settings is beside the point. Because there are bad universities, there is no erosion of the knowledge that there can be a Harvard University. Because there is a bad marriage, or an evil parent, mitigates in no way the importance of family and parenthood.

6. The idea that institutions are more efficient and less expensive than community settings is truly unbelievable. Does *anyone* believe that? The per capita expenditure for institutionalization in New York State today is at least $40,000 a year, and there are some state institutions in New York State which spend $100,000 a year per resident. Does anyone believe anymore that segregation is less expensive than normalization? In this regard, money has been less the issue than the culprit. Underneath our failures is how we conceptualize the value and the potential of other human beings. When all else fails, when money fails, our leaders must think better.

NORMALIZATION CONCEPTS

The institutionalization controversy has been both clarified and complicated by the intrusion of the "normalization concept" into the argument. Despite its popularity, "normalization" is widely misunderstood and misused. Thus, let me place before you a commonly accepted definition of the term, and a summary of the basic concepts which constitute its foundation.

First, normalization means making available to all mentally retarded people patterns of life and conditions of everyday living which are as close as possible to the regular circumstances and ways of life of their society.

Second, normalization means giving society a chance to know and respect mentally retarded people in everyday life, and to diminish the fears and myths that once caused society to segregate them (Perske, 1977, p. 5).

Perske also discussed the basic elements of normalization. What follows is my summary of that commentary:

1. The idea of a normal rhythm of the day. Retarded people wake up, dress, eat at normal times, and do other things people ordinarily do in the course of the day.
2. The idea of a normal rhythm of the week. People live at home, attend school or go to work, time for leisure, time for community activities.
3. The idea of a normal rhythm of the year. People take vacations, enjoy holidays together, visit the sick, attend celebrations.

4. The idea of a normal life experience. All people should have opportunities to live secure and nurturing lives, to have enriching early childhoods, to go to school, to be part of a family, to have friends through the growing years, to have lifetime friends, to work, to contribute, to spend one's later years in dignity and purposeful activities.
5. The idea that all people are entitled to respect from others. Retarded people should be paid attention to, should be in control of those aspects of their lives which they can reasonably handle (exactly as the rest of us want and need such freedoms).
6. The idea of living one's life in a heterosexual world. Boys should participate in activities with girls, and men with women. To the degree that one's life varies with these activities and the people one deals with and is associated with, life becomes not only more colorful but more meaningful.
7. The idea that mentally retarded people have economic needs, require the security and supports and legal guarantees which the rest of us require— during our growing years, during our working years, during our old age.
8. The idea that one's environment should be normal and should be judged on normal standards. People should live in ordinary homes and in ordinary communities, and the quality of those environments should be examined in light of the cultural mores and resources of society.

There doesn't seem to be much doubt that, long before the actual term "normalization" gained popularity, other scholars in the field used it (Wolfensberger, 1980). But those earlier examples appear to be rather casual and tangential to the main purposes of those works. Wolfensberger finds the earliest mention of the term itself in a 1966 edition of one of Maria Montessori's books. Tracking that clue to the original 1950 Italian edition, Wolfensberger was surprised to find that Montessori actually wrote about the normalization of children. Notwithstanding, even here its mention was quite tangential to the thrust of the main commentary. Wolfensberger also reports: the use of the term in a Swiss journal in 1958, its presence in a Canadian journal in 1964, and its appearance in the United States in 1966 in an article by a well-known practitioner in mental retardation, Simon Olshansky. To the best of Wolfensberger's understanding, the current usage and original stimulation for the widespread popularity of normalization should be credited to the work of Bank-Mikkelsen, once head of the Danish Mental Retardation Service and a world leader in the field. And, at about the same time that the concept enjoyed its beginning prominence in Denmark, it received strong endorsement and dissemination by Bengt Nirje and other Swedes. Of course, Wolfensberger himself is mainly responsible for the significant impact the normalization concept has had in the United States.

I have taken time to present a brief historical perspective on the normalization concept because it, possibly more than any other concept connected with de-institutionalization, provides the fuel for the philosophical argument against institutionalization. In a very real sense, to understand this controversy requires deep appreciation of normalization, what it is, and how it was developed. It is by no means accidental that Maria Montessori was one of the earliest proponents of the concept. It's also not accidental that Scandinavians—those colleagues abroad to whom we owe so much for their demonstrations of successful community life for the mentally retarded—embraced, refined, and implemented this concept with a firmness and certainty which we in this country have yet to achieve. Deinstitutionalization and mainstreaming are ideas connected intimately with the concept of "least restrictive environments." They were fostered after the institutional scandals of the '60s and the Civil Rights movements of the '60s and '70s. They are connected with the consumer movement, citizen advocacy, the civil rights movement, and the generally heightened political activism of the people.

RESEARCH AND THE INTEGRATION CONTROVERSY

Neither deinstitutionalization, communitization, normalization, nor mainstreaming—nor, for that matter, zero reject policy, Public Law 94-142, nor any other permutations of what has almost become an *Integration Revolution* in the United States—has been very much influenced by what research has been able to inform us about where people learn and grow best, what people want, and what people need. These particular arguments cannot satisfactorily be resolved by science, as they cannot be much better understood by what science uncovers. Stated another way, the integration controversy is not one of those dilemmas which present Man with a puzzle to solve as much as it is one which presents him with an opportunity to expose his values. The integration controversy has to do with how we want the shape of the future society to be, rather than with what the evidence is which will dictate the future society. The integration controversy is one of those arguments which is almost completely in our hands to decide. It has little, if anything, to do with what is "best" for people, and virtually everything to do with what people want to make their lives better.

After a visit to a traditional institution, the observer yet unhardened may ask how one endures that environment. The visitor may have also found inexplicable the attitude of the institution's superintendent, who appears to be bragging about his "failure"—the *decrease* of his institution's population. The visitor may have been astonished to find a happy man, one who talked and strutted like a musician enjoying his own virtuosity. And so the question: How does the institutional staff endure—appear to enjoy!—their lives? The answer is as paradoxical as the question. Consider the analogy of the institution to suicide, or to depression, or melancholia. Suicide is never a solution; it's the question. "Making the best of things" in the institution isn't the solution. That too is the question. So, while we can ask about how one endures—even prospers—in the institution, we know, or should know, that the "answer" cannot be in promoting institutional enjoyment and prosperity. Rather, the answer will be discovered when we better understand *why* an otherwise reasonable man can be happy and fulfilled in such places.

What I have tried to do in this chapter is tell the truth about segregation and freedom—not the precise truth as scientists like to tell, rather as I would see a more enduring truth. I have tried to imply that mental retardation is the fallen angel of science, because science can't solve these problems as well as ordinary common sense and not so ordinary decency. I have tried to say as gently as I could that mental retardation is the prodigal son of the professional, because the more we (the professionals) do for those with mental retardation, the more we alienate them from normal life. The institution is never the solution, only the question. And what about the "why" question, the "why" of it all? Is it temporary mass lunacy, horribly bad luck, or incredibly poor judgment? There has even been the suggestion that the mental retardation institution is simply the work of the devil. What's a plausible story to explain the inexplicable?

REFERENCES

Blatt, B. (1956). *The physical, personality, and academic status of children who are mentally retarded attending special classes as compared with children who are mentally retarded attending regular classes.* Unpublished Ph.D. Dissertation, the Pennsylvania State University, Ann Arbor: University Microfilms.

Blatt, B. (1963). *The education of handicapped children in Rhode Island.* Providence, RI: Legislative Commission to Study the Education of Handicapped Youth.

Blatt, B. (1971). *Massachusetts study of educational opportunities for handicapped and disadvantaged children.* Boston, MA: Massachusetts Advisory Council on Education.

Blatt, B. (1975). The integration-segregation issue: Some questions, assumptions, and facts. *Family Involvement, 8,* 10–14.

Blatt, B. (1981). Bureaucratizing values. In B. Blatt. *In and out of mental retardation: Essays on educability, disability and human policy* (pp. 327–347). Baltimore, MD: University Park Press.

Hungerford, R.H. (1950). On locusts. *American Journal of Mental Deficiency, 54,* 415–418.

Perske, R. (1977). *Improving the quality of life: A symposium on normalization and integration.* Arlie, VA: The National Association for Retarded Citizens.

Szasz, T.S. (1964). *Law, liberty and psychiatry.* New York: Macmillan.

Wolfensberger, W. (1980). The definition of normalization: Update, problems, disagreements, and misunderstandings. In R.J. Flynn & K.E. Nitsch (Eds.), *Normalization, social integration, and community services* (pp. 71–115). Baltimore, MD: University Park Press.

EDITORS' NOTE

The original manuscript version of this chapter was written by Dr. Burton Blatt in late August, 1984, and formed the basis for his invited address, "How to get a community imperative to work," delivered at the 47th Annual Conference of AAMD Northeast Region X, Kiamesha Lake, New York, October 1, 1984. The original title of the first draft of this manuscript was "Deinstitutionalization/Communitization/Normalization/Mainstreaming."

Dr. Blatt died on January 20, 1985, at Syracuse, New York without returning a revised version of his chapter. We have taken the liberty, based upon reviewers' comments, our conversations with Dr. Blatt, and our reading of his previous works, of editing the original manuscript to have it conform to the style and format of this book series. In total, we added fewer than a dozen words to the original manuscript, and, in so doing, have preserved both the richness and the intent of his presentation.

We are honored to be able to present this chapter to you in this book. It is fitting, we think, that this last written work of Dr. Blatt should challenge us once again to examine our own values, in order to find the truth about segregation and freedom of people who are mentally retarded.

Author Index

Subject Index

GUIDELINES FOR AUTHORS

Form

The reference for writing style, citations, and technical details will be the third edition (1983) of the *Publication Manual of the American Psychological Association* (APA). Technical questions should be addressed to the associate series editor: Richard F. Antonak, Education-Morrill Hall, University of New Hampshire, Durham, NH 03824, or phone (603)862-3720.

All parts of the manuscript, including references and notes, should be prepared double-spaced on one side of 21.6 × 28-cm white paper. Do not use onionskin or erasable paper, and do not attach anything to any of the pages. Leave 3-cm margins on all sides. Do not justify the right margin; that is, leave the right margin uneven.

A title page should include the title, author(s) name(s), and affiliation(s), an address and phone number for correspondence, and a running head of no more than 50 characters. A shortened version (2 or 3 words) of the running head should appear on the top line of each succeeding page. No author identification should appear on any page except the title page and author note page.

The first page after the title page should be an abstract of not more than 150 words, typed as a single unindented paragraph. Manuscripts should be no more than 40 pages, numbered consecutively starting with the title page and including all references, tables, author notes, and figure captions.

Terminology

Use the words ''retarded,'' ''disabled,'' ''handicapped,'' etc. as adjectives, not as nouns. The most recent edition of the AAMD ''Manual on Classification in Mental Retardation'' should be consulted for all definitions, levels, or categories of mental retardation. Because this series of books is addressed to many disciplines, unique technical terms should be carefully defined for readers not familiar with your field. Jargon should be avoided.

Statistical Analyses

For nonstandard statistical analyses, cite a reference or computer program. If necessary, identify an expert who can consult with the editors on the appropriateness of any unique or nonstandard statistical analyses.

Numerical and Illustrative Presentations

The metric system is used to express all measurements. Consult the APA manual for the preparation of tables and figures. Glossy prints or original line drawings will be required, but should be retained by the author until the manuscript has been accepted for publication and the editors call for them. Send a good photocopy of the figures with the manuscript for editorial review.

References
Consult the APA publication manual for the appropriate form for all references. Pay particular attention to the accuracy of the information in the references.

Author Notes
Do not use footnotes in the text. Use author notes sparingly to refer to (a) grant support, (b) acknowledgements of assistance preparing the manuscript, or (c) availability of more detailed information, related reports, or specific data.

Ethical Standards
All experimental investigations are required to have been approved by the human subjects review committee of the author's institution prior to initiation. The submitted manuscript should not be under review by any other publication outlet, nor should it have been published in whole or substantial part by any other publication outlet. Authors assume full responsibility for the factual accuracy of their contributions, and for providing proof of permission to use previously copyrighted material.

Submission of Manuscripts
Authors should submit three (3) good quality photocopies or wordprocessor copies of the manuscript to the series editor: James A. Mulick, Department of Psychology, Children's Hospital, 700 Children's Dr., Columbus, OH 43205. Copies will be sent to members of the editorial board for blind review. When a full editoral response is received, the series editor will communicate the decision to the author, together with requests for revisions or alterations.

Authors of accepted manuscripts will receive a copyedited version for review prior to publication. The authors should answer all queries on the manuscript and make any necessary corrections. Significant substantive alterations must be approved by the editors. Please refer to the APA manual for more information about copyediting and proofing manuscripts.

Once a manuscript is accepted for publication, the author(s) must sign a Copyright Assignment and Agreement conveying all copyright ownership to the publisher.